Taiwan, Hong Kong, and the United States, 1945–1992

Uncertain Friendships

TWAYNE'S INTERNATIONAL HISTORY SERIES

Akira Iriye, Editor
Harvard University

TAIWAN, HONG KONG, AND THE UNITED STATES, 1945–1992

Uncertain Friendships

Nancy Bernkopf Tucker

Georgetown University

TWAYNE PUBLISHERS • NEW YORK
MAXWELL MACMILLAN CANADA • TORONTO
MAXWELL MACMILLAN INTERNATIONAL • NEW YORK OXFORD SINGAPORE SYDNEY

Taiwan, Hong Kong, and the United States, 1945–1992
Nancy Bernkopf Tucker

Twayne Publishers
Macmillan Publishing Company
866 Third Avenue
New York, New York 10022

Maxwell Macmillan Canada, Inc.
1200 Eglinton Avenue East
Suite 200
Don Mills, Ontario M3C 3N1

Library of Congress Cataloging-in-Publication Data
Tucker, Nancy Bernkopf.
    Taiwan, Hong Kong, and the United States, 1945–1992 / Nancy
Bernkopf Tucker.
        p. cm. — (Twayne's international history series : no. 14)
    Includes bibliographical references (p.) and index.
    ISBN 0-8057-7929-9 (cloth).—ISBN 0-0857-9224-4 (ppr)
    1. United States—Relations—Taiwan. 2. United States—Relations—
Hong Kong. 3. Taiwan—Relations—United States. 4. Hong Kong—Relations—
United States. I. Series
E183.8.T3T83   1994
303.48'251249'073—dc20   94-12
                                                                 CIP

The paper used in this publication meets the minimum requirements of American National Standard for Information Sciences—Permanence of Paper for Printed Library Materials. ANSI Z3948–1984. ∞ ™

10 9 8 7 6 5 4 3 2 1
10 9 8 7 6 5 4 3 2 1

Printed in the United States of America

For Dorothy Borg, William E. Leuchtenburg, and Robert Huff,
who showed me the way

CONTENTS

ILLUSTRATIONS

FOREWORD

Twayne's International History Series seeks to publish reliable and readable accounts of post–World War II international affairs. Today, nearly 50 years after the end of the war, the time seems opportune to undertake a critical assessment of world affairs in the second half of the twentieth century. What themes and trends have characterized international relations since 1945? How have they evolved and changed? What connections have developed between international and domestic affairs? How have states and peoples defined and pursued their objectives and what have they contributed to the world at large? How have conceptions of warfare and visions of peace changed?

These questions must be addressed if one is to arrive at an understanding of the contemporary world that is both international—with an awareness of the linkages among different parts of the world—and historical—with a keen sense of what the immediate past has brought to human civilization. Hence Twayne's International History Series. It is to be hoped that the volumes in this series will help the reader to explore important events and decisions since 1945 and to develop a global awareness and historical sensitivity with which to confront today's problems.

The first volumes in the series examine the United States' relations with other countries, groups of countries, or regions. The focus on the United States is justified in part because of the nation's predominant positions in postwar international relations, and also because far more extensive documentation is available on American foreign affairs than is the case with other countries. The series addresses not only those interested in international relations but also those studying America's and other countries' histories, who will find here useful guides and fresh insights into the recent past. Now more than ever it is imperative to understand the complex ties between national and international history.

In this book Professor Nancy Bernkopf Tucker, author of the highly acclaimed *Patterns in the Dust* (a study of U.S. policy toward China during 1945–1950), surveys post-1945 United States relations with Taiwan and Hong Kong in an impeccably scholarly fashion combined with an accessible style. She chronicles the fascinating and often tortuous ways in which the island of Taiwan, for many years regarded as the stronghold of an archaic Nationalist leadership whose survival seemed to depend primarily on U.S. protection, steadily developed as an economically advanced and politically reformed entity, even as Washington reversed its policy and "de-recognized" Taipei. Hong Kong, on its part, started out as America's listening post when there was no diplomatic relationship between Washington and Beijing, but since the 1970s it has played a significant role in the resurgence of Asian economies. Even as the Crown Colony reverts to China in 1997, it may be expected that it, as well as Taiwan, will continue to be arenas of energetic economic activities in which the United States will find itself more and more deeply involved. To trace this story and to understand the contemporary challenges and opportunities facing America, there is no better place to start than this excellent volume.

Akira Iriye

PREFACE

When Akira Iriye asked me to write this book I imagined a simple task of short duration. That was then. Now I realize that the study of U.S.–Taiwan/U.S.–Hong Kong relations is not just a fascinating inquiry but also an arduous one. Scholars in the United States have been too absorbed with examining every wrinkled brow of mainland Chinese leaders to pay adequate attention to developments affecting the interests of the United States in Hong Kong or Taiwan. This volume quickly stopped being synthesis and became creation. I have tried to keep it a lively account for the general reader, placing the scholarly material derived from the research that became necessary in the endnotes, where detail does not intrude but does provide guidance and additional information.

A few items of usage need to be noted. Chinese names and terms in the text are rendered in two forms of romanization. People associated with Taiwan and places on the island follow the Wade-Giles system (with some variations according to common usage as with Chiang Kai-shek). People associated with the People's Republic and places on the mainland of China after 1949 follow the *pinyin* system. I have tried in all cases to provide the terms in the form that is most recognizable to the reader. All monetary figures in the volume are given in terms of U.S. dollars.

A few words about terms would also be helpful. The term *Nationalist China* derives from the name of the dominant political party in Taiwan, the Kuomintang or Nationalist Party. It came to power in China in the 1920s under the strong hand of Chiang Kai-shek, who "inherited" leadership of the party from Sun Yat-sen, "the father of the Chinese revolution" of 1911, which overthrew the Ch'ing dynasty.

The term *Taiwanese* is used here to refer to the roughly 85 percent of the inhabitants of the island who are descended from Fujian (Fukien) and Guangdong (Kwangtung) immigrants of the eighteenth and nineteenth centuries. Most of the remaining 15 percent arrived from various provinces in

China after 1944 and have been called *mainlanders*. There has also been a tiny minority of aboriginal residents, living primarily in the mountains. They have had no particular impact on U.S.-Taiwan relations.

ACKNOWLEDGMENTS

A number of generous friends and colleagues gave of their time and expertise in an effort to improve this book. Most notably, my wisdom in the choice of a husband provided an in-house consultant and editor: Warren I. Cohen took time away from his studies of East Asian art and of the cold war to advise and encourage me. Ralph Clough, Tien Hung-mao, Steven I. Levine, and Keith Neilson read the entire manuscript with great care, endeavoring to eliminate errors and to ask new questions. On the economic sections, Mira Wilkins and Carol Evans reassured me that I finally have come to understand some of that arcane science. I received help with locating and translating documents from Steve Phillips and Ke Yan, both of whom will soon emerge from graduate school with exciting manuscripts of their own. Eileen Scully performed not only the endless labors of a research assistant but also lightened the load with cheerful and intelligent conversation and the distraction of her remarkable dissertation. Carol Chin has been a patient and supportive editor, and Akira Iriye an understanding éminence grise.

Georgetown University helped further the research for the volume through the Father Edmund A. Walsh Fund and a summer grant from the graduate school. I have benefited from the financial support of the Lyndon Baines Johnson Foundation and the extraordinary efforts of archivist David Humphrey to locate and declassify documents. Kathy Nicastro at the National Archives has been an anchor through the years. Other archives, too numerous to single out, also assisted in my search for information, some more willingly than others. In the final days of assembling pictures for the volume R. Frank Lucas provided valuable advice and technical assistance.

Various actors in the relationship agreed to grant me interviews or engaged me in informal conversations: Shaw Yu-ming discussed his government's policies from his vantage point as director of the ROC Government Information Office, and Ding Mou-shih reflected on relations with the U.S.

from the standpoint of director of the Coordination Council for North American Affairs, as did Stephen S. F. Chen, his deputy director. I spoke with Winston Lord during his tenure as ambassador to China and with retired ambassadors Arthur W. Hummel, Jr., Leonard Unger, Marshall Green, and Harvey Feldman. David Dean and Natale Bellochi discussed their roles as directors of the American Institute in Taiwan. David Laux reviewed important issues during his tenure on the National Security Council in the 1980s and his subsequent responsibilities as head of the USA-ROC Economic Council. Michel Oksenberg also explored with me his National Security Council duties at the time of normalization with the PRC and his attitudes toward Taiwan. Various other State Department officers spoke of their experiences, including Ralph Clough, who served as deputy chief of the U.S. Mission in Taiwan and as director of the Office of Chinese Affairs; Roger Sullivan, who served as director of the Taiwan desk in the Ford administration; Paul Kriesberg, who headed the Asian Communist Affairs desk, 1965–70, and later as senior deputy director of the Policy Planning Staff participated in normalization. Ray Cline, who served as CIA station chief in Taipei, analyzed the cooperative intelligence relationship between Washington and Taipei. General Albert C. Wedemeyer talked about his assessments of Nationalist Chinese military capabilities in the late 1940s. On Hong Kong affairs, I benefited from insights given by Peter Lo and Susan Luke, minister and first secretary, respectively, of the Hong Kong Economic and Trade Office in Washington. Father John Witek, S.J., of Georgetown University explained the American Catholic missionary endeavors in Taiwan. I also had the honor of discussing American policy toward Taiwan with several high-level officials in the PRC, including Ambassador Han Nianlong, who had acted as an adviser to Deng Xiaoping; Ambassador Wang Bingnan, who served as China's representative at the Warsaw talks; Ambassador to the United States Zhang Wenjin; and Zi Zhongyun, a specialist on Taiwan affairs and, at that time, director of the Institute of American Studies of the Chinese Academy of Social Sciences.

In the end, of course, the mistakes were mine to make, and the enlightenment imparted by others did not always persuade me to abandon my theories—which may or may not have been a good thing. I hope that others will learn half as much from reading the book as I learned in writing it.

ABBREVIATIONS

ABMAC	American Bureau for Medical Aid to China
AID	Agency for International Development
AIT	American Institute in Taiwan
CAT	Civil Air Transport
CCNAA	Coordination Council for North American Affairs
CCP	Chinese Communist Party
CIA	Central Intelligence Agency
DPP	Democratic Progressive Party
GRC	Government of the Republic of China
IAEA	International Atomic Energy Agency
JCRR	Joint Commission on Rural Reconstruction
JCS	Joint Chiefs of Staff
KMT	Kuomintang (Nationalist Party)
MAAG	Military Assistance Advisory Group
NATO	North Atlantic Treaty Organization
PL480	Public Law 480: Agricultural Trade Development and Assistance Act, 1954
PRC	People's Republic of China
ROC	Republic of China
SEATO	Southeast Asia Treaty Organization
TRA	Taiwan Relations Act
UNRRA	United Nations Relief and Rehabilitation Administration
USIS	United States Information Service

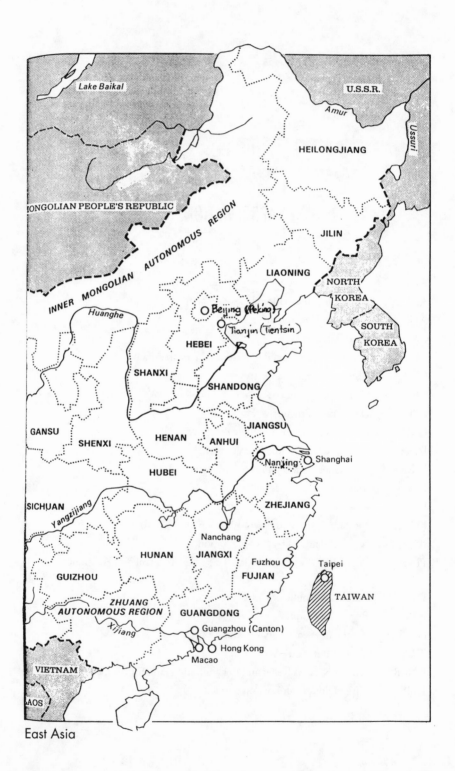

East Asia

chapter 1

INTRODUCTION: AID AND INFLUENCE

In 1989 the peoples of Taiwan, Hong Kong, and even the United States learned important lessons about the past, the present, and the future from the euphoria and terror that swept Tiananmen Square, at the heart of the Chinese Middle Kingdom. For a few brief weeks throngs of students, workers, and Communist party members believed they could change China, rectify corruption, and grasp a measure of freedom that had long eluded them. But ideology, history, and the lust for power in the hands of a few frightened old men crushed the movement, leaving behind alienation and despair among the Chinese. The horror of Tiananmen, however, became a defining moment not only for China. The disillusionment felt by many outside, who thought China had made a more basic commitment to democratization, refocused relationships between Washington, Taipei, and Hong Kong. At almost the same time the collapse of communism in the Soviet Union and Eastern Europe ended the cold war, altering the global environment within which Washington, Taipei, and Hong Kong interacted.

Thus, in the aftermath of Tiananmen, Americans awoke to the illusory nature of their expectations for China and, for the first time in many years, looked beyond the People's Republic with some interest and sympathy to Taiwan and Hong Kong. Massive demonstrations in Hong Kong protesting the Tiananmen massacre made Americans painfully aware of the human rights dilemma inherent in Britain's agreement to return the colony to Beijing in 1997, a dilemma particularly poignant for the United States, a nation fundamentally committed to self-determination. For the first time in years, American leaders began to think about devising political, as well as economic, policies toward Hong Kong.

1

A fresh appreciation of Taiwan also inspired the United States. Americans who had lost interest in the island when opportunities to travel in, trade with, learn from, and cooperate militarily with mainland China opened up once again saw in Taiwan a freer, more desirable China. Having long viewed the island as no more than a sanctuary for aging Kuomintang (KMT) reactionaries, they discovered that it had become a promising experiment in democracy. Perhaps, it had become an essentially different entity, one worthy of independence. Tiananmen seemed to underscore the liberalization that had characterized the 1980s in Taiwan, rendering its new internal and external policies still more meaningful to American observers.

That Americans should come to see Taiwan and Hong Kong differently after the terror in Tiananmen Square ought not to be surprising given the enormous contrast between what appeared to be happening in China—that is, a rejection of Western values and institutions—and what seemed to have been accomplished in Taiwan and Hong Kong—the increasing modernization, democratization, and, perhaps, Westernization of politics, economics, and culture. Of course, in many ways the image belied a far more complicated reality. In neither Taiwan nor Hong Kong could there be said to have been a wholesale adoption of Western or American ways; in neither place did a desire exist thoroughly to abandon tradition. In Taiwan, in particular, the effort to amalgamate Chinese thought patterns, philosophies, styles of human interaction, and ways of organizing society with sharply contrasting Western forms continued to trouble people in all walks of life. Harking back to the nineteenth-century dichotomy, encapsulated by scholar-official Chang Chih-tung as "Chinese learning for fundamental principles; Western learning for practical application," the tension remained.

To Americans the internal struggle within these cultures often seemed less important than the obvious changes that made interaction with the people of Taiwan and Hong Kong simpler. Indeed, accusations made by Beijing that the three shared malevolent motives, having helped to instigate, encourage, and then shelter dissidents who threatened the Chinese state, highlighted the bonds of sympathy and common purpose felt in Hong Kong, Taipei, and Washington. There was, in fact, a measure of truth in China's charges. Taiwan officials hoped that the Beijing Spring meant the final erosion and fall of communism in China, suggesting, at least for some, the possibility of a triumphal Nationalist return to the mainland. Hong Kong anticipated that the transformation of China could make the 1997 reversion of the colony to Beijing's control, upon expiration of Britain's 99-year lease over 92 percent of Hong Kong's territory, a brighter prospect. And Americans, having brought, consciously and unconsciously, liberal political and market principles to China since the early 1970s, celebrated what they saw as a democratic revolution. Media in Taiwan, Hong Kong, and the United States did rejoice in and stimulate criticism of the Beijing regime, and, when the crackdown came, governments in all three places welcomed the fugitives.

More extensive commonalities existed. In a rapidly changing environment, the similarities ranged from the growing physical resemblance of cities, whose steel and glass towers rendered them largely interchangeable, to the intertwined worlds of scientific research, trade and commerce, and artistic expression. Americans found that Taiwan's economic miracle and the continuing dynamism in Hong Kong created problems of deficits and intellectual property infringement but, more important, nourished an interdependence that would pave the way to enhanced prosperity for all. Things had come a long way from the days when Taiwan, and even Hong Kong, needed U.S. support simply to survive.

Declarations of American interest in Taiwan or Hong Kong ought, however, to be qualified by an acknowledgment of a fundamental apathy toward and ignorance of Asia specifically and foreign affairs more generally in the United States. The American people focus on domestic issues of employment and wages; they do not care very much, except in times of crisis, about developments overseas. When they have looked abroad, it has been across the Atlantic to Europe whence most of their ancestors came and not to Asia. Although Asia has recently loomed larger in economic terms, compelling greater attention, this has yet to erode the basic contours of American indifference to things Asian. Given their usual disinterest in Japan, China, and Vietnam, places that have for various reasons evoked passions and captured headlines, it need hardly be said that the superficiality of knowledge about Taiwan or Hong Kong is far greater. But tightening economic links make this condition precarious, inducing a measure of urgency in coming to understand the texture and limits of American relations with Taiwan and Hong Kong.

Given the disparities in size, resources, population, and power, it would appear obvious that in the relationship between the United States and Taiwan, Washington would have dominated, dictating policies and determining directions that Taipei would then slavishly follow. Reality, of course, could hardly have been more different. The United States has been able to set broad parameters for acceptable behavior in military, economic, and political arenas, but the Nationalist Chinese have been exceedingly adept at maneuvering within these constraints to shape relations that meet their needs for security, trade, and psychological support. The manipulation of the United States, a skill developed early by Chinese Nationalist leaders, became fundamental to Taiwan's foreign policies, and the nature of the American political system, as well as the larger international environment, made it effective. The Nationalists might not have practiced democracy at home but found it expedient and rewarding to exploit Washington's division of powers and sensitivity to public opinion.

Taiwan could, in fact, be the archetypical weak, small ally whose ability to evade great power dictation and shape a dominant ally's decisions political scientists have admired.[1] Although dependent on Washington, the Nationalist Chinese relied upon the existence of the cold war to eliminate alternatives for the U.S. and, therefore, give license to policies independent of and sometimes contrary to American interests. The Nationalists repeatedly courted danger and would happily have sparked global conflict to expedite reunification of China after having been driven from the mainland in 1949, irresponsibly assuming that their great power benefactor would fight the fight and manage the larger ramifications. Moreover, as political scientist Robert Keohane argued, Americans invited exploitation since "leaders who believe in domino theories not only have to talk to the 'dominoes,' they have to listen to them and believe them as well. Small allies are thereby enabled to use American ideology against the United States itself."[2]

Thus, weak players like Israel and Taiwan have penetrated the American government in their own version of "divide and rule," while at the same time rallying interest groups and U.S. public opinion on their behalf. Agencies such as the Central Intelligence Agency, the army, the navy, and the air force have at various times spoken for or provided information to the Nationalist Chinese to defend the parochial needs of Taiwan—and those agencies—against broader American goals. The legendary "China lobby" embarrassed and harassed successive administrations, utilizing congressional sympathizers and the voting public to prevent executive branch action inimical to Taipei. Whether it actually could have delivered on its threats of political retribution was not important so long as it could sustain the illusion that it would.

Taiwan, as the recipient of American military and economic largesse, proved not to be a predictable ward. Its ambitions remained large,[3] and among the major motivations for the United States' alliance with it was the determination to circumscribe its reach and ability to wreak havoc in international affairs. The association between them also balanced precariously on the unstable foundation of conflicting intermediate goals. If anticommunism cemented the basic bond, agreement did not necessarily follow on the means to pursue that objective. The United States repeatedly begged, threatened, and cajoled Chiang Kai-shek to reduce the size of his military establishment and to curtail his military activities, but Chiang accepted restrictions only under extreme pressure and then only partially, stretching the alliance as far as it would go without breaking.

Ultimately, of course, it did "break" because, as Machiavelli warned, weak, small allies are in the end at the mercy of their strong protectors.[4] Eventually, American priorities shifted, and Taipei could no longer offer strategic advantages comparable to what Beijing would provide. But even when the United States finally "abandoned" Taiwan by recognizing the People's Republic of China on 1 January 1979, the reality behind the formal move demonstrated that much of the preexisting relationship, and even Taiwan's ability to manipulate it, remained intact. The Taiwan Relations Act of 1979, the U.S.-Taiwan trade imbalance, and Taiwan's accumulation of foreign reserves attest to the acuity of a vulnerable client state that political scientist Steve Chan aptly characterized as "The Mouse that Roared."[5]

Furthermore, not only did Taiwan hold its own politically, it also avoided the trap of economic dependency that foreign penetration hypothetically ought to have imposed. In stark contrast to theoretical presumptions, Taiwan managed one of the highest sustained growth rates in the world through years of American aid and American investment. Neither the givers of aid nor the subsequent investors drained off profits needed to expand the economy. They did not undermine the ability of the government to direct economic development. On the contrary, according to sociologists Martin K. Whyte and Richard E. Barrett, "economic dependency seems to have been an essential element in maintaining a strong state apparatus in Taiwan, rather than one keeping it weak."[6] This strong state effectively barred imports, rendered Taiwan a production platform rather than a market for foreign goods, and cleverly adapted to fluctuations in the world market rather than being victimized by its volatility. Finally, it did not create an economic elite to collaborate with American business interests, which would arrogate benefits and prevent the wider distribution of profits and technology, but rather fostered a society with an exceedingly high degree of income equality whose commercial sector came to be dominated by small and medium-sized family concerns.

Although dependent upon the United States for sales of its goods, Taiwan used its talents for manipulation to avoid crisis. It learned to cope with protectionism by offering concessions on principle, so long as Washington agreed to flexibility in practice. Although it crafted an economic system more akin to Tokyo's than to Washington's, it proved more adaptable than Japan and better positioned to avoid American sanctions than its Japanese rival.[7]

What Taiwan never could do was to dissuade Washington from pursuing a "two Chinas" policy. Americans saw the Nationalist Chinese as only part of a story, invariably tied to the Communist Chinese. Having been responsible for salvaging the doomed Nationalist regime, Washington refused to fight to restore its control, making impossible either claimant's final assumption of total power. The United States not only stopped the Communists from crossing the Straits to liberate Taiwan but also refused to help the Nationalists try to return to the mainland. Containment in Asia faced both ways, restricting the "free" as much as the Communist Chinese.

For American leaders, a "two Chinas" policy made it possible to protect allies and innocents on Taiwan while also accepting the reality of communist domination on the mainland. It did not matter that neither China welcomed the fragmentation, the loss of territory, political legitimacy, or military security. Washington was not, in the end, much disturbed by the Chinese response and successfully fended off efforts to exact retribution. American policy seemed realistic and practical to each succeeding administration, and so it was sustained.

The history of relations between Taiwan and the United States, then, encompasses a broad journey. The Nationalist Chinese have looked to the U.S. for military, political, and economic support during the war with Japan, the civil war, and after their escape to Taiwan. Even with Taiwan's attainment of prosperity, political diversity, and a significant measure of respect from the world community in the 1990s, the American tie retained a conspicuous centrality. The Nationalists did not, however, allow their needs to overwhelm their sense of purpose, direction, and self. Nationalist goals remained different from those of the American government, and if the United States deterred some actions it acquiesced in others. For Washington the relationship yielded problems ranging from risks of war and depletion of resources to domestic political interference. The benefits, at the same time, proved both concrete and intangible. The United States nurtured an allied military arm, a trading partner, an international relations pawn. But, more important for the presidents and their advisers who took part, Taiwan became a symbol of victory in the cold war. In spite of a forceful challenge and precarious circumstances, the United States protected Taiwan from attack militarily across the Straits and politically at the United Nations. It did so to preserve a bastion of democracy against the evil empire of communism. The true nature of the Nationalist regime was inconsequential in contrast to its image. Moreover, the substance of the relationship—what Taiwan could do for Americans—was far less significant than the testimony it gave to the credibility of American commitments just by surviving.

Taiwanese on the island also urged American aid and secured it in three important ways despite Washington's greater commitment to the mainlanders. Promotion of private enterprise in the early years assisted Taiwanese to establish their dominance over the domestic economy. Sympathy on the part of many Americans for unencumbered political expression, even if that meant independence, allowed its advocates a U.S. base for operations and a sanctuary when flight proved necessary. And American concern for human rights helped put occasional limits on the martial law regime that existed after May 1949 and pressed Nationalist authorities for its eventual end. As time passed, these themes of development, self-determination, and human rights triumphed over all others, effectively altering whom the American government and the business community dealt with and whose future they emphasized when thinking about Taiwan.

By contrast, Americans rarely compromised their commitment to the British in order to take an independent stand on London's colony of Hong Kong. To begin with, the United States' alliance with Great Britain far exceeded in importance any relationship that Americans enjoyed in Asia. If they did not always approve of London's policies in Hong Kong, these were decisions of little real consequence. Sporadic objections to the continuation of colonialism notwithstanding, Americans generally accepted the British presence and lived comfortably within its limitations. In fact, after the advent of communist control on the mainland of China, Washington shared Whitehall's determination to preserve the colony and assisted the British in a variety of ways economically, politically, and even militarily.

The single most important American interest in Hong Kong, of course, remained the economic connection. The American ability to benefit or damage the economy proved second only to London's and at times overwhelmed even that tie. Ironically, as Hong Kong prospered, enjoying the most unrestricted market in Asia, its success produced frictions with the world's rhetorical champion of free trade. Thus, while Taipei maneuvered the United States into concessions, Hong Kong tried to embarrass it into adhering to its principles.

Finally, Hong Kong, even more than Taiwan, lived in the shadow of China. The dominant geographic reality made Hong Kong an incomparable window on mainland affairs, but also subjected it to the vagaries of China's internal politics. Americans used the vantage point, even when this engendered conflict with London, creating a strategic dimension to the relationship and increasing Hong Kong's value to the United States.

For the United States dealing with the problems of Asia often meant involvement with Taiwan and Hong Kong. Washington spent the years from 1945 to 1992 seeking to reconcile its European focus with the persistent political conflicts and growing economic opportunities that demanded attention in the East. The cold war and America's great power convinced policymakers that they could not ignore strife on the Korean peninsula or in Indochina. Still more strongly, they felt themselves obligated to Japan whose strength they intended to shape and use to serve American interests. To this end, they resurrected Japanese industry, reformed its politics, and redirected its foreign relations to encompass Taiwan and exclude China. Over the years United States priorities, of course, shifted, adversaries changed, and arenas of conflict moved from security to economic affairs. But it was never a one-way relationship. Taiwan and, to a lesser extent, Hong Kong supported the United States, reaching beyond their separate identities to play broader roles and justify Washington's continuing efforts to sustain them.

The future promises to be no less complicated than the past. Taiwan and Hong Kong have shared the uncomfortable distinction of being the two outlying territories that the Chinese Communists wanted most to recover after the success of the revolution in 1949. A partial resolution of China's quest was reached in 1984 when London and Beijing agreed on reversion. The arrival of 1997, with Hong Kong's metamorphosis from colony to special administrative zone inside the People's Republic of China, forces

Washington to derive new ways of promoting and protecting American interests in the territory. Reaching a balance between demonstrating concern and practicing intervention will tax imaginations throughout the American government.

Even more challenging, and far more dangerous, is the emerging reality on the island of Taiwan, where those who once dominated policymaking and dictated staunch adherence to the idea of reunification with the mainland have begun to disappear. The trend toward independence, although a minority movement, increasingly captures the imaginations of people who want the international status that ought to accompany their domestic successes. It haunts the minds of people who have traveled to the mainland of China and reject the political and economic conditions that they have observed there. But even were China to change and the disparities grow less pronounced, the idea of independence captivates those who believe that Taiwan has traveled far enough down a road different economically, politically, and culturally from the mainland that formal disengagement would only confirm the actual separation that has already occurred. Determining what the United States ought to do in response to this dynamic requires that Americans put aside assumptions and prejudices and devote considerably more attention than they have in the past to the effort to understand the history of the U.S. relationship with Taiwan. Peace in the Pacific may depend on it.

chapter 2

"TAIWAN" ON THE MAINLAND

The history of United States relations with Taiwan began on the mainland of China. Through the demoralizing 1930s and 1940s, when Chiang Kai-shek sought ineffectively for ways to stave off Japanese invasion, disintegration, and Communist triumph, Americans remained engaged, providing military and economic assistance despite the progressive bankruptcy of the Kuomintang regime. In those years the United States discovered that its advice would be ignored, that its ally could not correct basic problems, and that Nationalist requirements for aid vastly exceeded its capacity to give. Nevertheless, the United States did not abandon the Nationalist Chinese when defeat forced them to flee. But the lessons so sorrowfully learned on the mainland henceforth colored American attitudes toward Chiang and determined the Nationalists' strategy for managing both the Americans and future developments more successfully on Taiwan.

From the beginning of military confrontation between Japan and China, leading to full-scale war in 1937, the United States demonstrated the dismay and inaction that would characterize its behavior toward events in Asia until Pearl Harbor. In the 1930s Americans concentrated their energies and resources on dealing with the internal economic upheaval caused by the Great Depression. If they worried about foreign affairs, it was to berate European nations for not paying their First World War debts or to wonder about the significance of the emergence of Hitler's National Socialist Party.

Japan, meanwhile, anxiously watched as Chiang Kai-shek led the Kuomintang party and army to unify China in 1928. Chiang, an austere and autocratic figure with a veneer of Christian piety, derived his power from a personal network established at the Whampoa Military Academy, from Shanghai gangster affiliations, and from his association with Sun Yat-sen, the "father" of the modern Chinese state. Although politically conservative, he tolerated and utilized Sun's alliance with China's fledgling communist movement to win popular support and rid the country of foreign privilege. But the emergence of a strong China would, inevitably, curtail development of a Japanese empire on the Asian mainland. In September 1931, Japan's ambitious military leaders resolved to forestall unification by taking over the northern most provinces of China, an area known as Manchuria.

Neither the League of Nations nor the United States demonstrated any willingness to stop Japanese depredations. While the League studied the problem, Secretary of State Henry Stimson rejected the idea of U.S. economic sanctions because of President Herbert Hoover's reluctance to impose them and the strength of the Japanese economy. Instead, on 7 January 1932, Stimson settled for a public statement of nonrecognition, the so-called Stimson Doctrine, which refused to acknowledge the legality of any situation that infringed upon U.S. rights in China, denounced violation of the Kellogg-Briand Pact outlawing war, and, notably, lacked any means of enforcement. The Japanese consolidated their control over the area and in March declared the birth of a new state called Manchukuo.

Despite the obvious bankruptcy of America's response to Japan's blatant aggression, Washington's Asian policy continued largely unaltered for the rest of the decade. Franklin Delano Roosevelt, who assumed the presidency in early 1933, claimed to harbor warm feelings for the Chinese based on early commercial contacts the Delano family had established with China, but emotion did not shape policy. The president moved further than Stimson and Hoover in appeasing Japan by cutting back on economic aid to China. Continued Japanese advances in north China were met by perfunctory protests.

Worse, in 1934, Roosevelt blithely undermined China's economy to placate American business interests. Congress passed a silver purchase act which sucked silver dollars out of China creating a serious recession as currency became scarce. But Roosevelt, familial sensitivity notwithstanding, decided that the political risks of undermining the domestic silver lobby were too great and that any effort to compensate China through economic assistance would simply anger Japan. The best American policy would be no policy. China must resolve the crisis on its own. In 1935 America forced China off the silver standard.

The lack of American compassion for China stemmed in part from a growing sense that the Chinese were not doing enough for themselves to merit outside assistance. Although under fierce attack from abroad, they remained divided among different factions within the ruling party and opposing camps outside it. Chiang Kai-shek assumed increasingly dictatorial powers and surrounded himself with conservative advisers whose solutions for contemporary problems involved reviving Confucian traditions. The

1934 New Life Movement enjoined a code of Confucian behavior (demanding proper posture and banning spitting) that seemed wildly out of touch with pressing political problems. Chiang coupled this with a fascist determination to militarize the populace so that through discipline they could learn to endure suffering. He created his own Blue Shirt corps of secret police who rejected democracy as the root of chaos and blamed foreign powers for all of China's troubles.[1] Reforms launched during the Nanking decade, 1928–37, did further the modernization of China's economy, and Americans participated in carrying forward the transformation. But reforms remained firmly under Chiang's control and were pursued only to the degree that they did not threaten his predominance.[2] His closest advisers reinforced his most reactionary instincts. Although Chiang would not spell out his beliefs until 1943 with publication of China's Destiny, the policies and impulses were there far earlier. Washington could not help but see that Chiang's Christian facade did not prevent him from being anti-Western and that his need for American assistance did not diminish his anti-Americanism.

Even the actual outbreak of war between China and Japan in 1937 generated nothing more than studied American nonintervention. Henry Luce, whose missionary roots in China made him a lifelong campaigner for Nationalist China's salvation, tried to rally support by putting Generalissimo Chiang Kai-shek and his wife on the cover of Time magazine as man and wife of the year but generated no concrete assistance. Roosevelt did refrain from invoking the Neutrality Act, by refusing to recognize that a state of war existed, so the U.S. did not have to interrupt sales of arms or munitions to China, halt the use of American shipping, or decline the making of loans. But the Chinese did not have the funds for major purchases, and no loans were granted to them until the end of 1938.

Despite growing sympathy for the victims of Japan's brutal aggression, the United States remained caught in a pacifist mood that precluded any effective response to growing turmoil. The American people wanted to stay out of war, whether in Europe or Asia, and their leaders had become convinced that policies to the contrary would bring political punishment. When, on 5 October 1937, Roosevelt issued his famous call to quarantine an "epidemic of world lawlessness," he sought to ascertain the limits of presidential action through a major foreign policy address in the heart of the supposedly isolationist Midwest. He concluded immediately, and perhaps falsely, that his vision had not carried the day and abruptly abandoned the venture.[3]

Efforts to curb Japan's ability to conquer China came only slowly. Not until July of 1940, after the fall of France and the launching of Tokyo's southern strategy, which projected Japanese troops into Indochina, did Washington embargo aviation fuel and high-grade iron and scrap steel. In the interim Washington inadvertently heightened Japan's ability to acquire war matériel through cash-and-carry measures designed to assist Great

Britain. Moreover, despite termination of the U.S.-Japan Treaty of Commerce and Navigation, American sales of petroleum products to Japan escalated significantly during 1940.

The Chinese government found the American attitude incomprehensible and intolerable. Japanese troops ravaged the countryside and drove resistance forces back into the inaccessible hinterlands of far western China. Trading space for time, Chiang abandoned the modern, industrialized portions of the country, placing his government's fortunes in the hands of China's most tradition-bound landed elites. Further, this was warlord territory in which Chiang's control was challenged repeatedly by local military and political figures.[4] As the obscurantist and repressive features of his regime deepened, American criticism of the Kuomintang deepened as well. The United States found it difficult to reconcile the narrowing of political discourse in China with expectations of a liberal political order, which U.S. assistance was intended to promote and defend.

In an attempt to coerce the United States into being more responsive to China's desperate need, Chiang went so far as to threaten a separate peace.[5] Aware that Washington reserved its central attention for turmoil in Europe and that support flowed most abundantly across the Atlantic, Chiang nevertheless flooded Washington with appeals both to resist Japanese demands and assist China's struggle. He also mounted a lobbying effort in Washington designed to keep the war in Asia a present concern of officials.

The wartime China lobby operated initially through an arm of the Chungking (Chongqing) government called the Universal Trading Corporation (replaced in 1941 by China Defense Supplies). Structured as a purchasing agency, UTC allowed the U.S. to provide funds for China without alerting or alarming Japan. At the same time, its broad mandate included creation of a network of paid agents and influential friends who could help to shape policy. T. V. Soong, Chiang's brother-in-law, headed the operation and recruited those—like Roosevelt-insider Thomas Corcoran—capable of bypassing the bureaucracy.[6] One concrete result of Nationalist efforts was the development of a volunteer air force, the Flying Tigers, under the command of retired army air force pilot Claire Chennault, which, although restrained from mounting incendiary attacks on Japanese cities, did damage Japan's forces in China.

But it took Tokyo to do for China's cause what neither Chiang nor pro-Chinese American groups like the Committee for Non-Participation in Japanese Aggression could do. On 27 September 1940 Tokyo joined Berlin and Rome in the Tripartite Pact, thereby merging images of the devil in American minds and simplifying Roosevelt's effort to mobilize the United States for war. The Axis alliance would, in fact, produce few benefits for Japan, but it did make Japanese-American accommodation in the Pacific much less likely. American aid to China escalated, and by May 1941 Chungking became eligible for lend-lease. Finally, in July 1941, with Tokyo's armies advancing into southern Indochina, the United States froze Japan's assets in the U.S. and embargoed gasoline. Although this measure made war virtually inevitable, Washington still hoped to avoid confrontation.

Throughout the late summer and early autumn of 1941, American and Japanese negotiators tried to find a way to prevent a final breakdown. Resolution of the crisis short of war, however, proved impossible. For the Japanese, minimal conditions included the end of American assistance to the Chinese and acquiescence in a peace settlement imposed on China, as well as guaranteed access to oil supplies from southeast Asia. Washington insisted on Japanese withdrawal from both China and Indochina and renunciation of the Axis pact. More important, the Roosevelt administration wanted to protect Australia and New Zealand so that their troops would remain in North Africa fighting the Germans and to prevent the Japanese from striking north, which would force Moscow to withdraw troops from the European front. In order to preserve European access to raw materials, the U.S. also needed to guard the colonial holdings of European allies that Japan might try to seize.[7] But pressures from China and the China lobby made it clear that Japanese aggression not only would have to be contained but also would have to be rolled back.[8] Thus a Sunday morning surprise attack on Pearl Harbor and four years of a brutal and costly war would be necessary to change the direction of American-Japanese-Chinese relations.

As much as Roosevelt's men had labored to avoid a fight, Chiang Kai-shek had hoped that the war would engulf the Americans since this seemed to be his only hope of victory. Marooned in his mountain fastness at Chungking and increasingly preoccupied with military campaigns against the Communists rather than against the Japanese, Chiang counted on Tokyo to stimulate American intervention. Indeed, upon word of the destruction at Pearl Harbor:

> the military council was jubilant. Chiang was so happy he sang an old opera aria. . . . The Kuomintang government officials went around congratulating each other, as if a great victory had been won. . . . Now China's strategic importance would grow even more. American money and equipment would flow in; half a billion dollars, one billion dollars. . . . Now America would have to support Chiang, and that meant U.S. dollars into the pockets of the officials, into the pockets of the army commanders, and guns . . . for the coming war against Yenan.[9]

In the contrast between America's distress and China's joy on 7 December could be gauged the degree to which these allies saw the world differently and would clash in the future. Although thrown together in a relationship that would last almost four decades, their national interests coincided only sporadically and superficially. But in December 1941 the disparity appeared less important. Necessity dictated collaboration.

Nevertheless, the American response proved not to be what Chiang had anticipated. A major commitment to the Pacific theater did not follow the Japanese attack. Aid did increase but not as much as China needed or wanted. Roosevelt quite consciously sought to prevent immersion in the Asian conflict and to that end planned the North African campaign to get U.S. troops engaged against the Nazis as quickly as possible. Until Germany's surrender in the spring of 1945, Washington consistently gave highest priority to smashing Hitler and provided the Pacific war the minimum attention and resources needed to keep the struggle there alive.

The public relations side of the effort compensated somewhat for shortfalls in material support. Madame Chiang Kai-shek received an enthusiastic welcome during her 1942–43 tour of the United States. Henry Luce put the Generalissimo back on *Time/Life* covers for an unprecedented four additional appearances before 1945. Where concrete assistance proved unavailable, gestures sometimes sufficed, including repeal of Chinese exclusion and the signing of a treaty in 1943 that relinquished extraterritoriality.[10]

Chiang Kai-shek, Mme. Chiang, and, later, the Generalissimo's son Chiang Ching-kuo symbolized "Free China" to many Americans and Chinese. *Courtesy of the Government Information Office and CCNAA, R.O.C.*

In the field, however, cooperation proved far more difficult than either side had expected. What Chiang wanted was money, not American advice. Specialists dispatched by Roosevelt could not get serious attention for their recommendations. More important, although Chiang complied with American wishes and agreed to have a U.S. military representative on his staff, foreign minister T.V. Soong made it clear that the KMT government preferred a general with no previous knowledge of China. Instead they got "Vinegar" Joe Stilwell, an acerbic, decisive, and pragmatic man, whose service in China dated back to the 1920s, who spoke Mandarin, and who happened also to be close to Army Chief of Staff George C. Marshall.

The result proved disastrous. Stilwell's highest priority became his effort to build a serious Chinese fighting force to be used in keeping land routes to Burma open.[11] But Chiang did not want a modern army with effective officers who owed their loyalty to the institution and the country rather than to him personally. He also did not want to squander men and equipment to retain land access when the United States could fly supplies in over the Himalayan mountains at no direct cost to the KMT (whatever the burden might be for Washington). Instead, Chiang husbanded his resources for the civil war and kept 500,000 of his best troops in the northwest blockading the Chinese Communists.

Chiang's recalcitrance aroused Stilwell's fury, and the General spent the next two years trying to use Roosevelt to force Chiang to fight the war "properly" and to undermine the Generalissimo's power when he refused to. Thus Stilwell took the highly questionable route of providing weapons to Chiang's rivals, mounting training projects for troops for the Burma campaign, and may even have explored ways to oust the Generalissimo. Stilwell's influence with Roosevelt grew, however, not because of his own activities but because of the spectacular failure of General Chennault's war plans approved over Stilwell's objections. As Chennault's air operation began to hurt the Japanese forces, they predictably turned on the air bases, wiping out seven in the spring of 1944 because Chennault and Chiang had not adequately protected them. Chiang's refusal to supply their defenders, because of uncertain lines of loyalty, allowed the Japanese to overrun the bases at great loss of life and equipment.[12] Roosevelt, possessed of an ally who would not fight in Burma and frequently not even on his own territory, grew sufficiently disgusted that he turned down new aid for the Nationalists.[13] The president also acceded to Stilwell's oft repeated proposal that he be given command of China's armies.

Stilwell's triumph proved fleeting. True to his acerbic personality and reveling in the opportunity to humiliate a man he despised, Stilwell presented Chiang with the new reality in a humiliating confrontation. Stilwell soon found himself forced unceremoniously to leave China, having affronted a head of state who refused to have any further contact with him. He left behind a victorious but marginalized Chinese leader. Washington's frustration and American military technology, which had made an island-hopping campaign viable, eliminated the need to rely upon the China mainland.[14]

But Roosevelt, while slighting China's wartime needs, did make plans for China as a postwar power. The president recognized that Asian politics would be fundamentally transformed during the conflict by the emergence of nationalism. Colonial empires that had long dominated the area would be swept away. The challenge posed for the United States by this inevitable trend would be to work with emerging local leaders to reform their societies through gradual change. Helping to bridge the cultural gap would be a strong, united China under the leadership of a modernizing, Western-educated elite. This China could better perform its role as one of the world's four policemen. Thus, the United States insisted that it be given a position, along with the U.S., Great Britain, France, and the Soviet Union, on the soon-to-be-created United Nations Security Council.

Compensating for wartime neglect with postwar political munificence did not sit well with the British. Prime Minister Winston Churchill found Roosevelt's demand that China be treated as an important world power absurd. The British felt little but contempt for Chiang Kai-shek and complained that the U.S. intended China to cast "faggot" votes on Washington's behalf in international organizations.[15]

China, in fact, not only was to be a pawn in international organizations of the future but also would enter the postwar era locked into a series of commitments made by Roosevelt with the Soviet Union at Yalta. Anxious to secure Soviet participation in the Pacific war, FDR had bartered Chinese political, economic, and security rights in Manchuria and Mongolia. Roosevelt acknowledged that he had no explicit authorization from Chiang to bargain but pledged to see to it that "these claims of the Soviet Union shall be unquestionably fulfilled after Japan has been defeated."[16]

China's weakness was manifested further as the Nationalist government struggled to reassert control over the Chinese mainland after Tokyo's precipitous surrender. In this effort American assistance proved essential but not sufficient. The U.S. agreed to fly KMT troops to east China so that they could liberate long-occupied areas. But whereas American advisers urged Chiang to focus his energies on recovering China proper, below the Great Wall, Chiang insisted upon retaking all Chinese territory. This made early and violent confrontation with the Communist Chinese inevitable, given their deployment in Manchuria.

The Americans wanted above all to avert the rekindling of civil war and believed that through American mediation a coalition government could be created. To this end, the president, now Harry S Truman, dispatched George Catlett Marshall, a World War II hero and trusted presidential adviser, to China. General Marshall embarked on his mediation effort with a sense of urgency sparked by his conviction that the Chinese Communists and the Soviet Union were working together. He believed, however, that if the

Wartime Cairo Conference, November 1943. Nationalist China was promised return of all Japanese-occupied territories after the war. From left to right: Chiang Kai-shek, Franklin D. Roosevelt, Winston Churchill, Madame Chiang Kai-shek. *Courtesy Franklin D. Roosevelt Library*

Chinese Communists could be brought into the government, they would be transformed by the redemptive power of constitutional democracy.[17] He labored diligently, therefore, to reconcile the Communists and Nationalists even though critical of Chiang and aware that by continuing to supply the Generalissimo with weapons the United States could hardly be characterized as impartial.

The Marshall mission's central purpose was to bring the warring parties together, avoiding fresh bloodshed through compromise. Although Washington and Moscow had already embarked on the road to confrontation in Europe, Truman did not yet determine policies in China on the basis of cold war assumptions. Instead, in advocating absorption of Communists into a coalition government, he demonstrated less concern about internal subversion than about unrestricted fighting.

Harry Truman's views on foreign policy remained flexible in these early days of his presidency even though he took delight in projecting an image of toughness. During his congressional career and as vice president, he had had little occasion to think about foreign affairs and knew virtually nothing about Asia. He left these issues to the State Department, rarely intervening directly in such questions unless he felt American prestige or national interests might be threatened by foreign or partisan attacks. Nonetheless, he did not see the communist world as monolithic and entertained doubts about the degree of control Moscow exerted over the CCP (Chinese Communist Party). Moreover, he became increasingly disillusioned with Chiang Kai-shek and the Nationalists, believing them to be corrupt and incompetent. Accordingly, the president could see advantages for the U.S. in cooperation between the warring factions in China.

During the anti-Japanese struggle, Americans had come to feel that they could work with the Chinese Communists. Journalists, military officers, and diplomats who traveled to their northwest headquarters at Yenan portrayed them as youthful, honest, energetic, patriotic, and popular. The CCP had implemented moderate land-reform policies and operated effective guerrilla units behind Japanese lines. Assistance in the rescuing of downed American flyers and celebration of the Fourth of July 1944 boded well. The Dixie Mission, a U.S. army observer group sent to "rebel" territory, found that planning for joint operations against the Japanese went smoothly.[18] Those Americans who had the opportunity to deal directly with Communist officials Mao Zedong and Zhou Enlai found them attractive, friendly, and inspired leaders whose eagerness to work with the United States actually occasioned an offer to travel to Washington to confer with Roosevelt on defeating Tokyo.[19]

Also positive were the implications of American conversations with Soviet leaders about the political complexion of China. Joseph Stalin assured Ambassador Patrick Hurley and others that the Communists in China were not serious communists and that Moscow would support the Chiang Kai-shek regime.[20] At Yalta in February 1945 Roosevelt secured Stalin's pledge to that effect, and in the summer of 1945, just as World War II ground to an end, the Soviets and Nationalist Chinese signed a Treaty of Friendship and Alliance. Americans and Nationalist Chinese celebrated this development as the death knell for the Communist forces. Coming as a considerable shock to the CCP, this agreement did suggest that Stalin would not provide aid vital to a civil war victory and significantly demoralized them.[21]

Nevertheless, in Manchuria the situation proved more complicated. Stalin had acted on his Yalta commitment to confront Japanese forces in Manchuria and occupied much of the area before Tokyo's surrender. Thereafter, he delayed withdrawing Soviet troops to allow the CCP to strengthen its hold on the territory. Although the Russians stripped factories, taking machinery, inventories, and heavy weapons to the USSR, they did leave the Chinese Communists light weaponry that proved useful in the subsequent struggle.

Marshall went to China with a presidential mandate to stabilize the situation and, miraculously, arranged a ceasefire. Trying to capitalize on success, he returned to the United States seeking a substantial economic assistance package with which to rehabilitate and modernize China. But neither Marshall nor Truman gave sufficient credence to the depths of the split between the Kuomintang and the Communist Chinese. The truce rapidly disintegrated. Chiang Kai-shek believed that with his superior numbers and equipment he could easily defeat the Communists. They, for their part, hoped to avoid immediate war but increasingly distrusted Marshall who, despite rhetoric about evenhandedness, in the end clearly favored the KMT.

The civil war that followed the collapse of the Marshall Mission arrested any serious efforts at restoration or modernization of China. To begin with, reimposition of Nationalist authority in eastern China proved not to be a happy experience for the newly liberated masses. Instead of being freed from oppression, they simply faced a new tyranny. The Nationalists treated those who had remained behind under Japanese control as collaborators and descended upon the cities of the east like locusts.[22] Inflation, already serious when the war with Japan ended, rapidly worsened. American attempts to encourage reforms had no impact.

Efforts on the part of the United Nations Relief and Rehabilitation Administration and its American successor organization, the Economic Cooperation Administration, foundered on the shoals of civil conflict. Chiang refused to allow aid to be distributed in areas not firmly under his control. Government agencies frequently misappropriated or misapplied limited resources.[23]

Chiang's insistence on dominating economic and military as well as political developments in China stymied more than economic recovery. In a surprisingly short period of time, the Nationalists squandered their tremendous advantage in men and matériel. Battle after battle ended in ignominious defeat. Nationalist soldiers fought badly, and their leaders provided little inspiration or guidance. Chiang threw 400,000 into a doomed effort to win back Manchuria and on the plains of Central China, late in 1948, sacrificed another 200,000 of his fighting men to the guns of better-trained and more ably commanded Communist troops. When the Generalissimo decided to bomb his own forces rather than to allow their weapons and supplies to fall into Communist hands, he made tragically clear the bankruptcy of his resistance effort.

Military disarray was but one symptom of the political disorder within the ruling Kuomintang party. It had long been evident to Americans that factionalism characterized the Nationalist government, preventing appointment of effective generals or competent bureaucrats.[24] Chiang Kai-shek encouraged the competition between groups so as to protect his own transcendent authority. He nourished corruption—although probably honest himself—to render subordinates vulnerable to punishment. Disputes focused on power more often than on policy and would have disrupted effective administration even without the pressure of the growing Communist threat.[25] In the face of that challenge the constant infighting proved disastrous.

This was true not just on the battlefield but also in the diplomatic arena where Nationalist representatives grappled to secure support adequate to pre-

HOW LONG?

Cartoon by Loring. *Courtesy of the* Providence Bulletin

serve both their own narrow interests as well as those of the failing regime. Chinese Ambassador to the United States V. K. Wellington Koo wrote plaintively to the Nationalist Foreign Ministry in July 1949 of the confusion created "from the fact that half a dozen groups have their special representatives pressing forward their own views all as being in the best interests of China. Our American friends both in the Administration and on Capitol Hill . . . regard the situation here as a 'miniature China' reflecting the disunity in our country."[26] Chronically uninformed, the ambassador could not coordinate appeals for aid to American sources and found it impossible to avoid the embarrassment of having embassy initiatives undermined from China.

The din of competing voices did not obscure the message to Washington policymakers, but it did diminish still further the desire of Americans to aid the Chinese. State Department officials viewed Nationalist maneuvers skeptically, seeing them as designed to draw the United States into China's civil war. Such schemes included approaching the United Nations to have Moscow declared in violation of the 1945 Sino-Soviet Treaty of Friendship, which had pledged Soviet support to Chiang, a coastal blockade of China coupled with bombing of Chinese Communist facilities utilizing American planes, and proposals for a Pacific security pact modeled on NATO. The UN initiative attempting to indict the Soviet Union, for instance, pressed in spite of initial State Department reservations, foundered when CCP demands for China's seat in the General Assembly and the Security Council led the KMT to the view that any UN appeal exposed its status to dangerous scrutiny. Minister Counselor Lewis Clark observed that "in this as in so many other heartbreaking experiences I have had with the Chinese in the past two years, the Chinese just seem unable to do anything positive themselves. They always want the United States to do it first and for them."[27] The State Department and the White House, recognizing the desperation of a collapsing regime, were loath to commit further resources or prestige to a doomed rescue mission.

But not all Americans shared their disillusionment or could countenance abandoning the Nationalist cause. A coalition of politicians, journalists, scholars, businessmen, military leaders, and missionaries tried to keep the Chinese Kuomintang government's survival an issue of national significance in the United States. Rooted in the World War II procurement effort, but dubbed the "China lobby" by the New York Communist Party in 1949, this loosely organized grouping worked with Chiang's emissaries to secure appropriations for economic and military assistance from Congress and to prevent political recognition of the Communist Chinese by the president. The motives of China lobby members ranged from genuine concern about Chiang Kai-shek to a desire for an election issue with which to best the Democrats in 1948 (and again in 1952). Some spoke sincerely about the importance of a special relationship between Americans and Chinese based on missionary endeavor and Washington's turn-of-the-century open door policy of equal commercial opportunity and territorial integrity. All feared the threat of Communist takeover because they would lose the profits of trade and manufacturing enterprises, the devotion of converts, or the opportunity to make of China a strategic bastion against the Soviet Union. In pursuing their ends, they did not hesitate to condemn their opponents as fools and traitors. They toiled to make support for Chiang and loyalty to the American government synonymous; in time, they succeeded.

The days of real power, however, had not yet arrived in the 1940s. The China lobby labored diligently through newspaper columns and letter-writing campaigns to influence public opinion, members of Congress, and officials in the Departments of State and Defense. Chiang's supporters gave testimony to congressional committees, arranged all-expenses-paid "research" trips to China, and made campaign contributions. The Chinese government also maintained a secret fund for such special projects as the recruitment of highly placed "advisers" who could "guarantee" support from the Pentagon.[28] The China lobby's bloc in Congress did succeed in preventing the cut off of aid to the Kuomintang by holding Marshall Plan funds and the Military Assistance Program hostage, but the volume of that support remained consistently well below what the U.S. proved willing to give to Europe. Never once did a China bloc member offer a constructive, coherent, and rational program for China prior to war in Korea.

In fact, throughout the 1940s and beyond, the power of Chiang's sympathizers to destroy remained greater than their ability to create positive policies. As early as 1945, Ambassador Patrick Hurley had been able to damage the careers of several Foreign Service officers by accusing them of unpatriotic sympathy for the Communist cause in China. Despite valuable expertise on Chinese affairs, they found themselves dispersed to posts in Latin America and Europe.

Nationalist Chinese officials concluded quickly that a Republican administration would be more useful than a Democratic one. They looked forward to a Dewey victory in 1948 and assumed that this would solve their financial worries. When Truman won, they were devastated. Having endured a Truman/Marshall arms embargo from 1946 to 1947, they had minimal faith in a Democratic White House.

The new secretary of state, Dean Acheson, confirmed their suspicions with his unsympathetic attitude. Having watched the Nationalists squander American aid and ignore American advice, Acheson, never a patient man, sought to minimize U.S. responsibility for Kuomintang fortunes. Throughout his tenure he remained a confirmed Atlanticist who had difficulty believing that China was important to Washington. And, although events forced him to spend a considerable amount of his time and energy on Asian problems, he never developed a serious interest in understanding the region, its people, or its politics. Although constrained by the political dangers of undermining

BEEN TO THE CLEANERS

Cartoon by Little. *Courtesy of the* Nashville Tennessean

an ally, Acheson redirected aid voted by Congress from China to China's periphery and published the China White Paper.

This 1,054-page document on U.S. relations with China released by the administration in August 1949 attempted to demonstrate that the United States had done all that it could for the Nationalists. Chiang Kai-shek's imminent defeat could not, it contended, be attributed to any lack of aid from Washington, which had contributed some $2 billion, but rather was due to military ineptitude and political corruption. The fact that Truman and Acheson allowed confidential cables and memoranda to be revealed testified to their own partisan concerns and gave ammunition to their opponents. Attacks from pro-Chiang sympathizers bitterly denounced the administration for delivering the final blow to an allied and dependent nation.[29]

The Truman administration had, in fact, been engaged in serious discussion about the future of Sino-American relations. Whereas the president refused to allow American Ambassador John Leighton Stuart to go to Peking to attempt to open negotiations with Chinese Communist leaders in July 1949, the U.S. did not close its diplomatic missions in Communist-controlled areas.[30] Acheson assembled a group of respected outside consultants to make policy recommendations and, in the autumn, hosted a roundtable discussion that tapped the views of scholars from around the country.[31] At the same time, Great Britain increasingly expressed concern regarding its economic holdings in China and made clear not only that it would probably recognize a new government in China but that it hoped the United States would do so too.

The issue could not long be avoided. On 1 October 1949 Mao Zedong declared the establishment of the People's Republic of China. The Communists had seized the mandate of heaven.

• • •

At the end of the 1940s, with the civil war on the mainland of China having resulted in a Communist victory, the United States looked back on more than a decade of reluctant and disheartening involvement in Chinese affairs. Americans generally had had minimal interest in Asia, and those who had sentimental or monetary bonds wielded little influence. Japanese aggression finally dictated Washington's commitment to helping China. Although Chiang Kai-shek celebrated, he remained unhappy with the amount of aid and resistant to American attempts to reform his armies or his government.

The differences in U.S. and Nationalist Chinese objectives, which complicated fighting the war against Japan, became even more apparent in the civil war years. The U.S., perhaps naively, wanted to bring about a negotiated settlement between the KMT and the Chinese Communists. It dispatched a series of diplomats, culminating with the Marshall Mission, to realize this goal by creating a coalition government. But neither Chinese side wanted a compromise peace, although the CCP was willing to accept a temporary one to buy time for self-strengthening. Chiang, however, recognized that Washington believed it had no alternative but to support him and remained intransigent. Kuomintang disarray on the battlefield, in politics, and in diplomacy, as well as in the economy, brought rapid defeat.

As a result, the Nationalists fled to Taiwan, and the United States faced the decision of whether to continue its diplomatic ties to the losers or to confront the political perils of choosing to recognize the winners. Given the largely frustrating, dispiriting, and fruitless association with Chiang, there seemed good reasons for a change of course. But ideological and domestic political concerns that had circumscribed past policies remained in place, and Chiang astutely utilized these factors to preserve his power and to manipulate his American connection.

chapter 3

COMMITMENT AND CRISIS: THE ALLIANCE, 1950–1965

The island of Taiwan became home to the Nationalist Chinese in 1949 at a moment of crisis and despair. No alternatives existed, but the vulnerable sanctuary seemed an inauspicious place to try to create a viable government and an economic engine that could drive a return to power. Most observers expected internal disintegration, quickened by external attack, leading to the final fall of the Kuomintang regime.

Taiwan had for centuries occupied a peculiar place in Chinese consciousness and Chinese history. Competed over by the Dutch, Spanish, and Japanese, it became a haven for Chinese adventurers as well as for Ming dynasty loyalists who fled there to escape the Manchu conquest of 1644. Although increasing numbers of mainlanders settled on the island seeking economic opportunity, the Ch'ing dynasty exerted control only slowly and reluctantly. For the central government, the large, mountainous wilderness, roughly the size of Massachusetts, Connecticut, and Rhode Island combined, presented only administrative and peacekeeping problems rather than a source of profits or prestige. To American Commodore Matthew Perry, whose orders were to open the more northerly Japanese islands in 1853–54, annexation of Taiwan seemed a logical next step.[1] Neither he nor his successor Townsend Harris nor Commissioner to China Peter Parker succeeded in convincing Washington that acquisition of even a portion of the island would be in the national interest. This remained true even after the USS *Rover* ran aground in March 1867, and aborigines murdered the crew. Chinese officials attempted to fend off demands by the belligerent U.S. consul at Amoy, Charles W. LeGendre, to punish the killers, fearing American efforts to seize the island might follow. But though LeGendre and others in the China service recommended such a route be taken, Washington remained unmoved. Similarly in 1875, after Congress supported establishment of steamship routes to Asia, coal samples sent to Washington from Taiwan could not overcome official lack of interest.[2]

The Sino-Japanese War of 1894–95 cut short any latent American designs on Taiwan and China's opportunities to develop the island. A decade earlier, a reformist governor dispatched from China had begun a program of modernization, making Taipei the first Chinese city with electric streetlights. But in 1895 as part of the Shimonoseki Treaty settlement, and over local protests, Peking ceded Taiwan to the Japanese. Resistance activities marked the early years of occupation, but in time it became apparent that Japanese domination meant prosperity. The inequitable distribution of land, resource and industrial ownership, and efforts to eradicate Chinese language and culture bred continuing hostility, but interest in returning to Chinese rule diminished as the comparative backwardness of the mainland became increasingly apparent.

Being part of the Japanese empire proved a very mixed blessing. During World War I demands for democracy arose on the island in response to the Chinese May Fourth Movement of 1919 and the principles of self-determination articulated by Woodrow Wilson in his 14 Points. Japanese leaders ignored such concerns, implementing aggressively assimilationist policies to make Taiwan a more reliable base of operations. Thus, in the Second World War, planes from Taiwan brought destruction to the Philippines, and, in turn, beginning in 1943, American aircraft waged a debilitating air war against Japanese forces on the island.[3] The U.S. Navy planned an assault on Taiwan and trained a large force of military and civilian personnel to take over administration immediately in the wake of Japan's expected surrender.[4] Ultimately, at the behest of General Douglas MacArthur, who emphasized the importance of recapturing the Philippines, American forces bypassed Taiwan, isolating the Japanese contingents on the island.

Allied policy toward the island, however, was to treat it as occupied territory and to return it to China. Roosevelt, Churchill, and Chiang Kai-shek agreed on this at Cairo in December 1943. Stalin accepted their decision at Teheran, and conferees at Potsdam in July 1945 reconfirmed the policy.

Reimposition of Chinese authority did not proceed smoothly. The people of Taiwan joyously welcomed liberation in 1945, but enthusiasm rapidly turned to bitterness. As on the mainland, returning Chinese officials treated the Taiwanese as Japanese collaborators, excluding them even more completely from political power than had been the case for Chinese in the eastern provinces of the mainland. Symbolic of Chiang's grim determination to dominate Taiwan was his appointment of a brutal crony, Ch'en Yi, as governor. Under Ch'en's unscrupulous administration, thoroughly predictable given his disastrous rule in Fukien from 1934 to 1941, the Nationalists systematically looted the island, stripping its people of as much as $1 billion in property. Relative prosperity gave way to inflation, unemployment, and a precipitous drop in production. The breakdown of local services such as sanitation, while officials concentrated on collecting booty instead of garbage, led to the emergence of plague, smallpox, and malaria.[5] Taiwan appeared to have passed from subjugation at the hands of an imperial government in Tokyo to a far more irresponsible and costly subjugation at the hands of an inept government in Nanking.

Disillusionment and anger generated by Nationalist policies ultimately exploded. At the beginning of 1947, Ch'en announced that, because of their inexperience with self-rule, the people of Taiwan would not enjoy the new constitution promulgated on the mainland. Instead Taiwan would remain under Kuomintang tutelage. At the same time, some 20 percent of government employees would be terminated for budgetary reasons, and 20 percent of loans to private merchants would be recalled.[6] In such an atmosphere, a relatively insignificant incident on 28 February 1947 escalated quickly into a mass uprising. Ostensibly a protest against the arrest of a woman for selling untaxed cigarettes, resistance spread quickly across the island and did not subside until large contingents of troops from the mainland brutally smashed the demonstrations. The executions and terror that followed eliminated thousands of opponents to Nationalist rule and deepened animosity between the Taiwanese and mainlanders.[7]

American observers in Taiwan found it difficult to report on these developments. A prominent exception was General Albert C. Wedemeyer who stopped in Taiwan in the course of his mission to assess Chiang's fortunes and warned that Taiwanese "fear that the Central Government contemplates bleeding their island to support the tottering and corrupt Nanking machine." He added that he believed their concerns to be "well founded" and spoke of interest on the island in either U.S. control or a UN trusteeship.[8] More commonly Chinese Nationalist officials withheld information and encouraged anti-American propaganda. In the aftermath of the 28 February Incident, they tried to pretend that the violence had been at least in part aimed at the U.S. Embassy. At the same time, according to George Kerr, who was serving with the American Embassy in Taipei at the time, the U.S. government was not eager to know what was happening. Determined to support the Chinese government and to avoid carping criticism that might weaken it, Washington disregarded evidence of turmoil.[9]

Willful ignorance became less possible when advocates of Taiwan independence appealed directly to U.S. officials to assist them. Some of those who survived the suppression fled to Hong Kong where they initiated a Taiwan independence movement demanding self-determination. Others, who chose instead to seek refuge in Japan, vigorously pursued the support of American occupation authorities working with the G-2 intelligence section of the Supreme Command for Allied Powers under MacArthur. Bereft of alternatives, they appealed for a United States takeover and custodianship until an indigenous government could be formed. But although Americans listened patiently, they never considered these proposals seriously and dismissed the desperate Taiwanese as irresponsible and unrealistic.[10]

Chiang Kai-shek, at the same time, turned Taiwan into a fortress and expected the United States to protect it. He refused to accept defeat and quietly go into exile in the Philippines or elsewhere, forcing American policymakers to devise a policy to deal with his remnant Republic of China (Taiwan) government tenuously ensconced on an offshore island. Various alternatives seemed to present themselves, but rapidly changing circumstances quickly narrowed American options.[11]

During the autumn of 1948, as military disasters unfolded on the mainland, political pressure on Chiang Kai-shek to relinquish the presidency had mounted. In preparation for his departure from office and eventual flight from the mainland, the Generalissimo had 100 cases of art treasures from the Palace Museum, originally moved to southwest China to save them from Japan, sent on to Taiwan. But cultural artifacts would not sustain his political fortunes the way money would, so Chiang also directed the Bank of China to transfer its assets to the island. Public outcry temporarily halted such shipments, preserving some funds for the successor regime, but Chiang had already managed to remove all the government's gold bars, and late in 1949 he convinced the Bank's governor to send the remaining funds to him before the Communists took over.

Li Tsung-jen, who assumed the presidency with Chiang's departure on 21 January 1949, found control over the government's money to be only one of many areas in which his newly acquired powers were severely circumscribed. Generals continued to take orders directly from Chiang; Li could not replace civil officials who refused to resign or be fired, nor could he prevent the Generalissimo from conducting diplomatic negotiations on behalf of the country without presidential clearance. Li appealed to American Ambassador Stuart for help. First, he tried to convince the ambassador to accept a lien on Taiwan in exchange for a silver loan. Then, he urged Stuart to invite Chiang to the United States in order to separate him from the levers of power. In both cases the U.S. demurred, believing that Chiang would not be so easily diverted.[12] At the beginning of August 1949, in his capacity as director-general of the Kuomintang, a position he had retained when he relinquished the presidency, Chiang, in fact, created a shadow government in Taiwan, thoroughly undermining what remained of Li's power.

By that time Secretary of State Acheson had concluded that efforts to replace Chiang or to support the Taiwan autonomy movement could not succeed. Anxious to find a way to preserve a "free China" without the discredited Generalissimo, Acheson, early in 1949, had dispatched Livingston Merchant to investigate conditions in Taiwan in order to assess the potential for new leaders. Rumors abounded of coup plots, usually featuring pro-American General Sun Li-jen as the head of a more effective and compassionate successor regime. Acheson also entertained fantasies of a strong independence movement among the Taiwanese, which could give Americans an excuse to intervene as champions of self-determination. But both Merchant and officials of the U.S. Economic Cooperation Administration in Taipei attested to Chiang's unbreakable grip on island politics.[13]

Instead, the Truman administration adjusted to the idea that Taiwan and the Nationalist government would fall. Military and intelligence assessments during the autumn of 1949 made it clear that without massive American intervention a Communist assault could not be prevented. This the Joint Chiefs of Staff (JCS) had ruled out despite their often expressed concern that Taiwan should not be allowed to pass under Soviet domination. However important guarding the sea lanes of the western Pacific might be, the JCS repeatedly stressed that the limited military resources available had to be devoted to Western Europe and the Middle East. By November 1949, the Chief of Staff of the U.S. Air Force advocated that the CIA begin to plan for the destruction of Chiang Kai-shek's air force as soon as the fall of Taiwan appeared imminent.[14] And, in December 1949, Acheson dispatched a confidential circular telegram alerting American missions to the impending demise of the KMT and urging that the significance of this event for U.S. foreign policy be deemphasized.

Public announcement of America's disengagement followed. Pressures from prominent Republicans like Senator Robert Taft and former President Herbert Hoover to save the Nationalists had to be countered as did continued appeals from Taipei. Moreover, MacArthur's Tokyo headquarters had leaked the State Department's warning telegram embarrassing the secretary. On 5 January 1950 Truman declared that the United States would not intercede to prevent a Communist takeover of Taiwan. Seven days later Acheson reiterated this policy at the National Press Club, placing Taiwan outside America's defensive perimeter in the Pacific. The United States, he warned, should not risk incurring the anger of the Chinese people for imperialist intervention in China's domestic affairs.

The winter of 1950, however, witnessed the efforts of the China lobby to reach a broader audience, and administration efforts to disengage the U.S. from the Chinese Nationalist cause gave impetus to their crusade. In February Alfred Kohlberg, whose battle against the Institute of Pacific Relations for its alleged distribution of communist propaganda had given him a reputation as "the China lobby man," met Joseph McCarthy and began feeding him information about America's betrayal of China.[15] The palpable result was to intertwine McCarthy's communists-in-government campaign with the China issue. McCarthy chose as some of his first targets the Foreign Service officers who had been persecuted by former Ambassador Patrick Hurley in the 1940s. John S. Service, for instance, who had been "Hurleyed" out of China, had also been arrested in 1945 for allegedly leaking classified documents to *Amerasia* magazine.[16] Although acquitted by a grand jury, Service was not to escape so easily. McCarthy dredged up the *Amerasia* case and denounced Service in the Senate. He would later add State Department Asian consultant Owen Lattimore and Foreign Service Asia specialist John Carter Vincent to his list of supposed Soviet agents and dupes. However humiliating and destructive, this proved not to be the worst blow. Motivated by fear, confused by innuendo, and driven by a combination of China lobby and Republican stalwarts, the State Department between 1951 and 1954 not only destroyed the careers of China hands but seriously handicapped the reporting its policymakers relied upon.[17]

The importance of the China issue to McCarthyism and more broadly to the Republican Party had little to do with China. Developments in Asia became controversial because of the personal and partisan aims they could serve. Joseph McCarthy, guided by China lobby contacts, came to see the communism-in-China issue as a boost to his flagging career. A ruthless politician, McCarthy launched an anticommunist crusade, which, through audacious public lies, domination of a surprisingly pliant media, and an unprecedented degree of simple rhetorical thuggery, demonstrated that a lack of vision or principle need not prevent a senator from pursuing a demonically influential congressional career. The Republican party, with the exception of a few individuals, similarly lacked genuine interest in China but needed a campaign issue to defeat the seemingly unbeatable Democrats who had monopolized the White House since 1932. The bipartisan consensus that had governed the disposition of other foreign policy questions, therefore, broke down over China. Republicans made it clear that they had had no role in determining China policy, that they did not approve of the administration's China policy, and that the policy was misguided, harmful, and probably traitorous.

Given the combative political situation in Washington, the Truman/Acheson decision not to defend Taiwan did not end debate. Congress extended economic assistance to Taiwan four months beyond the president's preferred deadline by holding emergency aid to Korea hostage. Defense Secretary Louis Johnson continued surreptitious meetings with Nationalist officials to keep them apprised of American military policy, and the JCS devised plans to save Taiwan in case of a wider war in Asia. There are suggestions, provocatively pieced together by historian and political scientist Bruce Cumings, that large caches of weapons were secretly sold to Chiang by the U.S. military or donated by various pro-Nationalist individuals and organizations. A group of retired U.S. military officers expedited such acquisitions after Admiral Charles M. Cooke established them in Taipei as advisers to Chiang.[18]

Even within the State Department, men such as George Kennan, Dean Rusk, John Foster Dulles, and Paul Nitze schemed throughout the early months of 1950 to try to oust Chiang or to make the island a United Nations trusteeship territory. To Kennan, the ideal solution required initiative, the way "Theodore Roosevelt might have done it," ignoring all obstacles and acting with "resolution, speed, ruthlessness and self-assurance."[19] Rusk would claim later even to have had an offer from the indefatigable General Sun Li-jen to act, if he could get American backing.[20]

Truman and Acheson, nevertheless, resisted the plots and plans, anticipating that Kuomintang collapse would resolve their problem and allow eventual diplomatic relations with the Beijing regime. Monies that pro-Chiang elements in Congress tried to vote for the Nationalists the administration managed to redirect to the "general area of China" and then spend on Indochina. Senate Democrats rallied and voted support for Truman's policy of disengagement. Even public opinion, although not in favor of recognition for the Communists, evinced growing disgust with Chiang Kai-shek.[21] As late as 23 June 1950 Dean Acheson insisted that the United States would not again take part in the Chinese civil war.

The cold war and civil strife in Korea led to a very different outcome. On 25 June 1950 troops of the communist North Korean army smashed through weaker defensive units and swept into South Korea. The shock galvanized American policymakers and completely altered the direction of American China policy. Military plans readied in the autumn of 1949 to provide options in case of crisis came into play as the president sought to contain fighting to the Korean peninsula. He immediately ordered the U.S. Seventh Fleet to patrol the Taiwan Straits to deter any Communist Chinese attack on the Nationalists. Faint hopes that Taiwan would be saved by the 90 miles of water separating it from Fujian province because the PRC (People's Republic of China) had no amphibious capability had faded with Beijing's 1950 island campaign. On Hainan island, fifteen miles off China's south coast, Kuomintang units dissolved before the Communist offensive and morale on Taiwan plummeted. In the frantic days following the unexpected attack in Korea, Truman stepped into the breach.

Korea, thus, miraculously saved Chiang Kai-shek's government from extinction. If not quite the global Soviet-American conflagration Chiang had anticipated for years, this war sufficed to bring American resources back into the China theater. The Kuomintang and its American supporters jubilantly set about exploiting their good fortune. Chiang offered Nationalist military contingents to fight as part of the United Nations coalition. In July he hosted a visit to Taiwan by General Douglas MacArthur, whose position as head of United Nations forces in Korea ensured that his consultations with Chiang would command considerable notice. MacArthur followed these talks, which had not been sanctioned by Washington, with a similarly unauthorized letter to the Veterans of Foreign Wars convention in August that contested administration policies and argued for the strategic necessity of preserving Taiwan as an "unsinkable aircraft carrier and submarine tender."[22] But, in fact, already on 27 July at an NSC (National Security

Council) meeting Truman had made it official, approving in principle a military assistance program and a U.S. military advisory mission for Taiwan.

Truman, nevertheless, still intended his support of Taiwan to be a temporary maneuver, occasioned by war but soon to be terminated by peace. His Seventh Fleet order served not only to protect Chiang but to bar any Nationalist action in the strait that could provoke a full-scale war with China. The president and his secretary of state repeatedly tried to reassure the Chinese Communist leaders of America's good intentions.[23]

Korea, however, heightened anxieties and stiffened policies in many directions. At the same time that the president elected to send the Seventh Fleet to the Taiwan Strait, he also dispatched American military advisers to assist the French war in Indochina. Reconsidering his earlier conviction that the nation's fiscal health necessitated low military budgets, he approved NSC 68, which called for a massive increase in defense spending. By the end of the year, the ceiling on presidential requests had risen 257 percent over his original 1951 defense budget.[24] The attack in Korea undermined Truman's satisfaction with the development of events in Europe, where the United States had surmounted the Soviet challenge over Berlin with an extraordinary airlift between 1948 and 1949, had implemented the Marshall Plan, and had created NATO. Was conflict on the Korean Peninsula a diversion or simply the first step in a new world war that would quickly encompass more important battlefronts in Europe? Even if intelligence estimates were correct in predicting that a Russian assault on Europe would not follow U.S. entanglement in Asia, the opportunity to fortify the critical European arena should not be missed. Thus, the administration gently coerced Britain and France to accept the remilitarization of West Germany and impelled Congress early in 1951 to agree to an integrated NATO defense force, including four divisions of American troops under the aegis of an American General.[25]

Various benefits accrued to the Nationalist regime on Taiwan from this deepened cold war atmosphere. Not only did U.S. military assistance resume, but Washington decided to push through a Japanese Peace Treaty without the adherence of the Soviets. Provisions of an accompanying security pact made it possible to maintain U.S. bases in Japan, increasing Taiwan's safety as well. Moreover, Washington forced Japan to agree to shun the Communist Chinese and open diplomatic relations with Taipei over Tokyo's protests that mainland trade would be vital to Japan's postwar recovery.[26]

At the United Nations Taipei's position improved further after China intervened in the Korean conflict and bloodied UN forces north of the 38th parallel. International involvement in Korea had been facilitated in June 1950 by a Soviet boycott of the UN, which prevented Moscow's envoys from vetoing UN action. The Soviet absence, dating back to January, hinged upon the UN having refused to throw the Nationalists out and replace them with CCP representatives. In reality, Moscow did not want China to be admitted, and its refusal to participate in UN deliberations through the winter and spring of 1950 effectively prevented reconsideration of China's case, keeping Beijing dependent on the Soviet Union. This served Moscow's interests but ironically those of the KMT as well. Washington had refused to use its Security Council veto to prevent Beijing's admission and anticipated that the Chinese Communists would be seated on a procedural vote in the not-too-distant future. From Taiwan's perspective, then, the Soviet position proved welcome, but a more reliable guarantee came with passage of the February 1951 resolution in the General Assembly that labeled China an aggressor and ended any immediate likelihood that Beijing might secure enough support to seize the China seat.

Finally, in a somewhat subtle change of emphasis, the United States altered its view of the international legal status of Taiwan. Washington had supported the return of Taiwan to China's sovereignty at various wartime conferences and assisted mainland Chinese troops and bureaucrats in recovering the island from the Japanese at war's end. On 27 June 1950 Truman suddenly declared the disposition of Taiwan to be undecided pending "restoration of security in the Pacific," leaving the issue to be decided at some future unspecified date by some future unnamed coalition of forces.[27]

Taiwan's bond with the United States drew impetus from the prisoner-of-war (POW) controversy that prolonged the Korean conflict. In the summer of 1951, General Robert McClure, the U.S. Army's chief of psychological warfare, suggested that not all Chinese soldiers in prison camps wanted to be repatriated—that, in fact, some claimed to have been forcibly recruited and would elect to go to Taiwan if given an opportunity to choose. President Truman instinctively sympathized with a voluntary approach to repatriation primarily on moral and humanitarian grounds, overruling objections from his secretary of state and the UN force commander, Matthew Ridgway, based on the 1949 Geneva Convention on POWs, which called for unrestricted return of prisoners.

At the armistice negotiations, the UN delegation provoked the Communist Chinese by remarking that, since two Chinas existed, prisoners would be legitimately repatriated even if they went to Taiwan. PRC representatives also objected vehemently to the presence of Nationalist Chinese propagandists in the POW camps where they trained those not willing to be sent to the PRC in the "right" answers to repatriation commission interview questions regarding their preferences. The American's even facilitated a 30 July 1953 broadcast by Chiang Kai-shek, distributed in written form by the UN command, which urged the men to "stand firm in your choice of freedom." To add incentive, the Chinese Nationalist Air Force flew in thousands of letters of welcome to Taiwan and 14,000 gift parcels, but also encouraged intimidation and violence to ensure defections.

As historian Rosemary Foot cogently observed, the POW confrontation relieved pressures on Washington to justify the costs of war, as it confirmed the wisdom of American China policy.

> For the new government in China, the specter of thousands of its soldiers' embracing what it saw as the illegal alternative regime on Taiwan struck at the heart of its contention that it had come to power . . . backed by the gratitude of a united populace. . . . For the United States, the allure of many Chinese voting with their feet for Chiang rather than Mao validated a policy toward Nationalist China that was unpopular internationally, at the same time that it demonstrated to Truman's domestic critics that his administration was taking action that gave succor to the Generalissimo.[28]

The Korean War, then, inaugurated a new era in Asia and a fresh chapter in Sino-American relations. Nations in the area, swept up in the struggle against communism, found their individual problems discounted but discovered that aid to solve those difficulties could be secured by claiming fear of a communist challenge. No government learned to manipulate the system more expertly than Chiang Kai-shek's Nationalist regime. Faced in 1950 with abandonment by the Truman administration, Taipei, by 1954, had woven a web of political, economic, and military ties that made the mutual defense treaty signed that year almost superfluous.

Nationalist ability to have such an impact on the relationship stemmed in large part from the domestic political climate in the United States. The world shaped by North Korea's attack seemed clearly to be a more dangerous place to Americans. But, having welcomed the strong response of the Truman administration to communist perfidy, the public grew weary of the long struggle that became more and more costly in lives and matériel. Increasingly, they were willing to believe that the communist onslaught had been a reaction to Dean Acheson's ill-conceived defensive perimeter speech and the American response a product of the machinations of Soviet agents who, Senator McCarthy claimed, had infiltrated the government.

Disillusionment and frustration bred a series of policies designed to stem an imagined tide of communist victories. Thus anger that some nations, in trying to solve their economic weaknesses, went so far as to "trade with the enemy" led Congress to pass the Kem Amendment and Battle Act. These measures punished countries exporting strategic goods to the communist bloc by cutting off U.S. aid. For those that adhered more closely to U.S. policy, Congress voted the Mutual Security Act, telescoping military, economic, and technical programs of assistance into a single package. The U.S. also signed security treaties, not just with Japan but also with the Philippines, Australia, and New Zealand.

The harshness of new Truman administration strategies did not prove sufficient to deflect Americans' dissatisfaction with the Democratic party.

During the 1952 presidential campaign, Dwight D. Eisenhower and other Republicans attacked the incumbents for softness on communism and dismissed the containment doctrine, which rested at the heart of Truman administration efforts to prevent communist expansion and eventually led to Soviet collapse, as "negative, futile and immoral." John Foster Dulles, soon to be secretary of state, advocated instead the liberation of benighted souls caught behind the iron and bamboo curtains.

Just such a policy appeared to highlight President Eisenhower's first State of the Union message in which he announced that he was "unleashing" Chiang Kai-shek. The U.S. Seventh Fleet, which under Harry Truman had protected Communist China from Nationalist assault would, henceforth, only provide a safe sanctuary for the KMT on Taiwan.[29] This appeared to free Chiang to attack the mainland, a possibility that the Nationalist leader welcomed but that frightened America's European allies who saw it as flagrantly provocative and foolhardy.[30]

In fact, neither Eisenhower nor Dulles ever really intended to sanction serious conflict in the Straits. Almost immediately they imposed secret restraints, actually withholding deliveries of jet aircraft to Taiwan until Chiang agreed to clear all large-scale operations against the mainland with U.S. officials.[31]

As would become apparent during the following eight years, rhetoric in this administration tended to be more belligerent than action. Moreover, foreign policymaking in the Eisenhower years truly did rest in the president's hands as well as in those of Secretary of State Dulles. The traditional picture of Ike as a good-natured bumbler who preferred to sneak off to the golf course than deal with national crises has given way to a portrayal of Eisenhower as statesman and politician. His grasp of world affairs was sophisticated, and, although he had a tendency to dismiss anti-Western nationalism as the product of communist conspiracy, he understood that the communist world was not monolithic. As a result he proved willing to consider better relations with the Communist Chinese. During the course of his presidency he contemplated ending trade sanctions against Beijing and concluded that American recognition of China would be simply a matter of time.

Evidence for this could be found by contrasting the stance of his China-related government appointments with those whom he actually relied on in making policy decisions. Eisenhower and Dulles dutifully named a series of pro-Chiang individuals to visible foreign policy posts. The sympathies of American Ambassador to the Republic of China Karl Rankin, the Assistant Secretary for Far Eastern Affairs Walter Robertson, and the director of the Office of Chinese Affairs Walter McConaughy seemed to symbolize the thrust of U.S. relations with China. The reasoning behind these selections, however, did not involve pursuit of a particular direction in China policy so much as it sought to protect the administration from attack by right-wing Republicans who had made conditions so difficult for the Truman presidency.

To fulfill this task there could not have been better choices than these three men. Karl Rankin argued, whenever given the opportunity, that Washington had no choice but to support Free China against Moscow and its Chinese puppets on the mainland. Drawing a parallel to Nationalist-controlled areas that had escaped Japan's grasp during World War II, Rankin and other KMT partisans insisted that Taiwan, too, was Free China and must be preserved outside the zone of Communist Chinese occupation so that Chiang Kai-shek could again fight his way back to power on the mainland. He loudly opposed China's admission into the United Nations and advocated the expulsion of other communist states. His uncritical views of the Nationalists made him fall prey to clientist advocacy of almost anything Chiang wanted. He intentionally filed alarmist cables from Taipei to strength the hand of his allies at the Department of State. Walter Robertson, for one, made good use of them. A courtly and well-liked Southern gentleman, whom even his adversaries thought honorable and honest, Robertson, nevertheless, allowed his horror of communism to cloud his judgment.[32] Thus, he assumed that a Marxist tyranny in China could not possibly prosper or survive. In this assessment he was joined by Walter McConaughy. He, like Robertson, had served in China but, unlike

Meeting of Secretary of State John Foster Dulles with Chiang Ching-kuo and Ambassador V. K. Wellington Koo, 1953. *Courtesy of the National Archives*

Robertson, initially rejected Chiang's bankrupt regime, worried about fueling Taiwan irredentism, and favored trying to cultivate a Titoist China. To McConaughy, as to many other State Department observers at the time, a China that was communist in ideology appeared tolerable so long as it, like Yugoslavia, remained independent of Moscow's control. Beijing's intervention in the Korean War, however, soured him and ensured that his subsequent views were comfortably aligned with those of Rankin, Robertson, and the China lobby.[33]

When it came to making policy, however, these men had only occasional influence. Dulles relied upon an inner circle of advisers less sympathetic to Chiang, convinced that isolating China was unproductive, and oriented overwhelmingly toward Europe where they believed the United States' energies should focus. Thus, more moderate officials, including Herman Phleger, State Department legal adviser; Livingston Merchant, assistant secretary for European affairs; Douglas MacArthur III, State Department counselor; and Robert Bowie, director of the policy planning staff, applied more measured strategies to Chinese affairs during the Eisenhower years.[34]

Eisenhower administration caution proved a source of great consternation for Nationalist officials. They had been primed since the mid-1940s to expect that a Republican government would do more for Chiang Kai-shek. They had anticipated and celebrated the prospect of a victory by Thomas Dewey in 1948, and they had supported various Republican candidates in congressional campaigns. After the election of 1952, in which Eisenhower seemed to make clear a determination to roll back communism, they eagerly awaited an escalation of aid and tangible support for their effort to return to the mainland. This they did not get, and although administration policy generally proved favorable, there was also ground for disillusionment.

John Foster Dulles, for instance, had appeared to be a staunch advocate of Chinese Nationalist interests. He had manipulated the Japanese in 1951 into signing a peace treaty with Taiwan. He had lavishly praised the Nationalist regime, adamantly perpetuated the trade embargo against China, and proffered military assistance. Fearful of suffering the same fate as Acheson, who had been pilloried by right-wing Republicans, Dulles drew on his religious roots for fire-and- brimstone attacks against the evils of communism.

But the Taiwan regime alienated Dulles by trying to lock him into dangerous commitments that threatened to draw the United States into an unwanted war. The most striking illustration of this tension involved the Nationalists' preoccupation with a mutual defense treaty. To Taipei's surprise, Dulles did not desire it, and to Dulles's dismay, the Nationalists got it anyway.

Nationalist Chinese determination to sign a mutual defense treaty with the United States yielded a draft agreement in the autumn of 1953 not long after Washington had concluded a similar pact with South Korea. But rather than welcome this indication of Taipei's affections, the State Department

THE LINE IS DRAWN

Cartoon by John Fischetti. *Reprinted by permission of Newspaper Enterprise Association, Inc.*

displayed reluctance to consider it seriously. Chiang Kai-shek thereupon marshalled his supporters both inside and outside the government to lobby for the agreement as a guarantee for his government's survival.[35] That effort appeared to be making little progress, however, given State Department preoccupation with the May 1954 Geneva Conference and the far more pressing problems involving Korea and Indochina. Dulles in particular objected to negotiations with Taipei that might alienate America's European allies. Not until the development of a military confrontation in the Taiwan Strait did the secretary relent. Only then, when an alliance became the necessary price for involving the United Nations in a crisis that might otherwise degenerate into war, would Dulles accept entanglement. In exchange for the Kuomintang's commitment not to exercise its UN Security Council veto to block a cease-fire resolution, Dulles authorized treaty language carefully circumscribing the advantages that Taipei would gain.[36] Once again the United States insisted that Taipei must not launch military operations against the mainland without American approval. Washington also refused to permit the treaty explicitly to cover China's offshore islands or to give Chiang any control over American troops stationed on the island.[37]

The imbroglio that generated even this limited alliance became known as the 1954–55 Quemoy-Matsu (Jinmen-Mazu) crisis (the first of three).[38] The Communist Chinese initiated shelling of Quemoy, an island group lying just off the Fukien coast in September 1954 on the eve of the Manila Conference at which the Southeast Asia Treaty Organization (SEATO) was to be inaugurated. The Chinese hoped both to dissuade Americans from participating in a collective effort at anti-Chinese containment and to deter negotiation of a U.S.-Taiwan defense treaty. They saw such a treaty both as completing a ring of encirclement around China and as permanently severing Taiwan from mainland control.[39]

But instead of discouraging the U.S., China gave impetus to American involvement. Washington concluded that Beijing intended to begin its long-feared assault on Taiwan or, at the very least, probe the extent of the U.S. commitment to Quemoy. American analysts exaggerated China's military capabilities and reacted with alarm to Beijing's strident rhetoric. Although two island groups off the Zhejiang coast, Yijiangshan and Dachen, were sacrificed, the Eisenhower administration never considered abandoning Chiang or reducing its involvement in the region.[40] Not only did SEATO materialize on schedule, but Washington acceded to the U.S.-ROC (Republic of China) Mutual Defense Treaty, and early in 1955 the U.S. Congress passed the Formosa Resolution. Eisenhower thereby obtained authorization to assist the Chinese Nationalists in defending Taiwan, the Penghu islands, and related positions. Congress accorded him such open-ended powers even though most members acknowledged the intrinsic unimportance of the offshore islands.

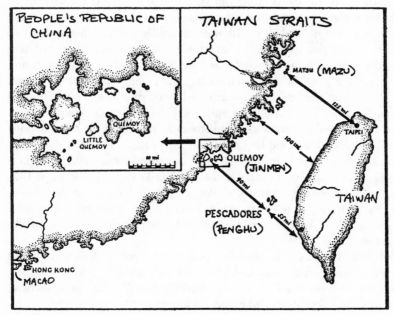

The Taiwan Strait

In fact, the inconsequential nature of the islands bore no relation to the progress of the dispute. The president believed that preservation of Nationalist control over not just Taiwan and the Penghus but also Quemoy and Matsu had become vital to Nationalist morale. Thus Washington went so far as to talk—publicly and, more ominously, in a March 1955 NSC meeting—about the possible need to use atomic weapons to stop the PRC.[41] In the long run, this would be the most consequential development of the crisis, since American threats spurred Beijing's decision to develop an independent nuclear capability.[42] Washington's review of its atomic option, however, proved disturbing enough to the Americans to occasion an effort to deal directly with the vulnerability of the islands. Eisenhower and Dulles sought to convince Chiang to abandon them in exchange for a joint naval blockade of the China coast. Chiang rejected the proposal, assuming that at the critical moment Washington would shrink from so provocative a maneuver as blockading the coast, which had the real possibility of causing a war.[43] Beijing, although unaware of all the details of U.S. policy, concluded that it had miscalculated the American reaction, and at the April 1955 Bandung Conference, influenced by consultations with delegates from various Asian states, PRC Premier and Foreign Minister Zhou Enlai abandoned the misadventure.

Confrontation in the Straits did not end there. In 1958 the dispute exploded again. Renewed American efforts in the intervening months to convince Chiang to evacuate his forces so as to diminish the impact if the islands were lost had failed. Eisenhower personally warned Chiang that "we do not consider that to invoke military force is an appropriate means of freeing Communist-dominated peoples and we are opposed to initiating action which might expose the world to a conflagration which could spread beyond control."[44] But neither the president's rhetoric nor Dulles's face-to-face encounter with Chiang could diminish the Generalissimo's conviction that these islands would serve as stepping stones to the mainland and remained the final link with a world he hoped one day to recover. Rather than scale down his commitment, by 1958 he had assembled some 100,000 soldiers composing one-third of his army to defend the islands.[45] Similarly, the U.S. Navy argued forcefully against a Dulles scheme to demilitarize the islands, asserting that the Communists would doubtless seize them once they were vulnerable. Then the U.S. would be reduced to letting them go or to attacking the mainland.[46]

What the Chinese Communists appear in retrospect to have objected to the most, and what prompted the renewed shelling, was continuing American attempts to follow a "two Chinas" policy. At the Sino-American ambassadorial talks, which had begun at Geneva in 1954 and had been regularized there between August 1955 and December 1957, the United States had insisted upon a Beijing pledge to renounce the use of force in its attempts to reunify China. Seen as a challenge to China's sovereignty, Beijing rejected this interference in its internal affairs. There was also a hollow ring to these demands as Kuomintang attacks on the Chinese coastline supported by the CIA continued, causing small but irritating losses on the ground and in coastal trade.

Moreover, in the summer of 1958 other factors spurred the PRC's leadership to action. They sought distraction from sacrifices demanded by the Great Leap Forward, Mao's effort to accelerate economic development through mass participation, and hoped to extirpate favorable assessments of American economic and military might held by disturbing numbers of Chinese. Also worrisome were criticisms of the communist system voiced during the disastrous Hundred Flowers campaign launched by Mao in 1956 to engage intellectuals more fully in socialist construction. When their complaints rapidly exceeded Mao's tolerance, he launched an antirightist purge, in the aftermath of which calls for patriotic unity against foreign encroachment were particularly timely. The leaders also took inspiration from Moscow's triumphal launching of Sputnik in 1957, which suggested to them that Communist bloc technology had surpassed that of the West. And finally the Lebanese crisis broke in July amid American fears of growing Nasserite and communist influence in the area. With 14,000 U.S. soldiers trying to prevent civil war in Lebanon, Beijing assumed that Washington would be sufficiently distracted not to mount an effective response to trouble in the Taiwan Straits. American inaction would then yield the further benefit of sowing dissension in relations between Washington and Taipei.

When the bombardment began, however, the U.S. did implement the defense treaty as well as the Formosa Resolution. Not only did American ships establish a convoy system to ensure that the offshore islands would continue to receive necessary supplies, but Washington also installed eight-inch howitzers on Quemoy capable of hitting China with atomic shells.[47] Pressure on the U.S. government, particularly from the JCS, sought to compel the president seriously to consider making use of nuclear weapons.[48] Dulles apparently commented to Chairman of the Chiefs General Nathan Twining that "there was no use of having a lot of stuff and never be[ing] able to use it."[49]

Mao's conviction, at the same time, that American power was in decline led China to prolong the confrontation. What finally convinced Mao to deescalate the crisis, in addition to international suasion and U.S. proposals through the ambassadorial talks for a cease-fire, was the success of his own attempt to cause friction between Taiwan and the United States.[50] Mounting demands from Washington upon Chiang to abandon the islands came to be seen in Beijing much as it was perceived in Taipei. If Chiang departed, then the last link between Taiwan and the mainland would be severed, and the "two Chinas" policy would be a reality. Mao, therefore, concluded that the recovery of the small islands should await the return of Taiwan to Beijing's control and in his 6 October 1958 "Message to Our Taiwan Compatriots" made this position clear.

Although the Taiwan Straits ceased to be a place of provocation for Beijing, it remained a flashpoint. The third and final Quemoy-Matsu crisis in 1962 again raised the specter of war. This time Taipei provided the impetus with troop deployments and rhetoric that indicated an intention finally to mount a major attack on the mainland. Chiang anticipated that a popular rising would occur in response to his assault given the economic crisis and political disarray left by the collapse of the Great Leap Forward and the fortuitous floods and drought wracking north and south China. Even Chinese Foreign Minister Chen I admitted, "This summer's harvests will not be very favorable. . . . Those opposed [to communism] are small in number. In the 600 million population, however, they may amount to several million. . . . In case Chiang Kai-shek drops paratroops and lands on the mainland with American support, these elements will come out of hiding."[51]

Beijing immediately mustered more than 100,000 men along the coast and prepared for resistance against a U.S.-Nationalist invasion. China's leaders, in a reportedly "panicky" state of mind, could not help but connect Chiang's threatening behavior with a general pattern of encirclement. Sino-Indian tensions were escalating toward an October war. Tibet remained unstable, with the CIA and Nationalist agents operating among refugees in

"Let's You And Him Fight!"

Cartoon by Richard Q. Yardley in *The Sun* (Baltimore) of 25 September 1958. *Courtesy of Susan Yardley Wheltle*

northern India. In Laos mobilization of American forces as well as remnant Chinese Nationalist troops in response to communist breaches of the cease fire appeared provocative despite the peace negotiations underway in Geneva. Meanwhile, in Taiwan a series of visits by high-level American officials and military leaders paralleled arms purchases, the levying of new "invasion" taxes, and accelerated conscription. The concurrent appointment of Admiral Alan G. Kirk as U.S. ambassador to Taiwan, given his World War II amphibious warfare experience, must have disturbed Beijing,[52] particularly when China also confronted a sharp increase in raids from Taiwan, U.S.-Nationalist joint military exercises, and incendiary rhetoric that predicted an imminent Nationalist victory.[53]

American policymakers recognized the volatility of a situation for which Washington would have to bear not only significant responsibility but possibly serious rescue obligations. However costly a fight would be for the Communists, they were likely to benefit from international sympathy and probable domestic loyalty in the face of aggression.[54] This was, after all, a chastened Kennedy administration, which just 14 months before had landed a Cuban exile force at the Bay of Pigs only to have it decimated on the beach without the slightest sign of sympathy from the Cuban people supposedly awaiting liberation. Convinced that the outcome would be equally disastrous here, officials notified Beijing privately at the Warsaw ambassadorial talks (sessions having been moved from Geneva in 1958) on 23 June 1962 that the U.S. would not support a Nationalist invasion of China. This assurance, followed by Kennedy's personal declaration to reporters that he opposed the use of force in the area, promptly defused the crisis.[55] Much to Chiang Kai-shek's chagrin, his return-to-the-mainland promises remained hollow, and the Taiwan Straits finally became a peaceful passageway.

The first effective use of the Warsaw forum in years during the 1962 crisis accentuated the role that Taiwan played in preventing progress in the face-to-face meetings between representatives of the American and Chinese governments. Dulles's decision to insist upon an explicit renunciation of force in the Straits ensured that no accommodation could be achieved despite Beijing's moderate foreign policy line between 1955 and 1958. Conversely, beginning in 1958, with the general radicalization of Chinese policy, Beijing determined that "pending the solution of the Taiwan issue, all other issues should wait."[56] Thereafter the Chinese scorned evidence of American flexibility, insisting for the next decade that a resolution of Taiwan's status was the most important question in Chinese-American relations.

Meanwhile, the need to support Taipei through a series of armed confrontations with Beijing over Quemoy and Matsu between 1954 and 1962 had important ramifications for United States domestic and foreign affairs. It gave impetus to the growth of the China lobby, it further politicized the China question, it complicated nuclear weapons control, and it delayed American recognition of the depth of the Sino-Soviet split. Although

America's attention largely remained fixed on events in Europe, Taiwan demanded intense if sporadic involvement by policymakers not always well schooled in the intricacies of Asian politics.

During the 1950s the Eisenhower administration concentrated on the Soviet-American cold war, devoting its energies to strengthening Europe economically and militarily but also, increasingly, competing among underdeveloped and newly independent nations for adherents to the "free world." This was an era in which neutralism proved difficult to defend and respect for nationalism was slow in coming. For Eisenhower and Dulles a country that rejected American free trade and investment as imperialism either was communist or might as well be. Thus, Washington intervened in Iran in 1953, Guatemala in 1954, Vietnam after Dienbienphu, the Middle East after Suez, and Cuba.[57] The same impulse made of Taiwan an ally in the anticommunist struggle despite bilateral frictions.

The China lobby reinforced administration concern about Taiwan as a bastion of freedom in Asia. Constituted in 1953 as the Committee For One Million Against the Admission of Communist China to the United Nations, it focused on the UN issue but stood guard in opposition to recognition of and trade with the PRC, along with defending Nationalist interests on other fronts. Its members comprised a diverse group, encompassing political liberals as well as conservatives, partisans of Chiang Kai-shek, and those who could be persuaded that the Red Chinese were unpalatable thugs. The Committee publicized its views through petition drives, radio broadcasts, newsletters, congressional testimony, and repeated success in securing congressional passage of resolutions opposing UN membership for Red China. Although it did not receive financing from Nationalist Chinese authorities directly, the Taipei government did fund many of its activities indirectly through donations to Committee secretary and right-wing organizer Marvin Liebman.[58]

More effective than the formless China lobby of the 1940s, the new organization held the line against flexibility in American China policy until at least the late 1950s. Symbolic of the effect that its intimidation had throughout the decade, and beyond, was the specialized language required when discussing Chinese affairs. Taiwan could be referred to only as Formosa, a Portuguese name, which emphasized the beauty of the tropical island but, more important, was not the name used by the Communists. No one in the U.S. spoke of the People's Republic of China but only of Red or Communist China. The city in which Red China's government sat was Pei-p'ing never Beijing as the Communists referred to it. The former term meant only northern peace, but the latter indicated the city was the northern capital therefore contradicting the reality accepted by all China lobbyists that the capital of China was Taipei.

Little latitude was allowed in the Manichean struggle against the evils of the communist bloc. Eisenhower and Dulles, for instance, failed to take advantage of changes in the Soviet Union after Joseph Stalin died early in

1953. Whereas Stalin in his last months had increased military expenditures and reconfirmed his conviction that war with the West was inevitable, a new leadership under the initial guidance of Georgi Malenkov declared that war was not the only solution to international disputes. The Soviet Union reestablished diplomatic relations with Israel, Greece, and even Yugoslavia. It renounced claims to Turkish territory. And in Korea it finally acceded to an armistice that had been under discussion for almost two years.[59] But neither Eisenhower nor Dulles knew what to make of the shift in Soviet rhetoric and policy. Instead of relief, they felt confusion and suspicion.

Similarly, although the signs of a Sino-Soviet rift began to emerge in the mid-1950s, Washington policymakers proved exceedingly slow to credit the phenomenon. Dulles hoped that the strain of Chinese dependence on the USSR would produce unremediable tensions between the two states. Eisenhower recognized clear advantages in portraying the Soviets as more reasonable than the fanatic Chinese Communists in his attempts to further the development of détente with Moscow. But top-level officials in the Kennedy administration such as the secretary of state and the director of the CIA doubted the depth of the split, and Kennedy himself dismissed it as an argument over how to bury the United States.[60]

The China lobby and the Nationalist Chinese government, of course, discouraged Americans from believing in the development. John Foster Dulles had said in his confirmation hearings in 1953 that if China changed its policies and broke from Moscow's grasp that recognition by Washington was possible. The Nationalists could not help but view any improvement in Washington-Beijing relations as catastrophic. Taipei encouraged reservations among Eisenhower administration officials, stressing the monolithic quality of communism, the deceitfulness of Moscow, and the oppressive nature of the CCP regime. Any evidence that Washington might be weakening elicited attacks deriding American naïveté or charging undue British influence on American policymakers.

Nationalist dependency on the United States made American attitudes of utmost importance to Taipei. Thus, the 1960 election campaign, pitting longtime supporter Richard Nixon against a sympathetic but less predictable John Kennedy, commanded serious attention in Taiwan. Kennedy had publicly attacked Truman for the loss of China in 1949 and shared the Kuomintang's inclination to blame the "Lattimores and the Fairbanks" for Chiang Kai-shek's misfortune. But he had also opposed passage of the Formosa Resolution in 1955. When, in three nationally televised debates and several campaign speeches, Kennedy declared Quemoy and Matsu indefensible and commitments to them "unsound militarily, unnecessary to our security, and unsupported by our allies," a heated debate ensued involving not just Republicans and Democrats, but also China lobbyists and Taipei.[61] Many, including Chiang rebutted Kennedy's contention that the islands would inevitably fall if attacked. ROC Ministry of Foreign Affairs spokesman

James Shen added that his government's leaders had "never requested any direct participation by the United States in defense of these islands" and that "we fully intend to continue to do our own fighting on our islands."[62]

But a Nationalist regime troubled by Kennedy's election victory and its implications for the offshore islands had, nevertheless, to be conciliatory, just as it had had to accept the contempt of Harry Truman and the occasional disloyalty of Dwight Eisenhower. The United States remained far too important to Taiwan's security and nascent prosperity. Moreover, the Republic of China's international standing depended in large measure on the United States.

The international ramifications could be seen most clearly in the context of the United Nations. Beginning in October 1949, Communist authorities had demanded that China's seat be surrendered to the new Beijing government. For the Nationalists loss of the dual positions in the Security Council and the General Assembly as well as various committee memberships would be devastating. Isolating Taipei from international forums, it would inevitably lead to a precipitous drop in the number of nations with which Taipei could maintain diplomatic relations or from which it could expect military support. Economic strangulation would accompany political exile.

Initially the American government indicated its opposition to the shift but chose to view the matter as a credentials question requiring nothing more than a simple majority vote. The United States would not veto a change of representatives. The Soviet decision to boycott the organization, allegedly to try to force the Chinese Communists in, actually complicated a matter that Washington was willing to see resolved. When the Korean attack materialized, however, to be followed by Chinese intervention, Washington's views altered radically. Now China was seen as a blatant aggressor, attacking not simply American troops but UN forces. China must not be allowed to shoot its way into the UN. Taiwan's position temporarily gained a reprieve.

Nationalist officials, lobbyists, and the Eisenhower administration managed to protect Taiwan's UN membership throughout the 1950s. Indeed, Congress began casting annual votes opposing China's admission, a practice that would continue through 1970. The Committee For One Million successfully collected its one million signatures on petitions opposing UN entry for China. The group then renamed itself the Committee Of One Million in order to remain a national watchdog. Administration officials devised a formula by which the General Assembly never even debated the substantive issue involved. Instead, the United States offered a moratorium resolution that prevented discussion of any proposal unseating Taiwan and admitting the Chinese Communists. Given American dominance in the General Assembly, change would await Washington's consent.

Administration views on the UN dilemma, however, were not as clear as its public position suggested. As early as 1953 Dulles told India's Prime

Minister Jawaharlal Nehru that, if a way could be found to substitute India for China in the Security Council, he would be willing to see both Beijing and Taipei seated in the General Assembly.[63] The Dulles State Department, moreover, took the stand that the United States could not exercise its veto in the Security Council to keep the Communist Chinese out. This would, it argued, set a dangerous precedent, potentially barring free world governments of importance to Washington from gaining admission.[64] Even when Eisenhower's UN Ambassador Henry Cabot Lodge passionately advocated a different approach, Dulles held the line.[65] He also weighed in forcefully against the threats of Senator William Knowland to pull the U.S. out of the UN if China gained entry.[66] Not until John Kennedy assumed the presidency did Chiang Kai-shek secure the guarantee he wanted regarding the UN. Whereas Dulles and the supposedly steadfast Republicans avoided commitment, Kennedy offered his pledge in order to avert the casting of a Taipei veto against the entry of Outer Mongolia into the UN.[67] The understanding remained secret on both sides. Indeed, Chiang offered Washington his promise through private CIA channels to the president before securing the backing of his foreign ministry.[68] Although Kennedy informed the State Department, neither the administration's UN ambassador, Adlai Stevenson, nor its ambassador in Taipei, Everett Drumright, were consulted.

The crux of the matter lay in two developments that could not be escaped but threatened thoroughly to undermine the Nationalist Chinese position. Kennedy administration officials, for one, recognized early in the spring of 1961 that the balance of votes on the admission issue had shifted dangerously. The influx of newly independent nations and the conviction that a China that would soon test an atomic bomb could be controlled only inside the UN had eroded the American coalition. The administration searched for mechanisms to shore up the Nationalist position. Believing that the moratorium approach was doomed, officials examined the possibilities of making the issue an "important question" requiring a two-thirds vote or introducing a "successor states" formula. The latter provided that both Taipei and Beijing should sit in the UN as successors to the single Chinese government of 1945. Washington assumed that the Chinese Communists would reject such a possibility and therefore the onus for exclusion would shift to Beijing.[69] This would be a difficult plan to implement since Washington could not make public its conviction that the CCP would not go along and therefore risked condemnation by the China lobby as it defended Taipei's "one China" position. Indeed, Kennedy met with Henry Luce in May to win his support for whatever solution the administration felt compelled to execute.[70] Kennedy also worried about the Congress and its potential for troublemaking.[71] As early as June, opponents of a "two China" solution, including Richard Nixon, Senator Barry Goldwater, the Young Republicans, Scripps-Howard press, and the *Los Angeles Times* began to mobilize.[72]

The second threatening development involved the pairing of Outer Mongolia and Mauritania for UN admission. Almost a facsimile of the 1955 standoff in which Taipei vetoed Mongolia and Moscow vetoed Japan, the changed balance of support for Nationalist China in the UN made this new confrontation far more serious. Taiwan depended heavily on the abstention of 11 French African nations to remain in the UN. If the Nationalists used their veto to exclude Mongolia, provoking the Soviets to veto Mauritania, most of the African states could be expected to abandon Taipei. Worse yet from the U.S. perspective, the infuriated Africans would probably line up against Washington on other issues, and the United States would face the growing likelihood that it might lose control of the General Assembly. This would, of course, be disastrous for U.S. prestige and its ability to dictate solutions to world problems. As for Taiwan, once expulsion from the UN appeared imminent, Kennedy feared a desperation attack on the mainland that could start a conflagration.[73]

In the end Kennedy eluded disaster. The General Assembly session elevated the Chinese representation issue to the status of an important question requiring a two-thirds majority and voted Communist China down. The General Assembly admitted Outer Mongolia, and Nationalist China abstained.

The issue, therefore, remained alive to bedevil subsequent presidents. Momentarily during the mid-1960s the radicalism of the Cultural Revolution led Beijing to pursue other goals. In 1965 it actually lured Indonesia away from the UN and threatened to establish a new organization that would be more responsive to Afro-Asian issues. Never a serious threat to the UN, this alternative died early and had no impact on the fortunes of the Chinese Nationalists. More serious was the growing sentiment within the American government that a "two Chinas" formula would be the only way to preserve a Nationalist Chinese seat. Although Lyndon Johnson pledged that he would honor Kennedy's promise to use the U.S. veto on Chiang's behalf, State Department advisers increasingly argued that such a stance might not be adequate to protect Taipei.[74] How long Washington could sustain a coalition strong enough to keep Taipei in and Beijing out became an annual and increasingly troubling question.

• • •

The United States approached the idea of an alliance with the Chinese Nationalists cautiously but, despite profound misgivings, undertook the commitment in 1954. The brutality with which the Kuomintang had secured the island of Taiwan as a final sanctuary in 1947 dismayed American observers. A widespread sense of Chiang as a discredited leader had provoked many in Washington to contemplate his overthrow. But Chiang's grasp on power was too firm, and the outbreak of the Korean War made dissatisfaction with him less important. American policy grew tougher on all fronts, benefiting the KMT. Chiang perfected his techniques for maneuvering Washington into granting him assistance. He secured American support in the Taiwan Straits crises, defied American efforts to reduce tensions by eliminating provocative troop concentrations on the offshore islands, obtained the Mutual Defense Treaty, held on to his UN seats, and blinded Americans to opportunities to improve relations with the Chinese Communists. The United States found itself undertaking policies and commitments that were not always in its national interest, but such obligations proved almost impossible to avoid. America's anticommunist crusade, which dictated norms of behavior and tried to impose standards on thought, provided an optimum environment within which an anticommunist, if autocratic, Chinese leader could flourish.

chapter 4

ECONOMIC, MILITARY, AND POLITICAL DEVELOPMENTS, 1950–1965

The continuing discussions between Washington and Taipei over a UN strategy provided but one of many issues requiring careful consultation during the years of close collaboration. From 1950 to 1965 the United States became intimately involved in Nationalist Chinese affairs, and the Taiwan government grew proficient at securing and utilizing American assistance. The combination of U.S. aid and the far-reaching policies of a Nationalist technocratic elite served to launch Taiwan into the modern world more firmly and more rapidly than anyone in either Taipei or Washington had anticipated.

Clearly relocation from the mainland of China to the island of Taiwan proved the single most important factor in the survival and eventual success of the Nationalist regime. The benefits included elimination of the Kuomintang's conservative, landlord constituency, acquisition of an arena of operations far more manageable in scope and complexity, and assembly of a significant body of highly educated and skilled refugee supporters to fill governmental posts and reorganize the economic and political institutions of the state. The outbreak of the Korean War added to these advantages the fortuitous circumstances of an anticommunist crusade in Asia, which revived the moribund United States commitment to the Kuomintang. And finally, the Nationalists inherited the socioeconomic infrastructure of Japanese colonialism, which, however exploitative it may once have been, endowed the island with communications, transportation, and industrial facilities vital to development.

The Nationalist leadership did not immediately respond to the challenge of a new environment, instantly discard the deleterious attitudes of the past, and implement fresh programs oriented toward more liberal and egalitarian goals. In fact, initially the Kuomintang viewed Taiwan as so temporary a home that it refused to think in terms of local improvements, which would squander limited resources needed to return to the mainland and rebuild control there.

Coupled with that barrier to change was the debate within the intellectual community over the appropriate techniques for pursuing the wealth and power that had eluded government authorities on the mainland. Although everyone agreed that Sun Yat-sen's three principles of the people, the San Min Chu I, would be fundamental, less accord existed on how these concepts (which spoke of nationalism, democracy, and people's livelihood) could be combined with capitalism to stabilize the regime and make it prosper. Should the Nationalists abandon tradition and plunge totally into an unregulated free market system? If the old-style, highly restricted, bureaucratized environment had failed, might not a mixed economy combining state enterprises and the guiding hand of government with the best of capitalist innovation serve the country most effectively? Rather than renounce the nation's Chinese roots entirely, leaders could sinicize elements of capitalism and socialism, undergirding the whole with Confucian precepts, while training a new generation of experts to implement economic and political reforms.

The United States further complicated the debate. Americans strongly supported the free enterprise system, casting aspersions on alternate models of economic organization. Furthermore, Washington had unmistakable expectations about what behavior could be exacted from a client state. Then there were also those elements in Taiwan who, in adhering too closely to the Americans and advocating total westernization, seemed to become disloyal, perhaps "less Chinese."

But, despite these dangers, American assistance could not be dispensed with and compromise seemed essential. Ironically, as on the mainland, concessions came as often from the dominant United States as they did from the weaker Taiwan regime. The Nationalists continued to hone their manipulative skills, insinuating Kuomintang needs into the American consciousness, deflecting Washington's demands, and selling their supposed strategic location and symbolism as a bastion of democracy for the money, guns, and technical support they required.[1]

THE ECONOMY

The economic sphere proved the most significant field for Sino-American cooperation and development. Confronted with destruction from the war and dislocations produced immediately after V-J Day by departing Japanese and incoming Nationalist authorities, the government had to undertake basic and thoroughgoing reform. Although this had proven impossible on the mainland, in Taiwan change began early and was not deterred by corruption, factionalism, or war.[2]

From 1950 to 1965 the United States provided an annual average of some $100 million to Taiwan in nonmilitary assistance.[3] This amount exceeded the per capita contribution made to any other government in the world during the same period. It comprised roughly 6.4 percent of Taiwan's gross national product and approximately 34 percent of total gross investment in the economy. In the especially important area of trade, U.S. assistance paid for 40 percent of Taiwan's total imports of both goods and services. The terms of United States aid were generous. From 1951 to 1955 Washington bestowed all assistance outright. Thereafter, in addition to grants, it provided loans at very low interest with extended periods for repayment.

American bounty did not come without strings, however, and conflicts over purpose and organizing principles complicated cooperation. Kuomintang officials did not welcome American interference in their internal affairs and correctly assumed that U.S. activism derived from distrust of Nationalist abilities and goals. Small matters like the need to hold meetings of Chinese government agencies in English for the benefit of American advisers rankled. More serious disputes that continued throughout the 1950–65 period of joint endeavor revolved around issues such as defense spending (to be discussed in the next section), privatization, the participation of the Taiwanese, and the general need to liberalize economic structures.[4]

Initial policies dealt with relief, stabilization, and rehabilitation rather than with economic development. Although bombing had taken a significant toll on the island's physical plant, Taiwan benefited from the extensive prewar and wartime development activities carried out by the Japanese in areas such as education, irrigation, and rural industry.[5] American programs succeeded in bringing inflation, which had devastated the Kuomintang on the mainland, under control, and this led to a significant surge in real per capita income. Under the Mutual Security Act passed in 1951, Washington's main focus was to assist the Nationalist government to build a strong military force. Congress appropriated economic assistance on an ad hoc basis with annual rather than long-term commitments to Taipei. Similarly, Chiang Kai-shek preferred to view economic policies in Taiwan as temporary measures designed to create a reliable base for efforts to return to the mainland. Since Taiwan's economy would then be reintegrated into that of China proper it appeared a waste to devote time, attention, and resources to island-specific plans. In fact, were affluence attained in Taiwan, it might diminish enthusiasm for returning to the mainland.[6] One Nationalist refugee confided to an American journalist: "You think about it every time you start to do anything, even such a simple thing as putting in a vegetable garden. Is it worthwhile planting these tomatoes? Am I not surrendering to despair if I put in trees—am I not admitting to myself that I may be here forever?"[7]

The primary exception to this shortsighted approach occurred in agriculture where the Joint Commission on Rural Reconstruction (JCRR), which had been established on the mainland in 1948, resumed its work. Composed of three Chinese and two American commissioners, the JCRR recruited a small but highly skilled technical staff, most of whom had studied in the U.S., to provide research, education, and extension services. Their efforts helped shape and implement the government's reform program that from 1949 through 1953 revolutionized landholding on the island. Derived from the thoughts of Sun Yat-sen, articulated most comprehensively in his lectures on the San Min Chu I in 1924, the policy had originally been promulgated by the Kuomintang regime in 1930. But, whereas the land law on the mainland failed, in Taiwan Sun Yat-sen's ideas received renewed emphasis and in an unencumbered environment proved successful.[8]

In the first stage the government reduced rents on the 41 percent of farmland operated by tenants from 50 to 37.5 percent of the annual major crop. In 1951 Taipei began sales of public holdings, mostly confiscated from the Japanese at the end of the war, to farm families. Finally in 1953, through the Land-to-the-Tiller program, tenants acquired the opportunity to purchase land at reduced rates over a 10-year period. Landlords whose property was seized to make this possible received payment in the form of government enterprise stock (30 percent) and land bonds (70 percent).[9]

That this policy could be realized signified the transformed nature of political support for the Kuomintang party. On the mainland the Chiang regime had been unable to foreclose on large landowners, who had composed the Kuomintang's political core, and so had not satisfied demands for a redistribution of wealth. The result had been a popular communist rebellion that had forced Chiang Kai-shek to flee. In Taiwan, by contrast, such holdings had been in the hands of either the defeated Japanese or Taiwanese. The Chiang regime's opportunity to undermine the status of Taiwan's elite at the same time as it carried out widely celebrated reforms could not have been more fortuitous.

The new patterns of land use coupled with the work of the JCRR proved extraordinarily successful in raising productivity. Although of obvious benefit in feeding the troops until they could attack China, the agricultural revolution profoundly altered economic relationships and laid a foundation for future development of the island. By 1964 aggregate agricultural output reached almost twice the 1950–52 level.[10]

The need to move beyond rehabilitation to the modernization and cultivation of the island's economy became evident in other sectors as well. Although Chiang Kai-shek remained reluctant to think in long-range terms, his American financiers shifted their focus toward building infrastructure, training personnel, and promoting industry as well as agriculture. Convinced that the Kuomintang would not be able to oust the CCP, Washington concluded that the time had come for developing and enhancing what territory remained to it. Chiang reached a similar conclusion more slowly and for a different end. As a showcase, Taiwan would provide great propaganda advantages that could facilitate retaking the mainland.

Agreement on interim objectives did not dictate accord on the means to realize development. In 1953 some 80 percent of Taiwan's industrial plant belonged to the state. From the Kuomintang's perspective, this seemed an ideal situation for reasons of political power and security. The government could dictate manufacturing priorities, control raw materials, exclude Taiwanese businessmen from leading industrial sectors, and provide jobs for political supporters. Moreover, such conditions accorded with Chinese tradition, which emphasized the necessity of a highly bureaucratized Confucian state, and took contemporary ideological legitimacy from the development plans laid out by Sun Yat-sen, including his concerns regarding the growth of unregulated capitalism.

To Americans, on the other hand, the encouragement of private enterprise seemed vital. It would assist in liberalizing the economy and entrenching free market principles as well as providing the Taiwanese access to wealth and status.[11] U.S. assistance in fact helped Y. C. Wang, a fledgling entrepreneur, to launch Formosa Plastics, among the biggest and most successful conglomerates on the island by the mid-1980s.[12]

Disagreement over the privatization issue, which dated back to Chinese-American reform discussions on the mainland, reached serious proportions in the late 1950s in the context of pressures on Taipei to open the island to increased foreign investment and trade. Americans emphasized the utility of foreign enterprise in injecting new funds, ideas, and technology into the economy. Government regulations designed to protect Taiwan from external competition, including high tariffs, tight credit, and harbor dues, however, militated against both the growth of domestic import/export firms and foreign participation. Even the encouragement of overseas Chinese investment languished in the early 1950s as Nationalist officials dismissed the desire to take profits off the island as unpatriotic.[13]

Legal and bureaucratic reforms introduced between 1958 and 1960, partly at American urging, began reconfiguring the economic order to accommodate foreign investment and to simplify expansion of the private sector. Not only had the domestic market been saturated, but local entrepreneurs continued to hesitate to put their capital into new ventures. When Chiang responded to the second Taiwan Straits crisis in 1958 by appointing Ch'en Ch'eng premier, Ch'en's protégés moved rapidly to free the economy from conservative stalemate and willingly undertook reform.[14] By 1960 they had devalued the Taiwan dollar, reduced restrictions on imports, introduced a single exchange rate, permitted repatriation of profits, and instituted more flexible terms of credit.[15] In 1959 the visit of Undersecretary of State C. Douglas Dillon spurred both Sino-American cooperation and Chinese government planning. Reformers used a modest proposal from the U.S. Agency for International Development (AID) as a basis for their own elaborate 19 Point Program of Economic and Financial Reform, which then elicited a $30 million American loan offer to ensure realization of the plan's ambitious objectives. Furthermore, in connection with the drafting of new investment regulations during 1963, the idea of special export-processing zones in which manufacturers would be granted privileges such as tax exemptions, originally broached by American advisers in 1956, finally received official encouragement. With impediments eliminated, trade, which had stagnated at only 4 percent growth per year between 1952 and 1959, expanded at 22 percent per year from 1959 to 1965.[16]

American companies also began to relocate to Taiwan. These included Singer Sewing Machine and the National Distiller and Chemical Corporation, whose experiences illustrated the government's role in encouraging particular types of foreign investment and specific directions for domestic industry to develop. Singer's entry in 1963 met vehement protest from local manufacturers. Officials countered that technology transfer and local procurement would compensate for initial sales losses. Similarly, the government mandated that National Distiller structure shareholding so that Chinese investors could buy into the operation after the first five years, export all surplus production, and refrain from diversification into related industries in Taiwan. At the same time, it willingly offered the American company tax concessions, a ban on competing imports, and unrestricted repatriation of profits as inducements. The U.S. government enhanced the offer with promises of cheap credit and insurance against loss due to war or expropriation.[17]

Analysts agree that the success of U.S. aid in Taiwan derived from three related conditions. First, officials on both sides managed to sustain a high degree of cooperation, which was facilitated by an uncommon continuity of personnel and institutions. Second, organizations that handled aid distribution and planning proved able to maintain considerable independence from regular government agencies, making it possible to shield both monies and programs from competing claims. The first of these agencies included the Council on United States Aid, launched as a counterpart to the U.S. mission in 1948, and the Economic Stabilization Board, established on Taiwan at the urging of the U.S. Mission in 1951. Working closely with American Embassy representatives, these and subsequent organizations dealt with responsibilities ranging from selection and supervision of aid projects to fighting inflation and allocating commodity imports.

And, finally, progress depended upon the success of the constituency in the United States that fought for aid to Taipei. The China lobby kept the question of Taiwan's survival a political issue in the United States, an issue that could not be ignored once the Korean War had made Asia an important cold war theater. The Department of State found itself in recurring battles against China bloc members of Congress such as Pat McCarran (R-NV), who in January 1951 proposed an aid package for Taiwan that the Department believed was beyond the capacity of the Nationalists to absorb. Moreover, officers in the Far Eastern division feared that "by making available to the Chinese Government enormous sums, we would remove the incentive to constructive Chinese leadership and forthright measures of self-help and, in all probability, merely undermine the self-reliance of the Chinese themselves."[18] Although both the Truman and Eisenhower administrations succeeded in keeping some control over the size of expenditures for Taiwan, they nonetheless found themselves increasingly committed to financial support for the KMT.

American money and advice clearly played an enormous part in advancing Taiwan's economy. Before U.S. aid resumed in 1950, the Nationalists

President Eisenhower on a visit to Taiwan appears with Generalissimo Chiang Kai-shek and Mme Chiang, June 1960. *Courtesy of Dwight D. Eisenhower Library*

had nearly exhausted their foreign exchange holdings and gold reserves. Recovery could begin on the basis of Taiwan's small domestic market, but access to the outside world held the key to sustained growth. This depended on the United States since Taiwan had virtually no foreign trade network and stood little chance of establishing viable connections given the dangers of civil war that made investment and even shipping risky ventures.

Among America's most significant contributions to Taiwan's development was encouragement of private enterprise, which became critical to economic expansion by 1965. Even had the government not been reluctant to enlarge the private sector, it lacked the knowledge to promote it. American advisers, therefore, guided the authorities during the 1950s and early 1960s in improving Taiwan's investment climate. In some instances, the U.S. took a more aggressive stance, blocking government plans to initiate expensive state-run projects such as a steel mill, an airline, and a nuclear reactor.[19]

U.S. assistance proved crucial in adding the financial flexibility that gave impetus to reform. Without American aid, inflation could not have been curbed quickly, and domestic savings vital to growth would not have been available, perhaps tempting the government to expand the money supply, thereby refueling inflation. American money, by subsidizing the purchase of capital goods and technical services, freed local resources to produce needed consumer items that increased government popularity. In fact, according to Neil Jacoby's admittedly self-serving U.S. government study, American aid reduced the amount of time necessary to reach 1964 living standards by 30 years.

The U.S. AID Mission at times also provided protection for those within the government in Taipei who wanted to move ahead with radical reforms. The opportunity to shift the blame onto unreasonable and demanding Americans enabled reformers to push forward developmental programs in the face of internal criticism and resistance. AID threats to reduce assistance levels constituted convincing leverage, since "both parties realized that, while the U.S. needed a stable and prosperous Taiwan, its interests did not necessarily require that the economy grow at the rate of 7.6 per cent a year."[20]

At the same time, American theory had a decisive impact on the study of economics in Taiwan. Young economists returning from graduate education in the United States reacted against outmoded ideas and irrelevant curricula. In 1955 Shih Chien-sheng, a professor at National Taiwan University, published his *Principles of Economics*, a volume that relied heavily on the insights of Paul Samuelson, and later the same year he also began to disseminate the ideas of John Maynard Keynes. Since Shih trained the better part of a generation of economists, his version of American economic principles had considerable influence in shaping thought and development. His efforts were supplemented by the American and Chinese-American lecturers and consultants who visited Taiwan frequently.[21]

American advisers, of course, did not always succeed in implementing policies they thought vital to Taiwan's growth. Nationalist officials sometimes had different priorities to which the Americans were not always sensitive. Certain fiscal restraints, despite American advice, reduced expansion. For instance, the government adamantly refused to reduce military expenditures, limit the money supply, or raise low taxes. Anxious to provide adequate national defense forces and determined to retain domestic support, which had been lost on the mainland in the 1940s, officials exceeded and severely skewed budgets, refusing to be deterred by prosaic economic arguments when they could count on American assistance to make up shortfalls.[22]

Nevertheless, it remains true that without the astute policies followed by the Taipei government even abundant U.S. assistance could not have accomplished so much. The Chinese throughout initiated project proposals and determined the direction that development would move. This they facilitated by utilizing not just talent recruited from the National Resources Council (NRC), which had controlled economic planning on the mainland, but also through adaptation of policies designed in the late 1940s. Thus, the Industrial Development Commission created under the Economic Stabilization Board and staffed with NRC veterans dominated economic affairs along with the Council for Economic Planning and Development, the two together making up Taiwan's "economic general staff."[23] The primary architect of the new order was K. Y. Yin, who, as vice-chairman of the Taiwan Production Board, secretary general of the Economic Stabilization Board, and then Economic Minister, determined priorities and oversaw implementation. Yin ranged widely from grand strategy to practical education to modernize his country and his countrymen. In 1954, for instance, he ordered destruction of 20,000 light bulbs in a central Taipei park to dramatize the importance of quality control.[24]

The most significant application of the government's guiding hand can be found in the adoption of export promotion to replace the import substitution regime of the 1950s. No longer would Taiwan strive only to protect domestic infant industries and reduce the quantity of goods that had to be purchased abroad, straining foreign exchange holdings, now it would seek to earn foreign exchange by selling overseas products manufactured at low cost on the island. If U.S. encouragement for this move played an important part in initiating the policy, Nationalist officials like Yin responded enthusiastically, and their execution of the policy took on a distinctively Chinese cast. The government exercised close control, abjuring American-style laissez-faire methods.[25] State planners persisted in selecting industries for promotion, sometimes contrary to objective economic advantages and the dictates of the free market, where security or other interests interceded. They occasionally utilized state enterprises to spearhead growth, and they never totally relaxed import controls or nontariff trade barriers. Decisions followed not from cooperation with the private sector but from the "vigorous policy network" created from "public enterprises, public banks, public research and service organizations, universities, foreign multinationals with operations in Taiwan, private consulting firms, and some 'special status' private manufacturing companies connected to the party, the military, or the economic ministries."[26] As quickly became apparent once U.S. aid ceased, Nationalist leaders were on the threshold of an extraordinary economic expansion.

Of course United States economic support for the development of the Nationalist Chinese economy followed from more than simple humanitarian concern for survival on Taiwan. In fact America's self-interested motives extended from security to commercial benefits. Washington's desire to strengthen strategic defenses in Asia against communist expansionism was paralleled by a determination to acquire markets, protect trade routes, and, increasingly, find low-cost sources of productive labor. The Chinese Nationalists have pointed out, for example, that U.S. food aid under the Agricultural Trade Development and Assistance Act of 1954 (PL 480) had as much to do with disposing of American farm surpluses as with the desire to assist Taiwan.[27]

Similarly, Taiwan's agricultural success and its experience with communist insurgency led Americans to see strategic cold war advantages in utilizing Nationalist expertise overseas. The first such effort began in 1959 with technical assistance programs in Vietnam. A farmers' association team helped establish cooperatives for providing credit and marketing outlets and educational extension services. Another group introduced Taiwanese varieties of soybeans, sugar cane, peanuts, and other produce, which increased yields by as much as 100 percent. Finally, irrigation surveying, planning, and training developed with the assistance of Taiwan specialists who worked in the fields alongside farmers. In 1964 the project added livestock improvement and expanded its staff, becoming the Chinese Agricultural Technical Mission.[28]

The idea proliferated quickly into a far more ambitious endeavor known as the Vanguard Project. Beginning in 1961, Taipei provided technical assistance to more than 20 governments, primarily in Africa but also in Asia and Latin America. Teams of agriculturalists organized educational programs in modern crop-producing methods, especially for rice, and animal husbandry. Thousands of technicians also traveled to Taiwan to attend training institutes. The United States funded the better part of the expenses through AID, and the CIA facilitated many of the initial contacts needed to convince governments to utilize Nationalist expertise. Taipei made annual monetary contributions, as well as furnishing the personnel. To American officials Vanguard appeared to offer several benefits, including enhancement of the ROC's prestige, solidification of its hold on UN representation because of the resulting African political support, dramatization of the success of American foreign aid, distraction of Taipei from its preoccupation with recovering the mainland, and hinderance of Beijing's efforts to establish its influence among the new African states.[29]

The decision, which began to form at the end of the 1950s, to terminate American economic aid to Taiwan derived both from the success of the effort and the domestic U.S. need to discontinue a costly enterprise in order to free funds for other programs. By 1960 preparations had begun to move Taiwan toward economic independence. Nationalist government officials protested that the end of economic support was coming too soon and too quickly but had no influence over the decision.[30] U.S. personnel, particularly those with the AID mission, saw the export boom of 1963 as confirmation that Taiwan would continue to prosper. When, therefore, the administration encountered unprecedented resistance in Congress to foreign assistance (producing a 34 percent cut in the president's proposed 1964 foreign aid bill), it decided to cite Taiwan's performance as evidence of great accomplishment and declare that no further appropriations would be necessary after June 1965.[31] Indeed, in mid-1965 as Taiwan graduated from the aid program, its economy was in the throes of an agricultural and industrial boom.

THE MILITARY

The overriding determination of the United States to deny the island of Taiwan to the USSR or any country allied with or dominated by it dictated the significance and longevity of the Washington-Taipei military connection. Americans intended to preserve Taiwan as a base for possible U.S. operations and a repository for potentially useful allied troops. Washington officially reached this conclusion in NSC 146/2 in 1953, recognizing that the neutralization of the island would not serve its strategic needs.[32] Americans noted, for example, that the cost of training and maintenance of each soldier on Taiwan came to $300 as compared to $5,000 for each American in uniform.[33] A $200 million expenditure annually for economic and military support was estimated by the American embassy in Taipei in 1956 to be less than the total price of equipping and feeding a single American division.[34] Despite the weakness of Nationalist forces, their very existence tied down substantial numbers of Communist soldiers along the coast from Guangzhou to Shanghai. Americans found this advantageous both during the Korean conflict and as Washington's interest in the Indochina campaign increased. The Nationalists, of course, advocated a more active policy. From 1950 onwards, they continually tried to goad the United States into supporting an attack on the mainland that would return them to power. In these efforts they received sympathetic consideration from various Americans in Taiwan and in the United States.

Among the most consistently enthusiastic exponents of an invasion were members of the U.S. military establishment. During the Korean War, even after President Truman had turned down Douglas MacArthur's proposal to

A 1955 airfield discussion between (from left to right) Assistant Secretary of State Walter Robertson, Chairman of the Joint Chiefs of Staff Admiral Arthur W. Radford, Ambassador Karl Rankin, and Major General William C. Chase, Chief Military Assistance Advisory Group, Formosa. *Courtesy of the U.S. Navy and the National Archives*

use Nationalist troops on the peninsula, both Generals Matthew Ridgway and Mark Clark renewed the request.[35] On a July 1953 visit to Taipei, Admiral Arthur Radford, chairman of the Joint Chiefs of Staff, discussed with Chiang a hypothetical attack on the mainland and got the Generalissimo's agreement that an American would be placed in charge of such an enterprise.[36] Clearly Chiang's hopes could only have been raised by planning of this nature with someone in Radford's position. Members of the American military establishment, as well as providing encouragement secretly, also on occasion made dangerous and embarrassing statements in public. Secretary of the Navy Dan Kimball, for instance, remarked during a visit to Japan in April 1952 that if the Nationalists struck the mainland, the U.S. Seventh Fleet would "cheer them on." As British analysts remarked, "the irresponsibility of some leading Americans is almost past belief!"[37]

Raids against mainland villages and shipping in the Taiwan Straits had the virtue of causing the Communist Chinese distress but not of risking war. General William Chase, chief of the Military Assistance Advisory Group

(MAAG), which had been established 1 May 1951 to reorganize, train, and equip Nationalist forces, proposed in February 1953 that General Chow Chih-jou, chief of the General Staff, Ministry of National Defense, mount a naval effort to blockade a portion of the China coast between Swatow and Dachen, increase the number of nuisance raids using contingents of less than 500 men conducted from the offshore islands as well as from Taiwan, and carry out more frequent and effective naval and air reconnaissance activities.[38] In March the Joint Chiefs of Staff approved a proposal by Chiang Kai-shek that the U.S. and the ROC undertake joint planning of offensive and defensive operations.[39] By the spring of 1954 the United States had begun to provide training for the guerrillas, and Chase had acquired a U.S. Army intelligence coordinator for such activities, whom he called his "Vice President in Charge of Pirates."[40]

Raids continued throughout the period from 1950 to 1965. The Nationalists landed whenever they could, while also sinking communist vessels and interferring with commercial shipping. The activity proved sufficiently disruptive to lead to repeated condemnation by Beijing, but by 1964 American military advisers concluded that the losses to the Nationalists might have become significant enough to curb future assaults. In just one incident, on July 11 and 12, some 150 men had been sacrificed along with four transport craft, reducing Nationalist lift capability by two-thirds.[41]

Covert operations in conjunction with and unconstrained by MAAG also proceeded under the direction of the U.S. Central Intelligence Agency. Beginning almost immediately after the outbreak of the Korean War and continuing until the 1960s, the Agency recruited guerrillas to return to the mainland to gather information and harass the Communist Chinese. Although President Truman had rejected Chiang Kai-shek's offer of uniformed soldiers for the Korean War effort, the CIA actively sought operatives to work behind Chinese lines on the Korean peninsula.[42] As early as 1951 the CIA supplied and coordinated the activities of as many as 100,000 Nationalist troops.[43] Working under the cover of a specially created commercial company called Western Enterprises, they provided training, logistical support, and the capabilities to carry out overflights, leafleting, and radio broadcasts.[44] Western Enterprises amassed fleets of ships and airplanes used to support guerrilla activities. By 1954, when Western Enterprises ceased operations and was replaced by the Naval Auxiliary Communications Center, the personnel of the CIA station had grown to more than 600.

The air arm of the CIA developed under the auspices of a proprietary airline called Civil Air Transport (CAT). Originally a private operation owned by former Flying Tiger Claire Chennault and Whiting Willauer, CAT made its way to Taiwan with fleeing Nationalist forces and undertook both overt and covert activities on behalf of the United States and Nationalist Chinese governments. In March 1950 the CIA actually purchased the airline and placed an intelligence operative in company headquarters in Hong Kong.[45]

By the end of the 1950s, its success had led to the creation of Air America, which serviced Southeast Asia and flew for AID and the State Department as well as the CIA. Air Asia, a wholly owned Air America subsidiary, ran the largest repair and maintenance facility in the Pacific region on Taiwan, relieving the U.S. Air Force of the need to operate its own workshops. CAT, meanwhile, coupled its secret missions with management of Nationalist China's domestic and international passenger airline routes until 1968.[46]

U.S. intelligence units also entered into agreements to exchange information with their Chinese counterparts, making Taiwan a major base for gathering material on developments inside mainland China.[47] This primarily involved technological eavesdropping on Chinese communications. Extensive electronic surveillance facilities were constructed by the U.S. National Security Agency. In some instances Chinese pilots took low- altitude flights over the mainland to record signals emitted by Chinese Communist radar and weapons systems. But, in the early 1960s, the CIA station chief Ray Cline persuaded John Kennedy to authorize use of the U-2 spy plane. After the disastrous flight by Francis Gary Powers in May 1960, which torpedoed the Eisenhower-Khrushchev summit, the U-2 could no longer be employed over Soviet territory. But the Chinese Communists had only a few of the SA-2 missiles Moscow had deployed to down the aircraft. Not until September 1962 did Beijing succeed in bringing down one of the spy planes, and the Chinese Nationalists continued to fly them, despite the loss of two additional aircraft, until the U.S. replaced the U-2 with SR-71s, which could fly far higher and faster.[48]

The U-2 proved instrumental in the U.S. discovery and monitoring of Chinese missile and atomic bomb production and test sites in northwest China. U-2 pilots, based in Taiwan, found a gaseous diffusion plant for uranium enrichment, and they tirelessly hunted for plutonium-processing facilities. President Kennedy, alarmed at the prospect of a Chinese bomb that could be used to threaten American allies and neutral powers throughout Asia, thought seriously about trying to arrest Beijing's progress toward a functional weapon. Among alternatives considered were an approach to Soviet Premier Nikita Khrushchev for a joint strike against Chinese research and development plants and dispatch of covert agents from Taiwan to blow up the critical installations.[49]

The Nationalists also ran a semicovert operation in northern Burma with at least initial cooperation from the CIA.[50] Chinese Nationalist troops had escaped to northern Burma as the civil war effort in China proper disintegrated in 1950. Rather than transport these forces to Taiwan, Chiang decided to keep them along the Chinese frontier, supplied and ready to fight. To Harry Truman these units offered the appealing possibility of distracting Chinese Communists from their war effort in Korea. In the summer of 1951, General Li Mi used his contingent of about 3,000 to stage an assault on Yunnan province, which was, however, quickly repulsed. The Nationalist

Foreign Ministry would subsequently claim that the effort had been launched prematurely because of American pressure. Although routed, Li Mi attracted perhaps as many as 20,000 followers, who fled to Burma with him and thereafter began seriously to threaten the stability of the government in Rangoon. Nevertheless, CIA and Taipei authorities welcomed Li Mi to Taiwan in the winter of 1951–52, agreed to continue to provide weapons, and, despite rhetoric about evacuation designed to appease the Burmese government, made it possible for him to continue harassing the Chinese Communists across the border.[51]

Halfhearted efforts at withdrawal finally began in 1953 after outraged Rangoon officials decided to appeal to the United Nations for relief from the chaos occasioned by the Chinese troops and refugees.[52] Taipei insisted that it had no control over Li Mi's troops, although Chiang Kai-shek did give him the title of governor of Yunnan province, and that it could not order these elements out of Burma. The Nationalist government also contended that there had been unprovoked and ruthless attacks by Burmese forces on Li Mi's men and that Burma generally did not present an effective barrier to expansion of Chinese Communist influence in southeast Asia.[53] American insistence that Taiwan remove at least some of the troops to avoid a crisis in Burmese-American relations seemed to the Nationalists as either intentionally deceitful or schizophrenic given the often voiced support for guerrilla activities elsewhere on the mainland.[54] In fact, Li Mi claimed to have received payments from the United States as late as July 1953, and private Americans may have continued supply efforts thereafter on a freelance basis.[55] John Foster Dulles, consequently, generated considerable tension by threatening to discontinue U.S. support for Chiang if some action did not follow to defuse the crisis.

The evacuation, when it came, did not solve the problem. Although as many as 7,000 people may have left, most were not able-bodied men, and few of these turned in their weapons upon departure. Subsequently, having undergone training in Taiwan, many returned to Burma. Supplies continued to flow from Taiwan despite an 31 October 1953 declaration at the United Nations disavowing the irregulars. And remnant forces increasingly supplemented these goods through opium smuggling. British military observers in the area affirmed that during 1955 Americans continued to air-drop weapons, although who the Americans were seemed unclear.[56]

After a period of quiescence, Nationalist support for the troops in the border region resumed in 1958 and escalated in the early 1960s. In 1961, paralleling expanded harassment of the mainland in the Taiwan Straits, Taiwan flew some 1,200 highly trained, well-armed men into northern Burma.[57] Moreover, Chiang's eldest son Chiang Ching-kuo personally began to direct operations, dramatizing the significance that the Taipei regime accorded the effort.[58] Although American matériel continued to be fundamental to supply efforts, direct United States involvement appeared by this time to have been abandoned. A joint Burmese-Chinese Communist military sweep of the border region in 1960–61 did uncover large caches of American arms, provoking a massive demonstration at the American embassy in Rangoon.[59] When an American airplane, supplied several years earlier by the U.S. Military Assistance Program, was shot down by the Burmese en route from Taiwan to deliver supplies to the guerrillas, Washington insisted Chiang mount another evacuation.[60] The Nationalists complied and brought more than 4,000 Chinese out, but Taipei never accepted American reasoning that retaining forces in Burma was a bad idea. In 1965 resupply activities resumed and bedeviled Americans through the rest of the Johnson administration. State Department officials, angered by the fact that Chiang "consistently disregarded" their entreaties and threats, sought ways to "force" compliance but found that "in each case we have run up against a basic limiting factor, that the amount of leverage available to us is in a practical sense very limited. This reflects the importance of the role that Taiwan plays in our strategic effort to contain Chinese Communist expansion."[61]

Taipei yearned to exploit, in every way possible, its pivotal position in the American defense perimeter in Asia. In 1957 and 1958 the Nationalists proposed the creation of a Taiwan rapid-deployment force that could act as a fire brigade to protect free world interests in Asia. The idea appealed to some high-level Americans, and the assistant secretary of defense sought serious consideration of the concept. The Joint Chiefs of Staff, however, rejected the creation of such a unit since it would look like a mercenary force, would drain resources needed in places such as South Korea, would not be welcomed by the countries of Asia it was meant to assist, and, most important, would be likely to bring Communist China into every incident to which it might be committed.[62]

On the other hand, Taiwan often served as a base for covert operations elsewhere in the region. In 1958 antigovernment forces in Indonesia were supplied from Taiwan.[63] The following year Tibetan insurgents received training on the island. In the early 1960s right-wing Laotians were drilled in Taiwan centers to conduct guerrilla warfare and Nationalist Chinese and American pilots flew CAT aircraft in support of military operations even after Laos was supposed to have been neutralized at Geneva in 1962.[64]

The American decision in 1956 to deploy Matador missiles on Taiwan introduced weapons having the capacity to carry nuclear warheads into the Straits area for the first time. The missiles, delivered in May and December 1957, gave Taiwan an all-weather, day-or-night capability and allowed the targeting of eight Communist Chinese airfields.[65] Initially, the United States sent the Matadors to Taiwan to soften Japanese opposition to basing these atomic weapons in Japan, proximity presumably likely to accustom the Japanese to their presence, rendering them less threatening. The Nationalists, however, saw the transfer as a sign of American confidence in and commitment to Taiwan and were cheered by it.[66] On the other hand, the Chinese Communists interpreted the Matadors as a mechanism to secure American control over Taiwan and to suppress internal opposition to what the Communists saw as the U.S. occupation of Taiwan.[67]

Beijing may have exaggerated the utility of the Matadors in asserting American ascendancy over Taiwan, but the Chinese Communists correctly saw military issues as a contentious element in the Washington-Taipei relationship. Military cooperation between the Nationalists and the Americans proved more difficult than did the joint efforts to develop Taiwan's economy. In the military arena, the differing objectives of the two governments clashed from the beginning and remained more or less incompatible throughout the period. Chiang Kai-shek devoted all his efforts to building forces for an attack on the mainland and maneuvered in the interim for opportunities to harass and sabotage Chinese Communist authority. Although the United States encouraged confusion and embarrassment of the Communists, it opposed Nationalist activities that threatened either to draw it into a war or to undermine Nationalist strength in Taiwan. Thus, questions of Nationalist military budgets, personnel recruitment and political indoctrination, attacks on the mainland, troops in Burma, and martial law in Taiwan all produced lingering frictions between Washington and Taipei.

From the first, American assessments of Nationalist capabilities made it clear that Chiang's forces could not retake the mainland. Without American protection it appeared certain that the Nationalists would be unable even to defend Taiwan from a Communist assault. Late in 1950 the Joint Chiefs of Staff described the Nationalist navy as "woefully inadequate"; the army as poorly led, inexperienced, and lacking equipment; and the air force as piloted by men insufficiently trained as well as demoralized.[68] Military incompetents had been promoted and officers at all levels deprived of command authority lest they contradict Chiang. Further, the services suffered from weak coordination stemming from Chiang's customary effort to divide and rule.

Nationalist claims regarding control over guerrilla units in China met strong skepticism from the State Department. Analysts believed that "in view of the general distrust and dislike of the Kuomintang on the mainland, it may be considered that the Nationalists have small influence with active or potential resisters." Thus a major effort to establish a bridgehead and bring down the Beijing regime seemed likely to end in yet another debacle.[69]

Washington decided to try to remedy Nationalist deficiencies after fighting on the Korean peninsula in the summer of 1950 produced a new and broader threat to Taiwan's security. In August 1950 the Department of Defense allocated the first shipment of ammunition to the island, designating it solely for defensive purposes. At the same time, Douglas MacArthur, despite Secretary of State Acheson's fierce opposition, dispatched a Far East Command Survey Group from his headquarters in Japan to assess Nationalist resources and requirements.

The resulting Fox report engendered controversy within the American government. State Department officers objected to massive appropriations recommended by the military, fearing that large amounts of equipment would land in Communist hands when Nationalist resistance collapsed.[70] Chargé d'affaires Karl Rankin in Taipei took issue with proposals to appoint military consultants who would not be subject to his authority.[71] Nevertheless, in May MAAG was launched and by September fielded a staff of 300, reaching a peak of some 2,300 in the late 1950s. Under the auspices of the Mutual Defense Assistance Agreement, moreover, Congress began a series of weighty appropriations for Taiwan, which between 1951 and 1965 totaled $2.5 billion, an average of $167 million each year.[72]

The result of American largesse, when coupled with the profligacy of Nationalist military spenders, produced a military budget equalling 15 percent of GNP with 85 percent of the government's total expenditures going to the military—a ratio double that of the United States.[73] Taiwan's military forces, therefore, could be maintained at approximately 600,000, which meant the proportion of uniformed troops to overall population was among the highest in the world. The equivalent in the United States would have meant a standing army of about 11 million. Not only was this costly in and of itself, but the drain on the general economy from siphoning off one-seventh of the able-bodied producers from farm and factory was severe. But, when civilian Nationalist officials expressed concern, they found it impossible to override the national military establishment, given the personal associations of Chiang Kai-shek and his sons Ching-kuo and Wei-kuo with the armed forces hierarchy.[74]

These connections also aggravated the ad hoc nature of military expenditures, which State Department officials, including Acheson, wanted curbed. Americans insisted that defense "charges on Formosan resources [need not] be so unpredictable, arbitrary, and irresponsible, in terms of the social and economic consequences they produce, as to render sound economic planning almost, if not completely, impossible."[75] But, some two years later, the American embassy continued to assert that the Chinese military and the government had "neither the will nor the intention to implement any program involving the establishment of strong budget controls."[76]

The problem as State Department officials saw it stemmed from "years of being financially assisted by the U.S. [which] has given most Chinese officials the attitude that the U.S. will pay the bill come what may." Thus, they concluded, "the most difficult job facing Formosa policy makers today in connection with developing aid programs is to convince Chinese officials that the U.S. cannot be pressured or cajoled into giving more aid than is considered compatible with U.S. security interests."[77]

It could be said, of course, that the U.S. in pressuring the Nationalists to reduce the size of their military establishment had arrogantly appropriated the right to dictate to a foreign government on an issue vital to its continued

Cartoon by Mauldin, 1958. *Reprinted with permission Chicago Sun-Times, © 1993*

existence. The MAAG advisers did not share Chiang's goal of retaking the mainland, nor did they propose to finance his effort to do so. The Nationalists, nevertheless, persisted and, in turn, defiantly sought to use U.S. funds for purposes that ran counter to U.S. policy. Repeatedly, officials stalled submission of estimates until the last minute, hoping to stampede Washington into additional appropriations.[78]

State Department analysts had anticipated that the effort to provide Chiang with advice as well as money would not work. Experience had taught them to believe that, beyond cash and equipment, the Generalissimo had no use for American expertise lest it make his manipulation of the armed services more difficult. "It may be doubted also," they asserted, "that American technicians would be welcome to the general run of responsible Chinese officers, who, despite their ineptitude on the mainland still consider themselves as superior to foreigners in military knowledge."[79]

U.S. plans and pressure to reorganize the Nationalist military forces to reduce costs, then, proved unpopular and met resistance. The Americans sought to cut down on the huge numbers of men Chiang insisted upon equipping, training, and feeding. Invariably, optimism in Washington that Taipei would comply was unfounded. Reductions that did occur failed to solve the fundamental problem. The greatest success involved retiring those too old or infirm to fight, but many of these were then replaced by Taiwanese recruits.[80] Instead Chiang thrust in quite a different direction. For instance, in 1954 he pushed for an expansion of his forces through the "Kai Plan" to make possible recapture of the mainland.[81] Not only did Taipei remain adamant about retaining a military establishment of 600,000, but Chiang also refused to listen to American insistence that heavy troop concentrations on the offshore islands be reduced. The Nationalist solution to disagreement was to keep the preferred number of men in uniform, use American supplies for as many as possible, and, in addition, field a series of under-equipped and poorly trained units.

The issue of political indoctrination among the armed forces proved to be a similarly sensitive one. Chiang Ching-kuo headed the Political Department, which ran a cadre of political commissars at every level of the army, navy, and air force. A useful mechanism for ensuring ideological purity and political loyalty of soldiers to the regime, it undermined the authority of line officers and penalized initiative among officers and men. To Chiang Kai-shek the negative features could not outweigh the ability such an arrangement gave him to eliminate potential rivals.[82] American advisers found the system politically, ethically, and functionally objectionable and struggled to eliminate it.[83] When that proved impossible, they devised a plan to complement political indoctrination with training in military discipline and the importance of command structures so that the commissars would be less apt to interfere detrimentally in military operations.[84]

Despite conflicting goals, by the mid-1950s it became clear that Nationalist military forces had begun to improve both in skills and morale. In addition to benefiting from American techniques introduced by MAAG, the services brought in Japanese military instructors. They also had better men to work with once near-universal conscription became the rule. Military missions traveled almost constantly between Taiwan and the United States. High-level American military officials came largely to build morale. Chinese groups, often in large numbers, traveled around the United States, visiting military schools, laboratories, and bases to learn about technology and organization. The striking result was demonstrated during the 1958 Straits crisis when the Chinese air force exceeded all expectations, destroying 31 MIGs and losing only 1 of its F-86F aircraft in combat.[85]

POLITICS

The United States played a far more modest part in the political development of Taiwan. American pressure sought to promote reform, broaden representation, and reinforce the liberal elements in the ruling Kuomintang party. Washington realized early, however, that it could exert little leverage on issues so complex and so vitally important to Nationalist leaders.

American hostility toward Chiang Kai-shek provided the clearest lesson in this regard. As mentioned earlier, Secretary of State Dean Acheson welcomed efforts in the late 1940s to eliminate Chiang and replace him with more progressive, effective, and cooperative leadership. But investigation of internal conditions in Taiwan made it clear that no viable alternatives existed, and Acheson relinquished the dream of ousting the Generalissimo. Although others in Washington revived that hope sporadically, Chiang's control only became more secure over time. The Generalissimo mounted a public relations effort, scattering portraits and sculptures around the island and ensuring that newspapers and posters constantly reprinted his nationalistic message.[86] In 1963 State Department analysts observed:

> Chiang's present power extends to virtually every area of activity in the Republic of China. One cannot exaggerate the extent to which political life in Taiwan today focuses on and emanates from the President, who not only makes every important decision but concerns himself with administrative details of the most trivial character. Access to the President . . . can give an individual political importance out of all proportion to his own rank and talent. . . . For years he has balanced one faction or leader against another, permitting no rival center of power.[87]

Americans feared that the Generalissimo's absolute dominance would lead, upon his death, to the succession of his sinister son Chiang Ching-kuo to the presidency. Concern about Ching-kuo stemmed from both his lengthy sojourn in the Soviet Union, where he absorbed totalitarian methods of political rule, perhaps even communist principles, and his subsequent tenure as the Nationalist's key enforcer of ideological purity through his mastery of the entire civilian and military security and intelligence apparatus.

Washington preferred the seemingly more liberal vice president and premier, Ch'en Ch'eng, with whom Ching-kuo was locked in an intense rivalry. Ch'en had proven instrumental in realizing the land reform program of the early 1950s and in implementing economic changes favored by the U.S. between 1958 and 1960. He appeared to lean toward development of Taiwan rather than recovery of the mainland and cultivated a cadre of American-educated, liberal economists and technocrats. Americans speculated that he might be sympathetic to democracy but worried about his ineffectiveness as an administrator. They tried to increase American interaction with him and strengthen the programs he favored. Ch'en, at the same time, did not reach out to the Americans for support, and his trip to the U.S. during the struggle over a seat for Mongolia at the United Nations hurt him politically because he proved unable to persuade the American government to change its position.[88] Whether Ch'en Ch'eng could have bested Chiang Ching-kuo became irrelevant when in March 1965 Ch'en died of cancer, leaving the field to the Generalissimo's oldest offspring.

Others who were more willing to be identified with Americans suffered for their audacity. Reflecting the uneasy relationship between tradition and modernization, Chineseness and Americanization, Chiang Kai-shek was suspicious of individuals who had been educated in the United States, too readily accepted American values and advice, and cultivated ties with Washington. The Generalissimo felt compelled at times to use these people to secure U.S. support, but he never trusted them and dispensed with their services as quickly as he could.

The result was a series of much publicized purges. After the violent February 1947 revolt of Taiwanese against the corrupt and repressive government of Ch'en Yi, Chiang appointed Wei Tao-ming governor. A former ambassador to the U.S., Wei's selection sent a strong message to Taiwanese and Americans alike that the Kuomintang recognized a need for radical change. But Wei, frustrated by Chiang's inflexible control, recognized that governance of the province of Taiwan could not easily be separated from governance of the nation when Chiang's national regime had only the one province to administer. Thus Wei suggested that the U.S. support him in separating Taiwan from the mainland. Chiang abruptly dismissed him in December 1948.[89] Wu Kuochen (K. C. Wu) similarly became governor to ensure U.S. assistance, explicitly bargaining with U.S. representatives for an exchange between reform and their assistance to him. Wu resigned under pressure in 1953 and, having survived a supposed assassination attempt, sought refuge in the United States. There he condemned Chiang's excesses and the absence of democracy on the island. Only two years later, General Sun Li-jen, commander in chief of the

Vice President Ch'en Ch'eng and his wife meet with President John F. Kennedy, Vice President Lyndon B. Johnson and Secretary of State Dean Rusk, 1961. Photo by Abbie Rowe. *Courtesy of the National Park Service*

army, who had long been seen by Americans in heroic terms as a Kuomintang anomaly—honest, competent, and liberal—was removed. Not only had he been critical of the government and Chiang Ching-kuo's political commissar system, but he had been American-trained, secretly promoted as a possible alternative to Chiang, and used by the Americans to champion their reforms.[90] When Chiang, possessed of the Mutual Defense Treaty, felt confident about United States money and protection, he moved against Sun, who was placed under house arrest and remained a "prisoner" until 1988 even though the Control Yuan (the government's investigative branch) had exonerated him from involvement in any plot against Chiang or the government.[91] Early in the 1960s, Chiang also cracked down on George Yeh (Yeh Kung-ch'ao) because of the way in which he handled the issue of Outer Mongolia's representation in the United Nations. Although Yeh had held portfolios as foreign minister and ambassador to the United States, his experience was less valuable to Chiang than the need to discipline an unreliable diplomat perceived to be too close to the Americans.

Chiang Kai-shek, feeling no compunctions about eliminating rivals at home, also attempted to eradicate opponents in the United States. In some instances he used the American China lobby to try to influence policymaking or by innuendo sought to tarnish the reputations of individuals who seemed too sympathetic to the Communist Chinese. Between 1950 and 1954 Taipei took a more direct hand by circulating three fraudulent documents implicating Americans such as Owen Lattimore, John Service, and even Eleanor Roosevelt in plots to turn the U.S. against Chiang. When asked for more specific information to help in the Justice Department's prosecution of Lattimore, however, Taipei supplied no evidence. The U.S. government finally had to drop its case in 1955.[92] Whether or not KMT officials actually believed that the U.S. government was riddled with "pinkos," they recognized this as an effective way to sow dissension and generate compassion. Later they would argue that since Joseph McCarthy had not succeeded in finding any communists in the halls of the State Department, such people must still be there, devising anti-Kuomintang policies.

Nationalist suspicions about American interest in the Taiwan independence movement further disturbed relations.[93] At various times, Taiwanese advocates sought American support and protection, urging U.S. military intervention or aid in arranging a United Nations trusteeship over the island. The controversial Conlon Associates Report, written for the Senate Foreign Relations Committee in 1959, and better known for its advocacy of relations with the PRC, also recommended that Washington re-recognize Nationalist China as the Republic of Taiwan.[94] In 1963, when Vice President Ch'en Ch'eng visited Washington, militants staged an embarrassing pro-independence demonstration.[95] The Nationalists, therefore, felt they did have reason to be troubled by the activities of Taiwan dissidents fearing any challenge to Kuomintang control of the Taiwanese masses.

Mainlanders had arrogated political power to themselves and ruthlessly excluded Taiwanese from all control over "national" policy to perpetuate the illusion of a government only temporarily lodged in a single province. They might jealously guard authority out of personal greed but were not wrong in arguing that any large-scale Taiwanese role in ruling would undermine the fantasy of a return to the mainland. Conveniently, they also ignored the injustice of compelling Taiwanese to serve in an army dedicated to recovering a mainland they had no interest in (except perhaps as a way to get rid of their persecutors) and of forcing them to pay heavy taxes to support the huge military budget.

Nevertheless, the independence movement developed primarily outside Taiwan, within exile communities in Japan, Hong Kong, and the United States. Beginning in 1956 it took on a formal presence, establishing the Provisional Government of the Republic of Formosa based in Japan, with Dr. Thomas Liao (Liao Wen-yi) as president. Nationalist officials insisted and perhaps believed that Liao was an American agent, despite the fact that American military police had arrested him for illegal entry into occupied Japan and briefly imprisoned him in 1950. Whatever their suspicions, they managed, possibly by threatening his family, to reach an accommodation and engineer Liao's return to Taiwan in 1965.[96]

The mainlanders' conviction that American officials harbored surreptitious sympathies for the Taiwanese was particularly ironic given Taiwanese exasperation at the unquestioning U.S. dedication to the Kuomintang.[97] Indeed, the political section at the U.S. Embassy in the mid-1960s operated under explicit instructions not to have any contact with individuals identified with independence activities.[98] The paradox was heightened by the fact that Beijing shared Taipei's certitude, seeing the independence movement as a device for ensuring the permanent occupation of the island by American soldiers.[99]

To prevent overseas activists from creating an underground network in Taiwan, the martial law regime on the island kept tight control over political expression, banning opposition parties, advocacy of independence, and criticism of officials and their policies. Hundreds of people went to jail for political crimes.[100] Americans sought to intervene in a few selected cases, pointing out that human rights abuses could lead the United States to resolve its China problem by dismissing Taiwan as a repressive police state no better than the communist dictatorship on the mainland.[101] Others feared that the hostility of the Taiwanese could be directed toward the United States if it did not take a strong position condemning government oppression. As Robert Scalapino, influential political scientist and Asian specialist, pointed out to the readership of the New York Times in 1966: "The time to prevent a Cuba in the Pacific is now."[102]

American interest in dissidents on Taiwan generally focused on the better-known intellectuals who followed careers in journalism or academia. Lei

Chen had been editor of a biweekly called *Free China* from 1949 to 1960. Developed originally under the guiding hand of the philosopher/diplomat Hu Shih, the journal represented liberal, American-influenced intellectuals from the mainland. It had benefited from financial underwriting by the Asia Foundation, whose secret CIA supporters enjoyed sponsoring mildly subversive ideas in Taiwan's rigid political environment. The United States Information Service (USIS) assisted with subscription promotion. *Free China*'s critical view of the Nationalist authorities became evident early, and its notoriety was assured in August 1957 when it published an editorial asserting that the likelihood of the Kuomintang returning to the mainland was highly improbable.

In 1960, still trying to resist KMT repression and make the best of living on Taiwan, Lei Chen participated in efforts, with a group of Taiwanese politicians, to establish the China Democratic Party. Hu Shih, who had initially supported the venture, retreated from political confrontation at the last moment.[103] Lei Chen and his confederates were promptly arrested on charges of sedition. Lei received a sentence of 10 years in prison.[104] The American government remained awkwardly silent, and calls from American intellectuals for Washington to take a stand and for Taipei to release Lei had no impact.

Lei Chen's experience epitomized the relations between Americans and the Nationalist Chinese during the years in which their alliance enjoyed maximum saliency. The United States exerted influence over military, political, and economic affairs, providing financing, encouraging reform, and occasionally supporting activities that challenged the rigid control of the Kuomintang regime. Washington, however, valued the strategic potential of Taiwan too highly to risk undermining mutual confidence by insisting upon the kind of liberalization that America's principles and traditions in theory demanded. At a time when most U.S. officials believed that anticommunism comprised the key to a successful American foreign policy, there existed a willingness to support conservative governments—however benighted or repressive—everywhere in the world. So Chiang Kai-shek and his Nationalist Chinese confederates found it possible to manipulate the U.S., adopting modernization policies that fortified their power, but fending off change that might threaten their control.

• • •

Between 1950 and 1965 relations between Taiwan and the United States reached their point of maximum cooperation and benefit. This proved apparent in the critical areas of economic recovery and military defense. Although other factors played a part, economic success on the island came largely as a result of massive injections of American monies and technical advice coupled with the policies devised by an astute group of Chinese technocrats, who effectively combined modern concepts with traditional norms. Building on land reform, which freed assets and labor, the government vigorously pursued industrialization and import substitution. Thus Taiwan passed from rehabilitation to reform and development more rapidly than could have been expected.

All the economic progress would not have saved the Nationalists had it not been for America's commitment to providing a defense umbrella and to creating an effective fighting force. Once the Korean War confirmed the image of an aggressive tyranny on the mainland of China, Washington felt compelled to protect "Free China" as a bastion of democracy and as a base for harassing the Communists and gathering intelligence on their policies and actions. But, whereas Chiang remained committed to creating a military establishment suitable to recovering the mainland, the United States favored a far more modest force designed for self-defense and guerrilla operations. Chiang as usual persevered and, for the most part, triumphed. Americans watched helplessly while aid was wasted and economic growth slowed by excessive military expenditures.

It was perhaps in the political arena that the difference between Washington's and Taipei's understandings of the relationship became most apparent. The Nationalists had no compunctions about interfering in American domestic politics and attempting to penetrate the U.S. government to gather intelligence and to influence decision making. The U.S. had far less success in, and more reservations about, influencing Taiwan's internal politics. Indeed, those in the Nationalist regime who most clearly advocated pro-American policies were purged. Others who attempted to expand the rights of the Taiwanese and to promote independence also suffered. Chiang Kai-shek kept a tight rein on political developments in Taiwan and insisted that the United States be a supporter, a banker, and a shield, but keep its advice and opinions to itself.

chapter 5

SOCIETY AND CULTURE, 1950–1965

The complex philosophical struggle between retention of tradition and commitment to modernization, or westernization, that had absorbed Chinese intellectuals since the late nineteenth century engulfed Taiwan after 1950. It became even more difficult to pinpoint how the essence of being Chinese could remain unsullied if Western knowledge and American assistance were to become still more crucial to the military survival and economic strengthening of the state. No longer sheltered by the vast population and territory of the mainland, the Chinese on the small island of Taiwan found themselves exposed regularly to values and behavior that would in the 1980s be condemned by the Communists in Beijing as "spiritual pollution." Thus the cultural interaction in the years of close collaboration from 1950 to 1965 produced benefits in areas such as education and health care, creative adjustment in fields such as art and literature, but also tension and violence where the two societies proved less compatible and least flexible.

Intellectuals persisted in trying to find ways to integrate Confucianism with science and democracy. In a 1958 manifesto published by the *Democratic Review* (Taiwan) as "Chinese Culture and the World," scholars urged the creation of a fresh neo-Confucian synthesis to revitalize China, imparting intellectual direction to rapid change. Such thoughts were echoed by the Nationalist ambassador in the United States, George Yeh, who told a meeting of the Sino-American Cultural Committee on 8 December 1958 that Chinese tradition had contributions to make to modern life in Taiwan. But the Confucius-Mencius Study Society established by the government in April 1960 to fight communism through renewed emphasis on Chinese ethical principles evoked little reaction and no enthusiasm from scholars or the public.[1]

79

The imagination of students and intellectuals responded more readily to the controversial ideas of Hu Shih, who in a November 1961 speech attacked Chinese culture as the main barrier to Chinese progress. Hu had brought home from his years at Columbia University in the 1910s the conviction that the search for truth through scientific thought was at the heart of Western achievement and a higher form of spirituality than the vaunted Eastern variety. Having argued those issues during the heady years of the May 4th era, 1917–21, when young intellectuals attempted to transform China by replacing Confucian ideas and methods with Western learning, Hu once again insisted that until the Chinese people stopped seeing science and technology as something alien forced upon them by the materialistic West, China would not develop and prosper. Publication of his lecture in the pages of the *Literary Star* (Taiwan) evoked blistering attacks from conservative intellectuals, joining a debate that would rage across the island and reach even to Hong Kong for the next two years.[2]

The dispute over the role that Western knowledge should play became a highly personal dilemma for students who elected to pursue advanced education in American universities. Aware of the benefits but also of the hostility that they would confront, most decided not to return to Taiwan. For many, the question of whether to go back was resolved by the lack of employment opportunities at home given the skills they had acquired. Intellectuals in Taiwan were generally demoralized in the decade of the 1950s, their resources meager, standards low, politics circumscribed, and scholarship isolated from developments elsewhere in the world.[3] To others the higher standard of living in the U.S. or the participation in democratic institutions determined their decision to remain in America. Less than half those who earned doctorates in American universities had returned to Taiwan by the early 1960s. Those who chose to remain in the United States acted sometimes as consultants to Taiwan on economic development projects. More routinely, they gave the American public an idea of what it meant to be Chinese, indirectly furthering Kuomintang efforts to portray Taiwan as the real China.[4]

Nevertheless, by 1965 American funding had facilitated the training in the United States of significant numbers of Taiwan's political and technological elite. These people would in the next decade become the core of a new leadership that would continue the transformation of Taiwan from a backward to a modern economy. They would also give impetus to development of a genuine rather than fictional democracy. Although at times they faced ostracism for their Western ways, as well as the suspicion that they no longer were loyal to the Kuomintang, they proved critical to the strength and prosperity of their island home.

Americans consciously joined in the cultural controversy through the creation of programs designed to explain the United States to the Chinese and China to Americans. The China Institute in America, for instance, dated back to the early years of the ROC, having been established in 1926 with Boxer indemnity funds extracted from the Chinese government as recompense for the destructive antiforeign violence of the Boxer Rebellion in 1900. Identified closely with Chiang Kai-shek's regime, especially in the 1950s, the Institute labored in the United States to make China's heritage accessible to Americans by promoting educational and artistic enterprises.[5] Similarly, most other cultural and educational ventures were devoted to assisting the Nationalists or serving some abstract Chinese community after U.S. access to the mainland largely ceased in 1950.

Funding of university study of each society by the other received support from various organizations. The Ford Foundation contributed as much as $30 million between 1955 and 1970 for projects on Chinese affairs at Harvard, Columbia, Berkeley, Michigan, and the University of Washington. The primary focus in these efforts tended to be on an examination of Chinese communism, with the exception of scholars at the University of Washington, who dedicated their efforts to Kuomintang China.

Foundations also devoted resources to the strengthening of research institutes and scholarly exchange. The Harvard-Yenching Foundation spurred creation of a China Council for East Asian Studies in 1957 to channel $30,000 into scholarly activities annually. With the help of John King Fairbank of Harvard University, the Institute of Modern History of Academia Sinica secured Ford Foundation monies in the early 1960s for scholarly travel programs and publication in the fields of Sino-American, Sino-Russian, and Sino-Japanese relations, as well as studies of modernization in education, law, and the economy. American scholars observed that Ford support assisted institute head Kuo Ting-yee to preserve the political autonomy of his research scholars.[6] Ford provided funding over a period of 10 years (1962–71) to the Institute of History and Philology, and Rockefeller helped the Institute build facilities and add to its historical collection.[7] At the same time, Columbia University's East Asian Institute assisted with the development of an oral history program that quickly began to capture the reminiscences of crucial Chinese political and military figures for use by Chinese and American scholars.

Ford and the Carnegie Endowment also took a leading role in financing the extraordinarily influential inter-university program for language study based at National Taiwan University. Over the next 30 years, it would train close to 800 Americans in Chinese language skills, profoundly affecting the development of research on and teaching about China in the United States. Promoted initially by Harold Shadick of Cornell University, the program was expanded by nine U.S. schools to create what became in 1963 the Stanford Center administered by Lyman P. VanSlyke.[8]

Recognizing the importance of science education for the modernization effort, Chinese and Americans collaborated in a series of educational and research activities. In 1959 they established the National Council on

Science Development with a budget heavily endowed by the U.S. Agency for International Development. In 1964 Tsinghua University, among the most prominent institutions of higher learning in Taiwan, broadened its nuclear physics program, which had been launched in 1955 using Boxer Rebellion compensation funds, into a cooperative research effort with the Argonne National Laboratory of the U.S. Atomic Energy Commission. Official collaboration between the U.S. National Academy of Sciences and the Academia Sinica also materialized in 1964 with the visit of a National Academy delegation headed by Dr. Joseph Platt. The two organizations created a Joint Committee on Science Cooperation to meet annually and decide priorities for cooperative ventures.

Organizations with political rather than scholarly purposes also participated in cross-cultural activities. The popularity of American studies in Taiwan helped boost the fortunes of the U.S. government's Fulbright scholarship fund. The Republic of China had been the first signatory to the Educational Exchange Program in 1947, but, because of the Chinese civil war, contacts languished until 1957 when the new U.S. Educational Foundation set up shop in Taiwan. Thereafter Fulbright awards helped disseminate American ideals and ideas through funding of teacher exchanges. A more clearly political agenda underlay establishment of the Asia Foundation in 1956. Conceived in response to cold war confrontation between the United States and the Eastern bloc, the Foundation enjoyed secret funding from the Central Intelligence Agency. Openly, it carried on programs of scholarly exchange, providing support for research at the Academia Sinica; for instructional programs in science, sociology, and agriculture; and for the distribution of thousands of volumes to several academic institutions. The Foundation also assisted the Taiwan government in carrying out tax reform between 1956 and 1973. At the same time, there were also covert efforts to recruit agents, provide cover for underground operations, disseminate anticommunist propaganda, and fund the research of sympathetic academics.[9]

The United States Information Service similarly sought to explain American society to people on the island in order to win adherents to the "free world." Its most successful years, between 1959 and 1969, saw readers besiege USIS libraries and flock to American films shown around the island by mobile units. Probably the most heavily exploited services were the radio broadcasts, magazines, and other materials that focused on English-language training.[10] Taiwan also heard more than 19 hours a day of Chinese- and English-language programs on American government broadcasting stations.

Projects providing books to China had begun in 1868 and were revived at the end of the Second World War with a nationwide appeal mounted by the American Library Association. Formal book exchanges, however, awaited relocation of the National Central Library (NCL) to Taipei and its 1954 appeal for donations. The Library of Congress quickly responded by depositing a full set of U.S. government documents. Between 1955 and 1990

American organizations supplied more than half a million volumes to the NCL, some 71 percent of all foreign donations it received, and Taiwan participated in some 48 book exhibitions in the United States, giving the items shown to host institutions to promote awareness of things Chinese.[11]

The school system on the island evidenced considerable U.S. influence as well. Americans tried hard to render education more practically oriented in order to create a citizenry with the skills crucial for participation in the modernization effort. Thus AID emphasized training in science, engineering, and medicine as well as helping to establish vocational schools. The Joint Commission on Rural Reconstruction focused on agricultural education, bringing in specialists such as the chief of the Mutual Security Administration's Agricultural Division, who reorganized the agricultural college of National Taiwan University during his brief consultative visit. Between 1958 and 1964 Michigan State University provided technical assistance for teacher training through agreements signed with the central and provincial ministries of education and AID.

Washington at the same time pressed Taipei to open educational institutions to overseas Chinese. In the competition with Communist China for the loyalty of these scattered groups, Taiwan would benefit by educating a new generation and preventing large-scale returns of impressionable youths to the mainland. Moreover, the U.S. Defense Department hoped to persuade the overseas Chinese to make contributions of money and manpower to the Nationalist cause.

Americans also saw advantages in providing succor to another type of overseas Chinese. These were intellectuals who, having fled the Communist regime, found themselves in inhospitable refugee camps in Hong Kong with no place to settle. Under the leadership of China lobby activists Congressman Walter Judd, B. A. Garside, and Marvin Liebman, and with funding from the Luce and Ford Foundations, Aid to Refugee Chinese Intellectuals (ARCI) began, in early 1952, planning for the removal to Taiwan of the most skilled and useful of these people.[12] To ARCI's surprise the Nationalists viewed the plan with significant reservations. Fearing that some displaced intellectuals might be communists plotting to undermine Taiwan from within, government leaders also opposed entry of those whose loyalty was sullied by support of the idea of a third force that could supplant both the Kuomintang and the Communists in controlling China. Furthermore, intellectuals safely ensconced on the island saw an influx of highly educated refugees as a threat to employment opportunities and status.[13] During the first year of operations, Taipei mandated strict screening procedures and refused to accept ARCI offers to hire additional investigators to speed processing.[14] If the Nationalists were skeptical and suspicious, Washington responded far more positively. Under the Refugee Relief Act, 600 families came to the U.S. to find new homes. In March 1953, the president authorized $250,000 to be placed at the disposal of ARCI to facilitate resettlement.[15] Nationalist hesitance, although it thwarted much of the propaganda effect of the original proposal, did not prevent the program from proving largely successful by the mid-1950s.

Mutual understanding between the U.S. and Nationalist China grew from the sharing of high art and popular culture. During World War II, Nationalist authorities, seeking to protect the country's art treasures, crated much of the collection from the Palace Museum and sent it south to escape Japanese bombing and looters. In 1948 those same boxes remained hidden in Sichuan, where Horace Jayne of the Metropolitan Museum of Art in New York City discovered them. Jayne found Nationalist officials interested in his proposal for an exhibition in the United States, given the potential propaganda windfall, and he immediately initiated an effort through the U.S. State Department to bring out boxes of imperial treasures. But the civil war rapidly undercut Nationalist control of the mainland, and 3,000 crates traveled instead to Taiwan, fleeing this time from Communist forces. Not until 1957 did the government display any of the items and then only because the Asia Foundation financed the construction of a small exhibition hall. Soon afterward, discussion began about creating a permanent home for the collection in order to free it from the caves and crates. Once again funding from the Central Intelligence Agency gave a critical boost to the project, making it possible for the building to open in 1965.[16]

American sympathizers with Chiang Kai-shek's cause had not forgotten the benefits that would follow from an American exhibition. Henry Luce and the Chinese Ambassador to the United Nations engineered a tour of the United States, which took Washington, D.C., by storm in 1961. As historian Warren I. Cohen has observed, "The study of Chinese painting became the center of the burgeoning field of East Asian art history. Private collectors and museum curators . . . doubtful if any work of value could be found on the market, rushed in." But there were political advantages too. Ambassador Wang Shih-chieh made Nationalist expectations clear in his preface to the exhibit catalogue: "In these troubled times of ours a fuller understanding of Chinese art and culture by the American people, on whose shoulders largely rests the future of the free world, assumes a new significance. This exhibition may also serve as a reminder that the free Chinese are fighting to save their cultural heritage as much as to recover lost territories."[17] In 1964 Taipei again sent treasures from the Palace Museum to the United States, joining on this occasion the 300th anniversary celebration of New York City's founding held at the World's Fair.

The film industry also contributed to perceptions entertained on each side of the Pacific by audiences willing to accept stereotypes. In the early 1960s Chinese villains dominated the underside of American movies, reflecting fears of Beijing in higher policy circles. Pro-Chiang organizations in the United States saw the medium as a perfect vehicle for building enthusiasm for the Nationalist regime. Propaganda films like "The Face of China," emphasizing the importance of the U.S. alliance with the Republic of China as a key to the defense of the entire free world, were distributed free to TV stations. "Fortress Formosa" ran at New York's Radio City Music Hall wedged between the feature film and the chorus line of sprightly Rockettes. Even NBC television's "Today Show" used footage of Nationalist troops on parade provided by a public relations firm hired by Taipei.[18]

Promoters of the KMT cause used mass circulation magazines to reach the same audience. The conservative Reader's Digest published articles such as Admiral Arthur Radford's "A Warning to the U.N." in October 1961 and Congressman Walter Judd's piece "Keep Red China Out!" in November 1964, encouraged and assisted by the Committee of One Million and Nationalist government officials. Marvin Liebman, for instance, provided Taipei's U.N. representative, Dr. Tsiang Ting-fu, with a preview copy of Radford's essay and assured him that the Committee would purchase 50,000 reprints for free distribution.[19]

Concern about the direction of American foreign policy more generally led William Lederer to follow up his triumphant first book, The Ugly American, with a further expose of public ignorance and official deception in 1961. A controversial and influential study, especially on college campuses, A Nation of Sheep asked readers, among other things, to think about "What We Aren't Told About Formosa." Charles M. Cooke, onetime commander of the Western Pacific Fleet and head of an informal military advisory group to Chiang, warned Nationalist Ambassador George Yeh that the book attacked Chiang and would be a disservice to the Kuomintang cause. Lederer did, in fact, accuse Chiang of brutality, deceit, and dishonesty, but his main target remained the U.S. government and people who Chiang "outmaneuvered" and "outsmarted."[20]

In scholarly circles efforts to explain history became mired in the partisan politics of the era. Ross Y. Koen was to have published a volume entitled The China Lobby in American Politics with Macmillan Publishing in 1960. The book was in production, with preview copies circulating, when word reached China lobby activists who immediately launched a countervailing effort called The Red China Lobby. Although the latter volume came out from Fleet Press in 1963, Macmillan refused to release Koen's book. It remained unclear whether Macmillan's retreat resulted from Nationalist Chinese, China lobby, or U.S. government pressures. Seemingly the crucial factor proved to be Koen's charge that the Nationalists had been smuggling narcotics into the U.S., an allegation to which both the U.S. commissioner of narcotics, Harry J. Anslinger, and Chinese Nationalist officials took strong exception. The book eventually emerged from its political travails in 1974, released by Harper and Row virtually unchanged.[21]

The United States also sent an assortment of arts and sports groups to Taiwan to allow the people on the island to experience American culture and welcomed delegations who could be immersed in American ideals. In 1957, for example, the Moral Rearmament Movement invited 100 boys and girls to its annual convention in Michigan. Some concern, however, was voiced in Taiwan about the pacifist and neutralist leanings of the organization, approaches seen by a government "at war" as not especially useful.

The wide-ranging involvement of Americans through aid programs and cultural exchanges inevitably transformed Chinese and Taiwanese society on the island. Modern institutions, greater access to education, privatization of the economy, all increased social mobility. New transportation links allowed people to move around freely. Land reform encouraged urbanization as it shifted the former landowning elite and excess rural laborers into the cities in search of new opportunities.

Though forced to operate quietly lest they become caught in political and cultural disputes, American aid officials also supported population control measures. Such efforts confronted the formidable barrier of tradition, which, operating just as powerfully in Taiwan as on the mainland, dictated not just large families but, more important, male children. Indeed, civil war politics added a fresh incentive. When in 1950 the JCRR issued a pamphlet advocating birth control, it was denounced as subversive of Free China's military strength.[22] The central government stubbornly ignored population pressures on the island, assuming that the problem would be alleviated upon recovery of the mainland and arguing that rising agricultural production in Taiwan would solve all problems in the interim. But the very high annual birth rate, approaching 3.7 percent, added to the influx of mainlanders who had precipitously enlarged the population in 1949–50, threatened seriously to reduce the economic benefits of reconstruction and expansion.

Unable to secure Chiang Kai-shek's cooperation until 1967, Americans and Chinese struggled unofficially through the 1950s and 1960s to change popular attitudes. The JCRR, along with Taiwan provincial agencies and private groups such as the Chinese Medical Association and the University of Michigan, established the China Family Planning Association in 1954 and focused their efforts primarily on education.[23] In 1962, with funding from the Population Council in New York, provincial health authorities established the Taiwan Population Studies Center to mount programs and evaluate results. Two years later, JCRR persuaded the Council for International Economic Cooperation and Development to appropriate $1,500,000 in counterpart funds (local currency accumulations generated by sales of U.S. aid commodities) to inaugurate a new five-year effort to disseminate birth control devices.[24] By mid-1965 the Lippes loop, a simple plastic intrauterine device, which cost two and a half cents to manufacture locally, had been implanted in 85,000 women. Population control activities proved so successful that AID coordinators from several countries traveled to Taiwan to learn how to implement family planning in the absence of central government authorization.[25] Between 1956 and 1966 the rate of population growth declined from 3.7 to 2.7 percent because of such programs and also, doubt-less, because of growing prosperity and urbanization.[26]

The JCRR also became active in the field of health care, utilizing monies donated by U.S. AID, the Rockefeller Foundation, and international organi-zations. An earlier Rockefeller effort to work with the Ministry of Health through a Taiwan Malaria Research Institute created in 1946 collapsed with the fall of the mainland. Between 1953 and 1965, however, the JCRR mounted a DDT spraying project to deal with the mosquito carrying malaria and succeeded in eradicating the disease on the island. JCRR technicians also carried out a bubonic plague control effort on Quemoy beginning in 1952.[27]

The American Bureau for Medical Aid to China, established in New York in 1937 to provide aid for Chinese forces fighting Japanese invaders, also relocated with the Nationalists after the Communist takeover. "The agency," according to its official historian John R. Watt, "became an active partisan in the Chinese civil war, strongly advocating American support of the Free China Nationalist government."[28] This could be attributed to the efforts of Dr. B. A. Garside, a onetime missionary educator whose dedication to Chiang's cause reflected the enthusiasms of board members Walter Judd and Alfred Kohlberg. Initially, Chiang Kai-shek invited ABMAC to operate an officially subsidized health program, but the board preferred to function on a more modest level. It became active in training medical personnel by provid-ing books, equipment, and drugs for programs at the National Taiwan University, the National Defence Medical Center, and the Provincial Junior College of Nursing. A school health program, involving physical examina-tion and treatment, sanitation, and teacher training, proved extremely suc-cessful. ABMAC activities also embraced relief work for the refugees from the Dachen islands following their evacuation in 1954. In 1962, in coopera-tion with the Chinese government, ABMAC provided half the funding for construction of the Alfred Kohlberg Memorial Research Laboratory, which undertook path-breaking work in the fields of protein metabolism, kidney failure, and hepatitis.[29]

Further assistance to health care efforts in Taiwan came from the U.S. National Federation of Business and Professional Women's Clubs. It had been a sponsor of the military nursing school on the mainland and now turned its efforts to reconstruction, helping to convert bamboo structures into housing for students. From there, it engaged in a series of money-raising efforts to provide the school with funding for equipment, training, and addi-tional building projects.[30]

American missionaries did not make a serious effort at conversion on the island of Taiwan until welcomed there by the Nationalist authorities in the 1950s. Absorbed in the primary battle to win over Chinese on the mainland, which they had begun in 1830, U.S. missionaries deemed Taiwan's smaller numbers a side show. The local population mirrored such disinterest, most often ignoring the foreign churches.[31] But, with the collapse of the Kuomintang on the mainland and the creation of refugee communities, the balance began slowly to shift. Early arrivals from the Baptist and Pentecostal denominations were tentative and poorly endowed, but, after the United States government placed the Seventh Fleet in the Taiwan Straits in 1950, a dramatic change began. Security justified investment. Missionaries, at the same moment, suddenly found themselves allies of the Nationalist regime, which looked upon their anticommunism as a guarantee of cooperation, their technical expertise as an excuse for their presence, and their access to American public, media, and official attention as an exploitable asset.[32] During the 1950s, most Protestant denominations made important gains among the disoriented and distressed population, although the Methodists had a clear advantage given the crusading zeal of their star devotee, Madame Chiang Kai-shek.[33]

The excitement of this striking upsurge dissipated within a decade, suggesting that much of the initial enthusiasm stemmed from the secular assistance that the churches, in cooperation with the United States government, had offered. Mission stations had acted as distribution centers for relief supplies and sources of education and advice for people eager to understand the West and modernization. When it became apparent that other agencies, such as U.S. AID, would provide support without requiring religious adherence, the growth of congregations dropped precipitously. The churches, nevertheless, continued to pursue their calling on the island through evangelism and through social service.

Their promotion of higher education through the establishment of Taiwan's Christian colleges proved to be among their most significant contributions. By 1 January 1950, all of the mainland Christian campuses had fallen under Chinese Communist control, and with the outbreak of the Korean War efforts by the United Board for Christian Colleges in China to sustain contacts with the schools rapidly collapsed. Attention shifted to the new Nationalist redoubt in response to a proposal in the fall of 1951 by church groups and refugee alumni from the 13 lost institutions to begin again in Free China. Tunghai University, launched with a February 1952 United Board appropriation of $50,000, received official sanction from the premier, secretary to the president Wang Shih-chieh, and the minister of education. Princeton-in-Asia provided financial support, earlier earmarked for Yenching University in Beijing, for professorial appointments, scholarships, and books. Similarly, faculty members provided by the Oberlin-Shansi Memorial Association, Syracuse University, and other American schools went to Tunghai in 1954. The United Board drew further on funds from the Luce, Rockefeller, and Harvard-Yenching Foundations to support library facilities at Tung Wu College and a student center operated by the Tainan Theological Seminary.[34]

Largely at the behest of Archbishop Paul Yupin, long a supporter of Chiang and the Kuomintang who had sought refuge in Taiwan under their auspices, the Catholic Church launched Fu Jen University in 1959. A slightly earlier venture, Providence English College, undertaken by the Sisters of Providence from Indiana in 1956, focused on the needs of women. Yupin's vision was broader. He solicited "seed money" from Francis Cardinal Spellman in Boston, which he then used to convince Pope John XXIII that loss of Fu Jen's Beijing campus left a vacuum in the Church's commitment to higher education. The new school proved an enormous drain on Church coffers and available faculty, leading to the unusual step of recruiting educators from a variety of orders across the U.S. and Europe.

The Catholic Church made a more innovative contribution to scholarship and public education through the support of the Kuang Chi Press and Television Service and the Tien Educational Center in Taipei. The Kuang Chi concept, borrowed from a successful program at Loyola Marymount College in California, trained writers and artists for the media and produced radio and television programs and motion pictures. The Jesuit order solicited equipment from the major American television networks and from the U.S. armed forces. Kuang Chi studios moved to larger quarters when the Tien Center was opened in the early 1960s. Designed to stretch resources and personnel, the Center was located between National Taiwan and National Taiwan Normal Universities so that students from both institutions would have access to a good library of English-language materials as well as English language instruction.[35]

Seminaries like Tainan and bible schools, such as those run by the American Pentecostal Assemblies of God, encountered greater problems with the Nationalist government than did the higher status and less clearly religious colleges. In the case of Tainan, for instance, despite close to a century of continuous landholding, the legitimacy of the Presbyterian synod's ownership was challenged during the 1960s.[36] Students were pressed to inform on the political views of their teachers, who carried on classes in local dialect rather than in Mandarin, and graduates found their degrees worth conspicuously less. Suspicion on the part of the government that missionaries were too sympathetic to ideas of Taiwan independence and too worried about human rights more generally led to frictions when institutions were less obviously concerned with the secular educational uplift of the island's population.

Missionaries and church groups exerted influence not simply on their parishioners or society in Taiwan but also on the American vision of Taiwan as Free China. Congregations across the United States solicited donations to help the "exiled" Chinese and to build Christian enterprises among people seen to be in particular need of spiritual guidance. Religious leaders, as in earlier periods, brought their concerns to Washington. They supported assistance to the Nationalist government, continuing to celebrate their connections to the Generalissimo and Madame Chiang. At the same time, increasingly, they worried about political repression in Taiwan and urged the leadership there to foster a more moderate environment. A few missionaries took such concerns to their logical conclusion and became advocates of independence.[37]

Efforts by those committed to preservation of a Nationalist China, whether they were missionaries, journalists, businessmen, publicists, or the Nationalists themselves, to make a salient case with the American people as to the significance of the island redoubt did not prove especially successful. Public opinion studies made it clear that a need for popular education remained. At the end of the period, in 1964, a poll by the Survey Research Center discovered that fewer than 4 in 10 Americans knew of the existence of the Nationalist regime, the name of its leader, or its location.[38]

• • •

Increasingly between 1950 and 1965, the people on the island of Taiwan found themselves besieged by the expectations of a modern world often alien to Chinese culture and hostile to their own particular needs and interests. Frictions inevitably accompanied the enormous American intrusion into Taiwan's daily life. Officials had ample grounds to resent American efforts to dominate strategic, political, and economic policy, while there also developed deeply rooted popular bitterness about cultural imperialism. Americans, who enjoyed their status in the island's society and saw their efforts as a positive force for change and as a necessary bulwark to protect the island, found it difficult to imagine that their presence could be resented. Incidents such as the 1950 search by the Peace Preservation police of island homes for copies of USIS materials and warnings to Taiwanese against subscribing to American publications startled a basically self-satisfied expatriate community.[39]

By the autumn of 1956 some American embassy staff members had, nevertheless, become uncomfortable about the "large centralized United States Government organization" that operated in Taiwan "in the colonial tradition." American civilian and military personnel lived not with the Chinese and Taiwanese but in compounds beyond the city's smog and noise and crowds. There they enjoyed the benefits of low-cost goods from military stores and had the disposable income to keep their lawns green and a staff of servants busy. The embassy recommended that advisers be better integrated into Chinese agencies and enterprises and that the entire International Cooperation Administration (ICA) mission be scaled down as quickly as possible.[40] The warning, however, came too late to prevent the dramatic backlash American behavior had engendered. On 24 May 1957 a mob of some 25,000 ransacked the U.S. embassy and the headquarters of USIS as well as threatening the U.S. Military Advisory Group offices. Successive waves of rioters tossed furniture, pictures, and government documents from the embassy windows and shredded the American flag. Although no

Severe damage was done to the U.S. Embassy and the USIS center in Taipei, 24 May 1957. *Courtesy of the National Archives*

Americans were seriously injured, several suffered cuts and bruises from rocks and debris.

The chaos clearly represented immediate anger and long-standing discontent. The proximate cause was the acquittal of Robert G. Reynolds in a U.S. military court of the murder of Liu Tze-jan who, the American insisted, had spied on his wife in the bath. The riot, however, was more than just a response to a perceived injustice. The prosecution had appeared perfunctory, and racism seemed to have influenced the proceedings. When the court announced the verdict, Reynolds received an ovation from the American audience. Analysts concluded that widespread antipathy toward Americans existed because of the living standards flaunted by an American community that numbered 11,000 and because of the immunity from Chinese laws, reminiscent of extraterritoriality, that Americans connected with the U.S. military enjoyed.[41] Astonished by the rampage, President Eisenhower remarked to Secretary of State Dulles that the administration would have to take "a very serious look at these Asiatic countries, and decide whether we can stay there. It does not seem wise, if they hate us so much."[42]

In fact, the destruction went on for some seven hours in a police state that routinely kept a close watch and tight control over political activity. In this instance official reaction proved largely ineffectual and belated in suppressing the violence against the government's closest ally. Normally sympathetic to Nationalist concerns, Walter McConaughy, director of the Office of Chinese Affairs, concluded that "the riots showed evidences of prior planning. . . . [T]he destruction was deliberate. . . . [L]aw enforcement authorities were either grossly negligent . . . or acted in collusion with the rioters."[43] CIA Director Allen Dulles also believed that the uprising was not spontaneous, although he told the National Security Council that the extent of the convulsion had probably exceeded official expectations. Despite the assertions of other American and Chinese observers, Dulles discounted speculation that Chiang Ching-kuo had instigated it.[44]

Nevertheless, there seemed to be good reasons to suspect officials at the highest level of complicity. The Nationalist government, faced with a dominating superpower for an ally, had few channels for expressing effective dissent. It could assert contradictory views through obstruction and noncompliance, which often characterized Taipei's behavior. It could also demonstrate displeasure through the willfulness of its citizenry. In May 1957 Kuomintang leaders were unhappy about the Warsaw talks and John Foster Dulles's efforts to get Beijing to renounce the use of force in the Taiwan Straits so that U.S.-China relations could be improved. They felt disappointed by the unwillingness of the U.S. government to commit its power to the defense of the offshore islands or to endorse their efforts to return to the mainland. Chiang Kai-shek sought to impress upon American military authorities his determination to retain full, autonomous control of his armed forces. The Nationalists could easily have rationalized the incident, reasoning that they had little to lose and much to gain from a chastened United States.

Washington-Taipei relations proved not to have been seriously disturbed by the violence. Apologies followed immediately, a few officials were cashiered, the Taiwan government repaired the damaged facilities, and the U.S. remained Taiwan's most generous and dominant benefactor. The events of May 1957 did, however, emphasize the limits of American power and culture in penetrating and reshaping a society—even one thoroughly dependent upon the United States. The Taipei government created the incident to make a statement about who would control Taiwan's affairs—political, military, and economic. That it had a citizenry willing to riot against

American institutions testified to the sometimes destabilizing social and cultural change. Growing Americanization stimulated discontent as it challenged values and undermined traditions. On the other hand, the burgeoning cultural ties between the people in Taiwan and American society enabled the relationship to survive the 1957 crisis and gave promise that it would endure.[45]

chapter 6

SHIFTING PRIORITIES IN ASIA, 1965–1972

Change in the United States' role in Taiwan heralded by the curtailment of economic aid to the Nationalist government in 1965 proved far more profound than Washington or Taipei had anticipated. Indeed, it appeared little had been altered given the continuation of military assistance, extensive economic ties, and political continuity in both capitals. But shifts in relations between China and the Soviet Union and between China and the United States would, by 1972, undermine the close collaboration with Washington that had sustained Taiwan for two decades.

As the period began, no clear signs of the approaching metamorphosis were evident to policymakers. The United States and the Soviet Union had not yet embarked upon détente, which haltingly materialized after 1967, nor had Sino-Soviet frictions reached crisis proportions. In Vietnam during the spring of 1965, armed with congressional consent under the 1964 Tonkin Gulf Resolution, Lyndon Johnson initiated a bombing campaign against the North called Rolling Thunder and bolstered it with the commitment of American ground troops. Developments in Latin America and Africa demonstrated a wider willingness of the United States to intervene in local conflicts, a willingness rationalized by the excuse that communists might otherwise triumph. Although in the Congo a confusion of tribal and European goals, coupled with a dearth of obvious American interests, made forceful, unilateral policy difficult, the Dominican Republic provided a seemingly simple arena within which to mobilize Washington's energies. Johnson defied the Organization of American States, sent in 23,000 American troops, and engineered the creation of a conservative government as a bulwark against a new Castroite regime.

For Taiwan, evidence of Washington's staunch anticommunism remained the best guarantee of stability and security. So long as American political leaders placed the cold war at the forefront and defined regional and local issues in terms of a free world struggle against an expansionist communist empire, then Taiwan would be protected. Indeed, Taiwan could continue bargaining its loyalty for American assistance, manipulating Washington to overlook or excuse internal political and societal abuses.

Also reassuring to Taipei in the mid-1960s was burgeoning chaos on the mainland of China as Mao Zedong's Socialist Education Campaign developed into the Great Proletarian Cultural Revolution. Angered by the retrenchment that had followed the collapse of his Great Leap Forward experiment, Mao wanted to eliminate rivals who, he believed, intended to return China to the capitalist road. The campaign rapidly escalated from a simple power struggle into a civil war with conflicting factions fighting for control in the streets. Mao gutted the party as well as the government's bureaucracy in the hope of reinvigorating revolutionary ideals among a new generation that had not experienced the hardships of the anti-Kuomintang campaigns, the Japanese war, or the Long March. Red Guard units of youthful fanatics, inspired by his call to battle, assaulted vestiges of old culture, pillaging libraries and museums as well as the homes of intellectuals and party officials.

From the vantage point of Taiwan, the disarray seemed a vindication of earlier predictions that the communist system could not survive in China and that the populace was ready for a Kuomintang-led liberation. It also strengthened Nationalist claims to be the repository of Chinese culture in the face of efforts to eradicate tradition on the mainland. Although there was always the possibility that Mao might use an attack on Taiwan to reunite a badly splintered nation, observers there generally saw the Cultural Revolution as a promising opportunity for Kuomintang political revival.

The logical outgrowth of that conclusion was to try to mount an effort to return to the mainland. The theme of recovery had provided the Nationalist raison d'être since 1949, had formed the patriotic core of each New Year's Day speech, and had shaped military budgets and plans for economic development. The missing ingredients consistently had been American assistance and Chinese Communist vulnerability.

Chiang Kai-shek's attempts to secure American backing had been legion. Throughout the 1950s, the Nationalists and their American supporters had held it as an article of faith that the moment would come and that Chiang's forces must be ready. American Ambassador Karl Rankin insisted to Washington that Nationalist morale demanded American collusion in the fiction of return, although he conceded there was little likelihood of action.[1]

When the failure of the commune movement and a series of natural disasters produced massive starvation on the mainland in 1960 and 1961,

Chiang's preparations became detailed and urgent, if still unwelcome in Washington.[2] He asserted that independently initiated paramilitary operations did not violate the consultative provisions of the 1954 Mutual Defense Treaty, by means of which the United States had consistently prevented an invasion of China. Although an emergency visit by Assistant Secretary Averell Harriman in 1962 squelched any imminent thrust, Chiang remained hopeful as Kennedy—in the interests of morale, domestic American politics, and possible future opportunities—kept his efforts to restrain the Generalissimo ambiguous.[3] Chiang insisted to the president in March 1963 that "it is no longer possible for the government to ignore popular sentiments."[4] In September 1963 Chiang asserted that "we shall so conduct ourselves as to make it unnecessary for American armed forces to be involved." The opening created by the Sino-Soviet split to carry out an invasion without Soviet intervention should not be wasted. Only a small force of air-dropped Nationalist guerrillas would be needed "to ignite an explosion."[5] But it was imperative to act quickly before a better harvest, or success by Khrushchev in subduing Mao, or Chiang's advancing age vitiated the opportunity.[6]

The advent of a new American administration did not diminish the Generalissimo's appeals. In the spring of 1964, he presented yet another elaborate plan for operations against the mainland, emphasizing the attractiveness of an incursion aimed against the five southwestern provinces paralleling American action in North Vietnam.[7] After Beijing exploded its first atomic device later that year, Chiang added proposals for eliminating Communist nuclear facilities. He made an even blunter request for logistic and military support in 1967, once again pointing to the advantages of disruption in south China for the American war in Vietnam.[8] Americans continued to say no,[9] having concluded that the Nationalists lacked the strength to carry off an effective attack and lacked the popularity to trigger an uprising. As the CIA warned in the summer of 1965, "the repeated failure of small scale . . . butcher and bolt raids by GRC [Government of the Republic of China] commando teams between late 1962 and mid-1964 points up the risks of attempting coastal landings." Analysts believed that the level of dissatisfaction with the Communist regime had been exaggerated, and, where popular ardor might be flagging, the anti-imperialist resentment sparked by an invasion would rekindle it.[10] No effective second front could be mounted by the Nationalists in China.

Chiang's attempts to link his future to the progress of the Vietnam war may not have induced the United States to undertake joint military action against the People's Republic, but it did serve to increase tensions between Washington and Beijing. Chinese Communist leaders shared with Chiang the recognition that the war provided opportunities for military cooperation on the battlefield. Mao saw Korea, Taiwan, and Indochina as the three vantage points from which American imperialism could challenge China, and, having committed forces at considerable cost in Korea, he watched the other fronts with trepidation.[11]

On the other hand, few things in the mid-1960s could attract Lyndon Johnson's attention as could offers of help in Southeast Asia. For the president the Vietnam War defined policy in Asia, and, increasingly, he insisted that America's allies back Washington's defense of Vietnamese democracy. During 1964, action officers responsible for generating "contributions" of men and matériel were appointed in each geographic bureau in the State Department, and the Joint Chiefs of Staff surveyed all U.S. embassies in nonbloc countries regarding the availability of support for Southeast Asia.[12] Harry Truman had artfully avoided Chiang Kai-shek's participation in the Korean conflict, but with different priorities Johnson gave the offer of Nationalist forces for the Vietnam theater serious consideration. It seemed a natural association since Johnson, along with many other Americans, held the Chinese Communists responsible for the continuing North Vietnamese aggression. A February 1965 Harris poll in fact showed 53 percent of respondents blaming China for Viet Cong attacks whereas only 26 percent held the North Vietnamese responsible.[13] Moreover, South Vietnamese officials, who were in continuing contact with Taipei, had begun urging Washington to enlist Chiang's troops as early as 1961.[14] Nevertheless, advisers ultimately persuaded the president that employing uniformed Nationalist fighting men would be too dangerous, arguing that Chiang could be useful in other ways.[15]

The ways proved multiple and only marginally less provocative. Nationalist officials provided small units of specially trained men for covert action conducted by the CIA and American military intelligence. They sent aircraft crews to fly transport and espionage missions, as well as technical maintenance teams, some of whom were camouflaged as Nung soldiers (an ethnic minority living along the Vietnam-China border) or given Vietnamese identities to hide them from both the Chinese Communists and the Vietnamese who were often bitterly anti-Chinese.[16] A large contingent served in southernmost Vietnam as part of the Sea Swallows unit led by a Catholic priest and supported by American aid.[17] In Taiwan the Nationalists set up training programs for Vietnamese troops. The United States also turned to Taiwan as a key staging area for operations in Vietnam: lengthening runways; stationing C-130 transport squadrons, KC-135 tankers, 13th Air Force fighter aircraft, and two fast-reaction F-4 nuclear bombers; establishing repair facilities; and using the island for armed forces' rest and recreation.

In addition to military collaboration other ties materialized. Nationalist officials argued that, just as the Korean War had boosted Japan's economy through procurement expenditures by the United States, the Vietnam War ought to aid Taiwan. Taipei's Council for International Economic Cooperation created a Committee on Overseas Economic Promotion specifically designed to increase Taiwan's share of the U.S.-financed commercial import program for Vietnam. Temporarily, until Washington decided to restrict purchases to U.S. suppliers, Taiwan secured a series of trade windfalls peaking at $89 million in 1966 as compared to $4 million in 1960. Nationalist technicians in agricultural, medical, and public works served in Vietnam, largely through AID financing, although Taipei also directly contributed a power substation, textbooks, seeds, fertilizer, prefabricated buildings, and over $800,000 of commodity assistance.[18] Each of these programs, whether military or economic, tightened bonds between Washington and Taipei and gave the Nationalist regime greater visibility in world affairs.

The Nationalists also adeptly exploited internal politics in southern Vietnam to promote a government there that would be cooperative. One of Saigon's most influential businessmen, Ly Luong Than, happened also to be a powerful member of the local Chinese community and a partisan of soon-to-be-president Nguyen Van Thieu. In 1966, when Thieu was maneuvering to capture political control, Than introduced him to Francis Koo, first secretary at the Taiwan embassy and a senior intelligence operative. Koo, thereafter, kept Thieu funded and facilitated his ties with U.S. officials. Thus Taipei ensured its links to power holders in South Vietnam and its commitment to the U.S. war enterprise.[19]

Nevertheless, Vietnam also played a prominent role in the shifting balance that would lead to Sino-American rapprochement. Several strands ran together. In the United States the decade of the 1960s witnessed both increasing involvement in the Vietnam conflict and growing public alienation from a government that insisted on sacrificing domestic reform to a foreign crusade. The mounting deaths of American soldiers galvanized an antiwar movement whose partisans confronted police clubs and gas in the streets of most major cities and eventually gunfire at Kent State and Jackson State universities.[20]

For Richard Nixon, elected president in 1968 in the wake of the Tet Offensive, finding a solution to the conflict became imperative. He bombed supply routes in Cambodia, withdrew soldiers to reduce American casualties, strengthened the Vietnamese resistance, and sought to open relations with China. Beijing, once seduced, would compel North Vietnam to negotiate seriously or at the very least shake Hanoi's confidence by its rapprochement with the United States.

Other factors contributed to Nixon's interest in China. Management of the Soviets had become more complicated as the Soviet Union graduated from a regional to a global superpower at the end of the 1960s. Nixon and his National Security Adviser Henry Kissinger proposed to use China to reduce Soviet strength and flexibility by confronting Moscow with a second, dangerous front against which constant vigilance and the expenditure of weapons, manpower, and money would be necessary. They also relished the political benefits that a foreign policy triumph would yield at home.

The likelihood of such benefits rose given that the American business community, which in the past had been indifferent or hostile to the PRC, no longer represented a barrier to better relations. China offered a vast market at a time when the American economy had to contend with its first serious deficits and the highest inflation rate since World War II. Vietnam-related expenditures, coupled with the aging of America's infrastructure, made the United States less competitive just as German and Japanese recovery surged. The Nixon administration raised interest rates, tightened the money supply, instituted wage and price controls, levied an import surcharge, and devalued the dollar. Businessmen, who often in the past had sought solutions to American economic problems in foreign markets, considered China's several hundred million customers as potential contributors to recovery.

It was ironic that Nixon, the cold warrior who had fashioned his early political career around vicious anticommunist attacks on his opponents and support for the China lobby, should pursue rapprochement with Beijing. But

As vice president, Richard Nixon had been a vociferous exponent of Chiang Kai-shek's cause. Here he greets students just before departing from Taiwan. *Courtesy of the National Archives*

Nixon and Kissinger, the Harvard professor, part of the intellectual establishment the president ordinarily disparaged, sought to discard unproductive confrontation in favor of détente.[21] Immune from right-wing denunciation, Nixon hoped to reshape the world balance of power, imposing greater American control while reducing American expenditures and commitments. In the process he shut the State Department out of policy discussions and angered the Congress whose role in foreign affairs he ignored. Ultimately, he resigned from office rather than face impeachment for his chronic abuse of power. His China initiative would long thereafter be seen as one of the few bright points in an ill-starred administration.[22]

Communist Chinese leaders came to consider rapprochement with the United States out of a different, but no less compelling, set of circumstances. Foremost was the urgent need to break out of the self-imposed international isolation following from the aggressive and unpredictable foreign policies of the Cultural Revolution. Beijing wanted the technological advances that foreign trade with the United States would bring and hoped to parlay better relations with the U.S. into liberalization of trade controls and broader access to European and Japanese markets. But economic imperatives could not compare to the crucial security dilemma facing China after August 1968.

The crisis started in Eastern Europe but soon engulfed China's border with the Soviet Union. The Kremlin had been confronted, beginning in the mid-1960s, with the increasing political disaffection and economic liberalization of the European bloc of states that it had dominated since the end of World War II. Leonid Brezhnev, trying to stabilize his domestic power through tighter central planning, more restrictive controls on intellectuals, and intensive militarization, chose to eliminate the ideological challenge developing in Czechoslovakia by sending in tanks to crush the Prague Spring on 20 August 1968.

To the Chinese Communist Party, Brezhnev's justification—that Moscow had fulfilled its duty to preserve the socialist system against external or internal subversion—appeared a potentially mortal threat to China, heralding invasion and an effort to install a more pliable regime in Beijing. Soviets and Chinese had been exchanging insults across their common frontier for years. Beginning in the mid-1960s, the Soviets moved nuclear-capable military units to the Far East and increased troop concentrations along the border from roughly 12 divisions to almost 40 by 1969. That March sporadic incidents developed into serious armed clashes, which continued into August. In the Soviet and Chinese press, talk of war became ominously frequent and made it clear that, given China's inferior military capability, a superpower ally would provide more security than scornful rhetoric and self-reliance.[23]

Observers in Taiwan, who had long insisted that the Sino-Soviet rift was pretense, quickly recognized the danger of this new situation in which Washington and Beijing could be drawn together by their antagonism to

Moscow. The Nationalists' inability to convince Americans to support an assault on the mainland had fueled suspicions that their government would be abandoned. Every moderate utterance made about the Chinese Communists, any suggestion that the world would be safer with Beijing in the United Nations or that commercial competition dictated an American presence on the mainland, occasioned sharp rejoinders. For years the Nationalists had been able to capitalize on Chinese Communist belligerence and point to aggression in Korea, or Tibet, or India. But the Chinese Communists as sober collaborators deterring Soviet expansion would be more difficult to counter.

In fact, although movement toward reconciliation with Beijing had been almost imperceptible, signs did exist pointing toward the Nixon initiative and justifying Taipei's long nurtured fears. During the Kennedy years, while the president worried about development of a Chinese bomb and intervention in Laos and Vietnam, China experts in the State Department devised policies aimed at loosening travel restrictions, offering food aid to ameliorate famine conditions, and opening diplomatic relations with Mongolia. Little actually materialized. Kennedy's fear of the Chinese was heightened by the efforts of Soviet Ambassador Anatoly Dobrynin, who persuaded Kennedy and Secretary of State Rusk that Khrushchev's adventurism in the 1962 Cuban missile crisis grew in part from goading by the more militant Chinese. And the contemporaneous Sino-Indian border war further distanced the United States from China. Here Kennedy had proof that the People's Republic was fundamentally dangerous and expansionist (although he failed to realize that Chiang Kai-shek shared Mao's determination to recover the territory in dispute). Ironically, proponents of better relations with Beijing, like Chester Bowles and John Kenneth Galbraith, identified more closely with New Delhi and once fighting began they disregarded evidence of Indian provocation and ceased speaking out for China.[24]

Other advocates, however, persisted, and in the Johnson years indications of interest in a new China policy multiplied. Roger Hilsman, assistant secretary of state, addressed the Commonwealth Club of San Francisco on 13 December 1963 with a speech that called for an open door policy toward a more pragmatic China. Taiwan would continue to be protected, but the possibility of a "two Chinas" policy ought not to be ignored. The Council on Foreign Relations stimulated public discussion through sponsorship of a series of publications on Chinese-American relations. Hearings conducted by the Senate Foreign Relations Committee in 1966 introduced the concept of "containment without isolation," suggesting inclusion of China in the world community.[25] Lyndon Johnson followed this with a speech on 12 July calling for reconciliation in Asia, and Senator Edward Kennedy pushed further with his thoughts on UN admission.

In Taipei these developments produced dismay and discouragement. The *China News* questioned how Johnson and his China advisers could have "forgotten Hitler and Mussolini and Tojo so soon" in their eagerness to placate Mao.[26] Rather than eliciting heated attacks on American duplicity or faint-heartedness from Chiang Kai-shek, these developments made him uncommunicative, convinced that U.S. resistance to Beijing would soon collapse. Taipei began to brace for American recognition of Outer Mongolia, the PRC's admission into the UN, and its own ensuing walkout.[27] Still more serious, Nationalist officials envisioned a day soon at hand when Washington would capitulate and abandon Taiwan completely.

The United States increasingly took the position that the improvement of relations with Beijing "detracts in no way from our support of the Republic of China." To strengthen that argument, the Johnson administration agreed to speed delivery of aircraft, continue exchanges of intelligence information, provide briefings on the Warsaw talks with Beijing, and invite Yen Chia-kan, the vice president, to visit Washington.[28]

Given this atmosphere, the article published by Richard Nixon in *Foreign Affairs* in 1967 did not alarm the Nationalists adequately. But Nixon made it clear there that the continued treatment of China as a pariah state must stop: "[W]e simply cannot afford to leave China forever outside the family of nations, there to nurture its fantasies, cherish its hates and threaten its neighbors. There is no place on this small planet for a billion of its potentially most able people to live in angry isolation."[29]

Acceleration toward a new Sino-American relationship began as soon as Nixon won the presidential election in November 1968. Zhou Enlai suggested even before the inauguration that the Warsaw talks reconvene.[30] In February 1969, the president let it be known through confidential channels that his administration would be undertaking a major review of China policy. Nixon lifted restrictions on trade and travel in July 1969. Secret probes via France, Pakistan, and Romania proceeded that spring and summer, and in August Secretary of State William Rogers made the first clear public statement of American interest in a dialogue with China.[31] The United States also assured Beijing privately and publicly that it would not join the Soviets in threatening China's security and would not tolerate the defeat of China in a Sino-Soviet war. Then, in November, Nixon terminated the operations of the U.S. Seventh Fleet in the Taiwan Straits.

The critical barrier to productive exchanges, however, continued to be Taiwan.[32] China had long since adopted the position that no breakthrough on any issue could be considered until the Taiwan situation was resolved. The United States had insisted that it foresaw no progress without a Chinese renunciation of the use of force in the Straits. Now, early in 1970, Americans in the State Department and White House came to terms with the fact that Washington could not impose either a "two Chinas" or "one China/one Taiwan" settlement. On 20 February 1970 at the second session of the new round of Warsaw talks, Ambassador Walter J. Stoessel pledged that "it is my Government's intention to reduce those military facilities which we now have on Taiwan as tensions in the area diminish."[33]

Despite the clear signal that the United States wanted rapprochement enough to make significant concessions, relations did not develop smoothly. The American invasion of Cambodia in 1970 and of Laos in 1971 provoked the Chinese, as did Nixon's public insistence that deployment of an American antiballistic missile system was necessary because of the threat from China. Mao and Zhou, at the same time, faced internal opposition to the moderation of Sino-American tensions. Not until the Lushan Central Committee meeting from 23 August to 6 September 1970 were they able to alter the official foreign policy line from one emphasizing that both the United States and the Soviet Union endangered Chinese security to one declaring that Moscow constituted the more profound menace. And only with the death of Lin Biao in a mysterious plane crash en route to the Soviet Union in September 1971, reportedly after failing in an attempted coup d'état, was effective resistance eliminated.

Nevertheless, once the United States shifted its position on Taiwan, rapprochement became almost inevitable. In negotiations undertaken by Henry

Washington's "two Chinas" proposal failed to save Taiwan's UN seat. Cartoon by Ranan Lurie, 1971. © 1993 Worldwide Copyright by CARTOONEWS INTERNATIONAL Syndicate, N.Y.C., USA.

Kissinger in a secret foray from Pakistan to Beijing in July 1971, Zhou Enlai presented China's three conditions for settlement with the United States. These involved acknowledgment that Taiwan was a province of China, withdrawal of American forces from Taiwan by a fixed deadline, and abrogation of the 1954 Mutual Defense Treaty. Kissinger readily agreed to the first demand, hedged on the third, and declared that troop reductions could begin once the war in Vietnam ended. He offered support for China's admission to the United Nations, although he added that Washington wanted Taiwan to retain its seat as well. Full normalization on the basis of the existence of one China would then follow in Nixon's second term.[34]

Kissinger also assured China, in this and subsequent talks, of Washington's eagerness to resolve the Vietnam conflict, its commitment to regional security, and its opposition to Soviet expansionism. To emphasize the latter point, Kissinger shared with Beijing extremely sensitive intelligence information about Soviet military deployments and assured the leadership he would keep them apprised of all discussions with Soviet officials.[35]

Public announcement of the breakthrough in Sino-American relations stunned the American people, Washington's allies in Europe and Japan, the Soviets, and, most particularly, the Chinese Nationalists. Richard Nixon had assured Chiang Ching-kuo during his 1970 visit to Washington that "I will never sell you down the river."[36] Having done just that, it seemed evident that the secrecy Nixon and Kissinger had imposed on Chinese affairs, although characteristic of their operating style, also served to protect their initiative from sabotage by Taiwan and the China lobby.

The Nationalist Chinese seat in the United Nations became an almost instantaneous casualty of Kissinger's July trip to Beijing. The trend toward admission of China had been accelerating in any case. In 1965 Taipei's position and confidence had been severely shaken when the vote on the annual Albanian resolution to expel Taiwan and seat Beijing produced an unprecedented tie. Although Taiwan still won the "important question" ballot, the United States felt compelled by the deteriorating situation to agree to a Italian initiative to set up a committee to study the entire representation issue. Washington's move so infuriated Chiang that he threatened to withdraw from the organization and reconsidered only under extreme pressure from the president and Ambassador McConaughy. Then, temporarily, conditions improved, as the Cultural Revolution made the Communist Chinese appear irrational and diminished the international desire to bring Beijing into the UN.[37]

But Kissinger's 1971 trip contributed to a refurbishing of China's image and severely compromised America's ability to control the issue. When the moment arrived, Washington attempted to propose a dual representation formula, persuaded Tokyo to cosponsor the doomed resolution, and coerced Taipei to accept it.[38] According to the *Far Eastern Economic Review*, Wash-

China's Membership in the United Nations: A New Seating Plan?

Cartoon by Don Wright. *Reprinted courtesy of Tribune Media Services*

ington actually flew "representatives of certain poverty-stricken countries, who would otherwise have been unable to attend" to New York for the balloting. Kissinger had, however, returned to Beijing at Chinese insistence, not coincidentally at the crucial moment, and Taipei refused to rally what supporters it retained for a formula that would reify a "two Chinas" solution. In the end, however, the dual representation resolution never came to a vote because the important question resolution preceding it failed (although by only four votes), and then the membership simply voted China in and Taiwan out. The U.S. Senate retaliated by withholding $141 million from the United Nations. But although offended by pro-PRC representatives dancing in the aisles, American fingerprints seemed so conspicuously on the "knife" that the funds were later restored.[39]

The expected panic in Taipei, accompanied by a collapse of the economy, did not in fact materialize. The Kuomintang convened an emergency session at which it approved a 15 Point resolution to shore up the government and adjust to Taipei's new status.[40] The Nationalist regime braced for a series of shocks, which were not long in coming.

Richard Nixon traveled to Beijing in February 1972 and, in the Shanghai Communique issued at the conclusion of his meetings, made clear that progress toward normalization of relations had begun. Beijing and Washington described in parallel statements their shared desire for peace and joint opposition to Soviet expansionism. China insisted on making plain its support for wars of national liberation in Indochina, and the United States spoke about self-determination there as necessitating its continued concern. The most significant remaining differences concerned Taiwan, even though there had been great concessions negotiated on this issue. The United States formally acknowledged the position of the Chinese on both sides of the Taiwan Strait that Taiwan was a part of a single China. This finally meant that Washington had discarded the notion, defended since 1950, that the future of the island had been left undetermined after World War II. China insisted on the withdrawal of all U.S. military support, but Washington made its agreement to do this contingent upon the diminishing of tension in the area. Kissinger avoided explicit reference to the Mutual Defense Treaty, and the Communique clearly suggested a continuing American interest in the security, stability, and welfare of the Nationalist regime.[41] Nevertheless, whether through ignorance or callousness, as Victor H. Li, a specialist in international law, has noted, Americans allowed the Communique to be issued on the 15th anniversary of the 28 February 1947 Incident.[42]

Privately, Nixon compounded the threat to Taiwan by providing Beijing with additional assurances regarding American intentions. These included pledges not to support Taiwan independence, not to aid any Nationalist attack on the mainland, and not to allow Japan to take over the American role in Taiwan as the U.S. reduced its presence. The United States would, Nixon affirmed, favor any peaceful resolution of the Taiwan problem.[43] But, even without knowledge of these confidential addenda, it was clear to Taipei and the world that, although American relations with the Nationalist Chinese remained intact, nothing would ever be the same again.

THE ECONOMY

The termination of American economic assistance in 1965 did not curb Taiwan's growth, which, in fact, accelerated without foreign aid. The most significant element assuring economic progress proved to be the shift away from a policy of import substitution designed to protect infant industries in the fields of textiles, chemical fertilizers, and cement production, which had characterized the 1950s. Instead, Taiwan took the risk after 1961 of orienting its policies toward export promotion. Initially this focused on labor-intensive light industry such as processed foods, wood products, and higher grades of textiles, but in the later 1960s it encompassed the chemical, electronic, and machinery industries.

Taiwan's gamble led it on a path quite different from, and more successful than, underdeveloped economies in Latin America, where advanced import substitution proved the rule.[44] Taiwan, along with South Korea, Singapore, and Hong Kong, sought instead to industrialize and focus production on foreign rather than domestic markets, benefiting from efficiencies encouraged by international competition.

The necessity for change had begun to be evident in the late 1950s after almost a decade of import substitution. The policy had been successful in fostering domestic industry by severely curbing the influx of foreign manufactured goods and through multiple exchange rates artificially reducing the costs of indigenous production. But the government found that Taiwan's small home market had become saturated, that industrial capacity was increasingly underutilized, that a balance of payments deficit had developed, and that limited levels of industrial exports kept foreign exchange earnings low. Although the national security considerations that had made self-reliance important still pertained, the government recognized that reforms could not be postponed. Between 1958 and 1960, officials laid the groundwork for a reconfiguration of policy, and early in the new decade, spurred by the U.S. desire to cut aid appropriations, Taiwan committed itself to an export-driven economy.

The key factor marking Taiwan's defiance of the limiting conditions so detrimental to countries in Latin America was the determination and vision of the domestic political elite.[45] Not circumscribed by the wishes of the indigenous business class, which was largely Taiwanese and therefore excluded from political power, the government could ignore their preferences for protectionist policies. Similarly, with U.S. pressures emphasizing the need for sources of income to replace aid appropriations, conservative voices in the leadership could be silenced. Officials saw their chance to capitalize on the fortuitously expanding world trade of the 1960s, inviting foreign capital in and encouraging foreign and domestic factories to orient themselves outward.

Contrary to dependency theory, however, Taiwan did not become the pawn of a hegemonic United States that distorted internal development to meet American needs, draining the island of profits, undermining regulatory structures, failing to assure price stability for exports, and neglecting to create jobs for the indigenous population.[46] Instead, the government successfully manipulated its environment, refusing to jettison entirely the import substitution approach with its beneficial mechanisms. Government authorities, convinced of the need for slow development under strict official management and aware of the discomfort and vulnerability of the business community, retained selective tariffs, subsidies, state enterprises, and currency controls. Labor-intensive, job-creating manufacturing preceded high-technology, capital-intensive ventures; the local economy was protected by a continuing emphasis on the development of agriculture; and, in accord with Sun Yat-sen's hallowed principles of the people as well as historical experience on the mainland, growth with equity of income distribution received priority.[47] The end result proved to be a mixed economy compatible with tradition but positioned to take advantage of a modern global trade environment.

Following from these decisions, the 1960s became a decade of very rapid industrial expansion. By 1966 industrial goods overtook agricultural commodities as Taiwan's largest foreign exchange earners, reflecting the fact that industrial production had appreciably exceeded agricultural growth in 1965.[48] In Taipei, the rice fields that reached almost to the gates of National Taiwan University began to be replaced by factories and highways. Foreign exchange reserves rose nearly every year between 1966 and 1973, making it possible to finance imports of goods and services virtually without loans from the World Bank and the Export-Import Bank.[49] For the period from 1965 to 1973 foreign trade experienced an average annual growth rate of 33 percent, compared with 4 percent for 1952–59 and 22 percent for the years 1959–65.[50]

Introduction of export-processing zones in 1965 at Kaohsiung and in 1970 at Nantze and Taichung further enhanced these developments. The idea had been under discussion with American advisers since the 1950s but had encountered serious opposition because the structure bore disturbing parallels to the exploitative extraterritoriality of the imperialist era on the mainland. Eventually the fact that regulations within the zones would be mandated and policed by the Taipei government rather than foreigners overcame resistance. In these areas businesses could import equipment or raw materials needed for their manufacturing operations without paying taxes or tariffs so long as they exported everything they made. As a further inducement Taiwan could assure abundant supplies of cheap and nonunionized but well-educated labor. Finally, the government also encouraged linkages with component producers outside the zones, who rapidly improved the quality of their output, absorbing new technology, meeting foreign standards, and reducing the need to bring in manufactured parts.[51]

The years 1965 to 1973, then, witnessed increases in private foreign investment seeking low-cost advantages in an intensely competitive international market. Approximately one half of the influx, which peaked in 1973 at $249 million, came from the United States, followed by overseas Chinese, Japan, and the European Economic Community.[52] The United States government explicitly undertook efforts to encourage an American presence in hopes of substituting private funds for the official allotments being phased out. Before AID departed in 1965, it contracted with the Stanford Research Institute to survey the Taiwan economy and pinpoint industries that could be effectively exploited by American investors. Government agencies in 1972 emphasized that, while skilled labor could command monthly wages of $272 in Japan, the literate and eager work force in Taiwan could be paid just $73.[53] Americans moved most rapidly into the electronics and petrochemical sectors with companies like Allied Chemical at the forefront. Liberalization of Taiwan's import regulations facilitated this expansion, rendering U.S. suppliers more competitive with the Japanese, whose proximity gave them significant advantages in shipping costs. As a result, an event like the November 1967 Industrial Machinery Exhibit, the biggest of its kind staged by the U.S. in Asia to that time, with an accompanying $5 million credit provided by the U.S. Export-Import Bank, generated significant sales of

American made machinery.[54] At the same time, Taiwan became a welcome haven for American multinational corporations, which had begun to suffer onerous restrictions from nationalistic Latin American governments. Nevertheless, private foreign capital remained confined to particular industries, and therefore its impact on the general economy continued to be relatively modest. Perhaps its primary benefit was the diffusion of technology and skills to workers and management.

More significant was the growth of private enterprises, which escalated substantially in this period, public ownership falling from 46 percent of industry in 1962 to only 19 percent in 1972. In contrast to the Japanese *zaibatsu* and the Korean *chaebols*, Taiwan's economy remained the preserve of small and middle-sized businesses. As American advisers had long argued, this development "enlarge[d] the area of creative individual decision making, encourage[d] entrepreneurship and innovation, improve[d] work and investment incentives, and contribute[d] significantly to the proper conservation of assets."[55] On the other hand, the state assured its ability to shape economic policy by retaining control over such vital sectors as utilities and banking through which it could manipulate private concerns when necessary.

The United States had its most significant impact on Taiwan's economic miracle by granting generous access to the American market. By 1966 the United States had replaced Japan as Taiwan's most important trading partner despite Tokyo's enormous advantage of proximity. More than any other people Americans eagerly consumed what Taipei had to sell, including plastic and wood products, textiles, canned foodstuffs, chemicals, and construction materials, thereby promoting Taiwan industry and, in turn, its standard of living.

Furthermore, American assistance did not end abruptly on 30 June 1965. The two governments negotiated a prolongation of cooperative work through the Sino-American Fund for Economic and Social Development (SAFED). This Fund directed some $200 million in local currency assets generated by established aid programs into economic development rather than allow such monies to be absorbed by other areas of the budget.[56] Roughly $172 million worth of surplus food and electrical generating equipment already committed before June 1965 continued to be delivered over the following three years. Washington and Taipei negotiated a new food agreement under PL 480 in December 1967. U.S. AID also maintained the Investment Guarantee Program, providing American investors in Taiwan with insurance against war damages and inflation. That American aid was predominantly in the form of grants (84 percent) and the rest in low-interest loans with long repayment schedules freed Taiwan from the heavy debt-servicing requirements so exhausting for many developing economies.[57]

Beyond strictly financial considerations, Washington also sought to provide experts and ideas. As Donald Hornig, the special assistant to the president for science and technology observed, "It seems unthinkable that after giving Taiwan $1.5 billion of aid we should withhold advice and technical assistance and abandon all influence over its future development."[58] President Johnson authorized a scientific team under Hornig's leadership to travel to Taiwan in 1967 and examine development needs. These he reported to be substantial, given the fact that "programs for strengthening the universities, improving vocational education, expanding industrial research, and developing skills in business management and marketing . . . have been pitifully undersupported." Although Chiang Kai-shek assured Hornig that he was thinking about a tenfold increase in funds for these programs (to $50 million), the special assistant urged Johnson to supply seed money, technical liaison through the embassy, and links to American laboratories and universities. The administration generally complied over protests by U.S. AID that renewed support for development activities in Taiwan contradicted all the publicity regarding Taiwan's graduation from the assistance program.

The JCRR, which had originally been intended as a temporary organization, also received continuing support under SAFED at the urging of the Taiwan government. Officials anxiously sought both reaffirmation of American interest in the island's prosperity and the concrete advantages of continued technical assistance. For the United States, despite the mandate to terminate economic assistance, collateral benefits appeared too good to surrender. As Congress noted, "The JCRR's contributions should not be measured alone in cold statistics of increased production. More significant, although less frequently recognized, is the training in leadership and democratic processes it has produced among the farmers and also among officials. Such values are bound to be reflected in the political evolution of the country."[59] Furthermore, the agency had accomplished its tasks using minimal amounts of capital. After 1965, the number of personnel was reduced, and the JCRR turned over much of its routine work to traditional government agencies but continued fostering innovative developmental projects.[60]

Private interests saw the end of official U.S. aid as an opportunity to provide technical assistance to Taiwan. Both the International Executive Service Corps and the Volunteers for International Technical Assistance, within months of the June 1965 termination date, dispatched engineers and businessmen on short-term assignments to aid Taiwan enterprises. Carried out on a nonprofit basis, support went to solve difficulties with financial control, production, and marketing.[61] American consulting and engineering firms, such as Arthur D. Little International, contracted with the government on a continuing basis.

The United States and the Republic of China also persisted in collaboration on ventures that made use of economic bounty and technical expertise to strengthen Taiwan's international political position. Building on the successful Vanguard project, Taipei proposed an "exchange of resources" program giving Taiwan commodity support under PL 480 so that it could extend its foreign assistance efforts. The United States agreed to dispose of surplus cotton, tobacco, and tallow on the Taiwan market and give half the currency generated (as much as $18 million) to Taiwan for its agricultural outreach efforts. As with so much else in the period, part of the attraction involved using the other half of the proceeds to offset Vietnam-related expenditures, reducing the outflow of dollars from the United States.[62]

In striking contrast to the previous period, in which assistance was generally one-way with money flowing from the U.S. to Taiwan, after 1965 the Nationalists began to reciprocate. The Johnson administration had to cope with a growing balance of payments problem and devised a partial solution that required help from allied nations. In the case of the Republic of China the agreement reached in June 1968 saw Taipei invest $20 million in medium-term, nonmarketable U.S. government securities and increase by another $20 million its longer-term bank deposits in the United States. It also agreed to increase its American holdings as its foreign exchange reserves grew.[63]

Taiwan pursued a series of policies designed to expand trade and foreign investment generally, but often including particular advantages for the United States. On 6 May 1967 the government cut its requirement for import exchange settlements by half, thereby reducing costs to importers. This benefited a range of trade partners but helped the United States more because American suppliers had to deal with the highest costs given their distance from Taiwan.[64]

Obviously, after 1965, although the explicit aid link had been largely severed, economic ties between the United States and Taiwan remained intricate and vital. Even where neither side adopted policies designed to assist (or punish) the other, the closeness of the relationship produced repercussions. For instance, in 1971 when the United States devalued its dollar, the Taiwan dollar fell too, producing a bonus for exporters whose goods suddenly were more competitive in international markets.[65] Continued economic involvement also suggested the need for military and political links that would help protect American investments.

THE MILITARY

Between 1965 and 1972, American military involvement in Taiwan proceeded along the lines of the previous period. The United States armed forces provided training, weapons, and encouragement. The size of American deployments grew as a result of the Vietnam war to the level of about 10,000 in 1970 and then began a long, slow decline. The military establishment, nevertheless, continued to see the island as a useful base of operations and as a source of potential troop strength.

Still Washington resisted Nationalist efforts to create an Asian military alliance based on American financial support and the possible involvement of U.S. air and naval forces. Chiang's desire to draw Taiwan, South Korea, and other nations in the area together dated back to the late 1940s, when the concept of a Pacific Pact was resisted mightily by State Department officials who saw it as a dangerous trap.[66] In its new guise, Chiang argued that such an alliance would counter growing Chinese militancy, which, he insisted, had accompanied development of Beijing's atomic bomb.[67]

Central to American assistance in Taiwan remained the effort to cut military spending before economic growth and social stability suffered. Military expenditures continued to average 10 percent of GNP and more than 80 percent of the central government annual budget.[68] Taipei put more money into the military than did any other nation not actively at war and fielded the largest standing army, proportionate to population, in the world. The Nationalists, however, resisted pressure to decrease forces by 140,000, making up for cuts in American military support with an increase in their own expenditures.[69] The strain grew when in 1967 the U.S. Congress reduced the entire military assistance program, and Taiwan's share fell by 50 percent. The U.S. embassy and MAAG could offer little hope for improvement, anticipating further contraction the next year. They soon renewed specific suggestions regarding ways to lessen expenses, including the cutback or removal of troops from the offshore islands. In response Defense Minister Chiang Ching-kuo finally agreed to engage in discussions about the reorganization of the military with the combined goal of shrinking the numbers of men in uniform while maintaining security.[70]

Taiwan's military preparedness acquired greater significance when in July 1969 Richard Nixon suggested that America's military posture in Asia would be changing. On a summer tour of East and South Asia, Nixon held a press conference at Guam where, in response to questions, he made an impromptu policy statement that quickly gained currency as the Nixon Doctrine. Declaring that commitments to allies would be observed, Nixon, nevertheless, asserted that Washington would in the future "look to the nation directly threatened to assume the primary responsibility of providing the manpower for its defense."[71] Although Nixon and Kissinger meant the doctrine as an assurance of continued American involvement in Asia despite withdrawal from Vietnam, it was interpreted by many governments as a warning that the United States would be pulling out.

In Taipei, officials insistently planned for greater not lesser American involvement. The Ministry of National Defense launched an expansion of airfields on Taiwan in 1969 at a cost of $30 million in hopes of providing permanent bases for B-52 bombers being shifted out of Okinawa. Sympathetic American military and intelligence officials tried to prevent suspension by the U.S. of jointly run intelligence-gathering flights over mainland China and protested against Washington's decision to stop Seventh Fleet patrols in the Taiwan Straits. Taipei further tried to heighten tension between the United States and China by increasing the frequency of guerrilla raids along the China coast. One of the most serious such forays came the very month of the announcement of the Nixon Doctrine, when the Nationalists provoked a naval engagement in the Min River estuary off Fujian province. And, clearly, combined pressures from Taipei and pro-Nationalist Americans had an impact as Washington secretly initiated negotiations for a substantial bulge in the 1970 military assistance budget.[72] Moreover, outright military assistance began to be supplemented by coproduction agreements such as that with Bell Helicopter.

Although the American presence in the area did not decline as significantly as some analysts had predicted and others had feared, Taiwan did have to deal with changing dynamics as Washington improved relations with Beijing. Richard Nixon, in his first foreign policy report to Congress on 18 February 1970, declared that the United States intended to abandon its "two-and-one-half-war" strategy, which had suggested that a conflict with the Soviets would automatically involve war with China. Aimed at conciliating Beijing and discomforting Moscow, the policy potentially endangered Taipei's security.[73] If Washington no longer saw Beijing as a vital threat, was no longer captive to the idea of the communist monolith, then Taipei could not assume the degree of commitment from the U.S. that had long underpinned its entire defense structure. Thus, when Sino-American rapprochement finally materialized, consternation in Taiwan about the impact on military relations between Washington and Taipei accelerated significantly.

POLITICS

After Ch'en Ch'eng's death in 1965, Chiang Ching-kuo quickly consolidated his hold on the reins of power, moving his own men into critical positions. Having operated largely in the security and military sectors, he now extended his reach into economic affairs, elevating American-trained technocrats who previously had worked for him into something of a shadow government. Lacking independent bases of support, they could be relied on to serve his interests at the same time that they allowed him to bypass entrenched Kuomintang conservatives. Symbolic of the shift underway from mainland-oriented to Taiwan-anchored policy was the "Declaration of the Tenth National Congress of the KMT" in 1969, which asserted that to recover the mainland, Taiwan must become a sterling example of the benefits of Sun Yat-sen's Three People's Principles.[74]

The United States government acknowledged Chiang Ching-kuo's new status by agreeing to his visiting the U.S. in 1970 and giving him high-level treatment throughout. Later in the year, Vice President Hubert Humphrey paid a return call to boost Nationalist morale further. State Department officials also began to use Ching-kuo as a foreign policy conduit to his less approachable father.

Dissatisfaction with Taiwan government policy, which had been muted in the past, found loud public expression in the "Protect Tiao-yu-t'ai Movement" in 1970 and 1971. The central issue revolved around a small group of rocky islets, which had been controlled by the U.S. since WWII, and had been of no particular concern to anyone until the discovery of oil in 1968–69. Taiwan immediately contracted with an American company to investigate the oil deposits further. At the same time, Japanese authorities unilaterally claimed the area, and American officials, who were already engaged in negotiating the reversion of Okinawa, announced that Tiao-yu-t'ai would be given to Japan along with Okinawa in 1972.

As the Taiwan government attempted to find a way to settle the matter through joint exploitation of the oil resources, the public reached a very different conclusion, interpreting Tokyo's position as aggression and Taipei's conciliatory approach as impotence. A series of demonstrations swept university campuses in Hong Kong, the United States, and Taiwan. In the U.S. a coordination network published pamphlets and organized protests in Chicago, Seattle, San Francisco, and Los Angeles along with rallies at the UN and, especially after the U.S. decision to turn the islets over to Japan, in Washington. Five hundred scholars living in the United States wrote to Chiang in March 1971 urging him to resist Japanese imperialism. For Taipei, the outpouring grew exceedingly uncomfortable both because there seemed little that Taiwan could do and because of fears that the movement would be manipulated by the PRC. Popular feeling that at a moment when national sovereignty had to be defended the authorities had flinched lingered even after the movement itself dissipated. Along with the other traumatic events of 1971–72, the Tiao-yu-t'ai Movement heightened a sense that political reform could not long be postponed.[75]

Opportunities for the Taiwanese did not improve significantly until late in the period. In 1967 mainlanders still held 82 percent of all jobs in the national security sector, including the police force, and more than one-third of positions in public administration and the professions even though they made up but 15 percent of the population.[76] Tight control over all criticism of the Kuomintang continued to lead to the persecution and incarceration of Taiwanese dissidents, stifling political activity. The trial of Peng Ming-min demonstrated this effectively to everyone on the island and to American observers.

Peng Ming-min had been among the few Taiwanese to earn an international reputation and the patronage of the Nationalist regime. A professor of international relations and law at National Taiwan University, Peng served briefly with Taiwan's UN mission in New York. In accordance with assumptions about his political reliability, he was even asked to inform on independence advocates in the United States. Instead he became radicalized in the United States and, after returning to Taiwan, gradually involved himself in dissident activities until he was arrested for writing and attempting to distribute a manifesto advocating the overthrow of Chiang Kai-shek. Nationalist interrogators insisted that he had acted as part of a secret U.S. agency dedicated to the overthrow of Asian leaders like Syngman Rhee of South Korea and South Vietnam's Ngo Dinh Diem. In fact, after he had been arrested, the American embassy in Taipei kept its distance, and government spokesmen took the position that Peng had in fact been guilty of sedition.[77] The primary distress felt at the State Department seemed to have been concern that the publicity the case had received would "complicate our efforts" in the regime's behalf.[78] American academics, on the other hand, protested fervently and, once Peng's eight-year term of imprisonment had been commuted, repeatedly extended invitations for him to come to teach in the United States. Eventually, he did flee the island and established residence in the United States where he became president of the World United Formosans for Independence (WUFI) and later of the Formosan Association for Public Affairs (FAPA). In Taiwan, his escape and the asylum granted him by the U.S. government most probably provoked the destruction of the Tainan USIS office.[79]

Independence activities in Taiwan remained a harrowing and furtive business. According to a former CIA agent who operated an espionage network on the island at the time, sentiment for independence had become extremely widespread even without any underground organization. All his agents were Taiwanese who happily spied on their mainland "colleagues."[80] But the inability to express such sentiments publicly energized a lawless element in the movement. In 1970 and 1971 bombs were planted at USIS and Bank of America facilities in Taiwan. More dramatically, during his 1970 visit to the U.S., Chiang Ching-kuo, having run a gauntlet of protestors whose signs proclaimed "Taiwan is neither free nor China" and "we represent the silenced majority," was attacked by an assassin at the doorway of the Plaza Hotel in New York City. Chiang escaped unharmed. The movement continued undaunted.

The United States' opening to the PRC, however, posed a serious challenge to independence advocates who divided over tactics and the significance of American policy changes. Some immediately rallied behind the Taipei government, believing both that unity was essential at a time of adversity and that the Nationalists might actually be more sympathetic to the idea of separation from the mainland under the new circumstances. In this sense the Nationalist Chinese departure from the United Nations seemed a promising development. To others, the moment seemed ripe for Taiwanese to take control. Even the New York Times declared that "China certainly is entitled to insist that Taiwan not continue as the seat of a rival Chinese Government or as a base for potentially hostile military forces. But Peking's legal right to Taiwan is not so clear. Far clearer—and in fact the overriding—claim is that of the Taiwanese people to self-determination."[81] The WUFI, among other groups, emphasized the urgency of saving innocent Taiwanese from communist rule by creating a new political entity. Demonstrators in New York City punctuated UN deliberations by chaining themselves together and calling for a new seat for a Republic of Formosa.[82] "We are no more Chinese than Americans are British," proclaimed a WUFI spokesman.[83]

From the American government's perspective 1972 did not seem a propitious time to tackle the complex and provocative issue of Taiwan's independence. Having just begun the process of reconciliation with China, Washington had no desire to raise incendiary questions, preferring to reassert its support for the Kuomintang regime while it directed its attention to mainland affairs. Efforts to influence Taiwan's internal political situation, accordingly, diminished.

CULTURE AND SOCIETY

The impact of the large American community in Taiwan on cultural and social conditions on the island continued to be significant despite the end of many U.S. aid programs in 1965 and the increasing redirection of U.S. interest toward the Chinese mainland. Despite the anti-Americanism evident in the 1957 riot and the concomitant recognition that too many Americans were calling Taiwan home, the community continued to grow during the 1960s, numbering almost 20,000 by 1967. Few encountered difficulties unless they raised the contentious subjects of communism and Taiwan independence or criticized the Kuomintang.

Resentment against and distrust of spreading Western contacts and values remained strong among conservative Nationalist government officials and intellectuals. When Chiang Ching-kuo was attacked in New York City, the USIS Taipei office was stoned, "possibly at the instigation of the government," speculated the *Far Eastern Economic Review*, and firebombs were thrown at vehicles driven by Americans in military uniforms.[84] Between 1966 and 1970, for instance, a bitter campaign raged against John King Fairbank, Harvard professor and dean of Chinese studies in the U.S., denouncing his influence in scholarly and popular circles in both Taiwan and the United States. Kuomintang critics harshly assailed his writings and congressional testimony, rejecting his suggestion that communism might have thrived in China because it was compatible with elements in Confucianism and traditional Chinese culture.[85] Scholars and political figures in Taiwan were berated for their association with him or for accepting money from the Ford Foundation, which conservative Taiwan magazines like *China* and *Modern Age* claimed was controlled by him.[86]

More broadly, in November 1966 the Kuomintang launched a Cultural Renaissance movement aimed at revitalizing the Three People's Principles of Sun Yat-sen as a basis for social relationships, cultural values, and political organization. Ostensibly a reaction against the Great Proletarian Cultural Revolution of the People's Republic, Chiang Kai-shek's Renaissance combined the rejection of Marxism with an equally vigorous denunciation of liberal democratic values that would lead to unbridled individualism.[87]

Ironically, the reasoning behind the Renaissance effort sprang from roots startlingly similar to the impulses that produced cultural uniformity on the mainland. Chiang Kai-shek and his colleagues, in analyzing their failure to retain the support of their countrymen, concluded that they had surrendered the moral and psychological high ground by not controlling intellectual life and literary expression. They would not make the same mistake again. Thus, beginning slowly in the 1950s and finally taking hold in the mid-1960s, government subjugated art to politics along guidelines disturbingly akin to those that Mao had issued at Yenan in 1942.[88]

The result could be seen in the complicated case of Bo Yang and Popeye the sailor man. Bo Yang, a satirical writer in the tradition of celebrated essayist Lu Xun, began harassing the government in 1967 with denunciations of what he called China's decrepit "soy sauce vat culture." He had at one time been a protégé of Chiang Ching-kuo and remained a patriotic opponent of extreme westernization. At the same time, he flayed his countrymen for their obscurantism, sycophancy, selfishness, and jealousy. In 1968 writing for the *China Daily News*, he tested the limits of official tolerance by translating an American comic strip of a crude but wise character who, when not slurping spinach or rescuing Olive Oyl from Bluto, critiqued human behavior. The particular strip in question portrayed Popeye as a tyrant, buying an island and forcing the only other resident to elect him president. Although Bo Yang clearly recognized the sensitivity of the cartoon and softened the dialogue, he still received an 18-year prison term. Petition drives and efforts to secure intervention from the Human Rights Commission of the United Nations as well as from the American government proved unavailing until 1977 when he was finally pardoned.[89]

In spite of the dangers inherent in self-expression, the "cultural desert" of Taiwan that Alexander Eckstein had described in his 1959 report to the American Council of Learned Societies had begun to be transformed by the mid-1960s. The Fifth Moon Group of artists led by Liu Kuo-sung produced abstract art that would not have been tolerated on the mainland. Although potentially unacceptable in Taiwan as well, the painters cleverly, and successfully, justified their movement as anticommunist. The arts also benefited from continued financial and technical support provided to the National Palace Museum by the Asia Foundation. At the same time as Nationalist China's leaders rejected American cultural influence as part of the politically driven renaissance effort, they happily accepted grants for training museum staff in the U.S. and for creating a joint master's degree program in art history offered by the museum in conjunction with National Taiwan University. The foundation similarly funded museum publications, collection inventories, and conferences on art.[90]

Indigenous effort and American assistance revolutionized the scholarly world as well. In the words of Academia Sinica scholar Chang Peng-yuan, "the revival of Chinese academic activities was closely related to [American] support . . . like a fresh rain ending a drought." The foundations, such as Rockefeller and Ford, continued to lavish patronage on academic exchange projects, library development, and intercultural research. In fact, during 1968, in a review of its China program, the Ford Foundation emphasized the need to go beyond established international relations programs and training for Taiwan's leaders to support different fields of inquiry, including economic development and science. Even the Asia Foundation, whose CIA affiliation was revealed in 1967, maintained its scholarly and governmental efforts, although increasingly with private funding, adding the reformation of Taiwan's judicial system to ongoing work on the tax structure, health care, and family planning.[91]

Science development moved firmly to the forefront after 1965 because of potential benefits for industry and the military. Leaders in Taipei also hoped that exciting research opportunities at home would begin to stem the "brain drain" that had been decimating the intellectual community for a decade. Following recommendations made by the 1964 American advisory mission of the National Academy of Sciences, six graduate research centers in the fields of mathematics, physics, engineering, chemistry, biology, and agriculture were established in the next 12 months. The director of the Chinese Academy of Sciences then traveled to the United States where he recruited faculty from among expatriate Taiwan Ph.D.'s to staff the institutes. The ROC National Council on Science Development (NCSD) received a renewed mandate in 1967 as the National Science Council with responsibility for guiding, coordinating, and evaluating research and development activities.

Lyndon Johnson's decision to dispatch Donald Hornig to the island in response to requests voiced during Vice President C. K. Yen's visit to Washington reinforced the scientific thrust. The State Department envisioned the mission as "fostering academic, intellectual and scientific achievement and development in Taiwan in order to strengthen moderate and cooperative elements in building up Taiwan as a 'torch bearer' of Chinese culture. Additionally, we believe that this tends to draw GRC interests to some extent away from military concerns."[92] Thus Washington proved willing to follow through with a series of joint projects and additional financial support. It hosted a delegation of scientists from Taiwan early in 1968, one member of which, in his guise as director of the Union Industrial Research Institute, conferred with the U.S. Atomic Energy Commission about the construction of an irradiator for treating food and construction materials. The administration created an interagency working group to coordinate such programs as the Industrial Research Workshop held in Taipei in August 1968 where 12 prominent American industrialists spoke about development and proposed linkages between private enterprise and Taiwan's scholarly community. Under the auspices of the Joint Committee on Science Cooperation, an Institute of Oceanography began operations in 1968, utilizing an American research ship and cooperating with the Woodshole Oceanographic Institute and the Smithsonian Institution. The U.S. Office of Science and Technology also sent a medical team to Taiwan that summer to extend cooperative ventures under U.S. naval auspices.[93]

Government concern led further to the recruitment of an eminent American scientist, Dr. Bruce Billings, to become science adviser to the staff of the embassy in Taipei in 1968. Rather than funnel government assistance into educational and other enterprises, his mandate involved establishing links for Taiwan-based companies and schools with American business both in Taiwan and the United States to encourage technology transfer.[94] At the same time, one of his first responsibilities was to complete negotiation of a cooperative agreement in January 1969 designating the National Science Foundation to work with Taiwan's National Science Council on joint research and topical seminars. During the next decade, the U.S.-Taiwan program would become the second most active of the 40 worldwide bilateral scientific exchanges in which the American government participated.[95] As Li Kuo-ting, cochair of the Chinese Joint Committee, remarked: "Directly or indirectly, all scientific education, scientific study and economic development received noticeable results from [Sino-American] cooperation."[96]

Since the sciences obtained some 80 percent of the NCSD budget, pressure mounted to create a group sensitive to the needs of other sectors of the scholarly community. In 1966 the Joint Council for Cooperation in the Humanities and Social Sciences, modeled on the parallel national council structure of the science committee, took up the challenge. Expectations about the work of the council, however, differed among its national constituencies. Americans hoped to use the organization not only to promote study of traditional Chinese history, politics, economics, and society, but also to facilitate research on Chinese Communist affairs using the extensive but secret documentary collection Nationalist authorities possessed. Resistance on the part of officials produced frustration among American scholars. Similarly, Chinese members were disappointed because they anticipated that the American Council would raise funds in the United States to support new institutes and other ambitious projects. The Americans preferred to move cautiously doubting the viability of some of the plans promoted by their Chinese colleagues. They also became caught in controversy over the political purposes to which some of the work of the council was being put. The late 1960s was not a time during which cooperation with intelligence agencies anywhere could go unnoticed. Some Americans also criticized bias in the organization toward senior scholars, which automatically meant exclusion of the younger and unconnected Taiwanese.[97]

Reflecting the political prejudice that intruded occasionally into exchange programs, studies revealed that in the 1960s the curriculum followed at most American high schools emphasized the goodness of the Nationalist Chinese on Taiwan and the inherently evil nature of those ruling the mainland of China. A typical example could be drawn from a high school unit prepared by historian Earl Swisher that asserted that Taiwan "preserves the rich Chinese civilization which is being destroyed by the Chinese Communists. . . . Taiwan is the only 'real' China left in the world."[98]

University programs faced fewer political pressures. Among the successful bilateral exchanges after 1965 was the collaboration between Michigan State and National Taiwan University (NTU) in the development of parallel American studies and Chinese studies curricula. Initiated by Michigan State professor Warren I. Cohen in 1965 the effort involved the recruitment of Chinese scholars from the departments of history and foreign languages and literature at NTU, who were then funded by Lynn Noah of the United States Information Agency (USIA) through the Fulbright program. After completing advanced study at MSU they returned to Taiwan where they became central figures in the development of American studies at NTU and, later, at the Academia Sinica, the government's premier research institution. Additional support for their training was offered by the American Council of Learned Societies, and the Rockefeller Foundation subsequently provided additional grants for American studies at NTU. At MSU meanwhile the fledgling Asian Studies Center was stimulated by the visiting scholars from Taiwan who helped to broaden course offerings and give greater depth to the program.[99]

Despite the flowering of intellectual pursuits in Taiwan and the vigorous cooperative environment cultivated by Americans, some of the best young minds continued to flee to the United States. Between 1965 and 1969, the number of students from Taiwan seeking to study in the U.S. almost doubled, rising from 6,780 to 12,029.[100] Ironically, facilitating this brain drain was the domestic education system, whose curriculum, which borrowed heavily from the United States, made adjustment to American universities less onerous.[101]

The numbers seeking to take up residence escalated after 1965. In that year, a new U.S. Naturalization and Immigration Act repealed the discriminatory ceiling for Chinese, substituting a reasonable quota of 20,000 from Taiwan and 600 from Hong Kong for the limit of 105 that had existed since 1943. From 1966 to 1975 some 205,000 immigrants from Taiwan and Hong Kong flooded American Chinese communities and forced the establishment of new settlements in places like Flushing and Elmhurst in New York, Monterey Park in Los Angeles, Richmond outside San Francisco, Miami, Houston, San Diego, and Argyle in Chicago.[102] Traditional organizations like the Consolidated Chinese Benevolent Association of New York had become closely tied to the KMT, joining with it in establishing the Chinatown Anti-Communist League and helping to stage annual protests at the UN opposing China's entry. Now they lost their dominance in the wake of the influx, the diaspora, and assimilation.[103]

In New York City, Chinatown also became more prosperous. During the 1950s and early 1960s, the community existed largely below the poverty line with inadequate health care, shoddy housing, and few social services. But as the garment industry elsewhere in the city floundered for lack of workers, imaginative entrepreneurs introduced clothing factories to Chinatown to take advantage of newly arrived women whose lack of English disqualified them for jobs outside the community. Although wages remained low and conditions in the sweatshops were often poor, the International Ladies Garment Workers Union secured health benefits. The new factories, making two-income families possible, quickly raised standards of living in Chinatown, and Taiwan immigrants helped return New York City to its leading position in the garment industry.[104]

Immigration to the U.S., although it accelerated after 1965, did not carry off enough people to solve the problems of Taiwan's burgeoning population. Family-planning activities, which finally had captured Chiang Kai-shek's interest in 1967, however, continued to make progress. In May 1968 local authorities actually hosted a 10-nation Conference on Population Programs in East Asia and agreed to join in establishing a regional training center in Taiwan.[105] A headquarters building for the Family Planning Association of China opened in 1969, having been constructed partly with ABMAC funds. ABMAC also contributed money to pay the association's director and run clinics. Further, it helped launch a maternity and child health demonstration project in association with the National Defence Medical Center and the Veterans General Hospital.[106]

ABMAC remained active in other health-related fields between 1965 and 1972. It engaged in two major building projects, a children's hospital wing for the Airforce General Hospital and, with support from U.S. AID, the American wing at the Cheng Hsin Rehabilitation Center. It also responded to the significant increase in the incidence of cancer on the island by establishing a cancer education committee in 1971, which would later be followed by organization of the ROC Cancer Society. ABMAC donated two mobile units to disseminate information and conduct gynecological cancer examinations.[107]

Alongside the developing ties in science and medicine, however, public opinion in the United States shifted slowly but perceptively away from support of the Nationalists during the late sixties and early seventies. As Joseph Kraft noted in the Los Angeles Times in August 1971: "There is almost no public resistance to the not very gentle letting down of Chiang Kai-shek."[108] Indeed, already in 1965 some 51 percent of the U.S. population was under 30 years of age with virtually no direct exposure to the wartime alliance with the Kuomintang. A Council on Foreign Relations survey established that only 43 percent of the American people had any knowledge about who the Nationalist Chinese were and why they were in Taiwan. All this remained true despite Taipei's efforts to educate Americans.[109]

The China lobby in the United States and officials from Taipei labored to keep the Taiwan issue in the minds of the American people throughout the period 1965 to 1972. The Committee of One Million Against the Admission of Communist China into the United Nations continued to lead the fight with the encouragement and advice of Nationalist government leaders. In 1965, for instance, the committee succeeded in getting Congress to make yet another commitment to oppose not just admission but also diplomatic recognition of and trade with Beijing and acquiescence in Beijing's expansionism. It published its signed clarion call in the New York Times as always and lobbied directly with UN members.

But the China lobby had aged, its influence weakened, and China policy got greater publicity from rather unwelcome quarters in the form of the Senate and House hearings on Communist China held during 1966. Marvin Liebman, on behalf of the Committee of One Million, insisted that Clement Zablocki, chairman of the House subcommittee on the Far East and the Pacific, include witnesses sympathetic to Nationalist China.[110] Although Zablocki agreed, a bandwagon effect developed not around the Free Chinese as in the past, but rather the idea that China policy ought to be reassessed; the alignment with Chiang Kai-shek reevaluated.

The outbreak of the Cultural Revolution in China temporarily halted the decline in enthusiasm for Chiang's cause. Public opinion polls indicated that, by early 1967, 70 percent of the American people had come to see Communist China as the main threat to world peace (only 20 percent chose the Soviet Union). In the UN, too, the voting supported Taipei.

Shifting congressional and public opinion hesitated only briefly in its move away from support of Chiang. Secretary of State Rusk sought ways to discourage further pro-Nationalist lobbying activities lest such propaganda accelerate disenchantment with the ROC.[111] Despite the organization of new support groups among students, the clergy, and businessmen, liberals, such as Senators Douglas, Ribicoff, and Javits, resigned from the Committee of One Million. By spring 1968 majorities sympathetic to the committee's work had ceased to exist in both houses of Congress. Between 1966 and 1969 support for the Mutual Defense Treaty with Taipei declined 10 percent, and opposition to it increased from 6 to 19 percent.[112] Rushed publication of The Amerasia Papers: A Clue to the Catastrophe of China with a vicious introduction by Anthony Kubek reiterating McCarthy era attacks on Jack Service failed to deter Nixon's initiatives toward the PRC or to generate support for Chiang Kai-shek. Even Anna Chennault, a longtime supporter, declared in 1970 that the time had come for a "more forward-looking" approach.[113]

The events of 1972 seemed to jeopardize the viability of the Nationalist regime on Taiwan as Washington appeared to turn its back on Chiang Kai-shek. The reality, of course, proved quite different. Not only did the United States remain tied quite closely to Taiwan for another seven years, but Taiwan itself had a much stronger grip on prosperity, unity, and stability than its dependent relationship with the U.S. had suggested. The future looked dark but not hopeless, and the developments of the following years would mandate a reformulation of the Washington-Taipei relationship rather than an end to it.

• • •

During the period 1965 to 1972 the close alignment of the United States and Taiwan very slowly disintegrated. To a large extent this followed from developments elsewhere, including Nixon's Guam Doctrine, which called for a reduction of America's presence in Asia; the total breakdown of Sino-Soviet relations linked to the Soviet invasion of Czechoslovakia and the Brezhnev Doctrine; and the American decision to move toward normalization of relations with the PRC. The latter policy, particularly, undermined the basis for friendship between Washington and Taipei and, at the same time, proved so exciting to Americans that they barely noticed Taiwan's distress.

Economic relations also experienced a profound change with the termination of formal U.S. assistance to the Taiwan government. In reality, various aid and cooperative programs continued, and the Taiwan economy did not suffer given the daring decision, made earlier in the decade by the Chinese with American encouragement, to move into the risky, but ultimately effective, area of export promotion. The U.S. further acknowledged its responsibility for Taiwan's economic stability and growth by preserving virtually unobstructed access to the U.S. market.

On the military front even greater continuity was evident. The Nationalists insisted, as often and as vehemently, on making an effort to return to the mainland, particularly in light of upheaval in Communist China linked to the Cultural Revolution. Chiang attempted to use U.S. involvement in the Vietnam War to persuade Washington that joint military operations would accomplish both their goals at once. Instead, the U.S. accepted small-scale assistance in Vietnam and maintained its pressures on the Nationalists to reduce the size of their military budget.

As before, cultural and political affairs showed the greatest evidence of the struggle being waged by conservative elements on the island to preserve the old ways and minimize American influences. In the political arena, the early signals of a growth in democratic representation could barely be seen. Independence activists continued to meet repression in Taiwan and to seek an American forum where it remained relatively safe to organize and proselytize. The government attempted to dominate the cultural sphere, reviving Sun Yat-sen's thought as a basis for self-expression and human interaction.

Political tests for artistic creations coerced most people on the island to repress radical ideas and made sure the rest would land in jail. Continued educational and scientific exchanges and immigration to the U.S. provided some of the few safety valves for the society. In retrospect, the era was not as bleak as it looked to many at the time. Serious political liberalization remained a decade away, but an opposition movement had begun to develop, and Chiang Ching-kuo would soon discover the benefits of change. There would also be prosperity. But first Taiwan would be forced to withstand further disappointments in its relationship with the United States.

chapter 7

THE END OF AN ERA, 1972–1982

Abandonment by Richard Nixon came as a blow, difficult to accept and harder to live with. It had long been assumed in Taiwan that American Democrats caused trouble for Chiang Kai-shek but that Republicans could be counted upon. Although Nixon had not actually opened diplomatic relations with Beijing and the U.S. embassy continued to operate in its shabby compound near the Taipei railway station, the prognosis looked grim and the outcome inevitable. That it took the United States another seven years to culminate the process, however, made it possible to prepare the island, its people, and the Washington-Taipei relationship for a new epoch.

In many ways the China opening had little immediate impact in Taiwan. Diplomatic contacts remained routine, business prospered, and military ties, although not as close, continued. The Taiwan economy experienced a greater trauma as a result of the 1973 oil crisis, which brought huge increases in the cost of energy and therefore manufacturing, a serious drop in foreign sales, and wildly escalating inflation.

Reconciliation between Washington and Beijing, despite the euphoria that had surrounded the signing of the Shanghai Communique in 1972, did not move ahead rapidly. On the American side progress stalled because of Vietnam and Watergate. In Beijing good feelings diminished because of American hesitancy, coupled with concern about Soviet-American relations, the deaths of Zhou Enlai and Mao Zedong, and the assumption of power by the hard-line Gang of Four. A process that some had thought would be completed in months virtually stopped.

The Vietnam War, which had dominated the calculations of policymakers in Washington for years, finally came to an end in a series of traumatic developments between 1972 and 1975. Nixon and Kissinger utilized the kind of secret diplomacy that yielded the China opening to bring Hanoi to the conference table and negotiated major concessions aimed at extricating the United States from southeast Asia. Just as they had excluded Taipei from participation in talks that undermined its status, they barred Nguyen Van Thieu from the deliberations that buried Saigon.[1] The South Vietnamese regime was, however, far less stable, far less creditable, and far less resilient than that of the Nationalist Chinese. Inefficiency, corruption, unpopularity, and mismanagement rendered the decent interval between the Paris peace settlement and the fall of the South Vietnamese government a short one.

Despite the chaos to follow in Vietnam, the February 1973 agreement that ended America's longest war might have been sufficient to make the Nixon administration one of the most popular in the twentieth century had it not been for Watergate. In mid-1973 the U.S. Congress launched an investigation into dirty campaign practices during the 1972 presidential election including a mysterious break-in at Democratic Party national headquarters. It soon became evident that the Watergate burglary had been carried out by a secret group of "Plumbers" created by Richard Nixon to plug information leaks in his administration. Nixon, already defensive about the war and antagonistic toward the press, had been infuriated by embarrassing revelations in the New York Times regarding the American bombing of Cambodia. He and Kissinger authorized a variety of criminal and coercive activities, Kissinger quipping, "The illegal we do immediately; the unconstitutional takes a little longer."[2] But Nixon's obsession with secrecy did what neither the destruction of Cambodia nor the destabilization of the dollar could have done—it provided sufficient grounds for impeachment, forcing Nixon to resign.

The ruin of the Nixon presidency made normalization with China impossible. Washington and Beijing did exchange quasi-embassies, called liaison offices in 1973, but nothing further developed. Fighting for his political life, Nixon could not risk losing the support of conservative Republicans in Congress. His successor, Gerald Ford, proved even more dependent, particularly once Ronald Reagan emerged as a main contender for the next Republican nomination and made clear his distaste for the country's China policy.

From the Nationalist Chinese perspective developments seemed hopeful if unreliably so. Officials felt that South Vietnam had been betrayed in 1973, demonstrating American willingness to jettison treaty guarantees, but believed that the disaster had, at least, given them "a breathing spell." James C. Shen, ROC ambassador, claimed that American officials felt "that 'selling one ally down the river was quite enough for one year without abandoning another.'"[3] As Watergate unfolded, Taipei could no more understand the ordeal than could Beijing, but it provided an additional welcome respite. The May 1974 appointment of Leonard Unger, a senior diplomat, as the new ambassador to Taiwan, when Beijing had anticipated a downgrading of the embassy there, seemed a significant gesture.[4]

To the political leadership in mainland China, who had risked so much in seeking better relations with Washington, the confusing events of the Watergate era seemed insufficient to explain the lack of progress in Sino-American relations. Beijing had expected more and disgruntlement turned to annoyance when Sino-American accommodation did not yield the palpable benefits obtained by the Soviets from détente with the United States. Further, the Chinese began to feel that Washington's appeasement of the Soviets, in the Middle East, for instance, demonstrated weakness and rendered the U.S. a less valuable ally in the era's triangular politics.[5] Indeed, Moscow began to escalate its deployments of land, air, and sea power in East Asia at this time. And Taiwan briefly played its own Soviet card, its foreign minister, Chow Shu-kai, suggesting to the press that the Republic of China might seek better relations with Moscow to balance the Beijing-Washington axis. Rumors alluded to a proposed Soviet lease of a naval base in the Pescadores Islands, speculation rendered more plausible when a squadron of Soviet warships sailed through the Taiwan Straits without interference for the first time since 1949.[6]

As important as PRC displeasure with Washington's policy toward the Soviet Union was their dissatisfaction with the impasse over Taiwan. Henry Kissinger consistently underestimated the significance of the Taiwan question, believing that the Chinese used it as a "control rod" with which to try to manipulate American behavior. In fact, Beijing proved exceedingly disappointed with the pace of American troop withdrawal from Taiwan, continued arms sales, and the opening of additional ROC consulates in the United States.[7]

Late in 1974, Kissinger attempted to refine American terms for resolving the status of Taiwan. Deng Xiaoping, recently resurrected from the obloquy heaped upon him during the Cultural Revolution and serving as acting premier, although still politically vulnerable, rebuffed the idea of establishing a liaison office in Taipei in place of the embassy when recognition shifted to Beijing. Deng also refused to provide a pledge renouncing the use of force in the Taiwan Straits in exchange for abrogation of the U.S. Mutual Defense Treaty with the Nationalists. In 1973, according to the U.S. secretary of state, Zhou Enlai had indicated a willingness to accept continued military, and perhaps even official, relations between Taipei and Washington if the United States would accept the idea of one China. Deng now dismissed such sensitive concessions, demanding instead a much tougher formula than the United States was prepared to accept: the severance of diplomatic relations and the defense treaty as well as withdrawal of all U.S. forces from Taiwan.[8]

To try to put Sino-American rapprochement back on track, Washington examined using the inducement of military assistance for Beijing as a complement to political and economic ties. The objectives sought included gaining increased leverage over the Soviets, obtaining a guarantee against Sino-Soviet reconciliation, and creating a Chinese strategic threat that would deter Soviet expansion. Public disclosure of this attempt came in an article by Michael Pillsbury, an analyst for the Rand Corporation, in *Foreign Policy* during the autumn of 1975. This frightened the Nationalists. Although the weaponry that the Americans contemplated giving Beijing was intended for use along the northern frontier, Taiwan argued fiercely that it could as easily be employed against them. Thus, they were not unhappy when James Schlesinger lost his position as secretary of defense, partly owing to his belligerent advocacy of military ties with China, while Beijing recognized his departure as a signal that Washington still would not tilt decisively toward China.[9]

Whatever the dissatisfactions with American policy, PRC accommodation with the United States failed to progress as much because of developments within China over which Americans had no control. Early in 1976, Zhou Enlai, the prime moving force behind Sino-American reconciliation, died, to be followed to the grave by Mao Zedong that September. Although the return of radical elements to the helm and the purge of Deng Xiaoping proved short-lived, the succession crisis focused attention on issues more basic than dealing with Washington. Of lesser foreign policy relevance, but also distracting, was the massive Tangshan earthquake that devastated portions of northern China in 1976.

Despite all this, during the 1970s, Taipei found a gradual alteration taking place in its relations with the U.S. Before its demise, the Nixon administration on some 50 occasions tried to reassure Taipei that relations would not deteriorate. But the liaison office that the People's Republic opened in Washington in 1973 functioned increasingly like an embassy and overshadowed the Nationalist diplomatic mission. Representatives of the Republic of China found it more and more difficult to see high-level American officials or to convince them to accept invitations to visit Taiwan. Ambassador Shen, feeling that his usefulness had been severely circumscribed sought to retire, but found the U.S. government unwilling to accept a replacement, forcing Shen to remain at his post four more unrewarding years.[10] The American presence in Taiwan meanwhile diminished, not only because the end of the Vietnam War meant fewer servicemen were needed there, but also because of agreements with Beijing and a sense of impending finality to the relationship. In 1974, Congress actually repealed the Formosa Resolution. And, when in 1975 Chiang Kai-shek died, President Ford tried to designate the secretary of agriculture as a sufficiently prestigious official representative to the funeral.[11]

Conditions grew considerably worse for the Nationalists when the Carter team assumed control of the government. Although the new administration opted to put the Middle East and a Panama Canal treaty ahead of advances in Sino-American relations, it became clear quite early that establishing

President Jimmy Carter and National Security Adviser Zbigniew
Brzezinski, who was eager to play the Chinese off against the Soviet
Union. *Courtesy of the Jimmy Carter Library*

diplomatic relations with Beijing was high on the agenda. A May 1977
National Security Council study known as PRM-24, which was leaked to the
press in June, contended that the main stumbling block to progress in relations had, in fact, already been surmounted; that is, during the Nixon and
Ford administrations the U.S. had accepted all concessions regarding
Taiwan: removal of troops, relinquishing of the defense treaty, and maintenance only of unofficial ties after normalization. Carter decided to move
ahead, although he concluded that he could demand of Beijing assurances
regarding the peaceful unification of China and acquiescence in continued
American arms sales to Taiwan.[12]

In Taiwan the attitude of the Carter administration produced accelerating
anxieties. No one could estimate what the impact on the economy might be
even if the People's Republic did not celebrate normalization with an immediate attack, which, of course, many believed was entirely possible. Ignoring
the dangers of lung cancer, government warnings on cigarette packages
focused instead on the more imminent political peril and counseled "Stay
calm in the face of adversity." Nevertheless, officials and businessmen
indulged in "toothbrushism," a practice whereby relatives were sent to live in
the U.S. so that a visa could be secured instantly for those remaining in
Taiwan in case of collapse.

Nationalist efforts to slow the pace of Washington's advance toward recognition of Beijing ranged from pleas to threats. Some 200,000 people joined in a letter-writing campaign appealing to Carter to stand by his Nationalist ally. Twelve residents of the president's home town toured Taiwan at Nationalist government expense so that they could remind Carter of the friendly people and wealthy ally he was abandoning.[13] High-ranking officials disparaged the idea of collaboration against Moscow, warning that "China is ideologically committed to the destruction of the United States as well as of the Soviet Union."[14] The English-language daily *China News* recalled that American advice to negotiate with the CCP in the 1940s had led to the loss of the mainland. Therefore, Taiwan's response in the 1970s would be "better dead than red."[15] Chiang Ching-kuo expressed similar sentiments, scornfully declaring that "except for battlefield contact in the shape of a bullet, I shall have nothing to do with [them]."[16] Moreover, the *United Daily News* thundered, "we will not sit tight and wait for . . . invasion; we will be forced . . . to take the initiative."[17]

Among the initiatives taken may have been increasingly elaborate intelligence gathering and disinformation activities in the United States. Taiwan intelligence organizations reportedly met in September 1971 to plan a program of disruption, briefly even considering use of letter bombs to discourage American academics who traveled to and spoke in behalf of the PRC.[18] According to Deputy Assistant Secretary for East Asian and Pacific Affairs William Gleysteen, the ROC embassy had mounted an "attempt to jump the White House," by trying "to provoke a serious crisis with the PRC, to preempt our moves, permitting Taiwan to rally its congressional troops and control the administration's approach to Congress."[19] These operations proceeded under the proficient hand of Rear Admiral Wang Hsi-ling of the National Security Bureau, who served at the embassy from 1975 to 1983 before becoming director of the Intelligence Bureau of the Ministry of National Defense. In Washington, he worked assiduously to infiltrate the U.S. government and pro-PRC and Taiwan-independence groups and to acquire classified information, technology, and occasionally weapons.[20]

President Carter became sufficiently concerned about penetration of government offices, such as the NSC and the Defense Department, and Taipei's efforts to provoke opposition to normalization that he placed Taiwan operatives on a list of hostile foreign intelligence services in 1977. He also had Taiwan diplomats targeted for surveillance and wiretapping.[21] Evidence of what the Nationalists were doing apparently was not difficult to obtain, however. Gleysteen's successor, Roger Sullivan, discovering that "documents presented on [sic] a [State Department] meeting on Thursday would turn up in Taipei on Friday," also found that ROC Foreign Ministry staff "just couldn't resist bragging about their access."[22] Ironically, investigation of Taiwan's covert efforts to derail accommodation between Washington and Beijing through espionage and dirty tricks revealed that some of the expertise making those undertakings possible had been imparted to KMT agents through CIA training programs, programs that continued even after the president designated Taiwan intelligence services as hostile.[23] But, in the end, although Taipei proved successful in stealing secrets and staging demonstrations, it could not stop the Carter administration.

After a false start in 1977, Sino-American talks gained momentum in 1978 in response to greater flexibility on both sides inadvertently encouraged by the Soviets and Vietnamese. Secretary of State Cyrus Vance on the first exploratory trip to Beijing in August 1977 had insisted upon Washington's maximum demands, including official U.S. representatives in Taipei and a renunciation-of-force declaration by Beijing. Both were met with flat refusals and subsequent complaints that the U.S. was backsliding and, as Deng Xiaoping told the Japanese, "playing two cards."[24] But strategic issues made each side more flexible. Americans worried about Moscow's involvement in Africa and expansion of its military forces, while the Chinese objected to a growing Soviet role in Vietnam (which would lead to the signing of a friendship treaty in November 1978) and the renewed buildup of troops, tanks, and missiles on the Sino-Soviet border.

Eager to capitalize on parallel anxieties, the United States avoided provocative behavior regarding Taiwan, further reduced access of Taipei's ambassador to the American government, and denied requests by Taipei to purchase advanced bombers or fighter aircraft. Carter also sought to keep American representation at the presidential inauguration of Chiang Ching-kuo low-key, generating a protest from 31 members of Congress. And aggravating that insult, National Security Adviser Zbigniew Brzezinski chose to arrive in Beijing, for what would prove to be critical talks, on the very day in May 1978 that Chiang was sworn into office.[25]

The U.S. Congress shared some of the distress felt by Nationalist government officials about Jimmy Carter's China policy. Aware that no popular groundswell demanded rapid progress on normalization, Congress could see from poll data that, on the contrary, a majority of Americans opposed recognition of the People's Republic if that meant sacrificing Taiwan. Still, there was less actual opposition to initiating diplomatic relations than resentment of the fact that the administration saw no need to involve Congress. Senators Robert Dole and Richard Stone (supported by 18 other members) thought that they had forced Carter to be more responsive by sponsoring a bipartisan amendment to the international security assistance authorization bill, which passed unanimously, calling for consultation prior to any change in the 1954 Mutual Defense Treaty. Thus the president's announcement on 15 December 1978 that problems with China had been resolved and that diplomatic relations would be formally inaugurated 1 January 1979 startled Congress. Clearly efforts to curb the "imperial presidency" and reassert constitutional checks and balances between the legislative and executive branches, upset during the Korean and Vietnam Wars, had failed.[26]

Although response was hampered by the fact that Congress was in recess, an angry debate began, encouraged by partisans of the Chinese Nationalists. Critics believed that Carter had conceded too much in order to reach an accord, that the administration ought to have insisted on an official liaison office for Taipei and on a guarantee that Beijing would not use force to reunify China.[27] Defenders noted that the PRC's leaders had long since rejected these demands and that Carter had preserved as much as could have been expected. Washington had agreed to withdraw from the Mutual Defense Treaty but asserted the right to terminate it after a one-year grace period compliant with treaty provisions. The U.S. upheld its commitment to sell armaments to Taiwan after normalization, although Carter accepted Deng Xiaoping's condition that a one-year moratorium be declared until the defense pact expired. China objected formally to the arms sales but did not let that issue prevent broader agreement. Similarly, Beijing declared that how and when reunification occurred was entirely a matter of China's internal affairs, yet Deng accepted the idea that unofficial relations between Washington and Taipei would continue.

Officials of the Republic of China, although cognizant that progress was being made in normalization talks, also had not anticipated Carter's 15 December bombshell. The secrecy maintained by the Carter administration, designed to prevent a Taiwan lobbying effort, proved effective. Taipei wrongly assumed, after watching the heated exchanges over the Panama Canal Treaties, that a change in relations would be preceded by impassioned congressional debate.[28] Brzezinski, who provided the main impetus behind normalization, dismissed Taiwan as a relatively minor casualty of an important strategic accomplishment that would significantly enhance national security.[29] The view of Taiwan as an inconsequential irritant marring a grand design could not have been more apparent when it came time to notify the Nationalist government of the impending change in American policy. Washington gave its ambassador in Taipei only some 12 hours warning, but because he was attending a party the minimal allotment diminished to 6 before he notified Chiang Ching-kuo. Chiang had to be awakened in the middle of the night to be told that Carter would make a public announcement of the new developments. For Taipei there could be neither appeal nor recourse.

The anger generated in Taiwan, not just by the event, but also by the inept and insulting manner in which it was handled, complicated efforts to salvage any relationship. Committed to creating an informal structure within which economic and cultural interaction could be continued, the Carter administration found its maneuverability circumscribed. When the president dispatched Deputy Secretary of State Warren Christopher to Taipei in late December to initiate negotiations for the new order, almost ten thousand demonstrators greeted his motorcade, pelting it with eggs, tomatoes, and mud and using crowbars to break some car windows.[30] At other anti-

Taiwan's ability to persuade Americans that it was China ceased abruptly in 1978. Cartoon from *Arkansas Gazette,* December 1978. *Reprinted by permission of the* Arkansas Democrat-Gazette

American rallies students trampled on peanuts to illustrate their disgust with Carter. The members of the Christopher entourage suspected government orchestration of the protests and were outraged by what they saw as inadequate police protection. Talks proved stiff and unproductive. Nationalist officials remained adamant that even economic and cultural exchanges required government-to-government relations.[31]

Meanwhile in Washington the administration prepared its Taiwan Enabling Act, anxious to submit it while Congress remained out of town for the holiday recess. The White House intended its legislation almost exclusively as a vehicle for the creation of informal exchange structures. It made no clear provisions for Taiwan's security, the intelligence community having assured the White House that there was no possibility of an attack by the People's Republic within the next five years. In addition, if the administration did not lock itself into a specific formula, alterations in levels of arms sales to Taipei might shape China's behavior toward peaceful reunification with Taiwan.[32] Perhaps most important, "the Carter administration made the judgment that China would be more forgiving if Congress rather than the Executive dealt with the security relationship with Taiwan. They were right. Congress enacted provisions that China accepted that the administration could not have initiated."[33] Neither did the Enabling Act include detailed stipulations to facilitate legal commercial interaction.[34] Drafting had, in fact, been hasty, begun only after the 15 December announcement and competed with both preparations for a Deng Xiaoping visit in January and the parties that customarily engulfed federal agencies for weeks before Christmas. Moreover, not all of those participating in the process appeared very concerned about Taiwan. A Senate staffer complained that Assistant Secretary of State for East Asian and Pacific Affairs Richard Holbrooke seemed at bottom a "PRC Zionist."[35]

Congress attacked the task of strengthening the bill with energy and alacrity. The coalition that insisted upon fundamental changes in the legislation, even altering its name to the Taiwan Relations Act (TRA), included Republicans and Democrats, conservatives and liberals. Hearings played to large crowds and gave a wide range of China specialists, businessmen, military officers, and government representatives opportunities to criticize and amend the bill. Administration concern that a new version would contradict commitments made to Beijing was ignored, as the focus shifted to stabilization of the relationship with Taiwan.

Congress also worried about providing reassurance to countries around the world that, they feared, might now question U.S. commitment to alliance relationships (Israel was mentioned often).[36] Finally their determination gained impetus from the invasion of Vietnam by the People's Republic of China on February 17. Not only did this seem clear evidence of Beijing's continued aggressiveness, but it was apparent that Deng Xiaoping had been planning the operation at the same time that he expedited normalization with the United States.[37] Worse, he had spoken during his January 1979 visit to the U.S. of the need to teach Vietnam a lesson, producing the impression that the White House concurred in China's subsequent action. Either American intelligence had failed to alert Washington or the administration had withheld the information. In either case, how safe could Taiwan be or feel?

The security dimension, accordingly, received the most serious consideration and the most significant revamping. The TRA made explicit that the use of force (including passive aggression such as embargoes and boycotts) against Taiwan would be of "grave concern" to the United States. To protect the island, the U.S. would enhance self-defense capabilities through continuing arms sales determined with reference to Taiwan's needs rather than China's objections. The president would be expected to report to Congress on any threat to Taiwan since it would retain oversight responsibility.

Alterations also were deemed necessary to strengthen provisions for economic relations. Congress mandated that American investors on the island would be permitted to receive Overseas Private Investment Corporation insurance, even though prosperity had placed Taiwan above the program's cutoff ceiling. Taiwan would continue to have the right to sue and be sued in American courts. Access to most-favored-nation treatment was preserved as was the right to contract for loans with the Export-Import Bank. Rumors that Taiwan would be forced to withdraw some $6 billion from American banks helped generate a provision protecting Nationalist assets in the United States from confiscation by the People's Republic.[38] Transfer of technology and fuel for Taiwan's fledgling nuclear power generation system also was assured.

Mechanisms for conduct of the relationship passed relatively intact from the Enabling Act to the final TRA. The United States government created an American Institute in Taiwan (AIT) staffed by Foreign Service officers temporarily detailed outside the formal State Department structure. The corresponding Nationalist organization became the Coordination Council for North American Affairs. Personnel in both organizations were to carry out consular responsibilities along with facilitating economic and cultural interaction. The TRA also called upon the administration to grant the CCNAA as many offices in the U.S. as the Republic of China had operated prior to derecognition. Despite the informality of all these arrangements, Congress maintained that the United States government would treat Taiwan under U.S. law as the equivalent of a nation and would continue to advocate Taiwan's inclusion in international organizations.

Members of Congress did more than just pass legislation. They also extended direct support by visiting Taiwan over the objections of the State Department, which feared for their safety in the wake of the Christopher mission fiasco and dreaded the negative publicity for Carter's China policy. The first such delegation went under the leadership of Lester Wolff (D-NY), chairman of the Asian and Pacific Affairs subcommittee in the House, and others soon followed.[39] Senator Barry Goldwater (R-AZ), along with six senators and eight representatives, filed suit in federal court charging that the administration did not have the right to abrogate the Mutual Defense Treaty without the Senate's assent. Winning the initial judgment in October 1979, and witnessing its overturn in November, Goldwater pursued the matter to the Supreme Court. In the interim an angry Senate passed a resolution declaring that abrogation of any mutual defense treaty would require Senate approval. But the inability of Senate members to agree upon whether they meant the resolution to be retroactive ironically contributed to the decision by the Supreme Court justices to dismiss Goldwater's complaint, freeing the administration to liquidate the treaty.[40]

Goldwater's legal challenge made up only a part of the program of a conservative coalition action plan devised within days of Carter's announcement. Determined to preserve the defense treaty and government-to-government relations, they proposed a full-scale and expensive lobbying effort. But Taiwan reined in their zeal, believing that compromise with the administration was probably wiser. Chiang Ching-kuo turned down an invitation proffered by Senator Robert Dole (R-KN) on behalf of the Coalition for Peace Through Strength to come to the U.S. immediately to confront the administration (although Premier Y. S. Sun encouraged Congress to take action). The executive director of the conservative Heritage Foundation, dismayed by Taipei's reticence, lamented: "You can't be more Catholic than the Pope."[41]

Negotiations between representatives of the Nationalist and American governments nevertheless did not progress smoothly. Taipei continued to try to find a formula through which some degree of "officiality" could be maintained in the relationship.[42] Borrowing from the approach used earlier between the U.S. and Beijing, the Nationalists suggested an "agree to disagree" contingency through which Taiwan would call the process official and Americans could refer to it as informal. Washington resisted that construction as inconsistent with promises to Beijing, but Taipei manipulated a press conference so as to put on record a statement that "elements of officiality" had been preserved. Similarly, the State Department objected, without result, to the transfer of the 26-room Victorian mansion in Cleveland Park, known as Twin Oaks, which had housed nine Chinese ambassadors, to the Friends of Free China when the PRC had already laid claim to it. The U.S. government took even stronger exception to Taipei's attempts to organize opposition among Americans against the recognition package. On 15 January 1979 the State Department asked for the recall of a Nationalist information officer in New York City who had published articles in the *New York Daily News* and the *Washington Star* trying to generate anti-administration sentiment. Tired of delaying tactics, the State Department was not above pressuring the Nationalists by threatening to close consulates in the

U.S. and warning that American operations would cease in Taiwan on 1 March if no agreement had been reached before then.[43]

The difficulties in these talks proved symptomatic of problems in the Washington-Taipei relationship during the remainder of the Carter presidency. Administration officials, eager to please Beijing, increasingly preoccupied with Soviet and then Iranian challenges, and angered by Taipei's obduracy, made few efforts to conciliate the Chinese Nationalists. In August 1979 Vice President Walter Mondale, while on a trip to China, revealed that several official agreements between the U.S. and Taiwan, including basic understandings like that covering civil aviation, would soon be canceled, despite earlier assurances that no such actions would be taken. The administration reduced the number of representation offices the Nationalists could operate in the United States from 15 to 8, also in contradiction to provisions of the TRA.

Once AIT's Washington headquarters were established outside the Department of State building in Foggy Bottom, Nationalist Chinese diplomats no longer could visit government offices. Republic of China officials were not permitted to schedule formal visits to the United States, and American officials ceased making regular trips to Taiwan. The Carter administration took no strong position when the World Bank and the International Monetary Fund expelled Taiwan. Further, the State Department tried to mandate that goods imported from the island would have to say "made in Taiwan" rather than the ROC.[44] Members of Congress complained that consultation regarding implementation of the TRA, particularly on defense-related questions, simply was not taking place.

Criticism of the way in which Carter had chosen to treat Taiwan became more caustic as the 1980 election campaign got underway. Republican candidate Ronald Reagan declared that Carter had made unnecessary concessions to the Communists, stabbing America's allies on Taiwan in the back and undermining the credibility of American commitments more generally. He, as president, would not pretend that U.S.-Taiwan relations were not official. He would not demean Nationalist representatives. He would not increase the vulnerability of the Free Chinese government in Taiwan. Even the Republican platform "deplore[d] the Carter Administration's treatment of Taiwan, our longtime ally and friend."[45] Once elected, Reagan appointed several officials known to be partisans of Taiwan, among them Richard V. Allen as national security adviser and Michael K. Deaver as White House deputy chief of staff, and invited Taipei to send representatives to be present at his inauguration.

Reality, however, preempted the quixotic nature of the new president's designs immediately, shattering the hopes that briefly cheered the Taiwan regime. Not only did the White House withdraw the inauguration invitations, but Nationalist officials found that admission to government buildings remained limited, that defense arrangements would continue to be discussed with Beijing, and that their own access to weapons and training would be circumscribed by what Communist China would tolerate. Sporadic statements by a president slow to understand the parameters of the permissible and the diplomatic angered Beijing but provided little relief for Taiwan.

Indeed Washington proved able to alienate both Chinas. In January 1982 the Reagan administration announced that it would not sell the advanced FX fighter jet to Taipei but that it would continue coproduction of the F-5E. In reaching this determination Washington had clearly bowed to pressure from Beijing.[46] Both Premier Zhao Ziyang and Foreign Minister Huang Hua had issued stern warnings to Reagan in October 1981. Beijing had, moreover, refused to accept opportunities to purchase weapons from the U.S. as a fair exchange for acquiescence in American sales to Taiwan. Having capitulated on the FX, Reagan pursued the effort to mollify Beijing, writing letters directly to Deng Xiaoping and Zhao in April 1982 explaining that his administration recognized legitimate reasons for their concern and expected that the need for weaponry in Taiwan would decrease as peaceful solutions were devised to the reunification dilemma. Further, he pointed to the 9 Point Proposal of 30 September 1981, an initiative by Beijing that had called for economic and cultural exchanges between the mainland and Taiwan along with direct talks regarding reunification, as promising a more peaceful future. The proposal offered an eventual compromise through which Taiwan would accept Beijing's sovereignty but would retain autonomous economic, social, and even military systems as well as participating in the central government.

Reagan simultaneously tried to reassure Taipei but left Nationalist officials profoundly unhappy with administration decisions. Having pushed for years to acquire a sophisticated fighter aircraft, they did not see the agreement merely to continue coproduction of a less-advanced airplane as a satisfactory substitute. They resented the blessing Reagan gave to the 9 Point Proposal, which Taipei had rejected absolutely. Chiang Ching-kuo asserted, "'To talk peace with the Chinese Communists is to invite death.' This is an agonizing, blood stained lesson that we and many other Asian countries have learned."[47] Nationalist officials subsequently acknowledged that their total condemnation of the offer, by appearing obstructionist, had been politically unwise, but this did not ameliorate their frustration with the United States.[48] The most telling blow, however, was delivered in August 1982.

Throughout 1982 Beijing focused intense pressure on the Reagan administration as the PRC tried to destabilize Taiwan and end American arms sales to Taiwan. Victory on the FX issue was only the first step. Having been disappointed in its expectation that normalization would demoralize Nationalist officials, forcing them to enter negotiations for reunification, Beijing sought yet again to convince Taipei of American unreliability. Thus Huang Hua presented a series of interlinked demands. The United States must decrease arms sales on a predictable schedule with a firm termination date, get prior approval of sales from Beijing so long as they continued, and not provide more sophisticated matériel than had been transferred in the past. Months of arduous negotiations followed, with Beijing unyielding on the fixed cutoff and Washington equally set on obtaining a renunciation-of-force pledge in return. Finally, the impasse led both sides to agree to an unsatisfactory but acceptable solution incorporated in the 17 August Communique. The United States conceded that arms sales would be reduced gradually leading to "a final resolution" and that at no time would sales exceed in quantity or quality those contracted in the base year of 1979. Beijing reiterated its "fundamental policy" that it would seek "peaceful reunification" and informally added the conditions under which it would employ force. These it limited to four developments: a declaration of Taiwan independence, Taiwan's inability to control its internal political situation, Taipei's alignment with an unfriendly power, or a prolonged unwillingness to negotiate with China.[49] Beijing spoke in general terms about accomplishing unification peacefully. The accord did not, in short, settle anything, but it did make gradual repair of strains in the relationship possible.

Once again, the news shook Taipei, particularly as it came from the supposedly sympathetic Reagan White House. The president did try to moderate the impact by pledging to the Nationalist authorities, even before the August Communique had been completed, that the United States had not compromised on a series of principles fundamental to the relationship:

1. It had not set a date for ending sales of armaments.
2. There would be no prior consultation with the People's Republic regarding sales to Taipei.
3. The United States would not undertake mediation between Beijing and Taipei.
4. The United States would not revise the Taiwan Relations Act.
5. The American position regarding the sovereignty of Taiwan had not been altered.
6. Washington would not pressure Taipei into agreeing to negotiations.

In contrast to the Carter administration's strict construction of agreements with Beijing, Reagan officials also utilized flexible interpretations that redounded to Taipei's benefit. Calculating what could be sold to Taiwan under the provisions of the new August understanding, the Reagan administration decided to index sales for inflation thereby significantly escalating the ceiling from which future transfer could be calculated. Then by using 1979 as the base, a year when Washington had increased sales to provide a boost before normalization, and converting that into 1982 dollars, the maximum rose from the $598 million actually sold in 1979 to a far more generous $830 million. The United States may have pledged to reduce sales, but in the short run it actually raised the value of the quantities shipped.

Members of the administration insisted that the August Communique did not controvert the Taiwan Relations Act. A communique was not, after all, the same as legislation, neither as binding nor as permanent. The State Department argued that the term "final resolution," when used with reference to arms sales, "should not be read as synonymous with 'ultimate termination,'" that, in fact, the communique did "not provide for termination of arms sales."[50]

Washington, moreover, skirted the obligation to place strict limits on the sophistication of weapons shipped to Taiwan. Although still reluctant to upgrade Taipei's offensive capabilities significantly, the Reagan administration did decide to make available more advanced weapons as older models became obsolete and could no longer be replaced or rehabilitated because the U.S. had stopped manufacturing either those designs or spare parts. In addition, the administration insisted that the agreement applied only to actual sales of goods and not to the transfer of technology. Utilizing that loophole, private industry could be encouraged to enter into coproduction agreements with Taiwan that would provide state-of-the-art equipment.

Contradiction, then, characterized Reagan-era policy toward China and Taiwan. Although clearly more concerned about Taiwan than had been the Carter people, the Reagan administration did not reverse normalization, nor did it negotiate a more favorable second-class, semiofficial status for Taipei. The basic characteristics of the triangular relationship between China, Taiwan, and the United States remained much the same as they had been since Richard Nixon shifted American priorities firmly toward the mainland. Nevertheless, Reagan's White House and State Department did not need congressional prompting to ensure that Taipei's security would be protected. They found ways to increase arms sales and provide an assortment of sophisticated equipment. They encouraged Taiwan's participation in the international community and fostered extended economic and cultural ties between the U.S. and the island. Moscow saw enough of a shift to believe that the "silly policy of the Reagan administration" regarding Taiwan meant that Washington had begun to lose Beijing, "and we are beginning to gain."[51]

THE ECONOMY

The economic dislocations anticipated in the wake of Richard Nixon's decision to go to China and acquiesce in Taiwan's expulsion from the United Nations did not materialize. Although there was an immediate and profound jump in the black-market exchange rate for U.S. dollars, conditions quickly returned to normal. Until late 1973 it appeared that anxiety had been overcome and that vigorous development would continue to characterize the economy. Had it not been for the worldwide recession caused by crisis in the Middle East, the decade of the 1970s could have been an uninterrupted period of expansion and optimism for Taiwan.

Among the reasons for Taiwan's calm and prosperity was Chiang Ching-kuo's energetic advancement of the 10 Major Construction Projects. Designed to overcome the uncertainties engendered by Taiwan's new and unwelcome status, the plan proved very controversial. It pinpointed sectors of the economy most in need of attention including energy, particularly the development of nuclear power, and transportation. Chiang's objectives embraced the betterment of the standard of living of Taiwan's people, the creation of employment, and the attraction of foreign investment capital. By inducing sizable loans, heavy investments, and liberal supply contracts, he hoped to give Americans a clear stake in continued relations with Taiwan. The United States government cooperated by encouraging and guaranteeing private investment. Roughly one-half of the $6.5 billion in financing neces-sary for these efforts eventually came from American sources.[52] The impact of this massive injection of capital and the improvement to infrastructure produced an unprecedented growth rate in the years 1975 to 1977 of 13.9 percent.

Private U.S. commercial enterprises invested enthusiastically in Taiwan's future. Cautious during the first year following the Nixon trip to China, thereafter they resumed expansion of production facilities, assumption of joint ventures, and the making of large loans. Taiwan's imports from the United States grew by 75 percent, and exports to the U.S. rose by 34 percent in 1973.

At the end of 1973, however, the global oil crisis brought on the econom-ic downturn that Taipei's leaders thought they had escaped. The October 1973 Arab-Israeli War and the American decision to provide emergency assistance to Israel led the Arab oil-producing states to impose an embargo, total against the United States and variable against other nations. The Organization of Petroleum Exporting Countries followed this in December with an enormous increase quadrupling the price of oil. Although the Middle East war provided the excuse, the escalation in prices was actually occasioned by profit seeking rather than politics, with non-Arab nations joining in the action. Even after the lifting of the embargoes, high prices did not fall.[53]

For Taiwan the shock proved destabilizing because of both domestic infla-tion and external financial dislocation. The decade had begun with a boost to Taiwan's exports produced by the devaluation of the U.S. dollar in late 1971. As the Taiwan dollar, linked loosely with U.S. currency, also decreased in value, Taiwan's goods and services found eager markets abroad, bringing in unanticipated cash surpluses, which began to fuel inflation. Inflation escalated further as foreign suppliers boosted charges for key com-modity imports owing to the burden of higher energy prices and adverse weather conditions that contributed to a scarcity of agricultural goods. Taiwan's surging growth suddenly slowed. Annual foreign investment, which had reached $249 million in 1973, plummeted to just $142 million in

1976.[54] Taiwan experienced a trade deficit of $1.3 billion in 1974, and its GNP, which had grown 12 percent in 1973, barely advanced at 0.6 percent in 1974.[55] The decline followed not only from the drop in exports and the rise in import costs (almost two-thirds of the energy used on the island had to be imported, driving up the local price of oil 300 percent) but also from the measures taken by the government to try to deal with soaring inflation, including restrictions on credit and stringent energy conservation.[56]

The 1970s brought other pressures that did flow directly from the new international position of Taiwan and the People's Republic of China. Several American companies with connections on the island became targets of discrimination by Beijing when they tried to conduct business on the mainland as well.[57] American Express, for example, discovered that its travelers checks could not be cashed in China, and Beijing excluded Union Carbide from participation in a delegation of chemical firms invited to examine business opportunities in China.[58] In June 1977 President Carter signed a law prohibiting U.S. firms from cooperating with boycotts declared by foreign governments, which, although a response to Middle East conflicts, provided some relief for a worried Nationalist regime.[59] Nevertheless, First National Bank of Chicago discontinued its operations in Taiwan in a well-publicized move to the mainland.

Despite all these difficulties, the 1970s saw significant growth in Taiwan's economy. Among the major changes was the replacement of largely light, labor-intensive, low-wage industries with higher-technology, capital-intensive manufacturing, which could pay more generous compensation to workers. Helping to facilitate this transformation was the implementation of the Generalized System of Preferences (GSP) in 1976 that emerged from the Tokyo Round of trade negotiations conducted under the auspices of the General Agreement on Tariffs and Trade. GSP lowered duties on certain manufactured goods produced by less-developed economies, the preferential treatment making their products more competitive. The United States utilized GSP to provide Taiwan with virtually duty-free access to the American market for a significant proportion of its goods, giving it 27 percent of the total quota, the highest for any individual country.[60] In a rather more wrenching way, the American consumer, who began to reject synthetic fibers during the mid-1970s, also exerted an influence on a shift from electronics to textiles, making it Taiwan's leading export by 1983 (and by 1988 surpassing textiles by 2 to 1).[61] As a result, Taiwan began to create its own area of dependency in Southeast Asia, relocating lower-level industrial production to cheaper labor pools as well as providing aid and trade.[62]

As Taiwan's status changed politically and economically, Nationalist officials and American businessmen (with encouragement from the Departments of Commerce and State) concluded that the new environment necessitated an institutionalized mechanism for facilitating commercial contacts. The American Chamber of Commerce in Taipei had already been heavily involved, not only in assisting American firms in Taiwan, but also in warning Washington of the problems that normalization with the People's Republic would create for American business interests, particularly if the administration did not plan carefully for the transition. Its 1976 position paper, "U.S.-ROC Economic Relationship: A Businessman's View," went so far as to argue that the China market had been highly overrated.[63] But the Chamber, a presence in Taipei, could not fulfill the same function in Washington. Thus, following a trip to Taiwan by former Treasury Secretary David M. Kennedy, the USA-ROC Economic Council was established in 1976 to give the U.S.-Taiwan trade relationship a vocal advocate in the United States and begin to offset the very successful National Council for U.S.-China Trade (later the U.S.-China Business Council).[64]

The Nationalist government also actively sought American loans and investments. In 1974 the U.S. Commerce Department opened a trade center in Taipei to assist in meeting those needs. During 1977 Taipei in turn established Industrial Development and Investment Center offices in Chicago and Los Angeles to generate interest in locating heavy industry in Taiwan. The Department of Industrial Development carefully courted regional banks in order to establish ties with rural and regional leaders and to bring in funds.[65] In August Taipei introduced 71 new measures to liberalize the investment climate, including extended tax holidays, multiple entry visas, and higher levels of profit repatriation.

But Taipei also had to accept some restrictions generated by the success of its export industries. Although the United States first experienced a deficit in its trade with Taiwan in 1968, this deficit did not begin to increase significantly until after 1975. As a result, in 1977 Washington forced the Nationalist government to comply with an "orderly marketing agreement" designed to curb supplies of low-priced footwear to the U.S. market. This was followed early in 1978 by a textile accord that targeted apparel shipments for a period of five years, cutting into some of the most profitable of Taiwan's clothing production.[66]

To ward off additional protectionist legislation, Taiwan mounted a series of "Buy American" missions intended, presumably, to reduce the growing imbalance in U.S.-Taiwan trade. The first such shopping spree began with a 50-day swing through 18 states in January 1978. Products particularly sought after included leaf tobacco, wine, liquor, fertilizers, and telecommunications equipment. A second group more than doubled spending to some $787 million in June. But despite plans for a third mission in September, Americans began to complain that the project was "chiefly window dressing." The vast majority of the contracts signed, they argued, would have been negotiated without the special mission. Further, private Taiwan entrepreneurs refused to participate.[67] Critics added that Taiwan circumvented the concessions it did make. After waiving restrictions on importing foreign cars, for instance, it taxed such vehicles so steeply as to render them prohibitively expensive.[68]

On the eve of the break in formal relations between Washington and Taipei, total trade had reached $7.2 billion. The United States provided a market for 40 percent of Taiwan's exports, thereby giving strong support to its GNP, half the value of which came from exports. American investment in Taiwan in 1978 had climbed to more than $500 million, comprising some 30 percent of total foreign investment, far outstripping Japan. Major firms with operations in Taiwan included RCA, Sylvania, Zenith, Gulf, DuPont, GM, Ford, Union Carbide, ITT, IBM, GE, Corning, Timex, Singer, Goodrich, and Mattel. They afforded employment opportunities at wages that averaged 20 percent above those of domestic companies, exerting pressure for improvement of salaries generally. They also provided the Nationalist government with revenues from taxes on income, real estate, and imports.[69] The Export-Import Bank held almost $1.8 billion in loans and guarantees on the island, making Taiwan the bank's third-largest customer after Brazil and Spain.[70] In addition, some two dozen private banks also had opened Taiwan offices, making American financial institutions the largest source of loan capital on the island. Nevertheless, when "asked by a visiting American in 1978 which aspect of Taiwan's economy caused him the most worry, Minister of Economic Affairs K. S. Chang replied: 'the United States.'"[71]

In fact, the impact of derecognition led to a mixed economic picture. The extraordinary growth rate of 12.8 percent achieved in 1978 declined in 1979 but far less than many had predicted, finishing the year at a strong 8 percent. Initial depreciation of the Taiwan dollar and a drastic fall in values on the local stock exchange turned around quickly. In 1979 Taiwan ranked as the world's 21st-largest trading country and the 9th-largest partner for the United States.

American business rapidly made it obvious that the absence of recognition would not undermine confidence in the continuing prosperity of Taiwan. During 1979, three additional American banks opened Taipei offices. Large companies such as General Electric, Chrysler, and Ford invested heavily in new manufacturing facilities. Bilateral trade continued to expand. In fact, businessmen under the energetic leadership of the USA-ROC Economic Council played a significant role in moderating the provisions of the administration's Taiwan Enabling Act to protect continued commercial interaction with Taiwan in the final bill. The Council also helped guard against subversion of the TRA's guarantees. In 1980 they effectively protested against State Department efforts to prevent goods labeled "Republic of China" from entering the U.S. and forced a compromise on the designation "Taiwan, ROC."[72]

More serious than the loss of formal relations with the U.S. proved to be the second oil crisis, which followed the beginning of the Iran-Iraq War in 1979. As before, the oil deficit led to significant inflation and disrupted foreign markets for Taiwan's goods. For the long-term, the government, therefore, sought new types of industrial development requiring smaller energy inputs. In the short-term, Taiwan's growth rates, although still high by international standards, fell appreciably from 1980 through 1982.

Worsening these financial and trade problems, Taiwan lost ground in international economic organizations in the wake of its departure from the United Nations. During 1980, the International Monetary Fund, the World Bank, the International Finance Corporation, and the International Development Association all decided to expel Taiwan in order to admit the PRC. These shifts meant a degree of economic isolation, although Taiwan's prosperity and its global trading ties moderated the detrimental aspects appreciably.

Taiwan, therefore, faced a new era shaken but basically strong. No longer able to rely on its alliance with the United States, it nevertheless had the assurance of trade and financial ties with a wide range of American companies. Lacking official access to the U.S. government, it still continued to enjoy legal guarantees designed to facilitate economic interaction. Shunned by most international organizations and governments, it remained a dynamic economy poised in 1980 to become what the press would term "an economic miracle."

THE MILITARY

U.S. troop reductions initiated in response to the Shanghai Communique continued through the rest of the decade. On the eve of normalization with China, the American military presence in Taiwan had fallen to just 600. Vietnam support units departed most quickly. Two squadrons of F-4 Phantom jets that had been transferred to Taiwan to make up for planes loaned to South Vietnam in the closing days of the war left in 1974–75. U.S. military advisers departed from Quemoy and Matsu in mid-1976 even though the Chinese Communists continued shelling on odd-numbered days and the Nationalists responded on even ones, prolonging the charade of a civil war. In 1974 U.S. military grants to the Nationalist government ended.

On the other hand, the United States sustained several cooperative ventures. Provision of military equipment continued but on a long-term credit basis instead of through grant funding. Some of these credits helped build a factory to produce F-5E Tiger single-seat fighter aircraft in Taichung under a joint agreement between the Nationalist government and the Northrop Corporation.[73] Small U.S. military contingents continued to train Nationalist troops, engage in contingency planning, and guard American missiles maintained on the island for emergencies. Neither the Shanghai Communique nor, in fact, the later break in relations arrested cooperation in intelligence-gathering activities. Both the Central Intelligence Agency and the National Security Agency sustained their operations, the latter continuing to staff a listening post outside Taipei that monitored radio frequencies used by the Chinese Communist air force.[74]

The Ford administration took seriously the injunction to give Taiwan a strong self-defense capability before normalization of relations with China interfered. In the mid-1970s arms transfers annually totaled between $200 and $300 million. Equipment included Hawk ground-to-air missiles and a highly advanced radar air defense system from Hughes aircraft that allowed the tracking of multiple targets simultaneously.

Nevertheless, the withdrawal of American forces from Taiwan compelled the Nationalists to think more seriously about alternate ways of protecting themselves. Already fielding a military establishment disproportionate to the size of the island's population and an enormous drain on the national budget, few options seemed available. It should not have been surprising, therefore, when rumors about development of a nuclear shield surfaced. The situation was, of course, complicated by the advent of a nuclear power industry designed to help Taiwan deal with its indigenous shortage of energy resources. Once the United States provided research reactors, trained nuclear scientists, and supplied enriched uranium, it became harder to be certain that surreptitious efforts to develop atomic weapons were not in progress.

Taiwan's nuclear assets were probably sufficient to build a small device by the mid to late 1970s.[75] Nationalist scientists had had an American research reactor since 1961 at National Tsinghua University and in 1973 acquired a new unit from the Argonne National Laboratory for training purposes. A Canadian reactor capable of producing enough plutonium for one bomb per year, and similar in design to the unit that yielded fuel for India's atomic device, came on line in 1973, just in time for Ottawa's decision to open diplomatic relations with Beijing, removing its active supervision from the facility. Moreover, one of two far larger U.S. reactors, comprising Taiwan's first nuclear power station, began operations in 1977. Taiwan had also purchased natural uranium from South Africa and had completed construction of a fuel fabrication plant in 1973.[76]

By 1976 Taiwan could boast some 700 nuclear scientists trained in U.S. universities or laboratories, and in that year 15 specialists came close to completing an inertial navigation program at MIT aimed at imbuing skills sufficient to build missiles capable of carrying nuclear warheads. That venture met a premature end when the press revealed that the 15 were under an obligation to work for the Ministry of National Defense at the secret Chung Shan Research Institute upon their return to Taiwan. But after 18 months in the $900,000 course of study, experts declared them capable of assembling missiles within 5 to 10 years that could hit within a one-mile radius of a target at 1,000 miles.[77] Furthermore, Taiwan had a pilot spent-fuel reprocessing plant under construction in 1976 from which it could recover plutonium.

Only under intense pressure from the Ford administration did Chiang Ching-kuo pledge to stop its development, without, he added, admitting that there had been anything wrong with the project.[78] Indeed, Chiang told the Legislative Yuan that consideration given to developing a nuclear arsenal in 1974 had been halted by Chiang Kai-shek, who "rejected it flatly on the ground that we cannot use nuclear weapons to hurt our countrymen."[79]

American concern about nuclear arms in Taiwan became evident when plans for redeployment of stockpiled weapons from Okinawa late in 1971 were canceled and two nuclear-equipped Phantom jets were removed from the island just prior to the Nixon visit to China. Washington protested vigorously against the expulsion of Taiwan from the International Atomic Energy Agency (IAEA) in 1972 when other international organizations were taking similar steps in response to PRC demands. In the case of IAEA, Washington saw the response as self-defeating and dangerous. Fears were not fully allayed by the fact that the Nationalists had ratified the Nuclear Non-Proliferation Treaty in 1970 or by Taipei's invitation to the International Atomic Energy Agency to continue inspections despite its official exclusion.

Washington's distress hinged, of course, on the desire to prevent Taiwan from acquiring an offensive arsenal. Taiwan's 1978 defense budget, which totaled 48 percent of the entire national budget, made that eventuality eminently possible. Early in 1978 the Carter administration notified Taiwan that foreign military sales credits would be cut from $80 million in fiscal 1978 to $10 million in 1979 and phased out completely in 1980.[80] It denied advanced bombers to the Nationalists at about the same time and blocked sale of a modified F-5E in October. The latter aircraft, the F-5G (which, in fact, had been built by Northrop specifically for Taiwan on Pentagon orders), arguably possessed sufficient range, speed, and radar capabilities to make it more than defensive. Although the White House announced that the decision was linked to 1977 administration guidelines against production or modification of weapons for sale that were not in American inventories, there was also the secret fact that normalization talks were in their final, sensitive phase and approval of the new airplane would risk unwelcome complications.[81]

The Nationalists did not, in all cases, take restrictions and cutbacks passively. Having been sold two WWII-vintage submarines by the Nixon administration, which stipulated that they could be used only for training and must not be armed, the government authorized covert agents to purchase torpedoes on the U.S. underground market in 1974. With help from criminal groups in San Francisco's Chinatown, Taiwan made it known that $100,000 would be paid for every torpedo found (even though each submarine only cost $153,000) and that it wanted 30. The FBI discovered the conspiracy, but no prosecutions or publicity resulted for fear that such a crisis would compromise U.S.-Taiwan relations too thoroughly in the eyes of Congressmen and the public.[82]

It was not immediately clear on 15 December 1978 whether derecognition had significantly worsened Taiwan's security. Among the few benefits that Taiwan received from normalization was Beijing's decision to stop exploding shells for propaganda purposes over Quemoy and Matsu as of 1 January 1979. In Taiwan a public campaign to emphasize unity and self-reliance raised $70 million for weapons purchases. More substantively, the Nationalist government increased defense spending by 12.4 percent for fiscal year 1980.[83]

The yearlong moratorium on arms sales mandated by the normalization accord between Washington and Beijing had a serious psychological impact on Taiwan's defense capabilities. Symbolic of the new relationship, it made clear that Taiwan's vulnerability had increased even though the United States would resume cooperation. High-level Nationalist military figures testified to the U.S. Congress that the hiatus in military supply had "tremendously affected not only the military buildup and readiness of the ROC armed forces but the feelings of our people and morale of our troops." Bitterness was palpable, despite continued deliveries of some $290 million in matériel already in the pipeline.

The United States government gauged Taiwan's actual risk as minimal. In line with assurances given President Carter by the Pentagon, neither the intelligence nor the diplomatic establishments believed that the People's Republic would launch an invasion of the island within the foreseeable future. Not only did China lack the amphibious capability, but it also had to contend with the ominous presence of major Soviet deployments along its northern frontier. A resort to a naval blockade to undermine Taiwan's economy courted disastrous confrontations with international shipping along critical routes in the area. China would also have to contend with a determined population, enjoying high morale, bolstered by ideological antipathy and domestic prosperity. The People's Liberation Army's performance in Vietnam during its 1979 punitive expedition embarrassingly showcased China's poor logistics, obsolescent weaponry, and ineffective command structure. Thus, Americans saw no significant military challenge on the horizon.

When the Carter administration embarked on new arms sales after the moratorium, it became apparent that, despite the clearly contrary language in the TRA, the White House would determine sales on the basis of which weaponry desired by the Nationalist regime would not provoke Beijing. Taipei was, therefore, denied the Harpoon ship-to-ship missile, Standard ship-to-air missiles, advanced jet fighters, and the training of military officers above the rank of major despite endorsements by the JCS. Although at the behest of seven Senators, U.S. contractors Northrop and McDonnell-Douglas were allowed to initiate talks with Taipei in the spring of 1980 regarding fighter aircraft sales, no authorization was forthcoming before the administration left office. The overall level of arms sales plummeted from $598 million in 1979 to $290 million in 1980.[84]

The advent of the Reagan administration did not solve Taipei's problems. Despite campaign rhetoric and a series of small sympathetic gestures, no decisive change in arms sales policy occurred with Reagan in the White House. Indeed in the first months of the Reagan presidency no new programs were undertaken, and the administration even stalled in sending appropriation requests for spare parts to Congress. Secretary of State Alexander Haig promised Beijing in June 1981 that PRC officials would be consulted before Washington sold fighter aircraft to Taipei.

Advocates of a stronger defense posture for Taiwan had anticipated that Reagan would resolve the pending Nationalist request for an advanced fighter jet (the F-16 or the F-5G), deflected by the Carter administration, with an immediate and positive response.[85] Instead, after months of study and debate within an administration badly split on the issue, the decision was reached in January 1982 to deny the FX (i.e., all of the sophisticated models under consideration) to Taipei and continue coproduction of the F-5E aircraft instead. Ronald Reagan had failed the "litmus test of . . . personal courage, credibility and strategic consistency" in the judgment of those who thought he shared their pro-Taiwan sympathies.[86]

The 17 August 1982 Communique, of course, went much further in demoralizing Taipei. Reagan surrendered the principle of perpetual arms sales to Taiwan that Carter had refused to give up in 1978 and that the TRA had instituted as law. And, although the administration interpreted the act broadly to benefit Taiwan, partisans of Taipei's interests, as described earlier, concluded that in the end Reagan's administration had been disloyal and shortsighted. Nationalist Chinese officials found themselves facing an uncertain future of economic upheaval and political vulnerability without a firm military guarantee.

POLITICS

After almost three decades of tight control over the political system on the island of Taiwan, the Kuomintang's grip began very slowly to relax after 1972. The primary moving force behind liberalization was an unlikely figure—the eldest son of Chiang Kai-shek and former head of the intimidating and brutal security forces, Chiang Ching-kuo. Perceived as a sinister influence by Taiwanese and Americans throughout the 1950s and 1960s, Chiang sought to recast his image in the 1970s. Observers found him cultivating the role of a populist politician, comfortable slurping noodles in the countryside, slapping backs, and dancing with aborigines.[87] Destined to assume the responsibilities of leadership after his father's death, Chiang Ching-kuo reached out gradually beyond the confines of conservative Kuomintang stalwarts who had given the Generalissimo unwavering support to new groups in the society. His most consequential and remarkable characteristic may well have been the wisdom he displayed in recognizing that the time had come to listen to dissenting voices whose continuing pleas for reform had always, in the past, been ignored.

Heralding change was the decision in 1969 to begin restructuring the legislature. Burdened with mainland delegates elected in 1947 and 1948, who no longer represented anyone and who were often too old to stay awake during official business, the legislature could not function efficiently. Therefore, in 1969 the government created extra seats in the chamber for which it could hold supplemental elections, a practice repeated periodically thereafter. This brought in not only younger men, but also Taiwanese who otherwise did not have a role in the central government.

Chiang Ching-kuo's concern with political reform became apparent after he assumed the position of premier in 1972. Among his first acts was enunciation of a 10-point program cracking down on corruption and inefficiency. Demonstrating the vigor and integrity of his rule, Ching-kuo claimed as an early casualty one of Chiang Kai-shek's personal secretaries. To enhance efficiency he brought a group of young men into his administration, some of whom were Taiwanese and most of whom were intellectuals and technocrats. He also decreed the release of significant numbers of political prisoners.[88]

Accompanying these official changes, a free speech movement of sorts sprang up among intellectuals. An unprecedented phenomenon in Taiwan, it was encouraged by Chiang Ching-kuo, who urged young people to criticize problems in the society. Articles quickly appeared calling for academic freedoms, greater income equity, and more access to government.[89] As with Mao on the mainland in 1956, however, the premier had not expected the deluge that followed his speech, and soon the Kuomintang curbed the "Taiwan Hundred Flowers," closing magazines and arresting particularly troublesome dissidents.[90]

Although Chiang clearly recognized the need for fresh policies and new directions, the 1970s proved a difficult time for innovation. Nationalist leaders felt themselves compelled to put a premium on political stability while Taiwan was buffeted by American policy toward mainland China. Reform could ensure support from fresh constituencies and sideline obstructionist Kuomintang diehards but could not always be safely channeled.

Anti-Kuomintang figures began slowly to have an impact on local politics. In 1973, Kang Ning-hsiang won election to the Legislative Yuan despite, or perhaps because of, flyers produced by the Justice Ministry's Campaign Inspection Office that accused him of inciting rebellion through his talk about Taiwanese-mainlander frictions and the independence movement. Kang stridently attacked the mainlander elite and the oppressive police force, and for his American audience, he proclaimed that the political and social status of Taiwanese was worse than that of Negroes in the United States.[91]

More dramatically, the Chungli episode of 1977 demonstrated that traditional politics had to change. The local elections of that year proceeded relatively free of their customary manipulation by the Kuomintang, in part, because of warnings by American Ambassador Leonard Unger that President Carter would be taking a particular interest in the human rights dimensions of the process. As a result, non-KMT candidates scored unprecedented victories. At Chungli, however, voters rioted against officials who had been caught tampering with the vote count, burning a police station and producing the most violent antigovernment incident in 30 years.[92] After Chungli, the opposition refused any longer to accept a self-imposed limitation to local offices and local issues. A national movement took form in the 1980s, contributing to and benefiting from substantive reform under the leadership of Chiang Ching-kuo.[93]

The Carter administration had given the issue of human rights an importance unprecedented in American foreign policymaking. Officials found it ironic, therefore, that among the charges leveled at the Carter White House at the time of normalization was its abandonment of millions of innocents on the island of Taiwan. Columnist George Will drew damaging parallels with the American mishandling of the desperate plight of Jews in Hitler's Germany during the 1930s. Carter, he declared, had done "more to jeopardize the rights of the Taiwanese than he had done to enhance the rights of any other people."[94]

In fact, both the administration and the Congress watched human rights conditions on the island carefully. The inauguration of the annual human rights reports to Congress compiled by the newly created Bureau of Human Rights and Humanitarian Affairs in the Department of State pinpointed abuses in Taiwan, providing information for occasional sanctions against the Nationalist government. Congress inserted in the TRA a reaffirmation of U.S. concern lest the disruption of official contact suggest a diminution of interest.

Taiwanese independence advocates had long addressed themselves to the United States on human rights grounds, even though American policymakers had generally been unimpressed by such appeals. In 1972 Taiwanese Presbyterians living in New York City had formed the Formosan Christians for Self-Determination, launched two periodicals, and staged public demonstrations. During Gerald Ford's visit to China in 1975, along with the World United Formosans for Independence and the Formosan Club in America, the Formosan Christians turned out some three thousand protestors for demonstrations in Washington, Chicago, and Los Angeles.[95]

Once Carter made clear both his concern for human rights and his determination to pursue normalization, independence advocates had a target and greater impetus for their efforts. In anticipation of Secretary of State Cyrus Vance's August 1977 trip to Beijing, the Council of the Presbyterian Church in Taiwan formulated "A Declaration on Human Rights" calling for Carter to keep in mind the responsibility to protect the security and freedom of the Taiwanese people by creating "a new and independent state." As the most active of the 80 religious organizations on the island with over 200,000 followers, the church's outspoken August 1977 appeal occasioned considerable anxiety on the Taipei government's part, prompting confiscation of the *Taiwan Presbyterian Weekly* to prevent dissemination of the message.[96]

Opponents of the KMT, seeking further to dramatize the issue of disenfranchisement, organized a demonstration at Kaohsiung commemorating International Human Rights Day on 10 December 1979. Riot police, unsuccessful in stemming the flow of people away from the authorized rally site, doused participants with tear gas and arrested some one hundred. Eight of the leaders, tortured into "admitting" that the event had been communist-inspired, subsequently received sentences of 12 years to life for sedition. The U.S. State Department protested the arbitrary nature of the charges, trials, and prison terms. The crisis had not ended with the demonstration, however. The head of the Presbyterian Church also was incarcerated for having provided sanctuary to one of the Kaohsiung Eight. Moreover, the mother of another supposed subversive, after trying to contact Amnesty International, was stabbed to death along with her son's seven-year-old twin daughters while he was in jail and they were under government surveillance.[97] In the aftermath of the confrontation, government officials slowed the process of reform, canceled scheduled elections, and returned to more severe repression of protest. In June 1981 this included the mysterious death of professor Chen Wen-chen from Carnegie Mellon University who had been visiting family in Taiwan. Having been taken for questioning by the Taiwan Garrison Command regarding political activities in the U.S., his body was later discovered on the campus of National Taiwan University amidst official denials that he had been killed while in custody.[98]

During congressional hearings sparked by the incident, witnesses made clear that spying by the Nationalist government in the United States had become an extensive and malignant adjunct to martial law in Taiwan. Informers had apparently been monitoring Chen's activities, as well as those of hundreds of other Taiwanese in the United States. Many had faced inquisitions upon their return, had found that their passports could not be renewed, had lost jobs, and had been imprisoned. Stories in university newspapers suggested that lively spy networks existed on the campuses of Columbia, Cornell, MIT, Berkeley, Iowa State, Princeton, the State University of New York, and the universities of Chicago, Florida, Minnesota, Hawaii, and Wisconsin. Students faced indoctrination sessions before their departure, under the guiding hand of the Overseas Work Commission, in which they were warned of the seductive danger represented by the CCP and independence activists. Then they were coerced into becoming informants. These revelations led Representative Stephen Solarz (D-NY) to sponsor and the House to enact an amendment to the Arms Export Control Act that mandated that the U.S. government must not extend credits or issue export licenses for weapons to any country that the president certified as being "engaged in a consistent pattern of acts of intimidation and harassment directed against individuals in the United States."[99]

The hearings, then, made clear that human rights abuses were not perpetrated solely in Taiwan but increasingly were intended to menace and demoralize Chinese in the United States. Nationalist officials had long exercised considerable influence in American Chinatowns. Not until the autumn of 1970 did communities in New York and San Francisco celebrate the founding of the PRC. Thereafter, competition between Kuomintang and Communist Chinese sympathizers began slowly to disrupt old patterns and relationships. Further instability arose out of the influx of large numbers of Chinese from Taiwan and Hong Kong, many of whom brought with them considerable financial resources, escalated rents, and drove small enterprises out of business. In 1977, rumors in New York City suggested that a private security guard service, recommended by the Nationalist consul general to combat street crime, actually was an enforcement squad for the KMT against pro-Communists and independence advocates.

To control these communities, Nationalist authorities also took an active role in questions of emigration and investment. Whereas authorities in Taiwan harangued citizens to remain on the island and put their resources into developing the economy there, the consul general in New York aided those politically reliable elements desiring to invest in the city. His influence could be seen not only in the launching of restaurants, trading companies, and banks but also in a Chinese-language pro-Kuomintang daily newspaper, the eighth in Manhattan.

More generally in the 1970s, as in earlier periods, the wealthier and politically connected people in Taiwan sought American "insurance policies" by placing family in the United States (Chiang Ching-kuo's daughter was among those who had relocated).[100] In December 1981 the United States government granted Taiwan an immigration quota of 20,000 annual entries separate from that of mainland China.[101]

SOCIETY AND CULTURE

With the signing of the Shanghai Communique, it became clear in Taipei that more vigorous cultural diplomacy would have to accompany economic and political pressure to try to salvage the U.S.-Taiwan relationship. The Nationalist government undertook concerted efforts to court members of Congress, invite influential Americans to see Taiwan, and reach out even to the average American whose sympathies could be put to use. Nationalist Chinese sought to picture themselves as the real Chinese, preservers of tradition in an open society.

During the early 1970s, the final outrages of the Cultural Revolution on the mainland rendered a favorable image of Taiwan far easier to draw. The anti-Confucius, anti–Lin Biao campaign of 1974, designed to eradicate reactionary thought by criticizing the former heir apparent to Mao as an exponent of Confucian ideas, unleashed vituperative attacks as well upon the decadent American culture foisted on the American people by the capitalist ruling class. In addition to indictments of sex and violence in films and on television, the Chinese media denounced U.S. ties with Taiwan. Taiwan utilized the opportunity to style itself not just as a bastion of freedom, but as the inheritor of Confucian thought and values, a place where great works of art were protected and the distinctive music, opera, theater, and writings of the past were treasured.[102]

The anti-Confucius campaign also generated a strident call on the mainland for the liberation of the island even if that meant the use of force. In 1975, China's temporarily belligerent position on the issue led to cancellation of the visit of a performing arts group to the United States. Among the repertoire of songs to be performed was one celebrating liberation, and the Chinese proved adamant about retaining it even at the cost of the tour's collapsing. Shortly thereafter Beijing retaliated by trying to bar the mayor of San Juan from an official delegation in an attempt to suggest that Taiwan was as much a part of China as Puerto Rico was of the United States. That visit, too, foundered on political grounds.[103]

Nationalist officials expended a great deal of money to reinforce the view of Taiwan as a more reasonable, democratic, and appealing place. In the first four months of 1973 alone the government was estimated to have paid *Time* magazine $250,000 for advertising.[104] Control of the Washington embassy passed to an air force general, S.K. Hu, and a group of young, American-educated functionaries who were determined to cultivate the U.S. Congress. To assist them, in 1974 Taipei created the Pacific Cultural Foundation, which as a private, nonprofit organization could extend invitations to members of Congress for all-expenses paid, first-class trips to Taiwan without violating regulations barring acceptance of gifts from foreign governments.[105] In spite of the nongovernmental cachet, the foundation could draw upon Foreign Ministry personnel to accompany visitors and easily arranged meetings with Chiang Kai-shek and other officials. The success of all these activities could be gauged by the Taiwan Relations Act, which responded in part to the embassy's importunings.[106]

Further help came from the remnants of the American China lobby, which in the aftermath of Richard Nixon's trip to China had reconstituted itself as the Committee for a Free China. Stalwart proponents of the cause, such as Walter Judd and Senators Strom Thurmond and Barry Goldwater, directed funds into projects on Capitol Hill and in the media to keep support for the Nationalist government viable. The committee conducted seminars for newly elected senators and representatives and even sought to influence college newspaper editors.[107]

Public relations efforts extended well beyond Washington, D.C. Three new consulates were opened. A continuing flow of entertainment and athletic groups toured the country. The Pacific Cultural Foundation helped organize visits of folk art troupes, costume exhibits, and more academically oriented workshops and symposia. Taiwan encouraged tourism, and in the mid-1970s some 140,000 Americans a year vacationed there, the third most numerous group after the Japanese and overseas Chinese.[108] Overseas Chinese in the United States, in fact, became targets of generously funded "study tours" that, "in addition to language and culture classes and the usual tourist sights," according to one young participant, "took us to visit hydroelectric projects and even a military camp, where they staged a mock battle with real tanks and colorful explosions. The transparent purpose of the trip was to impress college-aged overseas Chinese with the vitality, etc., of Taiwan and to make boosters of us." The embassy even helped arrange a sister-city agreement between Kaohsiung, Taiwan, and Plains, Georgia, Jimmy Carter's hometown.[109]

Taipei also hired paid lobbyists to make the case for Nationalist China. Among the more prominent of such firms was Hannaford Company run by Peter Hannaford and Michael Deaver, longtime advisers to Ronald Reagan. Attempting to emphasize the economic miracle and bypass human rights questions, the public relations thrust they employed targeted regional and small town newspapers and television stations where knowledge about Nationalist China was minimal but people were vitally concerned about economic growth.

Possibly some of these ventures contributed to the favorable readings that Nationalist China received in public opinion polls during the 1970s. A series of Gallup and Harris surveys taken between 1974 and 1978 demonstrated that not only did sizable majorities favor diplomatic relations with Taiwan, but they also backed the security treaty, although few advocated sending troops to defend the Nationalists should that prove necessary. The fairly significant support for recognition of the People's Republic dropped precipitously when respondents were asked to sacrifice Taipei in exchange. At the same time, pollsters found that many Americans proved to be entirely ignorant of Taiwan's status, and even half of the foreign policy elite did not see Taiwan as a "vital interest" for the United States.[110]

In the end administration secrecy prevented a final concerted push against normalization. Polls nevertheless made it apparent that the American people remained divided about Carter's policy. Recognition of the PRC was welcomed, but 56 percent of those questioned following the passage of the Taiwan Relations Act also supported continued protection of and informal relations with the island.

Further evidence of America's underlying commitment to a "two Chinas" policy came from United States' efforts to sustain Nationalist China's international profile, even as the U.S. moved closer to the People's Republic. In 1976 Washington threatened not to participate in the Montreal Olympic games when Canadian Prime Minister Pierre Trudeau barred Taiwan's athletes from competing under the name Republic of China. Acting to protect Canada's vital market for wheat in mainland China, Trudeau sparked sharp condemnation from the International Olympic Committee and almost destroyed the games.[111]

In 1980 the Nationalist government, seeking to stop the emigration of talented Chinese scientists and technical experts, as well as to bring in new types of foreign investment and facilitate technology transfer, created the Hsin-chu Science-Based Industrial Park. Modeled on Silicon Valley in California and Route 128 in Massachusetts, it emphasized the development of high technology and cooperation with nearby university centers having strong science and engineering programs. In contrast to the American experience, however, the government remained instrumentally involved, providing housing, schooling, and other support services for Hsin-chu workers. Officials linked Hsin-chu to the Industrial Technology Research Institute, which had been created in 1973 to monitor overseas developments, acquire methods adaptable to Taiwan's needs, and link academic and commercial technology development through recruitment of a first-rate cadre of researchers, many of whom had studied in the United States.[112] Nevertheless, research and development continued to be chronically underfunded, partly because of the disinclination of large private firms to engage in such speculative efforts, matched by the inability of small and medium-sized companies, the majority of the concerns in Taiwan, to afford it. Taiwan, as a result, remained largely dependent upon multinational corporations such as those welcomed to locate at Hsin-chu for technological advancement.[113]

The break in relations barely disturbed cooperative scientific endeavors and did not deter students from pursuing educational opportunities in the United States. Indeed, between 1971 and 1982 some 69 percent of all students funding themselves attended schools in the United States whereas only 25 percent went to Japan. U.S. government Fulbright fellowships increased the numbers particularly, between 1970 and 1978, in the humanities because of state support for those studying the sciences. As in earlier periods, the return rate for individuals going to the U.S. remained low. Between 1971 and 1982 only 8 percent of those with Ph.D.'s, 67 percent with masters degrees, and 12 percent of those undertaking other advanced work went back to Taiwan. This was true even though in roughly the same period some 148 institutions offering masters and doctoral degrees were launched in Taiwan.[114]

Interest in American culture was reflected in developments both of a serious and popular nature during the decade. The American mania for baseball, which had caught on in Taiwan during the 1960s, led to a series of world championships by Little League, Senior League, and Big League teams in the 1970s. Because of copyright infringement, American books were widely available, extraordinarily cheap, and enormously popular in Taiwan. The number-one best-seller on the nonfiction list in the summer of 1978 was Jim Fixx's *The Complete Book of Running*.[115] The Academia Sinica launched the journal of *American Studies*, which published articles on political and social as well as literary subjects and formally inaugurated a research Institute of American Culture in 1974. Four years later, the Institute helped to create an American Studies Association.

Literature in Taiwan made clear, at the same time, that Americanization did not suit everyone. The *hsiang-t'u wen-hsueh* (homeland literature) movement, which became the most popular trend in contemporary writing during the mid-1970s, rejected foreign techniques and espoused use of the local dialect, addressing itself to the working masses and using themes of social justice. Joseph Lau, author and literary analyst, attributed the movement's appeal to an islandwide disquiet that followed externally administered shocks, including loss of Taiwan's UN seat, U.S.-China rapprochement, and Japan's decision to recognize the PRC. Writers, some of whom, like Wang Chen-ho, had lived in the United States, pinpointed the vulgarity and patronizing behavior of the "Ugly American" and disparaged island residents who slavishly followed foreign models. Wang's satirical essay "Hsiao Lin in Taipei" published in 1973, for instance, demonstrated the absurdity of mimicking American customs such as drinking distasteful American beer (Budweiser), sending children to American schools, and throwing English words into conversation. Wang even had one of his characters fly to the U.S. so that her baby would be born an American. Ch'en Ying-chen's more melodramatic "Night Freight," published in 1978, ended with the abrupt decision to walk out on a job at an American electronics company after an American manager drunkenly belittled the "f___ Chinese."[116] For every character who made such a choice there seemed to be another, as in the story by Pai Hsien-yung, entitled "Winter Nights," who elected to run to the U.S. rather than away from it. Pai himself chose to live and write in the U.S. while, at the same time, becoming a leading literary figure in Taiwan.[117]

Such developments did not mean that government officials welcomed American scholars to work in Taiwan. During the 1970s some Americans had difficulty pursuing research; their notes were confiscated or their visas denied. In 1977 John K. Fairbank, the leading proponent of American China studies, was vilified by the press and ostracized by the scholarly community during a visit to Taiwan because he advocated better relations with the mainland and asserted that Sino-American accommodation would provide greater security than would the Mutual Defense Treaty.[118]

Asia Foundation assistance for domestic development projects continued during the decade. The foundation supported the initiation and refinement of legal aid projects, the training of judges, and legal education at the Soochow Graduate School of Law. It ranged more widely with the creation of an Urban and Housing Department in the Council for Economic

Planning and Development and major grants to the Pig Research Institute of Taiwan as well as continued assistance to family planning and health care projects.[119]

Similarly active in the health care field, ABMAC continued a variety of programs to fund training and research enterprises. By the mid-1970s, however, Taiwan's growing prosperity convinced the board to reevaluate its charitable impulses, shifting emphasis away from funding buildings and basic health care projects to involvement in sophisticated research on four difficult problems: renal failure, interferon, hepatitis, and toxic pollution. The new emphasis met some resistance from those who feared that rich Americans were using the Chinese as guinea pigs. ABMAC encountered greater enthusiasm for its efforts to place medical personnel in advanced programs in the United States. Aware of the risks that Taiwan bore in sending talented people abroad, ABMAC vigorously enforced its requirement that all participants return to the island.[120]

In addition to all the advantages accruing to the government from ABMAC's activities, Nationalist officials also availed themselves of direct consultative support from yet another American, Dr. Ivan Bennett. Appointed medical adviser to the newly formed national Science and Technology Advisory Group, Bennett had a mandate to try to bring technological solutions to health care problems.[121]

Although contacts continued to be plentiful and varied during the 1970s, interest in Taiwan dissipated as the romancing of mainland China captured the thoughts and philanthropy of government and private organizations. ABMAC and other groups found it increasingly difficult to solicit contributions for projects in Taiwan. Washington closed two of three International Communications Agency (formerly USIS) offices on the island and shifted personnel from one of these directly to Beijing. The United States even discontinued its participation in the JCRR, a symbol of successful cooperative development for 30 years. In 1973, when a group of scholars in the U.S. formed the Committee for Taiwan Historical Studies, they found attendance at annual gatherings dropped rapidly to less than a dozen even though they met among the throngs attending the Association for Asian Studies national conventions. Symbolic of the change was that among the most successful joint ventures between Nationalist China and the United States in the 1970s were the annual conferences focusing neither on ROC affairs nor U.S.-Taiwan relations but on mainland China problems held alternately in Taipei and the United States.

For Taiwan all this meant a fundamental readjustment of perspective. Optimism that the inauguration of a Republican president in 1981 would restore relations did not survive the early months of the Reagan administration. Instead, Taiwan discovered that, the worst having happened, life could go on.

• • •

Although hope for a reprieve remained throughout the decade following the signing of the Shanghai Communique between Washington and Beijing, the leadership in Taiwan had to confront the probability that the political landscape was changing in fundamental ways and that there would be no going back. Turmoil in Washington, because of Nixon's disgrace, and in China, after the deaths of Mao and Zhou, stalled progress toward diplomatic relations between mainland China and the United States. Nevertheless, the frequency and intimacy of contacts between the governments in Washington and Taipei diminished. Taiwan tried, in ways that had been successful earlier, to woo American businessmen, lobby with American politicians, and convince the American public that Taiwan, as the real, loyal, and productive China, ought not to be abandoned. But even had there not been a debate within leading circles as to the appropriate posture for the Nationalist government to take, little remained that Taiwan could do. Particularly after Jimmy Carter won the presidency, the U.S. could not be deterred from normalizing relations with the PRC.

In the aftermath of the break in formal relations between the U.S. and Taiwan, conditions on the island did not deteriorate as some had feared. Chiang Ching-kuo gave a boost to the economy, and to U.S. involvement in it, with the 10 Major Construction Projects. Although the U.S. subjected Taiwan's military to a one-year arms sales moratorium, no appreciable decline in Taiwan's defense capabilities resulted, and there were no indications of a serious threat from the PRC. Momentarily, the break in relations did lead to renewed political repression, arresting the slow liberalization of the 1970s, but the interruption could not last given the pressures within the society.

With the election of Ronald Reagan to the presidency optimists in Taiwan anticipated a restoration of some formal bond between Washington and Taipei, but the new president discovered the realities of power and could not carry through on his election promises. Not only did Reagan not restore recognition, he signed the 17 August 1982 Communique, which placed restraints on arms sales that went well beyond Carter's agreements.

The United States, long Taiwan's only supporter, had not, however, forsaken the island. With legislation of the Taiwan Relations Act, members of the U.S. Congress ensured continued routine, if informal, business, cultural, and economic ties. Even "diplomatic relations" were maintained through the offices of AIT and CCNAA. Much as Taipei tried to increase the officiality of these contacts, it failed to do so, but its ability to secure the benefits of access to the U.S. market, despite American protectionism, continued almost unabated as did its acquisition of military equipment, whether through direct sales or technology transfer that bypassed the August Communique. The sun had not set on the regime in Taiwan.

chapter 8

NEW CHALLENGES AND NEW ATTITUDES, 1982–1992

The shock and disappointment that characterized Taiwan's contacts with the United States in the 1970s and early 1980s led to a fundamental change in the dynamic of the relationship. Taiwan began to reshape its diplomacy, allowing for greater flexibility toward Beijing and cultivating broader connections, particularly among European nations. The dependency on the United States, which had produced frictions common to unequal alliances, began to dissipate. Economic prosperity, of course, facilitated greater decisiveness and increased stability. Americans felt less encumbered and the Chinese Nationalists less dominated.

Thus the two most important developments of the next decade, which profoundly altered and improved Taiwan's outlook, did not arise primarily out of Taipei's interaction with Washington, although American influence remained a significant subsidiary theme. The first was the extraordinary transformation of Taiwan from an authoritarian and often oppressive state to a fledgling democracy. The second, which fortuitously enhanced the benefits of the first, was the Tiananmen massacre of 1989. Not only did the image of Nationalist China change radically, but so, too, did the hopes that the People's Republic of China might emerge from a benighted era of communist dictatorship into a multiparty, free-market, modern society. Whereas earlier it had been fashionable to see Beijing as a more promising land of opportunity, after June 1989 Taiwan became a focus of hope, for the first time a genuine bastion of freedom in contrast to the communist dictatorship on the mainland.

During the 1980s, a network of informal contacts began to develop across the Taiwan Straits that defused much of the tension that had lingered in the area.[1] Initiated by Beijing, the positive approach eventually elicited grudging interest from Taipei. Deng Xiaoping followed articulation of the 9 Point Proposal of 1981 with an elaborated vision of "one country, two systems." He explained the details to a visiting Chinese-American scholar in 1983. Taiwan would be expected to accept the status of a special administrative region under the authority of the central government. Beijing would determine its foreign relations and provide defense against international threats. But Taipei would retain an unusual degree of autonomy, including maintenance of its own armed forces as well as a local government styled upon its own noncommunist principles. Neither civilian nor military authorities would be sent in from the center, but Taipei could participate at the national level. A version of the "one country, two systems" concept soon entered a period of prolonged practical testing when China and Great Britain adopted it in 1984 to resolve their impasse over the future of Hong Kong.

Taipei, on the other hand, rejected the idea, stridently enunciating a policy of the three noes: no contact, no negotiation, and no compromise with the People's Republic. The Republic of China's premier made it clear that Taipei would not recognize the Sino-British agreement and declared Taiwan a haven for Chinese fleeing Hong Kong as 1997 drew closer. Nationalist officials frequently referred to the lamentable case of Tibet, which after signing an autonomy agreement with Beijing in 1951 was brutally occupied in 1959.[2] Whenever possible they also pointed to the wishfulness of American thinking regarding development of the China market, political liberalization, or alliance politics, speculating that Beijing would reconcile with the Soviets on the principle that "relatives afar are not as helpful as next-door neighbors."[3]

In actual fact Taiwan's position did not prove absolute, especially in the economic arena, where the two societies began to explore openings for trade and investment. Taipei condoned expanded commercial relations so long as the pretense of indirection through Hong Kong was observed. Businessmen who risked supplying goods directly to the mainland rebels could face arrest, imprisonment, or even execution under strict sedition laws.[4] Trade via the British colony increased from $320 million in 1980 to roughly $9 billion by mid-1992. Taipei actually established its own trade office in Hong Kong designed to facilitate commerce with the PRC. Perhaps more surprisingly, behind the Hong Kong fig leaf, investment by Taiwan manufacturers in south China industry burgeoned, involving some 5,517 enterprises and $4.75 billion by mid-1992.[5]

Nationalist officials increasingly took pride in what they saw as the widespread influence of Taiwan innovations, such as export-processing zones, on the mainland. Government spokesman Shaw Yu-ming observed in 1985 that "it is no exaggeration to say that many of the economic reform programs of the P.R.C. today are direct or indirect results of the impact of R.O.C. achievements on Taiwan, a fact the P.R.C. leaders have openly, if reluctantly, admitted."[6] To many mainlanders in Taiwan, the means for the eventual

demise of communism and reunification with China lay with Taipei's tutelage, economically and politically, of this backward but promising country.
Professor Chao Chun-shun of the Institute of Asian Studies, and a graduate
of Georgetown University, remarked philosophically that "the Chinese are
very patient. . . . We can wait."[7]

The first publicly acknowledged direct political contact and the loosening
of restrictions on travel followed from the hijacking of a Nationalist cargo
plane in 1986 by a pilot anxious to visit his father in Guangzhou. Airline
officials from Taipei had no choice but to engage in direct talks with Beijing
authorities in order to retrieve the aircraft and crew members who did not
relish remaining in China. Further, they acknowledged the emotional yearn-
ings of mainlanders stranded on Taiwan since 1949 by relaxing prohibitions
on visits to China for family reunions. As of 16 October 1987, residents of
Taiwan who were neither government employees nor active duty military
men could travel to China once each year for periods of less than three
months. Subsequently, the categories of those who could go expanded, and
quickly familial motives were supplemented by business propositions and cultural exchanges.

Chiang Ching-kuo's death in January 1988 did not slow the trend. In
April the government approved mail service, and the following year authorized direct telephone connections. In April 1989 Taiwan lifted restrictions
against journalists going to the mainland to report on events there, and in
May Finance Minister Shirley Kuo became the first Nationalist official to
travel to the mainland since its loss to the Communists when she attended
an Asian Development Bank meeting that convened in Beijing. The leadership even gave brief consideration to a formula of "one country, two governments" to resolve the reunification impasse but buried it when attacked by
KMT conservatives for the implied recognition of the communist "bandits"
in Beijing and by the PRC for proposing a "two Chinas" policy.[8]

In April 1990 vice-premier Shih Chi-yang could, nevertheless, tell a conference of overseas Chinese that the Nationalists would permit establishment of an unofficial office in Taipei to facilitate communications and
business dealings if a similar informal representative agency were created in
Beijing.[9] President Lee Teng-hui convened an advisory National Unification
Council later in the year and created a Mainland Affairs Council to coordinate policy at the cabinet level. In 1991 a quasi-official Straits Exchange
Foundation was added to facilitate private interaction with the mainland as
trade climbed to $5 billion and investment to $2 billion.[10] And in 1992 officials such as Chiang Ping-kun, vice-minister of economic affairs, had begun
to assert that "it's high time for us to review our cross-strait trade policy and
make timely adjustments since our businessmen have become increasingly
reliant on mainland markets."[11]

To the United States the growth of contacts between Taiwan and the
PRC became a source of cautious optimism. The U.S. government, never-

theless, carefully adhered to a policy of neutrality, refusing to take on the obligations of a mediator, although it made clear its pleasure in the more constructive direction relations had taken. Deng Xiaoping tried in a 1986 CBS news interview to enlist Ronald Reagan to encourage the so-called three links in mail, trade, and transportation between China and Taiwan.[12] But the American government would go no further than the assertion by Secretary of State George Shultz, during a trip to China the following year, that the U.S. was eager to "foster an environment within which . . . a continuing, evolutionary process toward peaceful resolution of the Taiwan question . . . can continue to take place."[13] This did not mean that the Reagan administration would lessen its commitment to keep Taiwan supplied with military matériel or further reduce its informal connections in the United States—although officials in Taipei feared that it might—but rather that the United States viewed mutually desired betterment of relations across the Taiwan Straits with enthusiasm.

Beyond the creation of links to the mainland, Taiwan also began to follow a policy of flexible diplomacy. The Nationalist government decided to break out of its international isolation by dealing more expansively with the foreign policy needs of other governments. In 1984, when Surinam had expressed a desire to establish relations with Taipei in order to benefit from development assistance, the Nationalist regime insisted that it had to break relations with Beijing first. The result was to drive Surinam and other countries with parallel needs and interests away. After careful consideration over an extended period the Foreign Affairs Committee of the Legislative Yuan reversed that stand.[14] During 1989 Taipei welcomed ties with Grenada, Belize, and Liberia despite their formal recognition of the PRC.[15]

Thus flexible diplomacy has in fact meant acceptance of dual recognition by Taipei, although it continued to be rejected by Beijing.[16] By theoretically allowing simultaneous diplomatic relations with both Chinas, or parallel memberships in international organizations such as the Asian Development Bank, this policy allows Taiwan to surmount the ostracism orchestrated by the People's Republic since 1971. Where actual recognition has not been an option, Taipei has encouraged nations to upgrade their unofficial representative associations to make the relationship more substantive. Taiwan even placed a large advertisement in the New York Times to inform anyone who had not already heard of its flexibility and pragmatism.[17]

Taipei has also translated its economic might into greater international acceptance through participation in multilateral strategic action. During the Persian Gulf War, although the United States rejected a contribution from Taiwan of $100 million to support military operations, it formally requested Taipei's observance of sanctions against Iraq, and Taiwan did provide aid to Jordan, Egypt, and Turkey.[18] Exploiting this trend, a group of 80 Kuomintang legislators petitioned in June 1991 for government action to reapply to the United Nations "at an appropriate time."[19]

WITHOUT A FULL TEAM, IT'S UPHILL FOR THE U.N.

Why has the Republic of China on Taiwan, one of the world's strongest democracies, been banished from the world stage? Such exclusion from the U.N. and other world forums is unfortunate and detrimental to world affairs.

All because of rhetoric that ignores reality.

Communist China says the Republic of China on Taiwan does not exist. But that's a ploy which simply won't work anymore. How is it possible to ignore 21 million people, who make up the world's 20th largest economy. 14th largest trading nation, a blossoming democracy, and a colorful culture?

Communist China also argues that the U.N. is not big enough for two Chinese seats, even if only temporarily, until China's unification is achieved. But the U.N. was big enough for two Germanys, and is still big enough for the two divided parts of Korea. So much for that argument.

Rhetoric can't change reality. The Republic of China on Taiwan exists. The international community should not be bullied into playing along with any charade to the contrary.

It's high time the international community says "no" to Peking's attempts to block the Republic of China from assuming its rightful role as a responsible, charitable and key member of the U.N. family of nations.

Yes, The 21 million Chinese on Taiwan are ready, willing and able to assume a role in the U.N., to do their share in building a better U.N. and more harmonious world. Their continued exclusion is no longer justified. Reality and reason, not rhetoric, should make the world go round.

So, isn't it time for the U.N. to give the Republic of China on Taiwan a chance to participate in the most august of world bodies?

The Republic of China on Taiwan. We're Ready.

TODAY'S TAIWAN

REPUBLIC OF CHINA

Taiwan's determination to join the UN changed from being a demand of a minority in 1991 to a powerful political movement in 1993. Courtesy of the Government Information Office, R.O.C.

Beijing vehemently opposed Taipei's new pliant approach. Although, in a few cases, the People's Republic had accepted the possibility of both entities participating in intergovernmental institutions, no comparable tractability materialized regarding recognition. In fact in 1988 Beijing called upon members of the United Nations Security Council to rebuff flexible diplomacy in order to squelch any trend toward acceptance of two Chinas.[20] But Beijing's ability to command respect from the international community and elicit actions that accorded with its will declined precipitously in 1989. The military suppression of the protesters at Tiananmen Square that June undermined the regime's integrity and prestige. It also helped to highlight the new order on Taiwan.

The demonstrations ironically had grown out of dissatisfaction with both the conservatism of the regime and the rapidity of the economic reforms. As in Nationalist China, the 1980s had been a decade of growing prosperity on the mainland, but, unlike in Taiwan, benefits had not been as equitably distributed between the cities and the countryside, between coastal areas and inland provinces, or between private entrepreneurs and government employees. The caution of officials anxious about abandoning socialism in favor of reliance upon market mechanisms, coupled with growing corruption and inflation, discredited the leadership. Neither workers nor peasants nor intellectuals were eager to give up guaranteed jobs and wages when the durability of independent farming and private enterprise had not been assured, and the government seemed unable to articulate a clear rationale for future policy.

Added to these complaints was disappointment with the rate of political restructuring, which lagged notably behind economic change. Those who gathered at Tiananmen Square wanted greater freedom of expression, fuller access to a responsive government, and eventually, perhaps, political pluralism, although most envisioned it within the existing national framework. They found encouragement in a divided party leadership and used the fortuitously timed visit of Soviet Party General Secretary Mikhail Gorbachev to dramatize their demands through the international media that had gathered in China to record the historic moment of Sino-Soviet rapprochement.

When, on the night of 3–4 June, the government lashed out, sending the army to murder its own citizens, TV cameras graphically showed the world the bankruptcy of China's political system and the panic of its elderly and out-of-touch leadership.[21] That these events occurred on the eve of the revolution against communism in Eastern Europe, and eventually the Soviet Union, magnified the futility and perversity of China's retreat. Beijing's attempt to blame Taiwan and the United States for contriving the Beijing Spring merely added to the absurdity of the government's position. In those hours, as China's leaders seemed to toss aside the mandate of heaven, they also sacrificed their hold on the American mind.

Taiwan in June 1989 presented a notable contrast with political chaos on the mainland. Resuming the political reforms of the previous decade, Chiang

Ching-kuo had utilized Taiwan's greater sense of optimism about political and economic viability in the mid-1980s to tackle a series of sensitive issues. In 1984 he invited Lee Teng-hui, a Taiwanese and a technocrat with a Ph.D. in agricultural economics from Cornell University, to serve as vice president and presumptive successor. He made clear that no member of the Chiang family would run for the presidency and that there would be no military dictatorship. Early in 1986 he created a task force to discuss and implement more liberal policies.

Seeing an opportunity inherent in the new atmosphere, a group of politicians, who had deserted or never joined the Kuomintang, decided to abandon their *dangwai* (those outside the only substantial party, the Kuomintang) status and establish the Democratic Progressive Party on 28 September 1986. The move reflected the growing political aspirations of an emerging middle class no longer satisfied to substitute economic for political control, anticipating elections in December and inspired by the people's power movement in the Philippines. Illegal under martial law, then still in effect, at Chiang Ching-kuo's behest the DPP survived, despite its advocacy of self-determination for Taiwan. Chiang recognized the enormous domestic costs of suppression and saw solid political benefits to be garnered from the Americans in exchange for liberalization. Choosing his audience carefully then, Chiang pointedly told *Washington Post* publisher Katherine Graham, that so long as the membership upheld the constitution, remained staunchly anticommunist, and did not demand independence, it would be tolerated.[22] On 14 July 1987 Chiang lifted martial law, which had been in effect for 38 years. He also directed the government to moderate currency controls, remove restraints on the content of newspaper coverage, and, as noted previously, accompanied all of this with a relaxation of the ban on travel to the mainland.

At the same time, the Kuomintang leadership proved unwilling to relinquish the old order entirely. The delay in lifting martial law resulted from Chiang's determination to have a new national security law in place before revoking the 1949 emergency decrees. No serious reorganization followed in the intelligence services or the military establishment. Arrests of independence advocates continued.[23] The U.S.-based human rights organization, Asia Watch, disparaged election practices that denied the DPP access to the media (the newspapers, radio, and TV all were owned by the government, the KMT, or intimate allies) and that threatened arrest for discussion of restricted topics.[24]

Nevertheless, Taiwan's rapid evolution toward democracy stunned observers long accustomed to diatribes about the need for caution and control during a civil war. A smooth transition to the rule of Lee Teng-hui occurred upon Chiang Ching-kuo's death in 1988 despite Madame Chiang Kai-shek's effort to prevent him from becoming head of the KMT as well as president.[25] Even rioting by DPP members in the Legislative Yuan did not produce repression, despite flying teacups and wastebaskets, which injured upwards of 100 members and led to the death of at least one aged representative from heart failure.[26] Similarly a student strike at the Chiang Kai-shek Memorial Park in central Taipei during March 1990, exploiting the poignant images of Tiananmen, elicited promises from President Lee for a politically diverse convention to explore further political reform rather than violent reprisals.[27] Convened in July, the National Affairs Conference allowed delegates to wrestle in an unprecedented public forum over fundamental political questions, including direct election of the president. Representatives mirrored the diverse views of the island's political community, including those of various groups opposing continued Kuomintang dominance. Among the overseas Chinese invited to attend were well-known scholars from prominent American universities, including Tien Hung-mao, Kao Ying-mao, Chiu Hungdah, and Chang Fu-mei.[28] Furthermore, in May 1991 Lee ended the formal state of war between the Nationalists and Communists on the mainland and abolished "temporary" constitutional provisions that had allowed the president and the military to exercise arbitrary powers.

Paralleling such presidentially mandated changes, the Council of Grand Justices ordered all members of the Legislative Yuan, the National Assembly, and the Control Yuan who were originally elected on the mainland in 1947 and 1948 to resign by the end of 1991 so that constitutional change could proceed.[29] For many, the action came none too soon. Delegates were known to have arrived for voting sessions by ambulance. One elderly "representative" reportedly came to cast an election ballot for Chiang Ching-kuo only to be told that Chiang had been dead for two years.[30]

To Bo Yang, writer and longtime political prisoner, Taiwan had become a joyful place. "China has 4,000, maybe 5,000, years of history, but it has never had an era like Taiwan today," Bo insisted. "There has never been a time when people were so wealthy or so free. Living conditions are so great! I'm just glad that my wife and I have lived to see this period. It's a golden age."[31]

THE ECONOMY

By 1992 Taiwan possessed $82 billion in foreign exchange reserves, the largest such holdings in the world. Per capita income had reached $10,000 a year, exceeding that in Greece and Spain. The unemployment rate was just 1.4 percent, and the economy was growing, even at a time of worldwide recession, at 7 percent per year. Despite its small population and diminutive land area, its economic development had made it the 13th-largest trading power in the world. Moreover, it projected for the 1990s a series of infrastructural building projects, costing some $300 billion, designed to fuel the dynamo of economic growth, despite ongoing political and military insecurity.[32] The city of Taipei symbolized the island's success with its high fashion elite and volume of traffic that made "New York City look like a bucolic retreat."[33] The sounds of construction equipment kept tourists awake in the highest-priced luxury hotels as the cluttered, dirty, winding lanes of the old city disappeared beneath the glass and steel office towers and superhighways of the modern metropolis.

With the end of diplomatic ties and formal defense commitments, the heart of the American relationship with Taiwan came to rest in economic affairs. The Reagan and Bush administrations cultivated commercial links with Taiwan and helped to stabilize the Nationalist Chinese position in international finance and trade. Nevertheless, the burgeoning prosperity of Taiwan aggravated a set of frictions that had been overlooked in the past for political reasons.

The United States' role in Taiwan's economy remained crucial through the 1980s and into the 1990s. It continued to be Taiwan's leading trade partner, while Taiwan ranked sixth for the United States. Efforts to diversify into Japanese, southeast Asian, Chinese, Korean, and European markets suffered a halting start, and although these new markets for Taiwan grew rapidly, Americans in the 1990s still maintained a larger share in many areas.[34] American business surpassed other foreign countries in the amount of capital invested in Taiwan (at roughly 40 percent), although Japan held first place for the number of actual investments. Some six hundred U.S. companies maintained offices in Taiwan, and almost 12,000 American business people were living in Taipei and Kaohsiung at the beginning of the 1990s. Twenty individual states ran trade offices, and 35 had sister-state agreements. During 1991, according to the head of the USA-ROC Economic Council, Taiwan surpassed Saudi Arabia as the leading foreign purchaser of Cadillacs.[35] As the value of the U.S. dollar fell in the mid-1980s, the Taiwan dollar also dropped, leading to an export boom with growth rates reaching as high as 24 percent in 1986. Taiwan's prosperity, then, remained linked to the strength of the US economy, so that times of American distress had significant ripple effects in Taiwan, whether for good or ill.

Taiwan's tremendous economic boom rendered its status as an economic pariah state progressively more insupportable. When, in 1983, the Reagan administration threatened the Asian Development Bank with reduced contributions should it expel Taiwan, the United States was still ahead of general world opinion.[36] By 1986 the ADB itself sought ways to keep Taiwan within the fold even after admission of the People's Republic whose leaders insisted that Taiwan could not remain in the organization as the Republic of China. Although the invitation to continue as "Taipei, China" was initially greeted in Taiwan as unacceptable, under American pressure the Nationalists thought better of their position and in 1988 attended a meeting in Manila at the same time as they continued to protest the new appellation.[37]

Similarly, in the latter part of the decade, serious discussion materialized regarding inclusion of Taiwan in the General Agreement on Tariffs and Trade. The Nationalist government had rashly resigned its founding membership in 1950 and assumed a less demanding observer status between 1965 and 1971. But, with its departure from the UN, it had also been ousted from GATT, and Beijing had subsequently been adamant about keeping Taiwan out. For American policymakers the certainty of friction with China should they advocate GATT entry was paralleled by the necessary loss of trade preferences from Taiwan if it joined.[38] Thus Washington assumed a low profile on the issue refusing to risk either political or commercial loss.

In 1990 Taipei applied for membership as "The Customs Territory of Taiwan, Penghu, Quemoy and Matsu," hoping thereby to evade the sovereignty issue. Taiwan saw GATT as a way to circumvent rising worldwide protectionism. Members of GATT welcomed the opportunity to compel relaxation of Taiwan trade barriers as a condition for adherence. The central dilemma for both Washington and GATT was whether Taiwan should be admitted before, at the same time, or after the PRC. In the case of the forum on Asia Pacific Economic Cooperation, that question was resolved by admitting the PRC, Hong Kong, and Taipei together in August 1991.

George Bush shifted the American stance on the GATT dilemma in July 1991, making the United States the first major power in GATT to call for Taiwan's entry. He changed his policy in order to win votes in Congress for continuing most-favored-nation treatment for Beijing. Caught in the struggle, which had become an annual event following Tiananmen, Bush traded a promise to Senator Max Baucus (D-MT) that he would "work actively" in behalf of Taipei's application if Baucus and friends agreed to unconditional renewal of China's trade standing. Ironically, Foreign Minister Frederick Chien made clear Taipei's objections to linkage with China when Taiwan so obviously deserved admission on its own merits, notwithstanding his government's appreciation for the result.[39]

Prosperity in Taiwan, although welcomed by Americans, made the indulgence of previous years over issues like the burgeoning trade deficit and intellectual property rights less acceptable. Taiwan, of course, was hardly alone in either its rapid growth or the barriers it maintained against American access. But, given Taipei's need to assure arms sales, along with a continuing desire for technological assistance, it proved willing to try to mollify American business and congressional interests. Areas of particular friction included cigarettes, alcohol, foodstuffs, steel, and machine tools, as well as counterfeiting, tariffs, and export performance requirements.

General protectionist sentiment grew in the United States as the economy showed signs of strain in the 1980s. As a result of Ronald Reagan's determination to provide the country with a defense establishment second to none at the same time as he cut taxes, the federal government amassed a huge national debt. Washington's enormous appetite for loan capital forced interest rates up substantially, attracting foreign investors eager to acquire interest-bearing assets, which in turn pushed up the value of the dollar. Thus, beginning in 1982, American goods became far less marketable abroad, and the U.S. trade deficit soared by as much as $170 billion a year, eventually provoking Congress to take action.

The ensuing struggle between free trade advocates and protectionists directly affected Taiwan. The Jenkins bill, thwarted by a presidential veto in 1986, would have imposed an import-quota freeze on nine Asian suppliers of textiles. Some 80,000 jobs and $1 billion worth of sales would have disappeared for Taiwan. The House proved more successful in passing the Trade Enhancement Act, which demanded that Taiwan, Japan, and West Germany reduce their trade surpluses with the United States by 10 percent per year over a period of four years.[40] Also in 1986, the U.S. Congress voted to withdraw Taiwan's eligibility for Generalized System of Preferences support, eliminating its duty-free status on a range of exports to the American market.

A broader measure, passed in 1988 as the Omnibus Trade and Competitiveness Act, created a system, through Section 301, of identifying countries maintaining consistent barriers to U.S. trade and providing procedures for retaliation. Although Taiwan came close to provoking 301 action with regard to failure to fulfill the terms of an agreement on tobacco, wine, and beer, it escaped designation during 1988, nevertheless remaining high on the list as a possible target. Thus in 1990, when the United States mounted an aggressive campaign to force developing nations to purchase U.S. tobacco products, Taiwan resistance was interpreted as more of the same, that is, obstruction to protect the local economy. Washington threatened trade sanctions, provoking indignant protests from Taipei that the issue was really protection of human health. Indeed, at hearings held by the U.S. Senate Labor and Human Resources Committee in May, witnesses painted evil portraits of American companies circumventing restrictions against cigarette advertising in Asia by placing inducements on children's notebooks, kites, and chewing gum wrappers. Taiwan responded with its own ad campaign in major American newspapers protesting the incongruity of the United States using such pressure tactics while also promoting democratic rights.[41]

American anxiety surged because of the rapid and seemingly uncontrollable escalation of the trade deficit with Taiwan. From a level of $2.3 billion in 1979, it rose almost eightfold to $19 billion in 1987. When calculated on a per capita basis, this far outran the U.S.-Japan imbalance. Taiwan launched "Buy American" missions in 1978, which yielded more than $10 billion in procurements by the end of the 1980s. It also targeted purchases of products from companies located in the home districts of important members of Congress.[42] But Taiwan continued to purchase too little from the United States. Americans complained that Taiwan's markets were not truly open to their products. In the agricultural sphere, for instance, Taipei resisted change, contending that for reasons of national security the island must not become dependent on food imports. Possibly more central was the opposition

DON'T LET FRIENDSHIP
GO UP IN SMOKE

A Look At The US-R.O.C. Trade Consulting Talk From Our Side

I love America. I've spent most of my life studying the US, from your democratic traditions and Washington and Jefferson, to your latest pop movies and culture.

But one thing bothers me. Why is the US so bent on pushing American cigarettes onto the Taiwan market? I know the facts. Cigarettes can harm the health of smokers and non-smokers alike.

It's not that we don't like American products. We buy your wheat, your beef, your cars more GM models than anywhere else in the world, in fact. And we're using American materials and technology extensively in places like our six-year development program.

So why does your government persist in trying to open the Taiwan market to American cigarettes? This kind of pressure goes against everything I've learned about democracy and the rights of people and governments. For my sake, and the sake of those around me, please believe us when we say that we don't want American cigarettes.

We want to be friends with you, but how can we 'shake on it' when there's a lit cigarette in your hand?

Advertisement. *Reproduced by permission; Originally in the John Tung Foundation, R.O.C.*

of domestic farm groups, who dramatized their anger in unprecedented demonstrations at the American Institute in Taiwan in 1988 when Washington demanded an increase in imports of turkey parts.[43]

Other areas also produced frictions. American banks, insurance, and construction companies were either severely circumscribed or completely excluded from Taiwan. In industries such as petrochemicals, the government blithely banned imports in 1982 to foster domestic production, and they flung open the doors when local demand could not be met. To curtail the influx of American pharmaceuticals, authorities refused to accept certifications of health and safety from the U.S. Food and Drug Administration.[42]

Taiwan's foreign exchange holdings aggravated tensions further. Mounting at $1 billion a month in the mid-1980s, the reserves symbolized to American officials Taiwan's greed, defiance, and deceit. The U.S. Treasury Department complained to no avail that Nationalist officials kept their currency inappropriately undervalued to boost exports. Instead of permitting the Taiwan dollar to float and be traded on international exchanges, the government tightly managed its value, maintaining reserves that far exceeded levels sequestered by most nations.[45] Huge untapped resources made Taiwan's resistance to trade liberalization more than usually vexatious. "They give the U.S. this song and dance about how poor little Taiwan can't afford more imports," fumed one analyst, "then it produces these monstrous foreign exchange reserves."[46]

In addition to the political liability of angering Americans, the reserves also had concrete economic drawbacks. According to Nationalist foreign exchange control laws, businesses had to sell their foreign earnings to the Central Bank for local currency, forcing the bank to print excessive quantities of Taiwan dollars to buy up the flood of U.S. currency earned by the island's flourishing foreign trade. The resulting glut of local currency (a supply that grew at 44 percent annually as compared with 14 percent in the U.S.) began to threaten (although not yield) rampant inflation, anathema in Taiwan where memories of the 1940s remained surprisingly fresh. Moreover, the government insisted on keeping reserve funds almost entirely in the form of U.S. dollars and securities (some 88 percent in 1986 and still at about 60 percent in 1991). Taiwan thereby played an important role in helping to fund the United States deficit and earned enormous sums in interest payments. But the practice also led to substantial losses during 1985 and 1986 when, under American pressure, the New Taiwan dollar was allowed to appreciate, cutting the value in Taiwan dollars of monies on deposit in American banks.[47]

The Nationalists and some American entrepreneurs and government officials asserted that the trade imbalance could not be ascribed solely to nefarious practices by Taiwan. Among the major reasons for its existence was the refusal of U.S. manufacturers to modify goods to make them appropriate for the market in Taiwan. American businessmen did not study the local culture to refine marketing strategies, making them less competitive with indigenous and Japanese suppliers. Even the commercial unit at AIT agreed that few companies sent representatives specifically to Taiwan. Many businessmen who did visit were en route to other countries and, therefore, neglected to do the requisite preparatory work to understand the Taiwan market. Expectations of what the consuming public could absorb were also unrealistic so that Americans demanded increased sales of products already being shipped rather than working to diversify American exports to the island. Officials from the Taiwan Council for Economic Planning and Development (CEPD) insisted in 1987 that, per capita, Taiwan purchased $200 worth of American goods per year, whereas Americans bought only $10 each from Taiwan.[48] Increasingly, items produced by joint ventures also drove the export figures upward, although Taiwan per se could hardly be blamed for that part of the U.S. deficit. The electronics industry, for instance, held the distinction of being both the leading sector for U.S. investment and Taiwan's most significant export industry. In 1987 Taiwan's single largest exporter was General Electric.[49]

Nevertheless, as the trade surplus rose and alarm in the United States escalated, reduction finally received enough attention to be successful. The government overcame its reluctance to tamper with policies that clearly produced vigorous growth and that were almost universally popular in Taiwan.[50] It had become apparent that, as Ding Mou-shih, head of the CCNAA in the United States, observed, "we have now come to the stage where our trade surplus hurts also ourselves and threatens the long term health and stability of our economy."[51] Comprehensive tariff reductions pushed average rates down from 27 to 5 percent. Revaluation of the Taiwan dollar by 48 percent led to an exchange rate of 28 to 1 with the U.S., making goods from Taiwan less desirable to the American consumer.[52] These initiatives, along with import promotion, decreased the trade gap by $9 billion in 1988. Making the best of a difficult situation, Frederick Chien, chairman in 1989 of the CEPD, maintained, "The more Taiwan is pressured from without, the quicker Taiwan will move within toward its long-term goals of economic liberalization and internationalization, as well as political self-reliance."[53]

Relaxation extended to the financial sector. The government eased controls allowing foreign banks to accept savings deposits and make larger loans. American companies were finally permitted to issue credit cards, and nine U.S. insurance companies entered the previously closed domestic market.[54] Beginning in 1990 foreign securities companies gained access to trading on the highly speculative Taiwan Stock Exchange, with American giants Merrill Lynch and Shearson Lehman Hutton leading the way.[55]

The Nationalist government also decided to redirect some productive resources away from export manufacturing and into the provision of public services, redressing its long-term tendency to shortchange internal development. As part of the package it allegedly gave American companies preferential treatment in bidding on 14 new infrastructure projects slated for completion between 1988 and 1999. Unfortunately, as with other generous gestures, the reality belied the pronouncement. In fact, the planning stage of the $27 billion venture had progressed to the point where most procurement contracts had already been signed, many with European and Japanese suppliers whose equipment better met Taiwan's needs.[56]

If the $27 billion plan proved to be a chimera for American business, Taiwan intended far more concrete results from the decision to energize its somnolent commercial aircraft construction industry with American assistance. Taiwan Aerospace Corporation, a joint private and government venture, contracted with McDonnell Douglas in 1991 to purchase as much as 40 percent of the American operation at a price of $2 billion. For Taiwan coproduction of a new jetliner meant technology transfer and creation of new construction capacity; for the financially troubled St. Louis company the deal promised solvency. Nevertheless, 29 members of the U.S. Senate appealed to President Bush to bail out McDonnell Douglas with domestic capital for national security reasons, and the United Auto Workers urged government loan guarantees rather than welcoming foreign ownership into the industry.[57] American alarm proved premature. After tendering its offer and securing government approval (the government held a 29 percent share in the company), Taiwan Aerospace evaluators concluded that McDonnell Douglas was in far more serious trouble than previously imagined. Instead of buying a portion of the company, Taiwan Aerospace offered to purchase 20 jumbo jets.[58]

Yet another illusory opportunity proved to be Taiwan's Six Year National Development Plan (1990–96), described by Martin Lasater, long-term proponent of Taiwan's interests, as providing "many opportunities for American businessmen. A sizeable percentage of the $303 billion plan to restructure Taiwan's economy is open to U.S. bids." Indeed, Taipei advertised the plan as a way to alleviate trade imbalances. But according to Americans in Taiwan, evaluating progress early in 1993, only $50 to $70 billion would actually be awarded in contracts to foreigners, and, out of that fraction of the budget, Japan had been consistently ahead of the U.S. in bids accepted. Thus it appeared unlikely "that the high-level visit of U.S. Trade Representative Carla Hills in December 1992 had significantly affected sales to the United States."[59]

In a reversal of policies that characterized the expansive development of the previous 20 years, Nationalist authorities began slowly to dismantle their painstakingly erected export promotion structure. They stopped creating export-processing zones. They began to eliminate the tax benefits that favored exporters over companies catering to the domestic market. And they rewrote regulations to charge exporters the same harbor duties that importers customarily paid.[60]

President Lee Teng-hui met with U.S. Trade Representative Carla Hills in 1992 on the first visit of a cabinet-level American official to Taiwan since diplomatic relations were broken in 1979. *Courtesy of the USA-ROC Economic Council*

Another new thrust in the 1980s was the investment of Taiwan money in the United States. No longer simply a good prospect for Americans seeking cheap labor, Taiwan industry, with capital to spare, began to buy and build around the United States. Whereas in 1985 Taiwan invested only $107 million in the U.S., by 1992 official U.S. government statistics put actual investment at $2.87 billion for the year.[61] Petrochemical industry giant Formosa Plastics, for instance, began purchasing small, financially troubled companies in 1981 and in 1990 launched the largest offshore investment to date for a Taiwan firm, by building its own $1.7 billion complex in Texas. Y. C. Wang explained that he intended the new investment as a repayment to Americans who had provided the seed capital that launched Formosa Plastics in 1954. On a somewhat more modest scale, in 1990 Taiwan's largest food company, President Enterprises, purchased the manufacturer of Girl Scout Cookies, Wyndham Baking Company, and added Famous Amos Chocolate Chip Cookies to its holdings in 1992.[62] This activity linked the United States and Taiwan yet more closely together, although it also aggravated some American anxieties about the selling of America to foreign buyers.

Taiwan's overseas investment, of course, ranged far beyond the United States. Among the most frequent destinations for surplus capital between

1987 and 1990 was Hong Kong, where Taiwan emerged as the dominant for-eign investor. This reflected the growing economic integration of the two entities, which, along with the PRC, would come to be called Greater China (see chapter 9).

Complaints about intellectual property rights violations had long compli-cated U.S.-China commercial and scholarly intercourse. Taiwan never signed the International Copyright Convention and did not effectively pros-ecute local entrepreneurs who boldly offered pirated editions of books, records, and computer software for sale at huge discounts, costing Americans as much as $750 million a year in copyright infringements. The U.S. movie industry alone lost as much as $30 million annually in pirated films. Computer software manufacturer Microsoft Corporation released its new MS-DOS 5 package with great fanfare in June 1991, featuring a carefully cre-ated hologram system designed to deter falsification. Within two weeks a Taiwan counterfeiter had production under way with a holographer in China. Raids during January 1992 uncovered fakes in five languages and contracts covering more than three million sales with a potential loss to Microsoft of $150 million. Although the Legislative Yuan had passed a strong copyright law in 1982 and a rigorous amendment in 1985 increasing coverage and fines, the problem obviously remained.[63]

American business objected as much to trademark and patent violations. Union Carbide's Eveready battery, for instance, encountered competitors in Latin American and the Middle East that had been distributed from Taiwan and were named Everlight and Evershine. Until 1983, U.S. companies could not even bring legal action against infringements. When Union Carbide finally did obtain a judgment in its favor, the highest fine assessed amounted to $267, although the loss for the American manufacturer had been $500,000.[64]

In 1986 the U.S. International Trade Commission estimated that as much as $6 billion of the goods entering the United States each year were counter-feit and that Taiwan manufacturers were among the worst offenders. In com-puter software alone, Taiwan held the distinction of distributing some 90 percent of fraudulent materials produced worldwide. In April 1992 the United States Trade Representative cited Taiwan under provisions of Section 301 of the 1988 Trade Act.[65] But efforts to eradicate the problems encountered firm resistance. From Taiwan's perspective the copying of goods and ideas seemed smart not outrageous. Not only was it compatible with tra-dition, acceptable in the Chinese art world, for instance, in ways alien to Westerners, but it also had the advantage of accelerating diffusion of the most modern technology.[66] Early in the development of Hsin-chu Science-Based Industrial Park, at a time when Taiwan eagerly courted American companies, the government nevertheless demanded so much proprietary information without adequate protection or the payment of fees that Texas Instruments withdrew its application to locate facilities there.[67] Taipei conceded only where absolutely necessary, refusing to compromise on issues such as the payment of royalties for the use of copyright materials.

By the late 1980s, discussion in global economic circles had turned to the creation of trading blocs, prompted in part by the advent of European economic unity scheduled for 1992. To Taiwan, this trend could be dangerous were its political pariah status to lead to its exclusion from an Asian bloc or were a pan-Asian group to take a stance adverse to the United States. Therefore, economists from Taiwan began to tout the formation of an Asian-Pacific Free Trade Area, encompassing Taiwan, the U.S., Japan, ASEAN (Indonesia, the Philippines, Thailand, Malaysia, Singapore, and Brunei), and the newly industrializing economies of South Korea and Hong Kong, as well as Australia and New Zealand.[68] Indeed, in the 1980s the Pacific basin had become the fastest-growing trading region in the world, highly self-sufficient in commodities, capital, and industrial output, suggesting the viability of such an economic coalition. As a first step, Nationalist officials urged that the U.S. and Taiwan initiate a bilateral free trade accord modeled on Washington's agreements with Israel and Canada. Although Taiwan would sustain a large financial loss in tariff revenues, possibly approaching $400 million, it relished the benefits of increased trade volume, closer economic and political interaction with the United States, and elimination of frictions produced by protectionism on each side.[69]

The United States reaction proved guarded. An administration frustrated by the difficulties of widening market access with Taiwan through conventional trade negotiations found it difficult to imagine how talks about dropping all trade barriers would progress. Other reservations included resistance from a protection-minded Congress, the possible political perils of discussing a free trade association given Taiwan's anomalous status, and likely opposition from Beijing.[70]

A variation on the trading bloc theme did begin to materialize toward the end of the 1980s: the concept of Greater China. With the increase in trade and investment between the People's Republic and Taiwan, most of which passed through Hong Kong, the interlinking of the three economies changed the dynamics of regional trade and industrialization. Taiwan, for instance, reduced its trade surplus with the United States by transferring low-end production to south China and sending goods to the U.S. under quotas for mainland China.

To some Americans, the prospects of using this reality to force responsiveness from Beijing on issues ranging from human rights to weapons sales looked suddenly brighter. In a quickly infamous column in the *New York Times*, Leslie Gelb suggested that the Bush administration sought to warn Beijing that continued defiance could lead to "the ultimate sanction—a threat to the territorial integrity of the Middle Kingdom." According to Gelb, Secretary of State James Baker had implied "that instead of China eventually absorbing Taiwan and Hong Kong, as now prescribed in various solemn agreements, the exact opposite could happen—Taiwan and Hong Kong could absorb the southern tier of China," given the uneven impact of market reforms on the mainland.[71]

The Greater China phenomenon, more realistically, embodies a range of advantages and disadvantages for the United States. Given the tremendous growth of Taiwan's economy during the 1980s and early 1990s, its integration into a larger Chinese network has the potential, along with the dynamism of Hong Kong and the vast labor force and resources of China, for sparking creation of an economic giant offering tremendous trade and investment possibilities for the United States. At the same time, such a conglomerate would be more independent of the American market than any of the components had been in the past. The market access problems encountered to date could pale in comparison to the hurdles posed by a Greater China.

THE MILITARY

In spite of the 17 August 1982 communique, the United States continued to sell large quantities of equipment to Taiwan throughout the 1980s and into the 1990s. This proved true even with the annual reductions made on paper in compliance with Washington's agreement. Depending upon how the totals were computed and what value items were given, the volume actually could be said to have increased between 1983 and 1988. A genuine annual decrease of $20 million would, in any case, still prolong sales for 40 more years.[72]

Taiwan could also take consolation from the sophisticated weaponry provided. American officials argued that they were simply replacing decrepit equipment already in Taiwan's inventory with the closest existing American version of the item. In this way, the U.S. transferred Sparrow homing air-to-air missiles, C-130 transport planes, and Chaparral ground-to-air missiles to Taiwan. At the same time, American technology contributed to the development of a surface-to-air missile closely akin to Raytheon Corporation's *Patriot*, which would gain notoriety in the 1991 Persian Gulf War, and an air-to-air missile with an uncanny resemblance to the American *Sidewinder*.[73] Taiwan's desire to design and produce its own fighter airplane prompted the Reagan administration to license General Dynamics, the Garrett Corporation, and General Electric to assist in necessary technological innovations. The first operational indigenous defense fighter (IDF), essentially a scaled-down version of the F-16, was completed in December 1988, although problems with prototypes delayed actual production to 1994. A similar case of technology transfer in 1987 gave the Nationalists blueprints and data for construction of sophisticated frigates to replace World War II vintage antisubmarine warships. Assistance in constructing tanks followed.[74]

Nationalist officials also found it possible to utilize weapons sales to the People's Republic as leverage. When in January 1986 the U.S. sold some

$500 million worth of radar and navigation equipment to Beijing to be used in upgrading 50 F-8 jet fighters by giving them all-weather capability, Taipei demanded compensation.[75] Of course, the pressure did not always work or sometimes took effect only gradually. China's 1991 purchase of Soviet fighter aircraft led Taiwan to try to reopen discussion of F-16 sales, an effort stymied in 1991 but, as noted below, ultimately successful.[76]

In other cases the U.S. took strong restraining action. According to analyst Harlan W. Jencks, the U.S. attempted, early in the 1990s, to derail production of an indigenous ballistic missile, developed, most probably, with Israeli assistance and based on the *Lance*, a U.S. battlefield weapon. Washington also denied Taiwan missile booster technology in October 1990, disrupting Taipei's efforts to create a satellite-launch capability. Apparently, even before the U.S. took formal action, Taiwan undercover agents had attempted secretly to purchase forbidden missile guidance components through a Massachusetts company, reflecting Taipei's frustration with American prohibitions.[77]

In 1984 and 1985, efforts to ingratiate themselves with the Reagan administration led the Nationalists to become players in the strange game subsequently known as the Iran-Contra affair. When the U.S. Congress cut off funds for Nicaragua's anti-Sandinista rebels, retired army major general and former CIA operative John K. Singlaub apparently suggested to Taiwan and South Korea that they participate in a scheme to purchase arms at inflated prices, the difference being skimmed off for illicit Contra arms purchases. On a trip to Asia during January 1985, utilizing his Korean War vintage connections, he solicited pledges from each government of $5 million. Taiwan, however, refused to contribute directly to the Contras, insisting upon working through the CIA station in Taipei. At that stage National Security Council aide Oliver North and NSC East Asian specialist Gaston Sigur became involved, setting up meetings in Washington with the head of the CCNAA mission and directing surreptitious contributions to Swiss bank accounts.[78] Taiwan clearly acted only to please the Reagan White House, having no interest in Nicaragua, although some quiet promises were made that a future Contra government would open diplomatic relations with the Nationalists. In the end, as Taipei had feared, the entire business became public, but the greater sensitivity of Iran's participation kept Taipei largely out of the limelight.

Another brush with notoriety came in 1988, when the United States insisted that Nationalist officials close down a nuclear reactor. Constructed by the Canadians in the 1970s, the research facility attracted suspicion, despite regular IAEA inspections, when charges were made that some of its spent fuel was being reprocessed to yield bomb-quality plutonium. The allegations came from the deputy director of Taiwan's Institute for Nuclear Energy Research, who defected to the United States reportedly with assistance of the CIA and carrying documentation with him.[79]

The end of the cold war made it more difficult for the Nationalist military establishment to justify the need for Taiwan as an important strategic outpost for the free world. Even after U.S. recognition of the People's Republic, Americans had confronted a communist threat in Asia from the Soviet Union. In fact in the 1980s the Soviet naval presence had significantly escalated. Thus in 1985, the director of the government-supported Institute of International Relations, Shaw Yu-ming, argued in *Foreign Affairs* that Taiwan's position astride the most direct route for Soviet warships to Cam Ranh Bay in Vietnam meant that it should still be seen as a crucially important "unsinkable aircraft carrier."[80] The collapse of the Soviet Union undermined this reasoning, robbing political geography of its saliency, and stripping Taiwan's demands for military support from the United States of one element of urgency.

But Taiwan, having endured years of humiliation to ensure survival, did not allow the mere disintegration of Soviet power to nullify its efforts to strengthen military guarantees from the United States. Utilizing the Taiwan Relations Act and the support of sympathizers in the White House and the military, Taipei once again turned potential adversity into disproportionate gain, a pattern with considerable precedent and with many perils for U.S. interests in the future.

The issue centered on Taipei's desire to obtain advanced fighter aircraft from the United States. By no means a new matter, the Nationalists had tried to acquire such planes from both the Carter and Reagan administrations, but had been denied on the grounds that such fighters would be provocative, possibly violate arms sales agreements with China, and even be seen as having offensive properties. Taipei, however, took note of the burgeoning arms market developing in the wake of the Iran-Iraq War and the collapse of communism in the Soviet Union and Eastern Europe and pinpointed weapons purchases by the PRC as a new and dire threat to the island's security.

The decision by President George Bush to counter the threat and to sell F-16s to Taiwan became public on 2 September 1992. China immediately denounced the U.S., but Chinese displeasure could not compare with the pressures that had been building on the president, including the need to maintain a power balance in the Taiwan Straits, Nationalist lobbying, French competition, and domestic politics. In fact, the Chinese had been instrumental in pushing the U.S. toward the policy change. Beijing had become alarmed at the U.S. success on the battlefield in the Persian Gulf War, which demonstrated the obsolescence, not just of Iraq's armaments but indirectly of China's military capabilities. Dismay at the emergence of the United States as a largely unrestrained and possibly rogue hegemon led China to increase military budgets and secure sophisticated weaponry, including fighter aircraft such as the Soviet built SU-27.[81] Fortuitously for

China, its interest in acquiring weaponry intersected with Moscow's urgent need to turn excess arms into cash.

Washington analysts could not know with certainty whether Beijing's purchases were designed to give China the ability to exert its claims more effectively in the Spratly Islands or Mongolia, to endow China with improved defensive and offensive force projection capabilities in case of worsening relations with the U.S. or Japan, or to intimidate Taiwan.[82] To Taipei the answer seemed clear. Nationalist officials set out to manipulate the administration through appeals to Washington but also through a proposed deal with France for its *Mirage* 2000-5 jet.[83] In the end, Taiwan's persistence paid off even if Taipei's needs were only part of the equation.

As had often been the case for the Nationalists in the past, extraneous developments facilitated realization of their designs. During the summer of 1992, George Bush's campaign to win re-election to the presidency began to stall. On 29 July General Dynamics, builder of the F-16, announced that it would have to lay off 5,800 workers in Texas because of poor sales. Governor Ann Richards and Senator Lloyd Bentsen immediately raised Taiwan's wish to buy 150 aircraft as the solution to saving jobs—a critical issue in the election contest. They were joined on 5 August by 200 congressmen who presented a petition to the president.[84] Given Bush's identification with Texas as his adopted home state, the issue became even more personal, and the possibility that he might forfeit 35 electoral college ballots left no alternative.

Apart from the military equipment Taiwan received as a result of these events, Taipei scored an important symbolic breakthrough. In Taiwan, the Democratic Progressive Party, among others, objected to transfer of older F-16s rather than the newest models, but to American arms manufacturers and prospective buyers in Taiwan, the decision suggested a new era in which virtually any weapon could be justified for sale. Nationalist officials also anticipated that the American deal would help expedite negotiations with other countries for additional weapons systems.[85]

POLITICS

The energizing of the opposition, leading to the creation of the Democratic Progressive Party, transformed the political dialogue in Taiwan during the 1980s. Although it remained possible to be arrested for political crimes, new areas of discourse became acceptable in the public arena. Most prominent, because the vast majority of participants in the *dangwai* movement and the DPP were Taiwanese, became the questions of democracy and self-determination.

Explicitly pro-independence organizations still could not safely operate in Taiwan but prospered in the United States.[86] Some, like the Taiwan Revolutionary Party established in 1984, favored urban guerrilla warfare against the Kuomintang.[87] Others abjured the letter bombs and violent protest demonstrations of their colleagues and sought ways to propagandize peacefully. The Formosan Association for Public Affairs (FAPA), established in 1982, worked assiduously to generate greater interest in Taiwan among members of the U.S. Congress. With the Taiwanese community in the United States approaching 500,000 these groups had the potential of raising significant sums to support candidates for election. The large community also helped support two pro-independence newspapers, the *Taiwan Tribune* (Long Island City, N.Y.) and the Los Angeles–based *Formosa Weekly*.

Many in the independence movement continued to demand help from the United States, which, in the view of Kang Ning-hsiang, a leading *dangwai* figure, "has interests and has a tremendous impact on Taiwan's fate" so that it would be irresponsible for Washington not to take "a constructive position."[88] When independence advocate Hsu Hsin-liang tried to return to Taiwan in 1986 in the wake of the founding of the DPP, he enlisted former Attorney General Ramsey Clark to accompany him.[89]

Opposition figures also visited the United States to impress upon American constituencies the importance of U.S. support. They lobbied with members of Congress, sought out the media, and tried to strengthen ties with Taiwanese-American communities. Emphasizing their struggle for political liberalization, they urged American backing not for independence, but for the right to decide the future of the island. The pro-independence Presbyterian Church of Taiwan sent their own activists to the United States to attend specially organized university seminars to advance training begun on the island. Their tenacity in advocating independence, moreover, took on an added significance given the fact that head of state Lee Teng-hui was a devout Presbyterian.[90]

Members of Congress were particularly prone to becoming involved in efforts to shape the development of political and economic affairs in Taiwan. Late in 1987, for instance, Congress voted an amendment to the State Department Authorization Bill to "encourage" movement toward democracy.[91] Senators Claiborne Pell (D-RI), chairman of the Senate Foreign Relations Committee, and Edward M. Kennedy (D-MA) joined with Representatives Stephen Solarz (D-NY), chairman of the East Asian subcommittee of the House Foreign Affairs Committee, and his ranking Republican counterpart, Representative Jim Leach (R-IA), to form a Committee for Democracy on Taiwan.[92] In 1989 Solarz published a survey of Taiwanese living in the United States that indicated that 89 percent advocated independence for the island.[92] Such efforts, although rooted in American idealism, threatened a degree of interference in the Kuomintang's affairs that "might be seen as a direct challenge to the party's efforts to remain the dominant political influence on the island," warned Washington analyst Robert Sutter. "It could set the stage for a serious confrontation in U.S.-Taiwan relations that might not be easily resolved."[94]

But Congress worried less about the ethics of interference in Taiwan's internal affairs than about enforcement of a broader human rights agenda. During 1982 it held hearings on martial law in Taiwan in the Subcommittee of Asian and Pacific Affairs of the House Foreign Affairs Committee. In 1983 Pell convinced the Senate Foreign Relations Committee to endorse self-determination for Taiwan. The following year, Asian subcommittee chairman Solarz shepherded through a vote on a nonbinding sense-of-the-Congress resolution, calling for the end of martial law and the release of all political prisoners.

Solarz and others were outraged when, late in 1984, gunmen killed Henry Liu in front of his California home. Liu, an American citizen and émigré from Taiwan, had served as an undercover agent collecting information separately for Taiwan's Military Intelligence Agency and the FBI. Liu's mistake apparently was to believe that his connections would make it safe to publish a critical biography of Chiang Ching-kuo. Admiral Wang Hsi-ling, who had become head of Military Intelligence after returning to Taipei from his stint in the embassy in Washington, was determined to silence the troublesome journalist. He secured approval from persons at the top of the KMT hierarchy, possibly including Chiang Ching-kuo's son, to contract with an infamous Taiwan gang, the United Bamboo, to assassinate Liu. After the murder, the KMT turned on its erstwhile allies and blamed the entire operation on the United Bamboo, a fabrication that collapsed, forcing an indictment of Wang, but no one higher up in the KMT. In Congress, Solarz and others, dismayed by the lack of administration action, convened hearing in February 1985 pointedly, recalling similar proceedings three years before regarding the death of Chen Wen-chen. The Reagan administration, however, refused to allow the Liu killing or the hearings to interfere with arms sales to Taiwan or secret efforts to secure Taipei's financial support for the Nicaraguan Contras. Congress did pass a nonbinding resolution calling for extradition of those implicated in the case, but Nationalist officials ignored it. In 1993, on a visit to Taiwan for the Congressional Research Service, analyst Robert Sutter discovered that the three security agents (Wang and associates) imprisoned for the Liu murder had not only been paroled but had received jailhouse promotions.[95]

Following the Liu case, and the more notorious discovery in November 1985 of Jonathan Pollard's spying for Israel in the U.S. Office of Naval Intelligence, allied espionage commanded increased vigilance from the U.S. government. In 1988 David Tsou, a translator for the FBI in Houston, became the first person ever formally charged with spying for Taiwan in the United States. He was convicted in 1991 and sentenced to 10 years in prison. The impact on broader U.S. policy toward Taiwan, however, remained minimal with the entire case attracting almost no press or public attention.[96]

Also largely unnoticed by the American public, a group of Chinese dissidents in the U.S. and Europe, some of whom had escaped from China after

Tiananmen, turned to Taiwan for support in 1990 as money and enthusiasm for their movement withered. A series of scandals involving misuse of funds undermined the credibility of the newly formed Front for Democratic China, which was meant to provide unity to the badly factionalized prodemocracy cause, leaving its leaders with little recourse in the United States. Hong Kong's willingness to provide financing had declined under pressure from Beijing.

But the Kuomintang found the opportunity to embarrass and harass the CCP irresistible. It invested $3 million in the Grand Alliance to Unite China under the Three People's Principles, essentially a disbursement agency to prodemocracy agitators in the United States. A New York correspondent for the Kuomintang organ *United Daily News* asserted, "It is now public knowledge that all major democracy groups receive most of their funds from Taiwan." Of course, claiming such influence with the Chinese dissidents did not mean that the KMT really could shape the movement's policies or that all dissidents would deal with Taipei. Moreover, there was an irony in KMT backing of student radicals given its own history of suppressing student protests. Finally, to the opposition movement in Taiwan, the uncritical praise that mainland dissidents heaped upon Chiang Ching-kuo and the Kuomintang for prosperity and democracy on the island sounded more like Chinese nationalism than compassion for fellow sufferers in the struggle against autocracy.[97]

The events of 1989 to 1991 heightened the strains as they sweetened the successes for Taiwan. The havoc at Tiananmen cast a glow on liberalization in Taiwan as it provided terrifying evidence of why reunification with the mainland must not occur soon. Nationalist Chinese leaders could congratulate themselves on their peaceful transition to an increasingly democratic system and talk about their future role in helping China to achieve economic and even political reform. But opposition assertions that separation would be safer than unification proved harder to refute. The creation of a series of new republics in the former Soviet Union and Yugoslavia with far less claim to viability, not surprisingly, made Taiwan's anomalous position less palatable than before.

As a result, in the December 1991 National Assembly elections radicals in the Democratic Progressive Party proved able to dictate a platform calling for a Republic of Taiwan, turning the campaign into an explicit referendum on independence.[98] "We are asking people to recognize and legalize the status quo," declared the party's chairman Hsu Hsin-liang. "We think that if we say nothing now [given developments in Eastern Europe and the Soviet Union], the world might believe that we accept what Beijing and the Kuomintang claim people here want: reunification with China."[99]

Although Taiwan's voters produced a landslide victory for the KMT, suggesting that independence did not stir their hearts, their actions might have reflected prudence more than lack of desire.[100] People's Republic of China

President Yang Shangkun's threat that "those who play with fire will be burned to ashes" might well have skewed the balloting.[101] Moreover, the public had reason to reward the KMT for economic success, while preferring to avoid deciding difficult political questions. They had also become disgusted with repeated scenes of DPP violence in the legislature as it struggled to be heard in KMT-dominated deliberations. But the chastening of DPP radicals and the reemergence of more moderate opposition voices could not alter the fact that new generations of Chinese on Taiwan felt less and less loyalty to the idea of a single China.[102] Even the idea of returning to see relatives in the PRC, let alone reunification with it, dismayed more than 60 percent of those whose visits exposed them to the poverty, backwardness, and corruption of the mainland.[103] Awareness of this trend troubled analysts in Beijing where dedication to the "one China" ideal had not diminished. Chinese there of whatever political leaning—liberal or hard-line—remained determined to hold on to Tibet and to recover Taiwan. China, therefore, often denounced Washington as a "backstage supporter for . . . splittism" because of its willingness to allow the Taiwan independence movement to operate openly in the United States. It also continued to warn of the possibility of using "non-peaceful means" were Taipei to declare independence, asserting that most foreign countries would remain neutral in such an eventuality.[104]

The results of the December 1992 Legislative Yuan elections gave the PRC and the KMT reason for heightened concern regarding the political future of Taiwan. Early in the year, the Nationalist premier threatened the DPP with dissolution if it continued to campaign on a platform advocating independence.[105] The DPP ignored these warnings, the government did nothing, and the results of the election produced substantial gains for the opposition. Voters gave the DPP 51 seats in the legislature and in excess of 31 percent of the ballots cast, while the KMT came in with some 53 percent of the vote and 96 seats. Although the KMT retained its lead, this amounted to a serious decline in power for the ruling party. The fact that many middle-of-the-road voters, particularly professionals, turned to the DPP to support its position on independence gave impetus to the increasingly voluble calls for permanent separation from the mainland.[106]

SOCIETY AND CULTURE

Taiwan in the 1980s and 1990s wrestled as before with the clash between its desire to be, and be seen as, the keeper of the "Chinese cultural flame" and the increasing prosperity and westernization of society, particularly its youth. The competing impulses governed both self-image and efforts to influence American policy toward and perceptions of Nationalist China. For despite the wealth that appeared to assure Taiwan's place in the world, Nationalist China remained vulnerable and uncertain about its future.

Attempting to influence American policy, as always, remained a top priority. Disappointment with Ronald Reagan's approach to China led in 1982 to the appointment of a younger and more vigorous chief of the CCNAA office in Washington. Frederick Chien, a Yale Ph.D. in political science and a specialist in American affairs, quickly gave the mission a higher profile in the U.S. capital with, according to some observers, "a level of political influence in Washington that many countries enjoying formal ties would envy."[107] Chien proved adept at reaching audiences beyond the ideologically committed, generating new ties with state and local government and business interests. During his tenure in Washington visits by senators to Taiwan increased 360 percent over the previous four years and those by members of the House rose 250 percent. By the mid-1980s CCNAA was distributing more than $750 million to paid lobbyists for liaison with the press and Congress as well as for trips to the island.

More concretely, the Nationalist government sought to emphasize its essential "Chineseness" in 1991 through creation of a $6 million Taiwan Chinese Information and Culture Center at Rockefeller Center in New York City. Convinced that exposing the American people to Chinese civilization via Taiwan would strength bilateral ties, Shaw Yu-ming, head of the Government Information Office, designed a facility to present performing arts, such as opera and acrobatics. For specialists he included a 30,000-volume library on Taiwan affairs. Daylong opening festivities included speeches by Taiwan and American officials with a surprise videotaped message by former President Ronald Reagan. Reflecting on the purpose of the Center, a staff member observed that "if visitors . . . come away thinking that Taiwan is China and China is Taiwan, then so much the better."[108]

Meanwhile, in Taiwan, American incursions could be easily identified. The arrival of McDonalds in 1984 launched a fast-food craze that brought many of the most popular American junk foods to the island. Not only did this have an impact on eating habits, but it provided direct exposure for high school and college students to American culture through part-time employment at the outlets. Taiwan's fascination with baseball shifted from promotion of the Little League to the establishment of professional teams in 1990. As in most big U.S. cities, young American musicians could be found panhandling on Taiwan's streets.[109] According to *New York Times* reporter Nicholas Kristof in January 1992, "the fascination with American culture—more than with Japanese, European, or Hong Kong culture—is apparent everywhere in Taiwan. There are two English-language daily newspapers in Taipei, more than in most American cities. American films are frequently shown on television and in movie theatres. . . . Language schools are everywhere, and enormous numbers of small children go to English-language classes in the evenings."[110]

Cross-cultural contact benefited from increasing travel and better communication across the Pacific. In 1990, 227,000 citizens of Taiwan secured five-year multiple-entry visas for visits to the United States. Efforts to nourish links with Taiwan citizens living in the U.S., as well as interested Americans, led to an agreement between the Broadcasting Corporation of China in Taipei with C-SPAN for nightly one-hour programming.[111]

Scholars fortified those connections with a host of study societies, conferences, and political associations. The Committee on Taiwan Studies, which had encountered lean times shortly after its creation in the 1970s, was resurrected in the early 1980s and began publishing a successful and informative *Taiwan Studies Newsletter* under the editorship of Jack Williams, a geographer at Michigan State University. The Center for Taiwan International Relations in Washington, D.C., dedicated itself to informing Congress, the media, and human rights groups about issues related to the question of self-determination for the Taiwanese. The North America Taiwanese Professors Association sponsored research and symposia on questions of democracy, trade, environment, and human rights. The American Political Science Association launched a Conference Group on Taiwan Studies in 1991 to promote Taiwan area studies and encourage social scientists to take up the study of Taiwan and engage in scholarly exchange and collaboration.

Taiwan joined this academic outreach, using some of its newfound wealth to win friends through scholarly philanthropy. In 1989 it launched the Chiang Ching-kuo Foundation to provide research funding, conference support, institutional enhancement, and subsidies for publications. The first Foundation offices covered North America, Taiwan, and Hong Kong but subsequently reached out to Europe (1990) and the Pacific (1992).

Other projects assisted universities more directly. Nationalist funding created the Sun Yat-sen professorship at Georgetown University in Washington, D.C., and gave faculty from National Cheng-chi University the opportunity to study at Georgetown. In 1989 the Institute of International Relations of Cheng-chi helped to establish the first comprehensive Taiwan studies program in the United States. Based at Columbia University with a grant of $880,000, the program offered an extensive curriculum covering history, economic development, social change, political reform, and foreign relations. Between 1988 and 1990 the Nationalist government donated some 1,600 volumes to the University of Illinois at Urbana-Champaign, facilitating the establishment there of a new department of East Asian languages and culture. A $1 million grant to UC-Berkeley from the Ministry of Education made possible fellowships and grants to promote the study of Asia. And, at California State University at Los Angeles, Taipei support was symbolized by a "Street of the Arts, Republic of China" in the new campus fine arts complex.[112]

Joint efforts between Nationalist agencies and American foundations also flourished in the decade. Beginning in 1982 scholars were funded by Academia Sinica's Committee on Scientific and Scholarly Cooperation with the U.S., the Luce Foundation, and the Inter-University Program to pursue language study and research simultaneously.[113]

Efforts to interject the views of Taiwan international relations specialists into discussions of changing global realities led in 1991 to the creation of the Vanguard Foundation. Its explicit mission of academic cooperation and exchange focused on such politically sympathetic American organizations as the Heritage Foundation, the American Enterprise Institute, and the Hoover Institution on War, Revolution and Peace. Taiwan also provided direct financial support to AEI and Heritage in return for their efforts to circulate the government's message regarding the importance of America's commitment to Nationalist China.

American philanthropic activities also continued through organizations like the Henry Luce Foundation. In 1986 and 1989 two grants, totalling $375,000, went to the Inter-University Program for Chinese Language Studies in Taipei. Luce also helped to make possible the Taiwan History Field Research Project through a $100,000 grant in 1986 to Academia Sinica for a multidisciplinary examination of Taiwan history through archaeology, land tenure, architecture, and archival resources. The Luce grant not only funded the inquiry but also helped overcome resistance on political grounds to a Taiwan-focused investigation.[114] The Foundation also made it possible for scholars with U.S. citizenship to participate in the project and to conduct other research in fields as diverse as medicine and the arts.

The Asia Foundation received a renewed mandate from Congress in 1984 and continued support of projects that advanced understanding of democracy and the free market. Along with distributing books and journals to some 115 organizations, Foundation funding brought legislators from Taiwan to Washington to study the government and brought human rights activists to work with American organizations. Paralleling exposure of Taiwan citizens to American society in 1987, the Asia Foundation sought to heighten awareness of local history by providing money for a 20-volume annotated index of the holdings of the Taiwan affairs branch of the National Central Library in Taipei.

Educational institutions in Taiwan by 1990 were training 10 times as many high school students as in 1952 and 40 times as many university students. Scientific education received particular attention from the government, so that by 1989 advanced programs graduated four times as many engineers per capita as in the United States. In other ways, however, observed Hsu Cho-yun, of the University of Pittsburgh and Academia Sinica, the "educational system . . . is virtually a Xerox copy of the American system" and "remains an intellectual dependent of the United States."[115]

Nevertheless, students from Taiwan continued to join foreigners flooding American campuses in pursuit of a U.S. degree. During the 1990–91 academic year, some 230,000 came from around the world, out of which 33,500 were from Taiwan. Through much of the 1980s more young people from Taiwan left to study in the United States than from any other single point of origin, surpassed only toward the end of the decade by the People's Republic and

Japan. Moreover, of those who went abroad for higher education in the 1980s, the vast majority attended schools in the United States. The impact on Taiwan of this exodus was, of course, mixed. Twelve out of 20 members of the central government's cabinet, including the president, Lee Teng-hui, and his premier, minister of finance, minister of education, and the director-general of the health department, held American degrees. The number of doctoral degrees proportionately exceeded the number in the U.S. Cabinet. Examined historically, the pattern would be similar, with 37 percent of the total number of cabinet members between 1952 and 1987 having been educated in the United States. The number of those educated in the U.S. holding positions elsewhere in the bureaucracy probably surpassed the representation in any other government in the world.[116] On the other hand, according to *Forbes*, as many as 50,000 engineers and scientists from Taiwan settled in the U.S. instead of taking their degrees home.[117] This meant a significant drain of talent as well as an enormous financial loss.

But the pattern of sending bright young people off to the United States for college and graduate education never to be seen again changed in the 1980s; Taiwan finally learned how to bring them home again. In sharp contrast to the sometimes bleak conditions and absence of opportunities confronting those who returned in earlier decades, promising futures awaited the new generation. "Some of the young tigers are attracted home by Taiwan's new political freedoms," asserted *Forbes* in April 1989, but "the biggest draw is the red meat of money. Newly formed, government-promoted venture capital funds are underwriting entrepreneurs, and on the rampaging Taiwan stock market technology shares sell at over 30 times earnings." The Hsin-chu Science-Based Industrial Park, whose genesis derived in part from the need to lure talent back to the island, supported some one hundred companies by the end of the decade, one-third of which were established by Taiwanese-Americans and almost another third by U.S. companies. Between 1988 and 1991 some 2,250 high-technology specialists left jobs in the United States to work at Hsin-chu. Another large group returned to fill short-term needs sometimes making the pilgrimage from the U.S. to Taiwan repeatedly. Not only had the new enterprises been tremendously successful, producing goods valued at $1.7 billion in 1988, but, inspired by the philosophy of the park, they devoted 6 percent of their sales proceeds to research and development, 5 percent above the national average.[118]

American-educated students from Taiwan, coupled with Asian Americans more generally, also had a significant impact in the United States. Between 1977 and 1987 Asian Americans consistently scored higher on the mathematical portions of the Scholastic Aptitude Test (SAT) than did whites. Although only two percent of the population in 1986, they took the top five scholarships in the national Westinghouse Science Talent Search, the "Nobel prize" for high school science. In 1987 the *New York Times* singled out the Kuo family from Taiwan whose three sons were

Westinghouse competitors in consecutive years, two of whom went on to Harvard while the third was still undecided between Harvard and Stanford. The boys had been sent to the U.S. alone in 1976 when the youngest was six to benefit from American schooling. The intelligence, maturity, and diligence they demonstrated characterized Asian-American youth in the American consciousness.[119]

The problems created by the model minority stereotype that Asians and Asian Americans faced drew national attention during the 1980s. Accomplishments, such as those of the Kuo brothers, led to resentment about too many Asian faces on American campuses. In 1983, students accused several prestigious universities of imposing Asian quotas. By 1985, national newspapers had discovered the story, and, finally, in 1988, President Reagan spoke out against arbitrary Asian ceilings in university and college admissions. The stereotype produced problems off campus too. As young David Kuo observed, it meant that immigrant children in Chinatown who did not do as well tended to be overlooked by social service agencies because of the myth that all were high achievers.[120]

Other Americans, born in Taiwan or descended from immigrants, attracted public notice in these years. Elaine Chao, who emigrated from Taiwan at age seven, became the highest-ranking Chinese American official in the U.S. government in 1991 when President George Bush appointed her head of the Peace Corps. She had previously occupied important posts as deputy secretary of transportation and chair of the Federal Maritime Commission.[121]

Chinese Americans also found it possible to play important roles in Taiwan. Both the Kuomintang and the Democratic Progressive Party recruited supporters in the United States. In some cases, this included persuading American university professors to run for office in Taiwan or take up government positions. This was in addition to the overseas Chinese from the United States who for decades "commuted" between North America and Taipei to serve as consultants on economic, political, and social projects.

The development of an environmental consciousness in Taiwan began late and with an inadvertent spur from the United States. Government officials had long devoted themselves to issues of economic growth and believed that environmental protection would undercut development. In 1985 the government invited DuPont Taiwan to locate a titanium dioxide plant at Lukang, on the west coast in the vicinity of several operating chemical plants. Regulatory laxity eliminated the need for an elaborate environmental impact study or public hearings. Authorization for construction was obtained in just 18 days. DuPont's $160 million plant promised to be the most sizable single foreign investment to date in Taiwan and DuPont's largest factory in East Asia. But in the wake of the horrific disaster at Bhopal, India, in December 1984, when an American chemical plant exploded, killing and maiming thousands, the local citizenry decided damage from existing plants was quite enough and unexpectedly forced the authorities to retreat. Although DuPont subsequently mounted a more effective public relations campaign for a new location, the environmental movement had scored an important victory.[122]

In 1986 Taiwan's enormous trade surplus with the United States gave further impetus to government concern about the environment. Under pressure at home, and with growing international discussion of issues such as acid rain, the government decided to mandate that industry spend roughly ten percent of fixed capital investment on pollution controls annually. According to the chairman of the Council for Economic Planning and Development, Chao Yao-tung, this would address environmental problems at the same time as it reduced industrial output, thereby curbing exports to the U.S. and increasing imports of pollution control equipment from the United States.[123] The following year, the government published its first comprehensive environmental plan.

The environmental movement, nevertheless, had a long way to go. Thirty years of pollution had had a severe impact on the island. In the mid-1980s a massive study, carried out by experts from Taiwan, the U.S., and Western Europe and funded largely by the Asia Foundation and the Rockefeller Brothers Fund, compiled data on the enormity of the problems and the extensive cleanup needed. *Taiwan 2000*'s catalogue of horrors included the minimal sewer system of Taipei, where only three percent of human excrement was being treated as of 1989, producing some of the highest rates of hepatitis infection in the world from contaminated drinking water.[124]

Cooperative projects on environmental and other scientific issues continued to characterize the period after 1982. Unsure whether different procedures were necessary after normalization, the Taiwan and American governments pushed ahead undaunted to negotiate their first "new-style" accord to encourage scientific and scholarly exchanges. This resulted in an understanding signed by CCNAA and AIT in September 1980. Agreements quickly multiplied, until more than 40 cooperative projects were underway in the atmospheric sciences, geology, chemistry, civil engineering, health care, pollution control, and hazardous waste management. Taipei also launched a 10-year effort to underwrite greater research and development activity in both official and private laboratories.[125]

ABMAC, whose support of health care had been a consistent feature of scientific support for the government in Taiwan, recovered somewhat from the difficult financial straits it had been in as a result of recession in the United States, bracketed by the Nixon and Carter decisions to improve relations with the mainland. In fact, Taiwan's prosperity, and the initiative demonstrated in the founding of the Chinese Medical Advancement Foundation in 1982, convinced the board that its headquarters ought to be relocated from New York to Taipei to work more closely with medical and business people there. Despite the move, leadership remained in American hands, and programs continued to emphasize fellowships, research, and a new visiting professorship.[126]

Under the auspices of Academia Sinica and its energetic president, the physicist Wu Ta-you, a massive biomedical and molecular biology research center developed in the mid-1980s. With generous government funding, Wu recruited research personnel in the United States and provided them with newly constructed facilities and the latest equipment. Similar although less well-endowed programs were undertaken by Academia Sinica to refurbish facilities for other institutes in hopes of luring scholars back from the United States.[127]

Another environmental issue, that of population control, made even more significant progress. By 1987 the birth rate had declined to 1.1 percent. With the help of the Asia Foundation the Population Studies Center at National Taiwan University capitalized on success by reaching out to related concerns. In 1985 they launched the first research program on women in Taiwan to deal with questions of fertility, health, economic development, and family.[128]

As part of Taiwan's thrust into the world community, it relaxed its concern about using the title Republic of China, which had caused so many problems in the past, and accepted designations in various contexts as "Chinese Taipei." By surrendering its insistence upon employing a name, an anthem, and a flag that would indicate national status, it stopped provoking the PRC. This made it possible to participate in international organizations and sporting events such as the 1984 Olympic Games and the Thirteenth Asian Baseball Championship Series in 1985.[129]

In the 1980s and early 1990s as American society began to be more aware of its multiculturalism, the image of Chinese in films became more diverse. Movies such as The Year of the Dragon (1985) and True Believer (1988), which continued to portray Chinatowns, populated largely by immigrants from Hong Kong and Taiwan, as the haunts of brutal, sinister, and cunning crime lords, were somewhat balanced by those with more benign Chinese. Dim Sum (1987) by director Wayne Wong explored the importance of family ties and dealt with the effort to preserve old cultural values in contemporary society. Other films didn't try to present realistic Chinese experiences in America but showed a less frightening mainland China such as Iron and Silk (1991). The popular 1985 movie A Great Wall portrayed the trials of a very Americanized Chinese family that found the effort to return to China, and the past, more difficult than they had imagined it could be. These films began to bring Asian and Asian-American faces and images into a medium in which they had been largely invisible. As one Asian critic commented, "Over the years, Asians have been the form onto which white writers have freely projected their fears and desires . . . it can happen only when the people whose images are appropriated are in no position to object."[130]

Few films that focused specifically on Taiwan or highlighted the contribution of Taiwan artists to creative cinema captured the American mind in the 1980s. The stunning exception was the work of Hou Hsiao-hsien, Taiwan's leading filmmaker. Beginning with A Summer at Grandpa's (1986), his films were shown regularly at festivals in the United States. Among these were the first two vivid and poignant parts of his semihistorical Taiwan trilogy, A City of Sadness (1989) and The Puppetmaster (1993). Complex and somewhat overwhelming for an unschooled American audience, A City of Sadness, which emphasizes Taiwan's helplessness as a colonial pawn "eaten by everyone," proved a box-office success in Taiwan because of its extraordinary candor about island politics.

During 1989 public broadcasting made a more prosaic effort to tell Americans about the island on television. In a four-part series entitled "Taiwan: The Other China" filmmakers tried to explain Taiwan's history and emergence as an economic giant. Similarly, the Smithsonian Institution offered a lecture series in its "Campus on the Mall" in 1991, highlighting culture, development, travel, and politics.[131]

The popularity of works by Chinese Americans authors again held promise for writers from Taiwan, but none managed to make a significant impression in the United States. Novels by Amy Tan, The Joy Luck Club (1989) and The Kitchen God's Wife (1991), and the sadly captivating Spring Moon (1981) by Bette Bao Lord became best-sellers during the 1980s. But the most widely read "novel" about Nationalist China proved to be Sterling Seagrave's The Soong Dynasty, which remained on the New York Times best-seller list for 14 weeks in 1985. As an exposé of corruption and political deception perpetrated by members of Nationalist China's most powerful family, its popularity in the U.S. infuriated the Kuomintang and its American sympathizers.[132] Understandably banned in Taiwan, the book would make its way onto the underground market and become a "must read" for members of the political opposition. American interest in the travails of the Soong family led, in the summer of 1992, to the production on the off-off-Broadway theater circuit in New York City of a play called The Soongs: By Dreams Betrayed. An unusual dramatic examination of Nationalist China's elite, it staged performances alternately in English and Mandarin Chinese.

Music proved to be a more successful medium for cultural exchange in the period from 1982 to 1992. In 1983, Taipei inaugurated a magnificent concert hall and invited the Cleveland Symphony Orchestra, Isaac Stern, Yo-Yo Ma, and Emanuel Ax to participate in the opening festivities. That same year, the U.S. National Symphony Orchestra with conductor Mstislav Rostropovich also visited the island. The entire New York City Opera Company led by its general director Beverly Sills performed to enthusiastic crowds in 1987. Members of the company spent their off-hours getting lessons in singing Peking opera. The repeated tours of the Atlanta Ballet proved so successful that the company's director, Robert Barnett, received an invitation from the minister of culture to teach classical dance in a 1991 summer workshop.[133] In 1987 the Taipei Municipal Chinese Classical Orchestra toured the United States with concerts held in nine cities. Making such events a more accessible and common feature of the arts world in New York City, the Taipei Theater opened in mid-town Manhattan, close to the theater district but amid the office towers of corporate headquarters and Rockefeller Center, where opera troupes and dance companies from Taiwan could be ensured public notice and regular audiences.[134]

American disc jockeys brought American music more directly to Taiwan's listening public. Some ten percent of Taiwan's population reportedly tuned in to International Community Radio of Taipei (ICRT) in 1992, making it possibly the number one station on the island and bringing it a long way from its beginning as U.S. armed forces radio in the 1950s. Ten of Taiwan's best-known DJs, including some island celebrities, were Americans broadcasting for ICRT.[135]

Taipei also took the opportunity presented by the U.S. commemoration of the 500th anniversary of the voyage of Christopher Columbus in 1992 to join in a National Gallery of Art exhibition "Circa 1492: Art in the Age of Exploration." This was the first loan of Taiwan art treasures since 1964 and became possible only because of a congressional resolution protecting the National Palace Museum pieces from seizure by the People's Republic.

So the era ended with yet another testament to the interconnection between culture and politics. As in years past, the Nationalist authorities recognized that sharing their traditions and the best of their art and artifacts would predispose Americans to view Taiwan with compassion and interest. Such perceptions could then be translated, with skillful management, into a sense of obligation to sustain Taiwan militarily and politically as well as culturally. In 1992, the effort to win the hearts and minds of Americans had become easier than at any time since the mid-1960s. Culturally, economically, and politically, the changes wrought over the previous decade, particularly when contrasted with disenchantment over developments in China, brought the U.S. and Taiwan closer, yielding an unexpectedly happy equilibrium.

• • •

Developments after 1982 made clear that Taiwan would not simply survive the break in formal relations with the United States but would move rapidly to further its economic miracle, to advance democratization, and to develop a more realistic international posture. The most significant trends of the era involved the movement to liberalize internal politics to allow competitive elections, a freer press, and even constitutional reform. Paralleling these developments, Taipei also softened its stand regarding contacts with the mainland, permitting travel, indirect trade and investment, as well as ending the state of war with the Communist rebels. To deal with its growing international isolation, Taipei relaxed its insistence on being accepted as the only true Chinese government and began to practice "flexible diplomacy." This meant that Taiwan would tolerate name changes to enter international organizations, would put renewed energy behind diverse contacts short of formal relations, and would even admit the possibility of dual recognition with the PRC (which denounced the idea).

Among the results of these policy changes proved to be the growing economic integration of Taiwan with Hong Kong and the PRC, producing a phenomenon known as Greater China. Not only did this bring profits, it helped Taiwan to make major adjustments in its trade deficit with the U.S. by moving some industrial production to China, alleviating frictions in its primary market. Other measures that improved economic relations with the U.S. included efforts by Taipei to revalue Taiwan's currency, increase access to Taiwan's markets, and adopt less aggressive sales strategies. At the same time, Taiwan began to reduce its dependency on the U.S. by diversifying its trade profile, although it also used business dealings with Europe and Japan to manipulate Washington into allowing cabinet-level American officials to travel to Taiwan.

In spite of the growth of an economic Greater China, the era brought renewed military strains to the relationship between Taiwan and the PRC. The end of the cold war and the collapse of Soviet and European communism produced a new and copiously stocked world arms market. Beijing's efforts to improve its substandard military capabilities produced alarm in Taiwan, leading to renewed efforts to acquire high-technology weapons from the United States. As had been the case so often in the past, Taiwan proved astute in using external developments to advance its own agenda. Capitalizing on George Bush's campaign troubles, Taipei convinced the administration to sell F-16 advanced fighter aircraft to Taiwan. Whether or not the sale actually violated the August Communique prohibitions against increasing the quality of arms given to Taiwan or comprised transfer of an offensive weapon, the F-16 sale had enormous symbolic importance. It altered the dynamic within the U.S.-Taiwan-PRC triangle, reemphasizing the decline in relations between Washington and Beijing following the Tiananmen Massacre and asserting a new degree of cooperation between Washington and Taipei.

Finally, in the 1990s, an old theme received renewed attention. The independence movement began to wield a degree of political power not previously imaginable. Rising in importance with the flourishing of the Democratic Progressive Party, the idea of independence appealed to an increasing number on the island as the grip of the KMT weakened and the generations changed. The United States viewed this new development with a measure of anxiety lest the PRC be provoked to attack the island and the U.S. be called upon to intervene. For Washington the conflict between the principle of self-determination for the people of Taiwan and respect for China's national sovereignty presaged a discomforting dilemma.

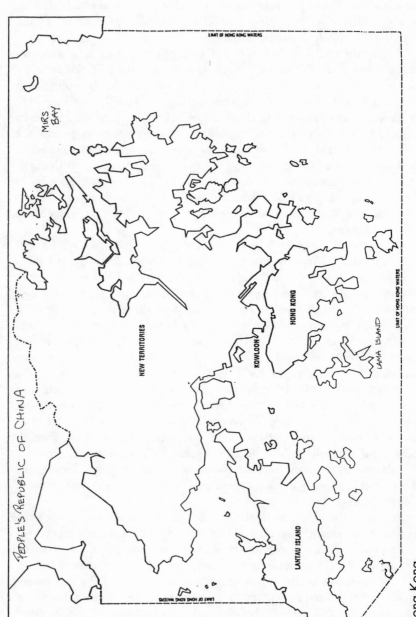

Hong Kong

chapter 9

HONG KONG: IN CHINA'S SHADOW

EARLY HONG KONG TO 1950

Hong Kong has lived on borrowed time since the British wrested it from Chinese hands in 1841 and confirmed possession of it in an unequal treaty ending the Opium War the following year. Although Hong Kong island and later (1860) the Kowloon peninsula were relinquished by China in perpetuity, the adjacent New Territories (92 percent of its land area) joined the colony in 1898, during the imperialist era scramble for concessions, on a 99-year lease.[1] London thus acquired a trading post and military encampment, encompassing possibly the best harbor in the world, strategically placed along the China coast, a little larger than New York City, with no natural resources and almost completely dependent on the outside world for food and water.

Cession of the land engendered resentment, of course, not just because of the challenge to national sovereignty, although that was important, but also because of the economic magnet that Hong Kong quickly became. A short-sighted British foreign secretary, Lord Palmerston, had been so angered by the acquisition of a barren rock rather than a fertile island that he relieved Charles Elliot of his post as London's representative, sending him to be chargé d'affaires in Texas. But, it soon became apparent that trade, which traditionally passed through nearby Guangzhou (Canton), gravitated to Hong Kong instead. Hong Kong prospered. Chinese nationalists came to see it as a major obstacle to the development of south China. In time, political dissidents, including Sun Yat-sen, would use it as a base of operations, seeking refuge there under British protection (although eventually British authorities banned Sun). Indeed, Chinese of all sorts emigrated to take advantage of the government's laissez-faire attitude and to enjoy the security provided by the British navy.[2]

Americans also saw benefits in the British presence at Hong Kong. The United States became the first foreign government to open a consulate in the colony in 1843, and Americans built the first church there. Although excluded from the economic and military advantages of the colonial relationship, Americans participated in commercial exchanges with China pioneered by the British including the opium trade and the lively exchange of tea and cotton. American firms, such as Augustine Heard and Russell & Company, headquartered their trade in Hong Kong where they could count on British protection from the instability besetting treaty ports such as Shanghai and Canton. Franklin D. Roosevelt's maternal grandfather, Warren Delano, was a partner in Boston's Russell & Company, which became one of the great trading firms in Asia. Roosevelt, as president, would insist that he felt a sentimental attachment to the Chinese because of this family exposure.

Hong Kong, although cocooned in the British Empire, was buffeted from these early days by United States economic influences. The 1849 gold rush in California produced a business boom in Hong Kong drawing laborers and supplies. Chinese also shipped out to work on railway construction in the American west from the port of Hong Kong. The great Hong Kong and Shanghai Bank, established in 1865, included Americans on its founding committee and became one of the first overseas banks to open offices in the United States, with a branch in San Francisco in 1875 and one in New York in 1880. In 1902 American banks formally joined the British financiers in the colony with the arrival of the Guaranty Trust Company and the International Bank of America. American speculation in 1905 about creating a new anchorage at Guangzhou and linking it by rail to Hankow forced the British to accede to Chinese desires, long ignored, to build a rail line from Guangzhou to Kowloon lest Hong Kong be replaced as an entrepôt.[3]

On occasion Hong Kong provided Americans with military advantages in the area without the responsibilities of colonial control. Commodore Matthew Perry wintered in Hong Kong in 1853–54 while waiting to force the Japanese to accept a treaty with Washington that would open their country to American contacts. In 1898, during the Spanish-American War, the U.S. Navy used Mirs Bay, just to the north, as a staging area for its attack on the Spanish fleet in Manila Bay. At the same time, the presence of the American Asiatic Fleet gave impetus to British fears regarding Hong Kong's security and their subsequent demands during the scramble for concessions for additional territory to shield the colony.

After war developed between China and Japan in 1937, Hong Kong authorities had increasingly to plan for the defense of the colony should the conflict travel down the China coast. In April 1941 American, British, Dutch, and Australian officials assembled at Singapore to determine what action to take in case of Japanese attack. Their ABDA Agreement provided for Hong Kong to become a major naval operating base, but neither American nor British military authorities regarded Hong Kong as sufficiently secure. And, in fact, when the Japanese arrived, the colony fell in just three weeks.[4]

During the Second World War, Americans played an important role in keeping Hong Kong a part of the anti-Japanese effort as long as possible. The China National Aviation Corporation (CNAC), 45 percent of which was owned by Pan American Airways after 1933 and which was piloted by Americans, kept routes between Chungking and Hong Kong open despite Japanese attacks on the unarmed civilian aircraft. When, on 8 December 1941 Japan besieged Hong Kong, CNAC flew a series of evacuation missions rescuing valuable officials and supplies.[5] The intelligence network that stayed behind under Japanese rule provided information throughout the rest of the war for the China-based U.S. 14th Air Force and the advancing Pacific assault units to help in selecting targets.

American enjoyment of the advantages of British colonialism did not deter disapproval of continued British imperial control of the territory. Convinced that the day of great empires must end, the United States government in the 1930s pushed London to relinquish its hold over various possessions including Hong Kong. During World War II Washington joined the Nationalist Chinese in their insistence upon retrocession once the Japanese had been defeated. In March 1943 Franklin Roosevelt assured Madame Chiang Kai-shek that Hong Kong, Manchuria, Taiwan, and the Ryukyu Islands all would be restored to China undoing the imperialistic gains of the past. In the case of Hong Kong, Roosevelt voiced his expectation that when the Chinese recovered it they would immediately turn it into a free port, a point he also made to the British in case they retained control.[6] Anthony Eden, the British foreign secretary, appalled at the idea of the "Chinese running up and down the Pacific," noted that Roosevelt did not appear to be making any similar goodwill gestures.[7] Chiang Kai-shek responded more positively, referring Roosevelt's proposal to his Supreme National Defense Council for consideration. He subsequently assured the president that China would follow his suggestion but as a voluntary act after rendition.[8]

At Yalta Roosevelt broached the subject with Joseph Stalin, who remarked that Prime Minister Winston Churchill "would kill us" for proposing it. Roosevelt brushed aside Stalin's concerns, responding that the British were "peculiar people" who "wished to have their cake and eat it too."[9] In fact Churchill insisted that "nothing would be taken away from England without a war" and specifically referred to Hong Kong.[10] So, when the conflict abruptly ended in August 1945, the British marched in to liberate their colony after all, and Chiang Kai-shek, committed to civil war against the Communists, found himself unable to act.

Pressure from the United States on Whitehall to cede Hong Kong, however, dissipated as it became apparent that the Communists would soon rule China. As late as 1947, the American ambassador to China, J. Leighton Stuart, still could suggest Britain take the initiative "by graciously and generously" returning the entire area to the Chinese.[11] But, as Nationalist political fortunes changed, not only did Americans oppose the idea of surrendering people and land to communism, but the colony assumed a new importance in the eyes of U.S. government personnel. By 1949 American intelligence operatives had established a listening post in Hong Kong, the first of many such espionage efforts in which the colony was used as a base.[12]

Concern about the possibility that the Communists would attack and overwhelm the enclave in the closing days of the Chinese civil war activated both the British and the Americans. As London reinforced the garrison in the colony, the U.S. Army placed a liaison officer in British defense headquarters, the first such peacetime appointment by Britain.[13] Although Secretary of State Dean Acheson refused to make an explicit pledge regarding military operations, he reminded reporters that any assault on Hong Kong would be a matter for the United Nations Security Council to deal with and that the United States would support Council decisions.[14]

1950 TO 1972

When the Korean War erupted a year later, the United States saw Hong Kong as an even more crucial pawn in the anticommunist struggle. The Chinese Communists had not tried to take the colony away from Great Britain during or after their victory in the civil war against the Kuomintang. Whether or not this initially followed from an aversion to confronting British troops and risking war with London, an even better reason arose soon thereafter. Hong Kong rapidly became a crucial entrepôt for Chinese trade with the noncommunist world bringing in needed goods and foreign exchange. Chinese entry into the Korean War, however, triggered a United States embargo on all trade with China followed by a United Nations ban on export of strategic commodities to China.[15] Convinced that Hong Kong's proximity to China made leakage inevitable, the U.S. applied strict licensing procedures to all American sales to Hong Kong. Washington also made sure that Hong Kong, however reluctantly, complied with UN prohibitions. Beijing retaliated by reducing purchases of whatever remained to Hong Kong to sell. Although the embargoes proved not to be impenetrable, the colony soon faced economic catastrophe as 50 percent of exports and 25 percent of imports that normally passed through Hong Kong disappeared.[16]

In severely straitened economic circumstances, and overwhelmed by masses of refugees from China, Hong Kong appeared exceptionally vulnerable to military assault. But, although the defense of Hong Kong seemed from the British perspective the most crucial of issues, it clearly ranked as one of the most difficult. British and American military figures acknowledged the impossibility of protecting Hong Kong against a determined Chinese effort to conquer the colony.[17] They also agreed that surrender must be avoided and that, therefore, the Communists should be deterred by rendering an attempt too costly.

To do this, the Americans proved willing repeatedly in 1950 and thereafter to make public their support for the British position, emphasizing the significance of Hong Kong for the prosperity and security of the region. In June 1951 Acheson told the Senate that "to have Hong Kong fall . . . into the hands of the Chinese Communists, would I think, have a very adverse influence on the United Nations interests and on ours in the Far East."[18] Truman's declaration in June 1950 that the U.S. Seventh Fleet would patrol the Taiwan Straits gave American assertions greater substance even though initially there were not enough ships to provide for a regular presence. The policy, nevertheless, testified to Washington's acceptance of the potential need to use force in the area.

Admiral Radford, serving as commander-in-chief of Pacific forces, believed the United States could go further. He dismissed assessments that considered Hong Kong indefensible and argued that with naval and air power the colony could be saved. He also raised, with Assistant Secretary of State for Far Eastern Affairs John M. Allison, an offer from Chiang Kai-shek to provide troops for Hong Kong in time of crisis, troops that Chiang would be willing to withdraw rather than use to wrest the territory from Great Britain.[19]

London took greater comfort from the conclusion that the Chinese would not try to recover Hong Kong. British intelligence asserted that Beijing would not attack given the "probability of precipitating a world war."[20] China also had too much to gain economically from trade with and through the colony.

Nevertheless, the British sought firm commitments from the United States to provide military assistance, which did not come, and suggested joint planning on numerous occasions, which did. In National Security Council series 73 on "The Position and Actions of the United States with Respect to Possible Further Soviet Moves in the Light of the Korean Situation," agreed upon during the summer of 1950, the United States set out the policy on Hong Kong that it would follow consistently, that is, a pledge to give military assistance in accord with "commitments and capabilities" at the time.[21] Prime Minister Winston Churchill and Foreign Secretary Anthony Eden still continued to press for more explicit guarantees.[22] John Foster Dulles tried to placate London in 1953, assuring the British of American willingness to help, but guarding against absolute guarantees.[23] Hong Kong's governor, Sir Alexander Grantham, nonetheless, told Americans on a 1954 visit to the United States that he anticipated U.S. air support were an attack to come.[24]

Precisely how promises were made or heard proved a point of contention. Did the Americans mislead London into believing that U.S. forces would defend Hong Kong or were guarantees offered at the highest levels and not communicated to diplomatic personnel conducting day-to-day exchanges? Alternatively, did the British make assumptions about Washington that allowed them simply to hear what would give them confidence? Or, perhaps, British officials thought they could manipulate Americans, whose diplomatic skills they often disparaged, into doing more than they intended. In January 1956, for instance, the Colonial Secretary Lennox-Boyd declared that the United States would come to Britain's aid in Hong Kong automatically as dictated by a secret accord. When U.S. embassy personnel expressed dismay to the Foreign Office, insisting that no such pledge existed, British officials alluded to some unspecified understanding reached in negotiations prelimi-nary to the establishment of SEATO (Southeast Atlantic Treaty Organization) in 1954. The Americans, convinced that no such commit-ment had been made, seemed unable to restrain their British counterparts.[25]

In fact, correspondence between Dwight Eisenhower and Winston Churchill may have embodied such a pledge. On 4 April 1954, Eisenhower, attempting to persuade Churchill to agree to a United Action collective security arrangement potentially including Australia, New Zealand, Thailand, and the Philippines to bolster the French position in Indochina, wrote, "The coalition we have in mind would not be directed against Communist China. But if, contrary to our belief, our efforts to save Indochina and the British Commonwealth position to the south should in any way increase the jeopardy to Hong Kong, we would expect to be with you." The president extended similar assurances in 1955, during the Quemoy-Matsu crisis, when Churchill expressed concern about U.S. involvement. Eisenhower noted that, as Washington needed support in this instance, London could require U.S. aid in the future: "It would surely not be popular in this country if we became involved in possible hostilities on account of Hong Kong or Malaya, which our people look upon as 'colonies'—which to us is a naughty word. Nevertheless, I do not doubt that, if the issue were ever framed in this way, we would be at your side."[26]

The United States and Great Britain did conduct exchanges of military information in Hong Kong. Initially stymied by an uncooperative British commander-in-chief, consultations became more frequent and fruitful with his replacement in late 1951.[27] Among the issues discussed appeared to have been a possible future role for Hong Kong in splitting south China from Beijing.[28] The British also pressured the United States to abandon aggressive thoughts of blockading the Chinese coast during the Korean conflict lest it provoke retaliation against Hong Kong. Dulles would not, however, include Hong Kong in the SEATO defense community.

United States economic pressure on the People's Republic in practice jeopardized the survival of Hong Kong far more than military threats. Robert

W. Barnett of the Office of Chinese Affairs admitted that the Commerce and Treasury Departments had treated Hong Kong as though it were a Communist Chinese port after trade and financial controls were imposed in December 1950: "the technicality of British sovereignty was brushed aside." Sharp protests followed. Hong Kong newspapers declared the practice "nothing short of calamitous." One of the two major American banks in the colony, Chase National Bank, announced it would close its branch office because of the "almost complete cessation of business."[29] The director of commerce and industry at Hong Kong, A. G. Clarke, rushed to Washington early in 1951 to argue that internal security would be undermined by the massive unemployment caused by the arbitrary and unwarranted restrictions.[30] London's accompanying aide-mémoire on 1 February, urging Washington to exempt Hong Kong from controls covering ordinary commodities, proposed that nonstrategic goods be automatically licensed at a level of 75 percent of sales in 1949. The Hong Kong government would, in turn, pledge not to export such goods to China or sell to China manufactured items primarily composed of raw materials from the United States.

State Department officials took the initiative in arguing that Washington ought to accept London's appeal because of the overriding need to protect Hong Kong. The Departments of Defense and Commerce, on the other hand, rejected it, with Defense insisting that the British had exaggerated both Hong Kong's predicament and the importance of retaining the territory.[31] Moreover, the Defense Department worried about strategic commodities that seemed to be finding their way to China in spite of U.S. and UN measures. Those concerns became public when General Douglas MacArthur testified to the Senate that Hong Kong had been shipping petroleum to the People's Republic. Congress launched an investigation with which the Hong Kong government provided grudging cooperation, amid protests that MacArthur's charges were entirely unfounded.[32] The immediate impact in the United States was to derail the State Department's efforts to eliminate barriers to trade for the colony.

American businessmen, as a result, continued to suffer often debilitating and sometimes ludicrous interference in their Hong Kong operations. Importers of dried ducks ran into trouble because their eggs originated in China, making the ducks communist. After much discussion, inspectors agreed that if they were present at the hatching and could brand the ducklings then the mature birds could be used.[33] A similarly absurd instance transpired in the summer of 1951 through the excessive vigilance of the Office of International Trade. Colonial Trading Company applied for a license to supply 10,033 phonograph records to Hong Kong but received permission for only 1,033 to be sent. Washington maintained that demand in the colony could not justify such a large order and that the remainder might end up in China. Colonial Trading insisted that Hong Kong businesses wanted 10,000 copies of Patti Page singing the "Tennessee Waltz," that the

CCP considered Patti Page subversive, and that it would be hard to imagine Beijing having any special use for the records. Consul General Walter McConaughy added that it would be a positive thing to have popular American music available in Hong Kong. His views did not immediately win over Washington, however, since in December he was still insisting that Hong Kong could absorb some 5,000 records per month.[34]

Finally, with the damage to Hong Kong increasingly obvious, Commerce Department officials reopened debate at the National Security Council. NSC 122 approved in January 1952 reduced the burden on Hong Kong without vitiating the effect of the restrictions upon China. Ignoring further attacks on Hong Kong by Senator Joseph McCarthy, the United States government agreed to tolerate liberalized controls. The colony could henceforth sell goods certified as not having used communist ingredients and buy commodities on condition that they would not reach communist markets.[35]

Far more important proved to be the decision to utilize Hong Kong's one plentiful resource—its cheap labor. This the colony accomplished by undertaking industrialization in order to have something to export besides prohib-

View from Victoria Peak toward Kowloon, July 1953. *Courtesy of the U.S. Navy and the National Archives*

ited goods from China. Handicapped by a lack of raw materials and energy, Hong Kong compensated with stability, low taxes, little regulation, abundant labor, and investment capital. Whereas in 1950 only 25 percent of Hong Kong's exports originated there, in 1962 some 70 percent had been manufactured locally.[36]

The development of industry in Hong Kong quickly induced protectionist responses from most of the colony's trading partners, even those within the British Empire. The United States government initially held the line, deflecting suggestions that tariffs should be raised against woolen gloves and watchbands from Hong Kong. But, building on the skills of engineers and workers who had fled Shanghai, Hong Kong's main focus became a textile industry that soon employed 46 percent of the colony's industrial workers. By early 1959, the United States had displaced the United Kingdom as the principal purchaser of textiles, putting Hong Kong in direct competition with domestic American manufacturers.

Colonial authorities, increasingly aware of pressures in Washington to curb imports, sought to persuade London of the merits of establishing a representative group in the U.S. to speak about the benefits of Hong Kong trade and parry criticism. In the autumn of 1959, they hired a leading Washington law firm, Covington and Burling, to study the problem and recommend action. London found itself facing conflicting factions in the Hong Kong business community, however, and hesitated between using members of the colonial elite (whose Chamber of Commerce operated on racial principles) or assisting rising Chinese entrepreneurs.[37] In the end, London postponed any action, deciding instead to increase the informational role of the British Embassy in the United States. To American policymakers, however, neither British nor Hong Kong officials appeared to be doing enough. At a June 1960 National Security Council meeting, Acting Secretary of State Douglas Dillon observed that though the colony had curbed its textile exports to Britain, it had been unwilling to take similar action with regard to the United States. That this could become a campaign issue worried the administration sufficiently to produce an approach to Hong Kong to impose more reasonable limits on textile sales.[38]

Notwithstanding domestic political concerns, less than a year later the new Kennedy National Security Council formally resolved to encourage Hong Kong's industrialization. The NSC, in March 1961, further directed government agencies to promote American business involvement. Recognizing the potential for trade frictions, however, the Council suggested that Hong Kong's manufacturers be stimulated to diversify production into areas less immediately competitive with domestic U.S. industry,[39] and consideration began in the government regarding curbs on fabric imports.

Hong Kong interests found the U.S. position untenable. Having sacrificed their entrepôt trade at American insistence, they objected vehemently to U.S. efforts to curtail indigenous exports. They pointed to the small percentage of American production Hong Kong had displaced and urged Americans to calculate U.S. cotton exports to the colony against textile imports. P. Y. Tang, a respected industrialist and MIT graduate, met with Walt Rostow in November 1961 to impress upon him that Hong Kong as the "West Berlin of the Far East" must not be undermined by the U.S. government.[40] American restrictions meant recession and frustrated efforts to employ the large numbers of refugees flocking to squatters' camps from China.[41] Nevertheless John F. Kennedy, having capitulated during the presidential campaign and pledged to impose curbs if elected,[42] forced Hong Kong to accept the first of many negotiated controls in 1961, at the same time as its growing trade volume made it the third-largest trade partner for the U.S. in Asia after Japan and the Philippines.

Making worse the frictions engendered by economic competition, Americans dismayed the British authorities by continuing to seek out and support anticommunist elements in the colony willing to contemplate subversive activities on the Chinese mainland. Americans financed efforts by Kuomintang and third-force guerrillas to assassinate officials, damage Communist property, and undermine confidence in the Beijing regime.[43] The CIA found Hong Kong a vantage point far too seductive to surrender despite British fears. No where else could Americans gain such immediate access to mainland communications or fresh information brought out by refugees. In fact, British intelligence organized a massive program for interviewing refugees and shared the results with the Americans.[44] But their efforts to hinder use of Hong Kong by passing their south China cullings to the CIA station in Singapore proved ineffective.[45] Although Washington recognized that it jeopardized the colony by using it as a safe haven—that this might eventually draw Beijing's wrath and end its tolerance for a foreign enclave along the coast—the gamble would have to be taken.

Circumstantial evidence suggests that the level of risk CIA agents were willing to incur sometimes was quite high. In 1955 a plane on which Zhou Enlai should have been traveling to the Bandung Conference exploded in mid-air, killing 15 people after having refueled in Hong Kong. Government officials in the People's Republic and Indonesia insisted that the bomb that destroyed the aircraft had been planted by a Nationalist Chinese paid off by the CIA. Zhou escaped because of a last-minute rerouting to meet with Gamel Abdel Nasser.[46] Less spectacularly, the CIA used Hong Kong routinely to secure large amounts of black market currency to help fuel the war in Vietnam and operated missions throughout southeast Asia from the station in Hong Kong.[47] The consulate general, at the same time, employed large numbers of people to translate and analyze Communist Chinese publications for Washington, occasioning repeated requests from local authorities to reduce the staff lest Beijing be provoked.

Colonial officials objected not simply to covert incitement but also to public rabble rousing. Operations of the Voice of America, which sent anticommunist Cantonese-language programs into China, provoked colonial authorities to shut down the signal without prior warning in early 1951.[48] In the summer of 1957, the impending visit of Marvin Liebman of the Committee for One Million to Hong Kong prompted a desperate appeal from local British authorities to the State Department asking that Liebman's rhetoric be restrained by formal warnings lest he "stir up the local political mud." Not in a position to bar prominent Americans from visiting, so long as they did "not seem likely to lead to a breach of peace," Hong Kong urged the British Embassy in Washington to discourage such trips as much as possible.[49]

Hong Kong officials also expected Washington to be able to control its Nationalist Chinese allies, who often ran elaborate operations from secret headquarters in the colony.[50] Since British officials had as little contact as possible with Taipei, to avoid angering Beijing, they required U.S. assistance. London's emissary retained in Taiwan (at Tamsui) pursued only consular functions, whereas efforts to control subversive activities demanded higher level representations. The British knew that Americans often were complicit in Nationalist plots, having uncovered large caches of American explosives in crowded tenement areas further suggesting an American obligation to be of assistance.

The colony frequently served as an arena for KMT-CCP competition. In 1956 a decision by the local government to take down Nationalist flags affixed to government buildings for the commemoration of National Day, 10 October, occasioned riots whose targets became communist organizations rather than British facilities. Beijing charged connivance between London and Taipei.

The dispute over disposition of China's fleet of commercial aircraft, complicated by American involvement, similarly, placed British authorities in the midst of a nasty Beijing-Taipei confrontation. Claire Chennault and Whiting Willauer, owners of a private American airline (CAT) that had flown missions for the KMT during WWII, persuaded Chiang Kai-shek to entrust them with the protection of Nationalist planes based in Hong Kong since the fall of Shanghai in May 1949. Willauer feared "that if [the Communists] got those transport planes and put them together with the Red paratroopers, considering the chaos which existed on Formosa [Taiwan] at that time, it would have been a pushover for the Reds to have taken Formosa."[51] The problem was that, with British recognition of the Beijing regime imminent, Hong Kong would surrender the aircraft. Although unable to get the CIA to underwrite a legal battle to block such an eventuality, Chennault and Willauer were made to understand that their effort was in line with U.S. policy, which opposed establishment of a Communist Chinese airforce that would endanger other parts of Asia.[52]

The legal contest became a prolonged ordeal for all concerned after the Hong Kong courts ruled that the 73 transport aircraft and associated properties sold in December 1949 by Chiang Kai-shek to Civil Air Transport had actually passed into Beijing's hands as of 1 October. The decision was appealed to the British Privy Council, and in the interim, Hong Kong Governor Sir Alexander Grantham refused to permit the planes to be flown to the mainland. At the same time, he also resisted pressure from the American legal team headed by Wild Bill Donovan, former Office of Strategic Services chief, to release the aircraft to fly to Taiwan. Having failed to convince airline executives to evacuate the aircraft from Hong Kong before Britain recognized the PRC, Grantham adamantly refused to relent in the uncertain legal situation.[53] In 1952, when the Privy Council decided in CAT's favor, mainland retaliation came in the form of nationalization of valuable British assets in Shanghai. Moreover, related clashes over "occupation" of warehousing facilities in the colony dragged on through the 1950s with Hong Kong assistance to Chennault being denounced by the Chinese Communist press.[54]

Tension between Washington and London in the 1950s impinged upon Hong Kong on a variety of occasions. Immediately after the outbreak of the Korean War, American officials tried to seize a Chinese Communist oil tanker under repair in Kowloon. Grantham attempted to hold out against Washington but found "London was adamant; evidently it was more scared of what the United States might do to Britain, than of what China might do to Hong Kong."[55]

Whether or not the governor correctly assessed London's motives regarding the ship, the British proved more willing to confront the U.S. when crises developed in the Taiwan Straits. Fearful of armed conflict between China and the United States, Whitehall urged Eisenhower to be realistic and not risk peace for inconsequential outposts like Quemoy and Matsu. British criticism of the U.S. position and assertions that the offshore islands ought to be abandoned induced American journalists, and sometimes officials as well, to remind London that Hong Kong too was an offshore island, only one mile from the coast, and truly indefensible.[56]

British reservations about American policy in East Asia assumed decidedly less significance after clashes in 1956 in the Middle East led London to seek ways to placate the United States. The Suez imbroglio left deep scars on leaders both in Washington and London. But London was willing to make concessions to try to revive the cooperative spirit of the World War II Anglo-American partnership, and President Dwight D. Eisenhower responded warmly. At Bermuda in March 1957 understandings were reached on a series of sensitive questions. Among these, two issues related to China policy commanded attention. Dulles pressed the British hard on the need to align London's political approach to China more closely with that of Washington. Not only should the British "wholeheartedly" support the American determination to keep China out of the UN, but the secretary of state also wanted the prime minister to withdraw diplomatic recognition from Beijing. Macmillan and his foreign secretary, Selwyn Lloyd, told Dulles they would consider a shift, noting that recognition had originally been declared by a Labor not a Conservative government. In return, Dulles acknowledged the need for Britain to relax trade restrictions.

British and American policy quickly changed. Britain announced that it intended to dispense with the China differential, which had kept restrictions against the People's Republic stiffer than those against the Soviet Union, and the United States acquiesced.[57] Discussions in Washington during October produced what historian Tracy Lee Steele has called a "declaration of interdependence."[58] The United States agreed to cooperate on atomic energy development and coordinate policies regarding Soviet expansion in exchange for Whitehall's pledge, made secretly in a letter shielded from public scrutiny, not to seek any alteration in the UN situation.[59] British efforts to encourage the United States to move toward relations with China stopped. Thus, in the 1958 Straits confrontation, Britain expressed sympathy for the American dilemma, Lloyd writing to Dulles "your troubles are our troubles."[60]

Anglo-American agreements also covered Hong Kong specifically. Having traveled a long cold war passage away from the anticolonialism of the 1930s and 1940s, Washington sought to encourage London to retain Hong Kong as a free world outpost.[61] To this end it proved willing to "regard Hong Kong as a joint defence problem."[62]

A June 1960 National Security Council document, numbered 6007/1, made the reasoning and intentions more explicit. The United States would support the British through "military deployments and high-level statements" should Communist forces threaten the colony, hoping that evidence of American determination and strength would deter Beijing. If this did not suffice, then the U.S. would decide whether to intervene directly based on British policy, existing conditions, and the extent of hostilities. It would, in any case, consult the UN and provide support for evacuation should that be necessary.[63] In NSC 6007/1 and repeatedly on other occasions, Washington also asserted its willingness to provide assistance to local authorities should civil disturbances threatened security, particularly if evidence existed that these had been Communist-inspired.

Refugees provoked instability that repeatedly challenged the colony's survival. The influx, sometimes of thousands fleeing political repression or natural disaster, strained resources. Under the 1842 cession accord, the British had agreed to permit unrestricted Chinese access. Nevertheless, in self-defense, the colony passed regulations in 1950 limiting arrivals from China to 50 per day and imposing a language test, which excluded northern dialect speakers, who, authorities assumed, intended to emigrate rather than pass the day on business and return home.[64] Even then, Hong Kong continued accepting political fugitives in greater numbers and those others who were not intercepted crossing the line. Thus in 1961 some 15,000 entered legally, while another 40,000 evaded border patrols to settle in squatter camps and eventually apply successfully for residence permits.[65] Americans looked upon this situation with ambivalence: on the one hand it was destabilizing for the colony, but on the other hand it proved fruitful for intelligence purposes and was a useful propaganda weapon against those who would try to picture Communist China as a new Eden.

A variety of refugee organizations, private and government-related, assisted those fleeing Communist China. The British governor used American generosity in providing relief assistance to embarrass London into taking action to rehouse squatters in the early 1950s.[66] From those difficult days just after the Communist victory until the autumn of 1960, Aid to Refugee Chinese Intellectuals, as noted in chapter 5, worked with educated Chinese who had fled to the colony, bringing some to the U.S. and helping others to relocate in Taiwan. Although the organization eventually successfully resettled large numbers, conditions in Hong Kong under American auspices proved difficult. The local ARCI representative confided in Consul General Julian Harrington that New York headquarters seemed too wrapped up in long-term programs to provide sufficient relief assistance and that this lapse had engendered much bitterness within the refugee community in the colony toward ARCI in particular and the U.S. in general.[67]

A new "assault" occurred in the spring of 1962 sparked by more liberal regulations regarding emigration on the part of the Communists. American analysts speculated that Beijing purposefully hoped to degrade the colony's ability to deal with the new arrivals and thereby remove some of the luster from this free world outpost along the China coast. State Department intelligence specialists also believed that Beijing wanted to demonstrate to London the vulnerability of Britain's hold upon the territory and the importance of Chinese goodwill in its survival.

Recognizing the potential for great propaganda benefits, Taipei responded to the outpouring of mainland Chinese with an unqualified invitation for all to come to Taiwan. On 21 May the Executive Yuan established a special committee under Premier Ch'en Ch'eng to work with Hong Kong authorities and the refugees, as well as to administer a fund for relief supplies. The American assessment of this proved very cynical, suggesting that Taipei did not intend actually to accept the refugees. First, the KMT would require screening of applicants to prevent spies from immigrating to or even transiting the island, and then they would demand U.S. financial support, the lack of which would allow them to rescind the offer. British authorities could, in any case, not agree to a stringent interviewing process by Nationalists in their territory, and so Taiwan would enjoy the good feelings generated by the gesture but not have to accept any people.[68]

In the end the refugees preferred not to go. Many disliked the KMT, saw greater economic opportunities in Hong Kong, and found the Cantonese-speaking population there more compatible than the Mandarin-dominated, authoritarian social and political order that awaited them in Taiwan. The few who made the move did so with U.S. government subsidies. Otherwise the U.S. minimized its involvement in the situation, providing some assistance through its PL 480 food aid program in the amount of $6 million annually and meeting, to a small extent, unprecedented British requests for money to construct housing for the refugees.[69]

The desire on the part of British officials to give the United States a greater sense of responsibility for Hong Kong led them to open the port as a rest and recreation oasis during both the Korean and Vietnam wars. Hong Kong authorities felt constrained to provide this support to American armed forces but did so unenthusiastically. Some worried that the Chinese Communists would see a large American military presence as threatening. Others focused on the disruption of law and order that rowdy troops were bound to bring, making of red-light districts like Wan Chai "a wildly liberated Las Vegas."[70]

Predictably, Beijing did view Hong Kong as being complicit in American imperialism. Foreign Minister Chen Yi told journalists in 1965:

> The fact that Britain and the Hong Kong authorities allow the U.S. to use Hong Kong as a base for aggression against Vietnam has caused the anxiety of local inhabitants. The Chinese government considers the question not only one of using Hong Kong as a base for aggression against Vietnam but also of preparing to use it in the future as a base for aggression against China. . . . This action of the British government is most stupid. We hope that it will choose a wiser course in its own interests. Otherwise, China will take measures.[71]

After delivering the same warning directly to the local government and printing a broadside in China's official newspaper *Renmin Ribao*, the Chinese succeeded in forcing a temporary halt to flights from Vietnam and frantic consultation between London and Washington. Analysts feared that the Chinese might take action in Hong Kong to demonstrate their militancy to Hanoi in the continuing competition with Moscow for Vietnamese loyalties. The British denied pressuring American officials to curb further visits, but their fear of provocation did lead them to reach an understanding with Washington that no more than 110 army soldiers would be in the colony at any point and that in the period between the PRC and ROC national days, 1 and 10 October, flights would be suspended entirely. No publicity was to be given to the arrangement, and the existence of a formal quota remained secret.[72] During 1966, drawing a distinction between ship visits and air transport directly from the battlefront, the U.S. allowed some 140,000 from the Seventh Fleet to take leave in the colony but only a total of 31,000 to arrive by plane from Vietnam, Japan, Okinawa, and other bases.[73]

U.S. sailors shopping in Hong Kong (here in 1953) became a familiar sight. *Courtesy of the U.S. Navy and the National Archives*

For Beijing, the continued existence of a British colony on Chinese territory posed a dilemma of principle versus economics. When India marched into the Portuguese colony of Goa in December 1961, New Delhi struck a blow against imperialism that Beijing could only applaud, heightening embarrassment over what the Soviet press colorfully condemned as a "urinal of colonialism" along the China coast.[74] But Hong Kong provided China some $210 million in foreign exchange in 1962 and as much as $500 million in 1965 or about 40 percent of its annual foreign exchange earnings. In fact, local Communist banks offered premiums for U.S. currency in large denominations for easier transfer to China, prompting the U.S. Navy to pay sailors on leave in the colony in small bills to staunch the flow.[75] Americans, who saw Hong Kong as a window into the communist heartland, also had to recognize that it acted as a "vantage point" for the Communist Chinese:

> China gets the benefit of the best harbor in East Asia for its trade and has the port managed for it for a reasonable fee by old and reliable hands. Hong Kong is a pressure release valve; a place to send undesirables and an extra feeding station in time of shortages. It is a good source as well as relay point, for gift parcels and remittances. . . . It is neutral ground for receiving capitalist businessmen. . . . The population is not unfriendly to Communist China. It adds nothing to the chances of the GRC [Government of the ROC]. Takeover would mean vanishing prosperity and foreign capital, an additional control problem and the possibility of a new subversive center.[76]

During the Great Proletarian Cultural Revolution, nevertheless, violence did spill over the border and challenge British control of Hong Kong. Industrial unrest, which the British tried to ignore, eventuated in clashes during a May 1967 factory strike involving Hong Kong police. Riots quickly spread through the colony but failed to arouse large numbers of people. These were followed by random bombings and terrorist attacks against police patrols. Although Beijing encouraged Hong Kong communists and even went so far as to cut off supplies of water in June, it did not send arms or attempt to expel the British. Even the water interruption was more show than substance, since deliveries for the period had already been completed and were not due to resume until October in any case.[77] Public confidence remained high, incidents were contained, and border guards kept troublemakers out of the colony.

State Department intelligence analysts noted that no disturbances directly involved Americans, although rioters did stone hotels along Nathan Road where U.S. servicemen on recreation leave in the colony regularly stayed.[78] There were also attacks on the Bank of America and two bombs planted at United States Information Service offices. American businesses, nevertheless, did not see the instability as long-lasting, few cut back or departed, and enterprises, including the Chase Manhattan Bank and Macy's department stores, expanded operations.[79] The influx of American tourists rose from the previous year, and the resident American community of 5,000 was shaken but not deeply troubled.

Washington worried, in the face of mainland chaos and unrest in the colony, that the United States might be called upon to assist in defending Hong Kong. Rusk secretly cabled Rice in Hong Kong and David Bruce in London warning them not to intimate any willingness to discuss joint military preparations, although they were to be as cooperative as possible short of this. He did not believe either that China would attack, given the economic costs, or that Britain would try to defend the colony or seek American help.[80] American analysts suggested that there were some 79,000 ground troops within 100 miles of Hong Kong and 170 aircraft ready to overwhelm Hong Kong's 8,000-man garrison and its three liaison planes.[81] What the United States government did do was to send a group of warships, including a nuclear-powered submarine, to spend the summer of 1967 in Hong Kong harbor.[82] Within the department, discussion regarding contingency planning did, of course, take place. Officials continued to maintain that Hong Kong should be preserved as an "independent and viable economic entity" that would offer the U.S. a market and a port of call for the navy.[83] And, although officials assumed that the United States would "probably not" commit forces, they did not absolutely rule out a role in defending it.

The idea of coming to Britain's rescue in Hong Kong, unappealing at all times, would have been particularly contentious, given London's refusal to meet Lyndon Johnson's troop requests for Vietnam. The president had so desperately wanted the symbolic support of the British flag on the battlefield that he beseeched Prime Minister Harold Wilson to send "a platoon of bagpipers." The British, however, could not spare the resources and in fact did not want to mire themselves in what seemed like an unwise and distracting struggle on the periphery. Bitterly, Secretary of State Dean Rusk remarked, "don't expect us to save you again. They can invade Sussex and we wouldn't do a damn thing about it."[84]

The Department of State, in fact, seriously considered the possibility that Britain would have to forfeit Hong Kong, some observers contending that "most Britons would accept it philosophically." The British announcement in July 1967 that they planned to withdraw their forces from east of Suez to concentrate their energies in Europe, in conjunction with their failure to stem rebellion in Rhodesia or to deal adequately with trouble in Arabia, made clear that London was having to accept "the fact of British impotence and . . . see the remaining overseas holdings as burdens to be got rid of rather than as elements of British strength."[85] In the end, pressure on Hong Kong subsided during September 1967 with London still very much in possession of the territory. For the next decade, Hong Kong did not present problems for Sino-British relations.

As the significance of Hong Kong as a pawn in the cold war diminished, its economic presence globally and for the United States began to increase. The United States soon outstripped Great Britain as a commercial actor in the territory. By the mid-1960s, the United States had become the colony's most important trading partner, with two-way exchange in 1966 reaching $560 million. The U.S. sold Hong Kong raw cotton, tobacco, foodstuffs, and electronic components. Hong Kong sent Americans electronic components, plastic flowers, and toys, as well as textiles and apparel, prospering both because of such diversification and because the United States chose not to levy truly burdensome tariffs.[86] Local investment totaled some $100 million, and 400 American companies operated there, including 150 regional headquarters offices.[87] The decision by Fairchild, a major U.S. semiconductor firm, to establish a factory in the colony in 1961, moreover, became, in the words of economic analyst Robert Wade, "a landmark in the history of East Asia." By transferring its labor-intensive assembly operations there, Fairchild initiated a "corporate strategy that came to be called global manufacturing . . . [that is] manufacturing or purchasing around the world wherever components could be obtained at lowest costs. Of all regions of the world East Asia . . . benefited most from this strategy."[88] Hong Kong benefited at the same time from military procurement, which proved a boon to the entire region. In 1966, for example, the colony earned $50 to 52 million by providing the U.S. matériel for the Vietnam theater.[89]

Hong Kong also became a major destination for American tourists during the 1960s. They quickly ranked first in the number visiting and expenditures made in the colony. The Hilton Hotel chain opened the largest hotel to date in the Far East there in early 1963. Costing some $14 million, it boasted 900 rooms, a stunning view of Hong Kong harbor, and, according to Conrad Hilton, was a "great act of faith" in the future of the colony.[90] On the other hand, Consul General Marshall Green found himself in the uncomfortable position of having to force the newly built hotel to strip rooms of $100,000 worth of Chinese decorations because they had been manufactured in China and therefore violated embargo restrictions that he, Green, considered foolish.

Green's embarrassment over the Hilton fiasco was just a silly symbol of a more profound reality. From the Hong Kong perspective, American policy often seemed shortsighted and inappropriate. Intimacy rendered those based in Hong Kong more flexible regarding American decisionmaking toward both Hong Kong and Beijing. Foreign Service officers vehemently opposed provocative activities such as the very operations their CIA colleagues secretly encouraged. They took the Sino-Soviet split seriously earlier than did many in Washington. They favored greater contacts with China, disparaging prohibitions against visits of reporters and scholars.[91] Although their reporting on developments inside China was valued, their recommendations for policy changes, to the chagrin of a series of astute officers, made little impression in Washington.

1972 THROUGH 1984

American policies toward China did, nevertheless, change after the inauguration of Richard Nixon. For Hong Kong the transformation held promise and peril. Sir Alexander Grantham, onetime governor of the colony, had predicted in the 1950s that Hong Kong would be most in jeopardy after Sino-American relations improved and the two opponents of colonialism began working together against British interests. By 1972 American impulses had shifted significantly, and although no one in Washington sought to push London out of the territory, Washington made no protest when China, as one of its first initiatives after admission, removed Hong Kong from the United Nations list of colonial territories entitled to self-determination.[92] Rapprochement, then, did unsettle established economic and political relationships in Hong Kong.

Moreover, by the 1970s British priorities had altered profoundly. London's determination to play a more influential role in Europe required, given its very limited resources, a further diminution of its presence in the East including Hong Kong. As a result of its 1974 Defence Review, the government in 1975 announced that it would withdraw additional forces from Singapore, Malaysia, and Hong Kong. American dismay at these decisions was reflected in the offhand comment of the chairman of the Joint Chiefs of Staff, reported in the London Times, that "they're no longer a world power, all they've got are generals, admirals and bands."[93]

Fortunately for both London and Washington the 1970s proved to be a peaceful decade along the Hong Kong–China frontier. The passing of the Cultural Revolution and the end of the Vietnam War eliminated major irritants. The United States, Great Britain, and Australia maintained their communications interception stations, which spied on China and the Soviet Union,[94] but the most troublesome security question became, once again, that of refugees. This time, however, the onslaught came from Indochina not China. After the communist victory in southeast Asia, thousands fled Vietnam, with the first ship carrying 3,743 people, arriving in Hong Kong in May 1975. Hanoi's pressures on ethnic Chinese escalated the numbers trying to reach Hong Kong, which peaked in the first six months of 1979 at 66,000, some 73 percent of whom were Chinese. Hong Kong's inability to handle the influx produced a burden-sharing agreement in 1979 designed to resettle refugees rapidly in Great Britain, Australia, Canada, and the United States, which agreed to accept the largest number. As The Economist magazine noted, "The sporting era of the 'touch base' policy, when an illegal immigrant was allowed to stay if he got as far as Hongkong's urban area, ended in October 1980." In 1982, to try to discourage continued arrivals, the authorities closed refugee camps, prohibiting the inmates from working in the colony.[95]

The drain on the economy produced by refugee demands made the colony less able to cope with pressures on its textile export trade. Tightening of the 1974 Multifiber Arrangement, under which bilateral agreements restricting trade in man-made fiber, wool, and cotton products were negotiated, hit Hong Kong with particular force. The local response coupled protest with efforts to shift production into new areas. The Hong Kong Productivity Centre, which had been established by the government in 1967, worked with new determination to attract high-technology investment from the United States as well as Japan, Germany, and Britain.[96] Strains were alleviated somewhat by Washington's decision to include Hong Kong in the Generalized System of Preferences in December 1975, qualifying it for tariff relief on certain commodities. Helping still more, during the 1970s and 1980s Hong Kong's service sector, particularly financial institutions linked to regional economic development, grew significantly, reducing industry's share of the gross national product.[97]

Americans joined this expansion despite warnings from the American Chamber of Commerce that soaring property values had made Hong Kong an unreasonably expensive place to house businesses and staff. Citibank became the fourth-largest bank in Hong Kong and the largest American enterprise in the colony in 1976, and several other banks and investment firms conducted business there, including American Express, Salomon Brothers, and Chase. Manufacturers Hanover Trust Company of New York headed a syndicate that financed construction of Hong Kong's subway system, which was completed in 1979. According to the project's originator, Hong Kong "learned what not to do from . . . San Francisco and, to a lesser degree, from . . . Washington, D.C. We have to offer service that doesn't break down."[98]

During the 1970s, Hong Kong business also increasingly sought to expand its foothold in the United States. The most prominent example of this new trend involved the Hong Kong and Shanghai Banking Corporation, the world's 68th-largest bank and the dominant financial presence in Hong Kong. In 1955 it had created a California subsidiary and by the 1970s controlled 10 branch banks in the state. But by 1978 its vision had broadened considerably, and, after selling the California operation as required by U.S. law, it acquired New York's Marine Midland Bank with its 350 branches, the 13th-largest bank in the United States. Although American competitors in Hong Kong disparaged the Hong Kong Bank's conservatism and the fact that none of its executives had received college educations, the acquisition made it the 15th-most-powerful bank in the world.[99]

Hong Kong's growing prosperity suffered a significant challenge in the early 1980s as political uncertainty and economic speculation combined to set back confidence and growth. On the political front, the colony's future seemed in jeopardy because of the expiration of the 1898 agreement, which had leased the New Territories to the British government. London, having concluded that Hong Kong island and the Kowloon peninsula would not be viable on their own, sought in 1982 to initiate talks with Beijing regarding the future of the enclave. In spite of Chinese nationalism, some in Britain entertained hopes that the colony could be retained since it yielded such high profits for Beijing. If not, then retrocession must be negotiated carefully to protect both the colony's prosperity and London's reputation. In either case, given the 1997 reversion deadline, there was some urgency, since increasing numbers of investors and companies found it impossible to decide upon long-term commitments.

Whitehall, of course, rapidly discovered that the talks would focus on surrender of British rights not on perpetuation of British control. The resulting loss of confidence led the Hong Kong dollar on 22 September 1983 to plummet. Faith in the ability of London to protect the community's freedoms fell victim to a growing sense of vulnerability and impending disaster.

On the economic front, surging property speculation, a balance of payments deficit, and a global oil crisis, coupled with rapidly rising interest rates in the United States, also contributed to the precipitous depreciation of Hong Kong's currency. The Hong Kong dollar declined at a rate of some 28 percent in 1982–83 as compared with just 4.1 percent annually between 1977 and 1982.[100] To prevent collapse, in October 1983 the government pegged it to the U.S. dollar, establishing an administrative exchange rate of 7.8, which rescued floundering financial institutions. The turn to the U.S. dollar reflected the reliance for virtually all trade and financial transactions on the American currency after the value of the British pound sterling began to fall in late 1971, forcing London to allow it to float in 1972.

1984 AND AFTER

In 1984 London and Beijing finally concluded the Sino-British Joint Declaration and embarked upon negotiations for a Basic Law (completed in 1990) to cover the status of Hong Kong during and after the process of retrocession of the colony to China's control. Under the provisions of the 1984 understanding, the Chinese guaranteed that Hong Kong would retain its economic, legal, and social institutions—its way of life—for 50 years beyond 1 July 1997. The colony would become a special administrative region responsible to Beijing in the areas of defense and foreign affairs but retaining a "high degree of autonomy" otherwise.

Throughout the 22 sessions leading to the Joint Declaration, the United States played a largely peripheral part despite its dominant role in trade. This did not signal a lack of American concern, but rather a lack of formal standing in the process. The 1984 Republican Party platform explicitly called for self-determination even though this contradicted Reagan Administration policy. Secretary of State George Shultz made clear to Beijing Washington's interest in the stability of the territory but accepted the idea of reversion. American Consul General Burt Levin, attempting to reassure residents of continued U.S. interest, asserted just four days after the agreement was signed that Washington would treat Hong Kong as a trading partner separate from China after 1997 including maintenance of independent textile quotas. Similar affirmations were voiced by other U.S. officials, including Vice President George Bush on a visit in October 1985, most of whom emphasized the 50-year guarantee.[101] The United States became the first government to take official note of the Joint Declaration and spearheaded the United Nations vote that marked it officially as an international treaty.

The changing status of Hong Kong made up but one component of the economic problems faced by the territory's entrepreneurs and their American counterparts. Mounting American trade deficits led to more aggressive American action against Hong Kong imports, especially in the textile area. Driven by the anger of the textile industry, which insisted that between 1980 and 1985 some 300,000 jobs had been lost because of textile imports, the Reagan administration forced Hong Kong into signing a restrictive bilateral textile agreement in June 1986. Not only did it impose ceilings on goods entering the U.S., but it significantly broadened the categories of textiles subject to limitation.[102] Nevertheless, early in 1989, Hong Kong became a target for a U.S. International Trade Commission investigation regarding dumping charges raised by the National Knitwear and Sportswear Association. The large potential losses to Hong Kong of new restrictions testified to its continued overreliance on the U.S. market. Some diversion promised to follow from Hong Kong's growing integration into what became known as Greater China in the late 1980s. In the short term, on the other hand, decisions by Hong Kong entrepreneurs, which began to move industrial production to mainland China to cut expenses, aggravated old controversies. The resulting low-cost textiles and garments passing through Hong Kong to the U.S. market occasioned renewed pressures to curb Chinese/Hong Kong manufactures entering the United States.

The massacre at Tiananmen in Beijing on 4 June 1989 worsened Hong Kong's political and economic situation, frightening residents and clouding forecasts for the post-1997 future. The more obvious political repercussions followed from the 1984 Sino-British Agreement. Hong Kong residents, who traditionally paid little attention to government and politics, realized suddenly that Communist rule after 1997 could be far more repressive than they had expected given the reform character of the Chinese regime under Deng Xiaoping. Some suggested fairly desperate schemes such as towing Hong Kong island out to sea, handing the territory back to the Nationalists instead of the Communists, or leasing the land to the United Nations to create the "Switzerland of Asia."[103] Pressure quickly developed[104] for more thoroughgoing democratization of the local government before 1997, a trend welcomed by the Americans, awkward for the British, and opposed vehemently by Beijing.

The United States Congress took up support for greater liberalization in the colony prior to Chinese resumption of control with several "support democracy" resolutions, the most comprehensive of which was the United States–Hong Kong Policy Act (S-1731) introduced in September 1991 by Senator Mitch McConnell (R-KY). Under provisions of this legislation, the United States would have undertaken to monitor the transition to Communist rule, encouraging full adherence to the Joint Declaration and the Basic Law, to protect the local citizenry. The United States would also revise its laws in order to prevent disruption of legal relations with Hong Kong after 1 July 1997. To the Chinese this constituted brazen "hegemonic" interference in a matter that ought to remain between Beijing and London. They called upon "all knowledgeable people who genuinely care about Hong Kong's future" to help defeat the bill.[105] Nevertheless, a modified version of the bill was signed into law in August 1992, the primary change being a requirement for the administration to report to Congress on general conditions in Hong Kong rather than specifically on implementation of the Joint Declaration to which the U.S. had not been a signatory.

In conjunction with efforts to pass such legislation, Congress also held hearings that gave Hong Kong citizens a platform from which to publicize their dilemma. One of the most prominent spokesmen quickly became Martin Lee Chu-ming, who told a House of Representatives human rights committee that "Britain's hand over of 5.5 million Hong Kong people to China may be likened to the hand over of 5.5 million Jewish people to Nazi Germany during World War II."[106] Called by some Congressmen "Hong Kong's Yeltsin" and by others "Hong Kong's Dalai Lama," Lee was rumored to have written the first draft of McConnell's bill.

Americans in the colony had fewer opportunities to exercise influence. Secretly, in the aftermath of the massacre, American officials in Hong Kong assisted Chinese dissidents who managed to reach the colony to find sanctuary in the U.S. or in other countries. They had less success in shaping policies followed by the Hong Kong government.[107] "Americans are not appointed in significant numbers to any of the consultative committees that are an important part of running the colony, have almost no representation in the all-important civil service, and are virtually invisible on the general commission of the Hong Kong General Chamber of Commerce. . . . Even today, when the Hong Kong government's official line is to favor more U.S. involvement, Americans are more likely to get lucrative contracts than a voice."[108] When Consul General Richard Williams spoke out in May 1991 on human rights concerns in the territory, only 2 of 30 government officials attended. Nevertheless, the American mission continued to assert the need for more rapid democratization of power holding and better preparation for Hong Kong's uncertain future.[109]

The economic consequences of Tiananmen threatened to be even more profound. Not only did the hemorrhaging of the colony's political and economic elite accelerate, but companies, in doubt about the environment for free enterprise under Beijing's control, took the 1989 repression as a signal that conditions might be far more restrictive than hoped. The loss of confidence became apparent in the steep decline of the Hong Kong stock market.[110] Real growth of the economy slowed from 13.8 percent in 1987 to just 2.5 percent in 1989.[111]

Then, too, there was the indirect but potentially devastating impact of U.S. economic sanctions against China. The American Congress sought ways to register its revulsion against Beijing's crackdown and demonstrate that it would no longer overlook Chinese policies challenging American principles or welfare. With few openings available, members of Congress pinpointed China's Most Favored Nation status as a vehicle for reshaping Chinese behavior in areas such as human rights, proliferation, and trade. For Hong Kong, circumscribing or eliminating MFN treatment of China, according to Hong Kong Chamber of Commerce estimates in 1991, would cost as much as $12 billion and the loss of 43,000 jobs. Havoc would result because of Hong Kong's central position as an entrepôt for China trade (annually it re-exports $8.5 billion worth of goods to the U.S.) and because of Hong Kong's financial and factory integration, through ownership and contract, with industry in South China. By the early 1990s, Hong Kong employed more workers inside the PRC than in the colony.[112] Thus the Hong Kong authorities mounted an energetic lobbying campaign in Washington opposing curbs that would hurt Hong Kong, an innocent bystander, so severely.[113]

Officials made the cardinal point of Hong Kong's appeal the enormous American stake in the territory. Hong Kong had become not only the United States' 13th-largest trading partner, with 900 U.S. firms operating there and $7 billion in investments, but also a regional headquarters for American companies in Asia. The United States was Hong Kong's largest market, and each Hong Kong resident purchased an incredible $1,300 worth of U.S. products in 1991. American banks had close to $99 billion in deposits there. Some 22,000 Americans resided in the colony, the largest expatriate community, and more than 600,000 visited in 1990. Eleven states maintained representative offices there. Even Jardine Matheson, one of Britain's oldest Hong Kong firms, named an American lawyer to head the firm in 1987. Yet, most Americans remained unaware that their role far exceeded Great Britain's, that, according to Hong Kong American Chamber of Commerce President John Kamm, "Hong Kong is an American outpost." Indeed, to service this American presence, the Chamber of Commerce operated the largest private business organization outside the U.S., and the government maintained the biggest foreign consular office in the territory, the second-largest such U.S. facility in the world.

Furthermore, Hong Kong had become a major source of investment capital in the United States, particularly on the West Coast. Already in the early 1980s, United States real estate had become an irresistible bargain, offering low prices and higher rates of return on rent than was possible in Hong Kong, as well as providing a hedge against possible chaos after 1997. The Department of Commerce noted that in 1980 and 1981 five times as much capital flowed into the U.S. from Hong Kong as moved the other way. This included the aforementioned purchase in 1978 by the Hong Kong and Shanghai Banking Corporation of Marine Midland Bank in New York. Hong Kong development and tourist offices operated in cities across the country, including New York, Miami, Dallas, Chicago, and San Francisco. In 1991 direct Hong Kong investment in the United States exceeded $1.2 billion. Should Hong Kong crumble owing to Chinese economic mismanagement and political repression, local officials insisted, the United States would have lost more than any other country except, perhaps, Japan and China itself.[114]

In reality, the ruin of Hong Kong, if annoying and damaging for selected businesses, would hardly undermine the United States' economy more generally. The actual percentage of American trade passing through Hong Kong markets remained small even as it grew rapidly.[115] The U.S. stake in the territory might be lucrative but not vital.

Although limited in the influence it could exercise over Hong Kong's future, the United States attempted to staunch the "brain drain" afflicting American companies and the colony's institutions (including schools and the civil service) by revising U.S. immigration regulations. The push for liberalization also gained support from the Congressional Human Rights Caucus which, in the person of members such as Congressman John E. Porter (D-IL), insisted on the importance of returning confidence to the people of Hong Kong and providing them insurance should China's promises of democratic rule prove illusory. The need for such measures grew out of the British government's unwillingness—inability it insisted—to absorb a potential influx of 3.5 million British passport holders.[116] The British authorities would go only so far as to extend full citizenship to 50,000 heads of households and their dependents whose service to the crown and skills would justify their resettlement in Britain. The United States tried to supplement London's policies with the 1990 Immigration Act, which increased Hong Kong's quota and provided that it would not be amalgamated with that of China after 1997. Thus Hong Kong's allotment, which had stood at 600 until 1987 and thereafter jumped to 5,000, rose to 10,000 with further escalation planned. More importantly, the Act freed applicants from the need to leave the colony immediately, giving them until 2002 to act on their immigrant visa status.[117] It also included a new immigrant category for employees of American businesses. As a result of the latter provision, American companies hoped to lose fewer workers, since the bill eliminated the need for them to flee abroad or shift to firms where managers could assure them of sanctuary in countries with more flexible admission regulations. The main draw-back, from the perspective of the Hong Kong employees, lay in the determination of who would be transferred to the United States, a decision that would rest with the employers, who might not live up to expectations. In a separate but complementary measure, the CIA offered U.S. passports to employees of the Foreign Broadcast Information Service through the 1991 Intelligence Authorization Act.

American openness proved less in evidence on the issue of Vietnamese refugees who had begun to overwhelm Hong Kong camps. By June 1988, the numbers being absorbed by the U.S., Australia, and Canada under the 1979 Geneva agreement had fallen enough so that Hong Kong saw itself forced to declare all the Vietnamese boat people illegal immigrants and to repatriate those not able to pass a screening for political asylum. Hong Kong contended that few were genuinely fleeing political or religious persecution. Most simply could not bear the poverty. Despite a significant labor shortage in the colony, estimated at some 200,000 jobs in 1989, officials insisted the high population density made absorption of large numbers impossible.[118] Voluntary returns began under the Comprehensive Plan of Action on Indochinese Refugees (devised once again at Geneva among 29 participating states), but fewer than 300 Vietnamese expressed willingness to go home. Thus on 12 December 1989 Hong Kong announced a policy of mandatory repatriation, to which it subsequently got agreement from Hanoi, Britain, and the United Nations High Commissioner for Refugees.[119] The United States, however, remained adamantly opposed to return, arguing that conditions in Vietnam would prevent the government from providing adequate housing and jobs even were its intentions honorable. At the same time, Washington refused British suggestions that a holding center be created in the U.S. territory of Guam to care for economic refugees until the U.S. determined that they could be sent home. American officials feared that such an arrangement would occasion a massive departure from Vietnam.[120] Hong Kong, not surprisingly, interpreted Washington's position as hypocritical, given its routine repatriation of economic refugees from all over Latin America. Moreover, Washington's embargo on Vietnam, they insisted, caused much of the suffering that spurred Vietnamese into boats. Fortunately, during 1992 the crisis appeared to have subsided on its own, with just nine Vietnamese arriving in Hong Kong between January and September as compared with more than 20,000 in the same period in 1991.[121]

As the 1997 transformation approached, Hong Kong looked increasingly toward an uncertain future and found that challenges to its stability went far beyond the question of how refugees would be treated. Trying to deal with the shock of Tiananmen and the reality that Hong Kong would be as vulnerable to government violence as Beijing after retrocession, residents of the territory saw the extension of democracy as a guarantee of sorts. People who had been content to live with London's benevolent "despotism" suddenly demanded far more.

Into this situation came, in the summer of 1992, a new governor, the outspoken and engaging Christopher Patten. Patten, a former chairman of Britain's Conservative Party, owed at least some of his pragmatism and unconventional flair, according to the *New York Times*, to his work as a volunteer in John V. Lindsay's campaign for the mayoralty in New York City in the 1970s.[122] Refusing to don the traditional regalia of the Hong Kong governor or to accept the constraints of a twilight colony, Patten quickly moved to launch a package of reforms, dismaying the local business community and distressing Beijing. Although he did not call for expanding the direct election of representatives to the Legislative Council, he did propose broadening voting rights and reducing the influence of interest groups as well as making large expenditures for education, social services, and the environment.

The reaction in Beijing attested to the fact that "China sees no reason for Britain to turn Hong Kong into a democracy now, since the British have ruled the territory without any for more than a century."[123] One observer noted that "to the mandarins in Beijing, often men from China's poor interior, Hong Kong represents everything they loathe: it is southern, urban, subversive, vice-ridden, rich, relatively free, and, above all, full of foreigners and their polluting ways. . . . [Thus] the hatred, awe, and envy inspired by Hong Kong is often extreme."[124] Many Chinese officials pointed to Shanghai as a model for what could be expected to happen to Hong Kong. But, during the 1950s, the Communists gutted its industries and laid waste its vibrant commercial trading sector, making it a disastrous model indeed.

In addition to the institutionalization of democracy, Hong Kong also looked to continued American economic involvement in the territory as protection beyond 1997. Post-retrocession American relations with Hong Kong involved the working out of several complex issues, including negotiation of United States–Hong Kong agreements to replace expiring Anglo-American accords. Import regulations required adjustment to assure Hong Kong access to advanced technology despite its inclusion into a state subject to restrictive Consultative Group Coordinating Committee (COCOM) rules on technology transfer.[125]

More pragmatically, the need to sustain commitment of the American business community to Hong Kong beyond 1997 led to several long-term commercial windfalls for U.S. companies. In 1989 the Hong Kong government awarded U.S. West Corporation a multiyear $700 million cable television contract to service the world's largest franchise of some 1.5 million people. During the first phase of contracting for Hong Kong's new airport, overall management of the $16 billion project, including the world's longest suspension bridge, a harbor tunnel, and a rail system, went to Bechtel Group of San Francisco. Hong Kong also awarded contracts to Morgan Stanley for financial management and Greiner Engineering to help produce a master

Hong Kong, 1992

plan.[126] Tied into projects that would not be completed until well beyond 1997, American companies might be expected to exert strong pressures to realize the Joint Declaration promise of 50 years of unchanged economic and political conditions.

CULTURAL INFLUENCE

American cultural influences in Hong Kong could not compete in volume or impact with the role that Great Britain played, but an American presence did make its mark. As early as 1889 Rudyard Kipling found Hong Kong "dressed by America, from the haircutters' saloons to the liquor bars" with the bordello girls all speaking with American accents."[127] In the immediate post-World War II period, British Hong Kong was not at all certain that American customs and styles ought to be welcomed. One of the main motives for reestablishment of the University of Hong Kong seems to have been "the promotion of British culture, British prestige, and British interests . . . in the face of growing American influence."[128]

Hong Kong educators after World War II also worried about Americans trying to use schools and colleges in the colony for propaganda purposes, particularly since hostility from China toward Hong Kong would be heightened thereby. Therefore, Alexander Grantham, then chancellor of Hong Kong University, advised London that "it would be fatal from the point of view of the University and the Colony if the University were to become an Anglo-American institution."[129] Contributions from the United States would be happily accepted but a genuine voice in educational policy should be discouraged.

Efforts by Americans to gain a foothold in higher education, then, were only moderately successful. Plans in 1951 by the American University Club to finance a new university, drawing upon Chinese alumni of U.S. universities for funding and perhaps faculty, were discouraged by the Hong Kong authorities. ARCI supported research fellowships at the University of Hong Kong, and the Harvard-Yenching Institute put up $5,000 per year from 1953 to 1958 to help purchase books and journals. Philanthropic organizations, although honoring British primacy, persisted in assuming some responsibilities for development of higher education and library projects. The Henry Luce Foundation made possible financing for faculty through the United Board for Christian Higher Education in China at Chung Chi College and, after Chung Chi joined New Asia and United colleges to form the Chinese University of Hong Kong (1963), the Luce Foundation provided a $175,000 grant to construct a library on the campus in 1965. It also supported the Universities Service Centre, established in 1963 as a research facility for scholars unable to travel to China. Through the 1970s and 1980s, Luce gave some $480,000 in funding channeled through the American Council of Learned Societies (ACLS). Further Luce projects included an innovative program of yearlong internships in business, medicine, and the arts bringing Luce Scholars to Hong Kong every year.[130]

Substantial grants also flowed from the Ford Foundation for a series of educational and societal programs. Ford joined Luce in subsidizing the operations of the Universities Service Centre with $300,000 in successive appropriations and provided the Chinese University with $805,000 for development of a research and graduate studies program. According to John K. Fairbank, intercession by the foundation proved critical to launching programs focusing on academic study of the People's Republic, since "somehow the use of trained minds to deal with such abstractions as social science and history was beyond immediate calculations of profit, so no one could afford to invest in it."[131]

Along with fostering the study of the PRC, Americans financed educational programs based in Hong Kong to turn overseas Chinese away from China. Throughout the 1950s and 1960s, the issue of the political allegiance held by Chinese populations scattered throughout Asia alarmed State Department and intelligence officers. To them there appeared to be a contest between Communist and Free China in which it was vitally important to dissuade young people from going to "Red China" for higher education.[132] Hong Kong became the coordinating point for the production of textbooks and other materials that would present the Nationalist experience in Taiwan and the economic, political, and cultural advantages of the West in ways seductive to Chinese students.[133] Of course, Beijing echoed such propaganda with its own denunciations of cultural degeneracy and crime in an American-influenced Hong Kong that contrasted so strikingly with the socialist virtues of China.[134]

The American desire to remedy the dearth of "institutionalized links of the kind which characterize bilateral ties between other countries, such as joint economic commissions, endowed chairs and study programs at universities abroad, or exchange programs" persisted into the 1990s.[135] The United States Information Agency in 1992 assisted in efforts to establish a Center for Hong Kong–US Educational Exchanges at the Chinese University of Hong Kong, and the U.S. government also initiated the process of creating a Fulbright program supporting study in the United States by Hong Kong residents.[136]

Significant numbers of students from Hong Kong traveled to the United States for advanced degrees during the 1970s and 1980s. Some of them returned to become key figures in the Hong Kong elite. Dame Lydia Dunn, the Chinese scion of colonial society, built upon a University of California at Berkeley education to become a director of the illustrious British trading house, the Swire group, and an appointee in 1982 to the Executive Council, the governor's cabinet and colony's most powerful ruling organization.

Popular culture reflected the American presence as Hong Kong Chinese increasingly copied the customs and habits of American expatriates.

American products became a fixation among local residents, who smoked in "Marlboro country" (the company marketed 6 billion cigarettes there in 1989 or roughly 50 packs per capita) and ate at Pizza Hut. McDonald's ran 48 local restaurants, with the busiest McDonald's outlet in the world selling burgers in downtown Hong Kong.[137] Other fast food chains, numbering around 660 all told, included Wendy's, Burger King, Chuck E. Cheese, and Dunkin Donuts. As early as 1967, a branch of the legendary New York delicatessen Lindy's began to supply the community with cheesecake. Coca-Cola arrived in 1965. Whereas in 1972 there were only about 50 American-style supermarkets, by 1985 people could shop in 600, which carried on roughly 50 percent of all retail food sales. Moreover, in the early 1980s, some 95 7-Eleven shops opened to cater to the increasingly busy Hong Kong two-job families.[138]

At the same time, Hong Kong, which never had made the development of the arts a priority, adopted little high culture from the United States. As journalist Ian Buruma observed in the *New York Review of Books* in 1990, "there are hardly any museums in Hong Kong, precious few libraries, no great historical buildings, and no monuments to speak of."[139] Recognizing the need to remedy this oversight, the government constructed an Academy for the Performing Arts in the mid-1980s, inviting Americans and British artists to help staff the new institution. But, like its predecessors, the philharmonic, the repertory theater, and the dance companies, all inaugurated between 1977 and 1981, the Academy's promotion of the performing arts remained tentative compared with the vigor of Hong Kong film.

The film industry of Hong Kong in its ferocious pursuit of profits more closely paralleled the cutthroat capitalism of the broader society. During the 1980s its studios released some 2,000 movies. According to critic Geoffrey O'Brien, "Hong Kong has the distinction of being one of the few places left whose population . . . prefers its own movies to the American product." Hong Kong, O'Brien asserted:

> makes the most raucous and least contemplative movies on the planet, movies which by turns recall the spirit of Abbott and Costello, George Raft, Bela Lugosi, Gene Kelly and Cyd Charisse. Hopping ghouls, cartwheeling comedians, heroines who sing and fire machine guns with equal flair, vampires kept at bay by chicken blood and sticky rice, passionate gangsters caught up in ruthless dynastic struggles, martial arts masters who set off cascades of special effects at the least flourish of their fingers: the hyperactive characters who inhabit Hong Kong cinema make the energy level of Hollywood types like Kevin Costner and Bruce Willis seem torpid by comparison.[140]

The martial arts fantasies that made media history in the 1970s got their start in Hong Kong. Bruce Lee, a San Francisco native and Hong Kong child actor of the 1950s, achieved stardom in Hong Kong in the early 1970s with his kung-fu films. Discovered by Raymond Chow, founder of the Golden Harvest studio, Lee "abruptly became . . . [possibly] the most recognizable human being in the world." His 1972 film *Fists of Fury* drew bigger crowds than *The Godfather* and made Lee an American superstar.[141] The subsequent box office smash *Rambo*, which was derived from the Lee prototype and energized by the cult of Vietnam War nostalgia, commanded crowds in Hong Kong as well as in the United States. Exploiting the American market for ultra-violent thrillers, Hong Kong's John Woo introduced a new line of cult films in the late 1980s such as *The Killer* (1989) and *Hard Boiled* (1992). Essentially choreographed blood-letting interspersed with bizarre humor and minimal melodramatic plots, Woo's films won critical acclaim and facilitated his decision to move to Hollywood. His maiden voyage, *Hard Target*, starring Jean-Claude Van Damme, suggested problems combining American and Hong Kong artistic visions.[142]

Television borrowed from the fascination with the martial arts. In 1972 David Carradine launched a three-year run in the series "Kung Fu" as a contemplative Shaolin monk driven to demonstrate his fighting skills in each episode by the villainy rife in the nineteenth-century American West.[143] As this supposedly Chinese view of the world captured U.S. audiences, the Hong Kong television market broadcast such preeminently American fare as "Miami Vice" and "Dallas" alongside Britain's "Masterpiece Theater."

Hong Kong's impact on American literature generally rose from its appeal as a setting for murder mysteries and adventure stories. A series of writers, from World War II onward, conveyed "a picture of Hong Kong as a den of iniquity and spectacular violence, a city living at fever pitch in an atmosphere of danger and excitement."[144] As early as 1937, Francis Van Wyck Mason, then the leading American author of espionage thrillers, placed an American military intelligence agent there in *The Hong Kong Airbase Murders*. Later versions included Franklin M. J. Davis, Jr.'s *Secret of Hong Kong: Spychase in a City of Sin and Death* (1962), James Hadley Chase's *A Coffin from Hong Kong* (1962), and Mignon C. Eberhart's *Message from Hong Kong* (1969).

Indeed, in fiction and film, Hong Kong became a presence in the cold war genre that developed in the 1950s, 1960s, and 1970s. Ernest H. Gann wrote in 1954 about an American wife who came to Hong Kong to orchestrate her husband's rescue from a Chinese Communist prison in *A Soldier of Fortune*. The movie version, released in 1955, starred Susan Howard, Clark Gable, Michael Rennie, and Gene Barry. Eric Ambler told of an American businessman in a *Passage of Arms* (1959) whose activities in Hong Kong underlined the constant opportunities for contact with the Communist Chinese and the vulnerability of the colony. In *The Bright Cantonese* (1962), Alexander Cordell's beautiful Eurasian, Red Chinese spy went undercover as a Hong Kong bar girl and became enmeshed in an inevitable Sino-American clash. A more intricate plot fashioned by Peter Driscoll in *Pangolin* (1979) involved a group of British and Chinese drifters with an American military deserter in a plot to kidnap a CIA agent. To authorities in Beijing such films were not especially welcome. In 1968, Communist officials objected to the making of the American espionage story *The Chairman*, which they saw as denigrating Mao Zedong, and in 1969 opposed filming of *The Girl from Peking* with its sequences of Red Guards shooting at a Russian trying to cross the Hong Kong border.

Other writers emphasized sin and social commentary along with danger. Emily Hahn highlighted the snobbery of small-town life in *Hong Kong Holiday* (1946) and *Miss Jill* (1947). Preston Schoyer, who helped found the Chinese University of Hong Kong, explored the cruelty existing behind the community's placid facade in *The Typhoon's Eye* (1959). And later best-selling books, such as Robert Elegant's *Dynasty* and James Clavell's *Taipan* and *Noble House*, exposed the corruption and decadence of Hong Kong's elite, both Chinese and Anglo-American. But probably the best-known of such novels was Richard Mason's *The World of Suzie Wong* (1957), which told the story of an American artist in love with a prostitute. The film version of 1960, based on the Broadway stage adaptation, starred William Holden and Nancy Kwan.

Hollywood movies clearly found Hong Kong's winding allies, tiny food stalls, and intermixture of classes, races, and customs endlessly evocative. A 1951 film, typical of the many second-grade movies made in the colony, told of a small-time thief trying to rob an orphan of a valuable antique. In the last minute the crook is converted, and the antique saved, leaving a young Ronald Reagan chastened but redeemed. *Hong Kong Affair* (1958) starred Jack Kelly as a U.S. veteran going to Asia to investigate his property holdings and getting caught up in the mysterious Orient. Similarly, *Hong Kong Confidential* (1958) used the city as a backdrop for British and American agents out to save an Arabian prince from kidnappers.

Cold war politics intruded into the realm of high culture too. The American embargo against trade with China, which had such a devastating impact on Hong Kong's economy, made acquisition of Chinese treasures more difficult. The U.S. Treasury Department refused to exempt works of art, ensuring that American museums and collectors could not acquire any piece that could not be proven to have left China before 17 December 1951.[145] The consul general in Hong Kong argued during the Cultural Revolution that, at a time when Chinese mainland officials were attempting to eradicate vestiges of traditional culture, the United States ought not to prevent Americans from acquiring Chinese artistic works in order to preserve a Chinese heritage from communist tyranny.[146] He too failed.

Mixed with various kinds of innocent entertainment that Hong Kong exported to the United States was a more insidious form. Not surprising, given the early opium trade with which Britain established its presence in the China market, Hong Kong developed in the twentieth century as a major transshipment point for drug traffickers bringing heroin to the U.S. market. At conferences instigated by the U.S. in 1909, 1911, and 1924, Washington had tried to press Britain, among others, to curb the dangerous trade, which by the early 1920s held some one million Americans in thrall. Resistance to the suppression of opium and its derivatives rested mainly among the British Asian colonies, where administrators feared that eradication campaigns would cause domestic unrest and discourage the influx of workers. Not until 1945 did the British Foreign Office finally triumph over the colonial service and mandate complete prohibition. Even then, according to historian Norman Miners, the decisions was "primarily motivated by the need to conciliate opinion in the United States."[147]

But prohibition did not dampen the heroin trade for long. From at least the 1950s onward, Hong Kong became a pivot for opium lords from the so-called golden triangle of northern Thailand, Laos, and Burma. By the 1980s, no longer content with just supplying drugs, traffickers began to build complex criminal organizations in America to compete with the Mafia and other long-established gangs. According to William Sessions, FBI director, "Chinese criminal organizations . . . [in 1991] pose[d] the most serious threat among all of the Asian criminal groups." The Department of Justice ranked Asian crime networks as second in law enforcement priority to the Cosa Nostra.[148]

The growing presence of syndicated Asian crime in the U.S., particularly on the West Coast, owed much of its inspiration to Hong Kong. Triad secret societies, whose roots lay in the subversive political organizations that had attempted to destabilize China's last dynasty, flourished in the colony. The San Francisco-based Wah Ching (Youth of China), for instance, formed strong links during the 1980s to the best-organized crime group in Hong Kong, the Sun Yee On triad. California's attorney general reported in 1987 that Chinese triads controlled as much as 30 percent of the heroin smuggled into the United States.

The most active Chinese gang in lower Manhattan's Chinatown demonstrated the reach of Hong Kong's underworld. Until 1985 a former Hong Kong policeman, who had fled the colony in the midst of a corruption inquiry carrying some $19 million, headed New York City's Ong Leong Tong.[149] In New York, Eddie T. Chan took a prominent role in local politics and became an intimate of Queens Borough President Donald Manes, who later committed suicide after evidence of his involvement in illegal activities became public.[150] Chan also operated on the national scene, becoming chairman of the Reagan/Bush Re-election Chinese American Voters Registration Subcommittee. As chairman of the Chinese Welfare Federation, he lobbied Congress to liberalize immigration quotas. Chan organized Asian-American protests against the killing of Vincent Chin, a Chinese bludgeoned to death by irate automobile workers in Detroit who mistakenly believed him to be Japanese. It was Chan's connections to international crime, however, that led novelist Robert Daley to use Chan as his prototype for the villain in his best-seller *Year of the Dragon* (1981). "Fast Eddie" turned his talents to support of the KMT and the distribution of heroin, possibly, according to journalist David Kaplan, supplied by the Intelligence Bureau of the Ministry of National Defense of Taiwan, which used the proceeds to finance intelligence gathering in the United States.

Others who ran illegal empires in both New York and Hong Kong included Johnny Kon, one of the world's most successful heroin traffickers, a resident of the colony but owner of $20 million worth of U.S. real estate. Kon was arrested in New York in 1988 by drug enforcement agents. Authorities proved less able to control street gangs, which increasingly imposed protection rackets and general thuggery on Chinatown merchants.[151] Between 1965 and 1975, the FBI asserted that Chinese youths, mostly from Hong Kong, had the fastest growing crime rate of all racial groups in the United States.[152] As 1997 approached Triad societies sought with greater vigor and increasing success to gain footholds in American Chinatowns.

A new, lucrative type of international smuggling, developed in the early 1990s by criminal organizations in Hong Kong and the U.S., involved the transportation of illegal immigrants. Benefiting from the worldwide increase in migration occasioned by political and economic upheaval, gangs derived as much as $3 billion annually by moving mainland Chinese, Vietnamese Chinese, and Taiwanese to the U.S. at $25 to $30,000 per person. Volume dictated bold action, and the syndicates began to move shiploads such as the *East Wood*, a merchant ship that departed from Hong Kong loaded with 400–500 Chinese but was seized by the U.S. Coast Guard in December 1992. Given the lack of resources possessed by most immigrants, the illegals also became part of the criminal enterprise in the United States. For instance, in the 1980s, one operation set up a seven-city call-girl service using newly arrived Taiwanese women.[153]

Even the more benign impact of Hong Kong immigrants on Chinatowns disrupted these communities after the implications of the Sino-British Accord became apparent. Commercial rents in New York's Chinese community soared in the mid-1980s to the levels of midtown Manhattan, making "operators of vegetable stalls . . . pay more rent per square foot than the owners of Tiffany & Company at Fifth Avenue and 57th Street."[154] The pressure of numbers also led to offshoot communities in Queens and Brooklyn as the constricted space of the original settlement failed to accommodate all the new people and money.

• • •

American policy toward Hong Kong followed three separate paths in the years from 1945 to 1992. In the first period between 1945 and 1949, Washington sought to honor its commitment to the principle of self-determination and its respect for national sovereignty by restoring Hong Kong to the Chinese state. Having concluded that the colonial era had ended and that Britain's imperial control must be terminated, U.S. government officials pressured London to withdraw. The impulse passed, however, when it became apparent that communists would determine the destiny of China for the foreseeable future.

American policymakers renounced their earlier efforts and sought instead from 1949 to 1984 to strengthen Britain's position politically, economically, and even militarily. Hong Kong became for the United States a free world outpost and, happily, a perfectly designed window for monitoring developments in China. Over time it also became a commercial center, yielding trade and investment opportunities and profits. The United States approached its involvement in Hong Kong with far greater circumspection than it pursued its activities in Taiwan out of respect for Britain and the legal framework of British colonial control. Nevertheless, American influence was significant in all areas. The American economic embargo challenged the community's very survival in the 1950s and helped shape its transformation from an entrepôt into a manufacturing center. Later the American business community made important contributions to the prosperity of the colony and eventually became the largest group of non-Chinese residents there. Culturally that presence led to a small, if powerful, degree of Americanization of lifestyles, with fast food restaurants as only the most obvious example. American foundations and universities played a role in intellectual affairs. The U.S. military helped give the territory a sense of security. The degree of U.S. commitment to the colony's defense may not have been clear, but the continuing presence of the U.S. Navy, and even of the rowdy troops on leave from Vietnam, reinforced the idea of U.S. concern and availability. Washington also utilized the area as an intelligence gathering point and, at times, a base for operations in different parts of Asia.

The third phase began with the announcement of the Sino-British Joint Declaration in 1984, which heralded the end of relations with Hong Kong as a British possession and the realization of the earlier American ideal of a return to Chinese sovereignty. In such circumstances, the United States had to reassess its interests in Hong Kong and identify concerns of lasting importance. Since Hong Kong would, after all, revert to the control of a communist China, Americans began to see the territory as more than just a marketplace. If no longer an operational base for espionage against China since normalization in 1979, it nevertheless was imbued with a strategic importance for the stability of the region. Chaos in Hong Kong would demoralize neighboring states and produce a new refugee crisis at the same time that it would be likely to cause serious financial turmoil within China. After Tiananmen, Americans awoke to the fact that imminent retrocession of Hong Kong might mean surrendering its people to a tyrannical China rather than the liberalizing China that had negotiated the Joint Agreement. The American response was to increase immigration quotas and to try to assert an official, if low-key, interest in human rights and democratization, reserving for itself a continuing and more assertive role in the territory's future even after 1997.

chapter 10

CONCLUSION: POWER, CULTURE, AND COMMERCE IN THE PACIFIC

In the last half of the twentieth century, the United States shaped its relations with Asia to meet the requirements of cold war politics. Since few Americans had roots in the region, understood its dynamics, or cared about its problems, Washington remained relatively free to impose on relationships there the larger demands of ideological loyalty and military alignment. Bilateral ties took on an urgency and purpose that excluded the more normal assessments of cultural affinity, economic compatibility, or political interdependence. Thus, although the United States remained a nation and a people oriented toward Europe, it took a progressively more active role in what Americans had always considered the Far East.

In the case of Hong Kong this meant that Washington interfered in a British colony to a degree not often attempted or allowed. During the closing days of World War II, the United States, convinced that the colonial era had come to an end, sought to restore the territory to China and expunge imperialism from Asia. Shortly thereafter, Americans inadvertently brought economic chaos in the form of an anti-Chinese embargo designed to further the war effort in Korea. But, once reconciled to the necessity of continued British control and convinced that Hong Kong could function independently even in China's shadow, the United States worked to strengthen Britain's hold.

Hong Kong emerged in time as a commercial and financial center, as a haven for refugees and with a not-so-secret life as a base for espionage. American business became entrenched, with trade and investment outstripping virtually every other foreign presence, and an expatriate community that eventually dominated numerically even over the British and increasingly shaped the colony's cultural assumptions. The American military and intelligence communities appreciated Hong Kong's harbor and land border with China for different reasons. They fully exploited its geographic propinquity to spy on the Chinese, interviewing those who fled the People's Republic and listening to radio traffic. Sometimes they collaborated with the Nationalist Chinese to harass Beijing. Often they anchored elements of the Pacific fleet there to provide Hong Kong protection or to support ventures in Korea or Vietnam as well as Taiwan.

Anglo-American policy in Asia diverged substantially after World War II. Britain followed its tradition of pragmatism and established relations with China in 1950. Washington, true to its Wilsonian heritage, rejected the Communist Chinese and prayed for their overthrow. Yet both countries shared in the perception of Hong Kong's political, economic, and strategic value to Britain, the United States and the so-called free world. London may have found some of America's compulsions foolish and might have preferred Washington to be more flexible and realistic, but in the compelling battle against fearsome communist tyranny, Hong Kong had its role to play.

Taiwan came much more fully under American control than did Hong Kong, reaping wider benefits and paying higher costs for the relationship as, indeed, did the United States. Committed to the preservation of democracy when communists challenged a republican government, Washington ignored the fact that Chiang Kai-shek was no democrat and that efforts to meet the needs of the Chinese peasantry, the vast majority of China's people, were championed by Mao Zedong, not America's allies in the Kuomintang. The United States, therefore, accompanied Chiang into exile on the island of Taiwan where it sought to transform the KMT to create a bastion of freedom and to act as an alternative model for the Chinese people.

Surprisingly, the Nationalists proved able to devise a regime far more successful than anything even hinted at in years past on the mainland. Officials made a more serious, if not thoroughgoing, commitment to modernization. They eliminated corruption and ameliorated the most destructive aspects of factionalism. They carried out land reform, industrialized, and adopted strategies that turned Taiwan into a dynamic export-oriented economy that distributed its resources equitably among the citizenry. After years of struggle, the new Taiwan order even came to include Taiwanese in governance of the island, a role from which they had always been excluded.

Americans played a major role in helping to realize these changes. American money, in huge amounts, was crucial to the success of reform and the avoidance of obstacles. It prevented inflation, facilitated the growth of private enterprise, introduced scientific approaches to land use, and created badly needed social support such as health care. The United States also provided the security that a government absorbed in civil war required. Behind the protective screen of the U.S. Seventh Fleet, the Nationalists remained free of danger and able, once the psychological barriers were crossed, to devote their attention to developing the island. Although officials insisted upon squandering enormous percentages of the society's wealth on military preparations for a return to the mainland that never came, they gradually invested in industry and infrastructure.

Throughout these years, the Nationalist government also proved adept at manipulating the Americans. On a series of foreign policy issues where the interests of Taipei and Washington diverged, the Nationalists succeeded in advancing their goals. The signing of the Mutual Defense Treaty in 1954, over which American policymakers were divided, was only the most obvious such case. The U.S. continued to support the Nationalists in the United Nations long after it became politically deleterious to do so. And Taipei proved able to delay recognition of the People's Republic through the astute deployment of allies in the United States government, Congress, media, and business community.

When the end finally came, Taiwan again defied the prognosticators and emerged from derecognition in control of its future. Its government remained strong and gradually began to broaden its representativeness. The economy did not disintegrate. Taiwan became one of the most successful newly industrializing countries, a minidragon whose prosperity and productivity astonished, and troubled, the entire world.

Moreover, Taiwan managed to retain United States military ties. Through the Taiwan Relations Act, it preserved access to U.S. weapons and obtained an ultimate guarantee that Washington would not tolerate a Chinese attempt to take the island by force. Technology transfer and continuing arms sales reduced Taipei's sense of vulnerability despite Chinese efforts to isolate and intimidate it.

These complex relationships took a new direction in 1989 with the virtually simultaneous occurrence of the Tiananmen Massacre in China and the end of the cold war. Attitudes toward the Chinese were transformed by the combination of government brutality and the lessening of Beijing's strategic relevance. Disillusioned with the People's Republic, which suddenly seemed to have abandoned reform and liberalization for brutality and obscurantism, the United States rediscovered Taiwan and Hong Kong. After years of seeing both as appendages of China, Washington awoke to changes that made each entity more significant to Americans. Democratization and economic power in Taiwan dispelled lingering memories of an autocratic and dependent Kuomintang regime. In the wake of Tiananmen, the scheduled retrocession of the crown colony of Hong Kong to Beijing in 1997 brought home the human rights issues that American principles of self-determination made poignant and pressing.

The United States responded to these new challenges by taking stronger positions relative to the problems Taiwan and Hong Kong would face in the coming years. Washington became again an advocate of Taiwan's admission into international economic organizations such as the GATT. After years of discussion and hesitation, in December 1992, it dispatched an official cabinet-level mission to confer on economic issues with Taipei. And, for domestic political reasons as well as concern about Beijing's acquisition of arms from the former Soviet Union, it promised to sell advanced fighter air-craft to Taiwan, despite repeated refusals by previous administrations under both Democratic and Republican presidents.

Concerned also about Hong Kong, although more limited in its ability to respond by virtue of Great Britain's primacy, the U.S. Congress, nonetheless, legislated an American role through the U.S.–Hong Kong Policy Act. The Act mandated that Americans take more interest in the human rights situation there as the British colony was transformed into a Chinese special administrative region. Indeed, this American pressure would seem to have had an early impact in encouraging the more outspoken, democratizing policies of the new Hong Kong governor Christopher Patten in the closing months of 1992.

But these policies and approaches might well be overtaken by the new reality fundamentally altering relationships in Asia. Greater China, the fastest growing major economy in the world at the beginning of the 1990s, challenges the United States to approach Asia with fresh perspectives, assumptions, and policies. Accustomed to viewing each component part—Taiwan, Hong Kong, and the People's Republic—as related, but largely inde-pendent of the others, demanding of different treatment and open to distinct expectations, Washington confronts the need to reformulate outdated images and adapt to a rapidly changing reality. Whether or not Greater China ultimately complements commercial, industrial, and financial integra-tion with political federation, its existence alters the dynamics of the entire region.

Evidence of the profound impact the new order in Asia will have is already apparent. The United States has been confronted in the 1980s with unmanageable trade deficits that have contributed to a general weakening of the American economy. Under pressure to reduce those imbalances, Taiwan and Hong Kong found a solution in the transfer of manufacturing to south-ern China where the commodities produced, although still yielding profits to Taiwan and Hong Kong entrepreneurs, became incorporated into China's export profile instead of their own. Thus, the need to deflect American trade sanctions, as well as those imposed by European markets, helped spur interest in Taiwan and Hong Kong in the development of an interlinked Chinese industrial sector. The benefit to them of being able to disguise their produc-tivity and continued penetration of the U.S. economy was compounded by the advantages of low-cost labor, energy supplies, and physical plant.

On the other hand, if the consolidation of a Greater China adds complex-ity and danger to the Asian economic arena in which Americans must com-pete, it may also begin to moderate behavior that has been decidedly impervious to change. Taiwan and Hong Kong have actively lobbied Beijing to mitigate its resistance on market access issues. Indeed, they have discov-

238 • CONCLUSION: POWER, CULTURE, AND COMMERCE IN THE PACIFIC

ered independently that promotion of interaction with China demands the elimination of barriers Americans have long complained about such as inconsistent and ambiguous commercial regulations.[1]

These developments suggest the perplexing network of interdependence that the United States will be compelled to confront as it adapts to the emergence of a Greater China and to the growing importance of this Greater China in the world. In the past, United States decisionmakers shaped policies to meet the requirements of bilateral relations, whether that meant arming the Chinese Nationalists against Beijing or recognizing the Communist Chinese and abandoning a Mutual Defense Treaty with Taipei. If Hong Kong suffered because of an embargo against mainland China, that was lamentable but not critical. Few in Washington considered Hong Kong's interests of consequence in the context of armed conflict in Korea.

In the days to come, Washington needs to think in multilateral terms, recognizing that henceforth individual judgments will reverberate throughout the Greater China community with much more devastating results than before. Thus, reflecting only the most obvious instance, the implications of curbing most-favored-nation trading benefits for China promise, as in the early 1950s, to be more profound for Hong Kong than for the intended target, whose self-sufficiency protects it from the devastation that Hong Kong would endure. But in the 1990s not only would Hong Kong suffer. Such action would entail serious detriment to American and Taiwan businesses whose investments in both Hong Kong and on the mainland would be jeopardized. Furthermore, in Taiwan, government and business interests would see the destabilization of Hong Kong as a harbinger of disaster to come for the island.

The new economic alignments that force Washington to reconceptualize its approach to Taiwan and Hong Kong could eventually also moderate the political tensions that continue to trouble the area. There are analysts in the U.S. who suggest that economic integration could lead to political cooperation, even a federation of some kind that might bridge the question of reunification and the ideological differences among the participants. Others, particularly in Taiwan, remain skeptical.

Hong Kong's frictions with the People's Republic following Tiananmen evoked minimal interest among observers on Taiwan, the incident seeming to them entirely predictable. The idea that Deng Xiaoping's "one country, two systems" formula would prove to be effective in Hong Kong, thereby relieving anxieties on the island and reducing resistance to reincorporation, precipitously lost credibility after 1989. Beijing's angry rejection of efforts by the British to facilitate democratization of Hong Kong struck many in Taiwan as no more than expected and a clear harbinger of further repression to come.[2]

If an economically driven Greater China does not lead naturally to a larger political settlement, however, the United States can anticipate confronting some difficult issues in the years ahead. The return of Hong Kong to China promises to be disturbing if not devastating for the territory. Although China has good financial and commercial reasons for protecting existing institutions and conciliating the foreigners whose money keeps Hong Kong viable, there are also internal political pressures that militate against a successful transition. The United States may be faced with the loss of large investments. More significantly, it may find that watching the incorporation of a semidemocratic system into a communist state confronts it with unanswerable human rights problems.

More destabilizing yet would be the "two Chinas" question that is certain to arise with renewed force in the not-too-distant future. As the mainland refugees on the island of Taiwan age and die, a new generation no longer looks to recovery of or reunion with China as an ultimate goal. Sharing more with the Taiwanese than with the mainlanders, they think increasingly about independence. Were it not a hazardous idea, there is every reason to believe that it would be an exceedingly popular one. Clearly Chinese leader Deng Xiaoping fears this truth, believing that "it is better for both the mainland and Taiwan to establish contacts and realize the goal of the country's reunification when the senior leaders of the PRC and the KMT in Taiwan are still alive. The problems concerning the Taiwan issue can be resolved easier when people who know the history of both . . . are alive. If the issue is postponed, there are many questions the younger generation of the two parties do not understand. This is the reason behind the anxiety."[3] Emphasizing his concern, Deng, although an octogenarian in failing health, offered to travel to Taipei in 1991 to discuss reunification.[4] Moreover, it is doubtful, even were the Communists to lose power and a democratic government to take their place, that the rising tide of Chinese nationalism would be stilled and the mainlanders more willing to accept self-determination for Taiwan.

In Taiwan discussions of independence have become increasingly common as the DPP's growing power has made it safer to contemplate a path that the KMT rejects vehemently. Public patience with Taiwan's exclusion from international organizations such as the GATT has declined, and a demand for representation in the United Nations has emerged with surprising insistence. Although some of the rhetoric has been for political effect, there are those who are obsessed with the issue, unrealistic about the consequences, and conceivably within range, in the not too distant future, of grasping political control. Thus, even with a democratic government in Beijing, people in Taiwan, especially the Taiwanese, may well have no interest in surrendering their de facto independence.

The danger for the United States rests in the almost inevitable clash between long-held principles. The U.S. has emphasized through much of the twentieth century, in rhetoric if not always in action, the tremendous importance of self-determination. People ought to have the opportunity to choose for themselves the kind of government they will live under, the values they will live by, the goals they will live for. But the United States has also stressed respect for national sovereignty as a fundamental organizing precept addressing pragmatic and philosophical needs. So far, it has resisted demands that it intercede in Beijing-Taipei relations to broker a solution to political disjunction. Washington, while welcoming economic ties and developing dialogue, remains as neutral as possible lest it be forced to chose between violating freedom of choice or the sanctity of the state. This is a precarious position from which there seems no escape.

Should Taiwan take the next step and declare independence, the United States would have to choose between neutrality or assistance to Taipei in the military struggle almost certain to ensue. Washington has warned independence advocates that it takes Beijing's threats seriously, as they should, and that the U.S. advocates a peaceful solution to the so-called Taiwan question. Assumptions that the United States could ignore a PRC attack on Taiwan, even one occasioned by Taipei through a declaration of independence, however, may underestimate the tensions and passions that would be aroused in such a situation. Taiwan as an island might be seen as militarily defensible by U.S. naval power, and Taiwan as a symbol of democracy in Asia might not be so easily abandoned. The alternatives are sobering; a solution disturbingly out of reach.

The United States' relationship with Taiwan and with Hong Kong has come to a moment in history driven by tremendous change and fraught with opportunities and perils. The future could be prosperous and peaceful or there could develop crises of a most fundamental sort. Washington must focus its attention on Asia and on Greater China to a degree and with an intensity heretofore reserved for problems among its European allies and adversaries.

Only then will the United States begin to understand clearly the area's dynamics, its history, and its expectations. The American role in the Pacific region has diminished with the end of the cold war, but Washington has no choice but to remain involved to protect the security and prosperity of the United States and the world.

CHRONOLOGY

1945   February:

Roosevelt and Stalin agree at Yalta that USSR will enter the Pacific War and China will grant concessions in Manchuria.

September:

Japan officially surrenders, ending the Pacific War.

1947   January:

U.S. announces end of Marshall Mission and its mediation efforts in China.

February:

Rebellion of Taiwanese against Nationalist authorities suppressed brutally.

July:

Chinese Nationalist government orders total mobilization for war against the CCP.

August:

Wedemeyer mission.

1948   April:

China Aid Act ($570 million) signed.

December:

Madame Chiang Kai-shek visits U.S. to secure aid for Republic of China.

1949   January:

Chiang Kai-shek retires from presidency in favor of Vice President Li Tsung-jen.

April:

Congress extends China aid through February 1950. CCP crosses Yangtze river.

July:

ROC begins to withdraw troops to Taiwan.

August:

State Department White Paper on China.

October:

People's Republic of China established 1 October.
Mutual Defense Assistance Act provides $75 million for the general area of China.

December:

Nationalist government evacuated to Taiwan. State Department circular telegram warns of imminent fall of Taiwan.

1950   January:

MacArthur's headquarters leak circular telegram. Truman issues statement of nonintervention in Chinese civil war. Great Britain recognizes PRC. USSR walks out of UN to protest ROC retaining China seat. Acheson's National Press

Club speech places Taiwan outside the U.S. defensive perimeter.

February:

Senator McCarthy attacks communists in State Department at Wheeling, West Virgina. Sino-Soviet Treaty signed.

June:

Korean War erupts 25 June. Truman orders 7th Fleet into the Taiwan Strait. U.S. commits ground troops to Korea.

July:

MacArthur goes to meet Chiang on Taiwan.

October:

Chinese Communist troops intervene in Korea.

December:

New trade and financial controls against the PRC treat Hong Kong as though it were a communist port.

1952   January:

NSC 122 reduces restrictions on Hong Kong's trade with PRC.

1953   February:

President Eisenhower "unleashes" Chiang Kai-shek.

July:

Korean armistice signed 26 July.

October:

Committee for One Million Against the Admission of Communist China to the United Nations opens its first office.

November:

U.S. begins airlifting Nationalist troops out of Burma

1954   September:

PRC begins artillery shelling of the offshore islands, launching first Taiwan Straits crisis.

December:

U.S.-ROC Mutual Defense Treaty signed.

1955   January–February:

Chinese raids on Dachen islands, prompting evacuation. Formosa resolution becomes law.

August:

U.S.-PRC ambassadorial talks begin.

1957   May:

American Embassy in Taipei ransacked. U.S. decides to station Matador missiles on Taiwan.

1958   August:

Second Taiwan Straits crisis begins with shelling by PRC.

September:

Zhou Enlai suggests resumption of Warsaw talks. Secretary Dulles criticizes continued garrisoning of offshore islands.

October:

PRC declares temporary cease fire. Chiang renounces use of force to recover mainland. PRC begins alternate day shelling of offshore islands.

1960   June:

NSC 6007/1 approved, pledging to help Britain provide security for Hong Kong.

September:

Warsaw talks are stalemated on Taiwan question. Lei Chen arrested.

October:

Kennedy-Nixon campaign debate raises offshore islands issue. Conlon Report published.

1961   December:

US succeeds in making China representation issue an important question at UN requiring two-thirds vote majority.

1962   May:

Kennedy suggests possibility of food aid to China as refugees flood Hong Kong.

June:

US tells PRC at Warsaw that Washington will not support ROC attack on mainland.

September:

U-2 shot down over East China, first after two years of unimpeded overflights.

1963   December:

Roger Hilsman makes China policy speech seeming to open door to improved relations with PRC.

1964   October:

PRC first nuclear test. Peng Ming-min arrested and imprisoned.

1965   March:

Vice President Ch'en Ch'eng dies.

June:

U.S. aid to Taiwan ends.

1966   March:

Senate Foreign Relations Committee hearings on China.

November:

Cultural Renaissance Movement.

1967   May–December:

Cultural Revolution spills over China's border into Hong Kong.

October:

Nixon, in *Foreign Affairs* piece, hints at the need for better relations with the PRC.

1969   March:

Sino-Soviet border clashes.

July:

Nixon relaxes trade and travel restrictions on China. Nixon Doctrine articulated at Guam.

November:

7th Fleet terminates operations in Taiwan Straits.

1970   April:

Assassination attempt on Chiang Ching-kuo in United States.

1971   July:

United States announces Nixon China visit.

August:

United States declares support for China's admission to UN but opposes ROC ouster.

October:

UN votes to seat PRC in UN; ROC walks out.

1972   February:

Nixon arrives in PRC and joins with Beijing leaders in issuing Shanghai communique.

June:

Watergate break-in.

1973   February:

U.S.–North Vietnam agreement ends American participation in the Vietnam War.

April:

Liaison offices established in Washington and Beijing.

1974   U.S. Congress repeals Formosa resolution, ends military grants to the Nationalist government.

1975   April:

Chiang Kai-shek dies.

May:

First Vietnamese boat people arrive in Hong Kong.

1977   November:

Chungli incident.

1978   May:

Chiang Ching-kuo inaugurated president of ROC.

December:

Joint communique announces establishment of U.S.-PRC diplomatic relations and termination of Mutual Defense Treaty ties between Washington and Taipei; Senator Goldwater and 14 other members of Congress file suit in U.S. District Court to prevent termination. Christopher mission to Taiwan.

1979   January:

U.S. and PRC resume formal ties. Message from the Standing Committee of the PRC National People's Congress to "compatriots in Taiwan." Deng tells U.S. Senate delegation that Taiwan could maintain autonomy and armed forces after reunification. U.S. reveals agreement of one-year moratorium of arms sales to Taiwan.

March:

U.S. Embassy in Taiwan officially closes, to be replaced by American Institute.

April:

Taiwan Relations Act.

December:

Kaohsiung Incident.

1981   July:

Death of professor Chen Wen-chen under mysterious circumstances.

September:

PRC 9 Point Proposal for economic and cultural exchange across the Taiwan Straits and direct talks regarding reunification.

1982   January:

Reagan administration rules out sale of advanced fighter aircraft to Taiwan, approves additional F-5Es.

March:

PRC warns U.S.-China relations will suffer if U.S. insists on longterm arms sales to Taiwan.

August:

U.S.-China communique pledging reduction in U.S. arms sales to Taiwan.

September:

British Prime Minister Thatcher visits PRC for talks on Hong Kong.

1983   June:

Deng Xiaoping announces "one country, two systems" formula. Taipei announces 3 noes: No contact, no negotiation and no compromise.

1984   September:

China and Britain announce agreement transferring Hong Kong to PRC sovereignty in 1997.

October:

Murder of Henry Liu. Taiwan participates in the Olympic games as "Chinese, Taipei."

1986   February:

PRC enters Asian Development Bank; Taiwan, a founding member protests change in its name from ROC to Taipei, China.

May:

Taipei and Beijing conduct first face-to-face negotiation, over hijacked aircraft held in Hong Kong.

December:

First election effort for Democratic Progressive Party

1987   July:

Martial law, imposed in 1949, lifted in Taiwan.

September:

ROC lifts ban against travel to PRC.

1988   January:

Chiang Ching-kuo dies and is succeeded by Lee Teng-hui.

1989   March:

New voluntary repatriation program for Vietnamese refugees in Hong Kong.

April:

Hu Yaobang dies in PRC triggering Beijing Spring.

May:

Taiwan's finance minister Shirley Kuo attends Asian Development Bank meeting in Beijing, first ROC official to visit mainland China since 1950.

June:

Tiananmen Massacre in PRC.

July:

Demonstrations in Hong Kong against British refusal to grant Hong Kong passport holders refuge in Britain. Forcible repatriation of Vietnamese boat people from Hong Kong.

1990   January:

Massive demonstration in Hong Kong for democracy in PRC.

February:

Hong Kong Basic Law adopted.

March:

Prodemocracy demonstration in Chiang Kai-shek Square.

May:

Protest ship "Goddess of Democracy" is rebuffed by Taiwan.

1991   July:

George Bush calls for Taiwan's entry into GATT.

September:

Taipei police clash with 15,000 protestors demanding referendum on UN membership.

October:

Democratic Progressive Party renounces claims to sovereignty over mainland.

December:

In first full elections for National Assembly, KMT wins 71% and DPP wins 24% of the vote.

1992   April:

Christopher Patten named governor of Hong Kong.

August:

United States–Hong Kong Policy Act.

September:

George Bush announces F-16 sale to Taiwan.

December:

USTR Carla Hills visit to Taiwan, first cabinet-level official to go there since 1978.

NOTES AND REFERENCES

The following abbreviations are used in the notes:

bx	box.
CA	Records of the Office of Chinese Affairs, General Records of the Department of State, National Archives.
Columbia	Rare Book and Manuscript Library, Columbia University Libraries, Columbia University, New York, N.Y.
f	folder.
FBIS	Foreign Broadcast Information Service.
FEER	*Far Eastern Economic Review*.
FRUS	*Foreign Relations of the United States* (Washington, D.C.: Government Printing Office).
Georgetown	Foreign Affairs Oral History Program, Georgetown University, Washington, D.C.
Harvard	Harvard University Archives, Harvard University, Cambridge, Mass.
IKE	Dwight D. Eisenhower Library, Abilene, Kans.
JFK	John F. Kennedy Library, Columbia Point, Boston, Mass.
LBJ	Lyndon Baines Johnson Library, Austin, Tex.
MUDD	Seeley Mudd Library, Princeton University, Princeton, N.J.
NA	National Archives, Washington, D.C.
NSC	National Security Council.
NSF	National Security Files.
POF	President's Office Files.
PRO	Public Records Office, Kew, Great Britain.

RG   Record Group.
RG 59, NA   Record Group 59: General Records of the Department of State, National Archives.
SCMP   *Survey of China Mainland Press*.
WNRC   Washington National Records Center, Suitland, Md.
Yale   Yale University Archives, Sterling Memorial Library, New Haven, Conn.

CHAPTER 1

1. Robert O. Keohane, "The Big Influence of Small Allies," *Foreign Policy* (Spring 1971): 161–82; Robert L. Rothstein, *Alliances and Small Powers* (New York: Columbia University Press, 1968).

2. Keohane, "Big Influence," 163.

3. This is contrary to the assumptions of Robert Rothstein and Raymond Aron who believe a small power can only have defensive ambitions. Rothstein, *Alliances*, 27n24.

4. Machiavelli, *The Prince* (New York: Modern Library, 1950).

5. In the 1959 Peter Sellers film by that name, the Duchy of Grand Fenwick tried to manipulate the United States into taking care of all its needs by declaring war on it. Steve Chan, "The Mouse that Roared: Taiwan's Management of Trade Relations with the United States," *Comparative Political Studies* 20 (October 1987): 251–92.

6. Richard E. Barrett and Martin K. Whyte, "Dependency Theory and Taiwan: Analysis of a Deviant Case," *American Journal of Sociology* 87 (March 1982): 1073.

7. Chan, "The Mouse That Roared," 275.

CHAPTER 2

1. James K. Sheridan, *China in Disintegration: The Republican Era in Chinese History, 1912–1949* (New York: Free Press, 1975), 216–20. The debate over whether Chiang and the Blue Shirts truly adhered to fascism has been joined by Lloyd Eastman, "Fascism in Kuomintang China: The Blue Shirts," *China Quarterly* (January–March 1972), 1–31; with a reply by Maria Hsia Chang, "'Fascism' and Modern China," *China Quarterly* (September 1979): 553–67; and the rejoinder by Eastman in *China Quarterly* (December 1979): 838–42.

2. Paul A. Cohen, "The Post-Mao Reforms in Historical Perspective," *Journal of Asian Studies* 47 (August 1988): 529–32; James C. Thomson, Jr., *While China Faced West* (Cambridge: Harvard University Press, 1969), discusses the role of American advisers.

3. Dorothy Borg, *The United States and the Far Eastern Crisis of 1933–1938* (Cambridge: Harvard University Press, 1964), 387–98.

4. Although Chiang did secure the province of Sichuan, in which his wartime capital was located, frictions continued with Lung Yun in Yunnan. Wu T'ien-wei, "Contending Political Forces During the War of Resistance," in *China's Bitter Victory*, James C. Hsiung and Steven I. Levine, eds. (Armonk, N.Y.: M. E. Sharpe, 1992), 60–62.

5. John W. Garver, "China's Wartime Diplomacy," in Hsiung and Levine, *Bitter Victory*, 8–10, 20.

6. Michael Schaller, *The United States and China in the Twentieth Century* (New York: Oxford, 1979), 54–57; Charles Wertenbaker, "The China Lobby," *Reporter*, April 1952, 4–8.

7. Waldo Heinrichs, *Threshold to War* (New York: Oxford University Press, 1988).

8. According to John Garver, Chiang threatened China's collapse to keep Anglo-American forces committed to the theater even though he always intended to continue his resistance against Japan regardless of their actions; Garver, "China's Wartime Diplomacy," 19.

9. Han Suyin as quoted in Schaller, *United States and China*, 70.

10. A practice introduced in the 1842 Treaty of Nanking, which the U.S. acquired in 1844 in the Treaty of Wanghsia. Under extraterritoriality foreigners were not subject to Chinese law but rather would be punished under the laws of their own countries for crimes committed in China.

Exclusion had been enacted in 1924 following a series of laws tightening immigration restriction. Although Chinese could enter the U.S. after 1943, the Chinese quota was set at the absurd figure of 105.

11. Garver indicts Stilwell for poor leadership in Burma, suggesting Chiang willingly contributed forces to win there even though he suspected the British simply wanted to cover their retreat and see China weakened; Garver, "China's Wartime Diplomacy," 20–21.

12. Herbert Feis, *The China Tangle* (New York: Antheneum, 1967), 166. It also drew Japanese troops deeper into Chinese territory than they might otherwise have gone.

13. Warren I. Cohen, "Who Fought the Japanese in Hunan? Some Views of China's War Effort," *Journal of Asian Studies* 27 (November 1967): 115. A more sympathetic account of Nationalist China's effort appears in Ch'i Hsi-sheng, "The Military Dimension," in Hsiung and Levine, *Bitter Victory*, 157–84.

14. For Stilwell's views see his diary, Theodore H. White, ed., *The Stilwell Papers* (New York: William Sloane, 1948), 203–4, 304–5, 333; Barbara Tuchman, *Stilwell and the American Experience in China, 1911–1945* (New York: Macmillan, 1970), 215–20, 310–11, 335–39, 356–57, 458–59, 493–94; and for Chennault's account see Claire Chennault, *The Way of a Fighter* (New York: Putnam's, 1949).

15. Robert Dallek, *Franklin D. Roosevelt and American Foreign Policy, 1932–1945* (New York: Oxford University Press, 1979), 328–29, 389–90; Winston S. Churchill, *The Hinge of Fate* (Boston: Houghton Mifflin, 1953), 507–8.

16. Far Eastern Agreement on Soviet Entry into the War Against Japan, Yalta, 11 February 1945. In fact, according to John Garver, "although domestic political considerations required that Chiang later plead surprise and outrage at this Soviet-American diktat . . . Chiang . . . had indicated to Roosevelt general approval of several of the key elements which were embodied in the Yalta agreement"; John Garver,

Chinese-Soviet Relations, 1937–1945 (New York: Oxford, 1988), 209. No agreement had existed regarding Outer Mongolia; Garver, "China's Wartime Diplomacy," 27.

17.   Steven I. Levine, *Anvil of Victory: The Communist Revolution in Manchuria, 1945–1948* (New York: Columbia University Press, 1987), 75.

18.   Michael Schaller, *The U.S. Crusade in China, 1938–1945* (New York: Columbia, 1979), 181–90, 228–29; Joseph W. Esherick, ed., *Lost Chance in China: The World War II Dispatches of John S. Service* (New York: Random House, 1974); David Barrett, *Dixie Mission* (Berkeley: University of California Press, 1970).

19.   Barbara Tuchman, *Notes from China* (New York: Collier, 1972), 77–112; and see Kenneth E. Shewmaker, *Americans and the Chinese Communists, 1927–1945* (Ithaca: Cornell University Press, 1971). The most influential contemporary portrait was Edgar Snow's *Red Star over China* (New York: Random House, 1938), based on three months spent with the Communist leaders.

20.   Lyman P. Van Slyke, ed., *The China White Paper, August 1949* (Stanford: Stanford University Press, 1967), 94–96. Stalin told Ambassador Averell Harriman in 1944 that "the Chinese Communists are not real Communists. They are 'margarine' Communists"; Feis, *China Tangle*, 140.

21.   James Reardon-Anderson, *Yenan and the Great Powers* (New York: Columbia University Press, 1980), 103.

22.   Wu Kuo-cheng Oral History, Chinese Oral History Project, Columbia University, 1–12.

23.   George Woodbridge, *UNRRA* (New York: Columbia University Press, 1950), 430–36; "Summary Report on Operations in and for the Far East through February, 1946," UNRRA Records, PAG-4/1.0.4.0.0., bx 14, f: China Post Liberation, February 1946, United Nations Archive, New York, N.Y.

24.   Official American studies of Chinese factionalism appear often in the State Department records as in, for example, Office of Intelligence Research Report no. 4378, "The April 1947 Reorganization of the Chinese Government," 26 May 1947, OSS/State Department Intelligence and Research Reports, reel 4, pt. III: China and India, University Publications of America, Washington, D.C.

25.   Lloyd E. Eastman, *The Abortive Revolution: China under Nationalist Rules, 1927–1937* (Cambridge: Harvard University Press, 1974), 20, 83, 304–5.

26.   V. K. Wellington Koo to George Kung-chao Yeh, 20 July 1949, V. K. Wellington Koo Papers, Box 168, Columbia University, New York, N.Y. (hereafter cited as Columbia).

27.   761.93/11–749 Memorandum Clark to Philip Jessup, Record Group 59: General Records of the Department of State, National Archives (hereafter cited as RG 59, NA).

28.   V. K. Wellington Koo Oral History, J (section 5), 396, Koo Papers, Columbia; Koo Diary, 2 March 1949 and 4 January 1950, Koo Papers, Columbia; analysis of Pawley Memorandum by W.W. Stuart and Philip D. Sprouse, folder: Civilian Advisors to China, Records of the Office of Chinese Affairs, RG 59, NA; interview, General Albert C. Wedemeyer with this author, 30 November 1977.

29.   Van Slyke, *The China White Paper*, was originally published as *United States Relations with China, With Special Reference to the Period 1944–1949*, Department of State Publication 3573.

30.   U.S. Congress, Senate Committee on Foreign Relations, *The United States*

and Communist China in 1949 and 1950: The Question of Rapprochement and Recognition (Washington, D.C.: Government Printing Office, 1973), 10n28; U.S. Department of State, The Far East: China, 1949, vol. 8 of Foreign Relations of the United States (Washington, D.C.: Government Printing Office, 1978), 741–802 (hereafter cited as FRUS).

31. U.S. Department of State, Transcript of the Round Table Discussion on American Policy toward China, October 6, 7, and 8, 1949 (Washington, D.C.: Government Printing Office, 1949).

CHAPTER 3

1. Huang Chia-mo, Meiguo yu Taiwan, 1784–1895 (The U.S. and Taiwan, 1784–1895) (Taipei: Academia Sinica, 1966), 135–37.

2. Sophia Su-fei Yen, Taiwan in China's Foreign Relations, 1836–1874 (Hamden, Conn.: Shoe String Press, 1965), 49–55, 69–70, 126–31.

3. Walter E. Gourlay, "Hong Kong and Taiwan: The Colonial Heritage," in Jack F. Williams, ed., The Future of Hong Kong and Taiwan (East Lansing: Michigan State University, occasional paper #9 of the Asian Studies Center, 1985), 1–32; Leonard Gordon, "American Planning for Taiwan, 1942–1945," Pacific Historical Review 37 (May 1968): 201–28.

4. Among the most outspoken and influential proponents of self-determination for Taiwan has been Senator Claiborne Pell, chairman of the Senate Foreign Relations Committee, whose dedication arose from his experience as part of that group; Pell, "I Fully Support Self-Determination," Taiwan Update (March 1987): 1. For details on the Formosan Research Unit see George Kerr, Formosa Betrayed (Boston: Houghton Mifflin, 1965), 19–31.

5. Kerr, Formosa Betrayed, 174–75; Van Slyke, China White Paper, 308–10.

6. Kerr, Formosa Betrayed, 240–48.

7. Different interpretations of these events are discussed and evaluated in Lai Tse-han, Ramon H. Myers, and Wei Wou, A Tragic Beginning (Stanford: Stanford University Press, 1991), 3–11 and passim. The government of Taiwan has published its own investigation of the event, entitled "A Special Report on the February 28 Incident," prepared by the 2-28 Incident Research Task Force commissioned by the Executive Yuan in 1991. Among other things it criticizes lack of discipline in the military, unequal treatment of the Taiwanese, and exaggerated Taiwanese expectations of the government; Tammy C. Peng, "Official '2-28 Incident' Report Readied," Free China Journal (14 February 1992): 1. It should be noted that Lai Tse-han, a coauthor of A Tragic Beginning, also headed the government task force.

8. Van Slyke, China White Paper, 309.

9. Kerr tells the story in detail in Formosa Betrayed.

10. 894A.01/2–949 and 894A.01/4–1249 Sebald to Allison, RG 59, NA.

11. The remainder of this chapter draws upon Nancy Bernkopf Tucker, Patterns in the Dust: Chinese-American Relations and the Recognition Controversy, 1949–1950 (New York: Columbia University Press, 1983).

12. John Leighton Stuart Diary, 20 and 21 February 1949, Washington, D.C.; 893.001 Chiang Kai-shek/2–2149, #440, Stuart, Nanking, FRUS 1949, vol. 8, 142.

13. NSC 37/2, "The Current Position of the United States with Respect to

Formosa," 3 February 1949, *FRUS 1949*, vol. 9, *The Far East: China* (Washington, D.C.: Government Printing Office, 1972), 281–82; 893.50 Recovery/4–2949 Economic Cooperation Administration to Assistant Secretary, ibid., 319–20; 893.50 Recovery/5–449 Merchant, Taipei, ibid., 324–26.

14. JCS 1966/20, "Possibility of Communist Acquisition of Chinese Air Force Aircraft Presently on Taiwan," 29 November 1949, Army Intelligence Document Files, Record Group (RG) 319, bx 154, f 091: Formosa (4), Washington National Records Center, Suitland, Md. (hereafter cited as WNRC).

15. For further discussion of the role of the China lobby and the Chinese government in the U.S., see Tucker, *Patterns*, 59–99, 161–68; Ross Y. Koen, *The China Lobby in American Politics* (New York: Harper & Row, 1974).

16. Service had followed a common practice of sharing factual information with a journalist, not knowing that Philip Jaffe, *Amerasia*'s editor, was under FBI surveillance. Esherick, *Lost Chance*, xix–xx, 388–91.

17. E. J. Kahn, Jr., *The China Hands: America's Foreign Service Officers and What Befell Them* (New York: Viking Press, 1972), examines the experiences of several victims; Robert P. Newman, *Owen Lattimore and the "Loss" of China* (Berkeley: University of California Press, 1992), 123–492; O. Edmund Clubb, *The Witness and I* (New York: Columbia University Press, 1974).

18. Bruce Cumings, *The Roaring of the Cataract, 1947–1950*, vol. 2 of *The Origins of the Korean War* (Princeton: Princeton University Press, 1990), 509–31.

19. PPS 53, "United States Policy toward Formosa and the Pescadores," 6 July 1949, *FRUS 1949*, vol. 9, 356–59; 794A.00/5–3150 Memorandum by Howe, Deputy Special Assistant for Intelligence to Armstrong, Special Assistant to the Secretary of State for Intelligence and Research, *FRUS 1950*, vol. 6, *East Asia and the Pacific* (Washington, D.C.: Government Printing Office, 1976), 347–51.

20. Cumings, *Cataract*, 531–44.

21. Leonard A. Kusnitz, *Public Opinion and Foreign Policy: America's China Policy, 1949–1979* (Westport, Conn.: Greenwood Press, 1984), 34.

22. 794.00/8–2650 Memorandum by Lucius D. Battle, Special Assistant to Acheson, *FRUS 1950*, vol. 6, 453–60; *New York Times*, 28 August 1950, p. 1, and 29 August 1950, pp. 1, 3, 17.

23. The CCP made apparent in its newspaper commentary that it was not comforted by Truman's order to withdraw MacArthur's letter. *Hsin-hua yueh-pao* (New China Monthly) 3 (November 1950): 16.

24. John Lewis Gaddis, *Strategies of Containment* (New York: Oxford University Press, 1982), 113.

25. The most persuasive case regarding the significance of the Korean conflict was made by Robert Jervis, "The Impact of the Korean War on the Cold War," *Journal of Conflict Resolution* 24 (December 1980): 563–92.

26. Dulles worried that the British would convince an Anglophilic Dean Acheson to have Tokyo follow a policy less hostile to Beijing. He threatened Prime Minister Yoshida with congressional refusal to ratify the Japanese Peace Treaty. Historian Warren I. Cohen maintains that Yoshida was happy to be coerced since he favored relations with Taiwan but wanted to trade acquiescence for other benefits. "China in Japanese-American Relations," in Akira Iriye and Warren I. Cohen, eds., *The United States and Japan in the Postwar World* (Lexington: University of Kentucky Press, 1989), 40–42.

27. Rao Geping, "Taiwan Diwei Weidinglun de Falu Toushi" (A legalistic examination on the thesis of the status of Taiwan as undecided), in Zi Zhongyun and He Di, eds., *Meitai Guanxi Sishinian* (Forty years of U.S.-Taiwan relations) (Beijing: People's Press, 1991), 78–107.

28. Rosemary Foot, *A Substitute for Victory* (Ithaca: Cornell University Press, 1990), 87–92, 97, 192–93, 219–20.

29. According to Pu Shan, aide to Chinese Premier and Foreign Minister Zhou Enlai, the CCP leaders saw "unleashing" as a pejorative epithet and as an indicator of frictions in U.S.-Taiwan relations. Interview with Pu Shan, Beijing, China, summer 1987.

30. State Department Study of Reactions to Unleashing, 11 February 1953, Records of the Office of Chinese Affairs, bx 40, f 410: Chinese Nationalist Armed Forces, RG 59, NA.

31. 139th Meeting, National Security Council, 8 April 1953, *FRUS 1952–54*, vol. 14, pt. 1, *China and Japan* (Washington, D.C.: Governmment Printing Office, 1985), 181; 794A.5/4–1653, #848 Dulles to Rankin, ibid., 191; 794A.5/4–2353, #1118 Jones, Taipei, ibid., 193.

32. Nevertheless, Everett Drumright remarked in retrospect that as U.S. ambassador on Taiwan he "usually took a strong line in defense of the ROC [Republic of China] position. I had the feeling that my superior, W. S. Robertson, felt I was inflexible; perhaps I was." Letter, Drumright to the author, 5 July 1989.

33. Nancy Bernkopf Tucker, "A House Divided: The United States, the Department of State, and China," in Warren I. Cohen and Akira Iriye, eds., *The Great Powers in East Asia, 1953–1960* (New York: Columbia University Press, 1990), 36–38.

34. Tucker, "A House Divided," 39–41.

35. See memoranda of conversations that Ambassador V. K. Wellington Koo had with men such as Congressman Walter Judd, Senator William Knowland, and Vice President Richard Nixon in July 1954, Koo Papers, bx 191, Columbia; Foreign Minister Yeh to Nixon, 18 December 1953, bx 3, f: KMT Troops in Burma, China Post Files, RG 84, NA.

36. 793.00/10–154 Dulte 15, *FRUS 1952–54*, vol. 14, pt. 1, 670.

37. Nancy Bernkopf Tucker, "John Foster Dulles and the Taiwan Roots of the 'Two Chinas' Policy," in Richard H. Immerman, ed., *John Foster Dulles and the Diplomacy of the Cold War* (Princeton: Princeton University Press, 1990), 241–44.

38. For an interesting perspective on the offshore islands crises see He Di, "The Evolution of the People's Republic of China's Policy toward the Offshore Islands," in Cohen and Iriye, *The Great Powers*, 222–45. In a more recent piece He Di and his coauthor Gordon H. Chang argue that from the Chinese perspective the events of 1954–55 never were perceived as a crisis. "The Absence of War in the U. S.-China Confrontation over Quemoy and Matsu in 1954–1955: Contingency, Luck, Deterrence?" *American Historical Review* 98 (December 1993): 1500–24.

39. Interview with Ambassador Zhang Wenjin, Beijing, China, July 1987; He Di, "The Evolution," 224–25.

40. Chiang and others claimed that the U.S. pledged to defend Quemoy and Matsu when officials agreed to evacuate Dachen. Jonathan Trumbull Howe, *Multicrises* (Cambridge: MIT Press, 1971), 170–71; #417 Hoover to Taipei, 29 January 1955, Eisenhower Papers, Whitman File, International Series, bx 9, f:

Formosa Area U.S. Military Operations (3), IKE, Dwight D. Eisenhower Library, Abilene, Kans. (hereafter cited as IKE).

41. Memorandum of Discussion, 240th NSC Meeting, 10 March 1955, *FRUS 1955–57*, vol. 2, *China* (Washington, D.C.: Government Printing Office, 1986), 346–50.

42. John Wilson Lewis and Xue Litai, *China Builds the Bomb* (Stanford: Stanford University Press, 1988), 34.

43. Memorandum by Rankin, 29 April 1955, *FRUS 1955–57*, vol. 2, 529–31.

44. Letter Eisenhower to Chiang Kai-shek, 17 May 1956, *FRUS 1955–57*, vol. 3, *China* (Washington, D.C.: Government Printing Office, 1986), 361.

45. Eisenhower to Dulles, 5 April 1955, Eisenhower Papers, Whitman File, Dulles-Herter Series, bx 4, f: Dulles, April 1955 (2), and Eisenhower Diary, bx 10, f: April 1955 (2), IKE; Memorandum for the Record, Karl Rankin Papers, bx 26, f: Chiang Kai-shek, Seeley Mudd Library, Princeton University, Princeton, N.J. (hereafter cited as MUDD).

46. Op-00 Memo 000416–58, 7 September 1958, Burke to Twining, CCS 381 Formosa (11–8–48), sec. 38A, U.S. Department of Defense, RG 218: Records of the Joint Chiefs of Staff, NA.

47. According to Richard P. Stebbins in *The United States and World Affairs* (New York: Harper & Brothers, 1959), 322, the U.S. assembled "the most powerful air-naval striking force in its history." McGeorge Bundy observes that that fact had "a special resonance at a time when memories of the armada of World War II were still fresh"; *Danger and Survival* (New York: Vintage, 1990), 673n107. The armada included 6 aircraft carriers, 3 heavy cruisers, 40 destroyers, a submarine division, and 20 other ships; Gordon H. Chang, *Friends and Enemies: The United States, China, and the Soviet Union, 1948–1972* (Stanford: Stanford University Press, 1990), 185.

48. Official military doctrine sanctioned the use of nuclear weapons in limited war situations; Howe, *Multicrises*, 166n13.

49. Chang, *Friends and Enemies*, 189. He wrote much the same thing to British Prime Minister Harold Wilson on 4 September 1958. Eisenhower Papers, Whitman File, International Series, bx 10, f: Formosa (1958) (2), IKE.

50. Jacob D. Beam, *Multiple Exposure* (New York: W. W. Norton, 1978), 127–28.

51. This section relies on the analysis provided by Allen S. Whiting in *The Chinese Calculus of Deterrence: India and Indochina* (Ann Arbor: University of Michigan Press, 1975), 62–72 (quote taken from p. 67).

52. Memorandum of Conversation Averell Harriman with Anatoly Dobrynin, 22 June 1962, JFK Papers, President's Office Files, bx 113a, f: China Security 1962–63, John F. Kennedy Library, Columbia Point, Boston, Mass. (hereafter cited as JFK). According to Ralph Clough, former Foreign Service officer and historian, Kirk's background was seen as giving him the authority necessary to dissuade Chiang from attempting an invasion; interview with Ralph Clough, Washington, D.C., May 1993. Ambassador Harvey Feldman suggested that Kirk, a crusty character, was meant "to lay down the law to Chiang Kai-shek"; interview with Ambassador Harvey Feldman, Virginia, April 1991.

53. According to Allen S. Whiting, who was on the State Department's Intelligence and Research (INR) staff in 1962, the CIA knew about and facilitated

Chiang Kai-shek's weapons buildup and kept it secret from the State Department. Interview with Allen S. Whiting, Beijing, China, 1988.

54. Roger Hilsman (INR) to Secretary of State, 18 January 1962, Roger Hilsman Papers, bx 1: Countries, f: China-OSI Crisis, June 1962, JFK.

55. Thomas G. Paterson, "Fixation with Cuba: The Bay of Pigs, Missile Crisis, and Covert War against Fidel Castro," in Paterson, ed., *Kennedy's Quest for Victory* (New York: Oxford, 1989), 131–36; Paterson is skeptical about the degree to which the administration was chastened. John M. Cabot Diary #24, 23 June 1962, 52–54, Tufts University Library, Medford, Mass.; *Public Papers of the Presidents: John F. Kennedy, 1962* (Washington, D.C.: Government Printing Office, 1963), 276–77, 509–10.

56. Wang Bingnan, *Nine Years of Sino-American Ambassadorial Talks* (Beijing: World Knowledge Publishing House, 1985), 71.

57. See Richard H. Immerman, *The CIA in Guatemala* (1982); William Stivers, "Eisenhower and the Middle East," in Richard A. Melanson and David Mayers, eds., *Reevaluating Eisenhower* (Chicago: University of Illinois Press, 1989), 192–219.

58. See Stanley D. Bachrack, *The Committee of One Million: "China Lobby" Politics, 1953–1971* (New York: Columbia University Press, 1976), 60–61, 190–95. See also the papers of Marvin Liebman, Hoover Institution Archives, Stanford, Calif.

59. Although the North Koreans sought to continue the war, China's economy was suffering and its leaders appealed to Moscow in the autumn of 1952 to agree to end the conflict. Dependent upon Soviet help to finance and provide technical assistance for domestic development, the Chinese could not negotiate an armistice if Moscow refused. Stalin apparently approved in 1952, but rapid progress awaited his death. Robert R. Simmons, *The Strained Alliance* (New York: Free Press, 1975), 223–35; Foot, *Substitute for Victory*, 181–83, 218, and passim.

60. Theodore Sorenson, *Kennedy* (New York: Harper & Row, 1965) 726. In July 1963 Secretary of State Dean Rusk, CIA Director John McCone, and Undersecretary of State for Political Affairs Averell Harriman agreed at a National Security Council meeting with Kennedy that "although the differences between the Russians and the Chinese are very great," they were not "very deep" nor would "a final break between the two powers . . . occur." Summary Record of NSC Meeting, 31 July 1963, National Security Files, M&M: NSC Meetings, 1963, no. 516, bx 314, JFK.

61. Excerpts from speech, 12 October 1960, James C. Thomson Papers, bx 14 FE 1961–1966, f: Communist China Letters, Articles, Speeches, Commentary, 1960, JFK.

62. Press statement by James Shen, 14 October 1960, Thomson Papers, bx 18: FE 1961–66, f: Taiwan OSI 1960 Campaign Issue, JFK.

63. William P. Snyder, "Dean Rusk to John Foster Dulles, May–June 1953: The Office, the First 100 Days, and Red China," *Diplomatic History* (Winter 1983): 86.

64. "Views of the Department of State on Certain Questions Relating to China," Dulles Papers, bx 79, f: China, People's Republic of, MUDD.

65. 795.00/6–953 #786 Lodge, *FRUS 1952–54*, vol. 3, *United Nations Affairs* (Washington, D.C.: Government Printing Office, 1979), 661–62; 330/6–1053 Memcon, ibid., 663–65; 310.2/6–1153 Lodge to Dulles, ibid., 667, and reply on 679–80. Lodge nevertheless assured the Chinese Nationalist ambassador to the UN

that he would cast a veto should the issue arise. Telephone conversation, 10 June 1953, Koo Papers, bx 187, Columbia University.

66. 310.2/7–654 Memcon Dulles and Knowland, *FRUS 1952–54*, vol. 3, 735–36.

67. Bundy to Cline, 11 October 1961, and Cline to Bundy, 14 October 1961, NSF Countries, f: China General CIA Cables 7/61–10/16/61, JFK.

68. Cline to Bundy, 16 October 1961, NSF Countries, f: China General CIA Cables 7/61–10/16/61, JFK.

69. Battle to Bundy, 30 June 1961, NSF Countries, f: China General 6/28/61–7/7/61, JFK; William H. Sullivan Oral History, 1–3, JFK.

70. Memcon President, Rusk, Stevenson, Cleveland, 24 May 1961, NSF Countries, f: 5/1/61–6/12/61, JFK.

71. Komer to Bundy and Rostow, 15 June 1961, NSF Countries, f: China General 6/13/61–6/27/61, JFK.

72. Department of State Daily Opinion Summary, White House Central Files, bx 387, f: IT47/CO1-CO 50–2, JFK.

73. Memcon President, Stevenson, Schlesinger, Cleveland, 5 August 1961, Schlesinger Papers, bx: WH-22 Subject Files, f: UN Speeches 8/3/61–8/11/61, JFK.

74. Airgram Taipei to Washington, 27 April 1964, NSF Country File, bx 237–38, f: China memos, vol. 1, 12/63–9/64, Lyndon Baines Johnson Library, Austin, Tex. (hereafter cited as LBJ).

CHAPTER 4

1. For a discussion of the ability of weaker states to control their stronger allies, see Chan, "The Mouse That Roared," 251–92.

2. The following analysis depends heavily on the outstanding work of Neil H. Jacoby, *U.S. Aid to Taiwan* (New York: Praeger, 1966).

3. The total for all aid, 1951–65, was $4 billion; K. T. Li, *The Evolution of Policy Behind Taiwan's Development Success* (New Haven: Yale University Press, 1988), 55.

4. Denis Fred Simon, "External Incorporation and Internal Reform," in Edwin A. Winckler and Susan Greenhalgh, eds., *Contemporary Approaches to the Political Economy of Taiwan* (Armonk, N.Y.: M. E. Sharpe, 1988), 139.

5. Shirley W. Y. Kuo, Gustav Ranis, and John C. H. Fei, *The Taiwan Success Story: Rapid Growth with Improved Distribution in the Republic of China, 1952–79* (Boulder: Westview, 1981), 43.

6. Robert W. Barnett to Harriman, 3 March 1964, James C. Thomson Papers, f: Far East: Taiwan 1958, 1962–64, JFK.

7. Emily Hahn, "Our Far-flung Correspondents," *New Yorker* 29 (24 October 1953): 124.

8. A. James Gregor, et al., *Ideology and Development: Sun Yat-sen and the Economic History of Taiwan* (Berkeley: China Research Monograph, University of California, 1981), 18, 30–32.

9. T. H. Shen, *The Sino-American Joint Commission on Rural Reconstruction: Twenty Years of Cooperation for Agricultural Development* (Ithaca: Cornell, 1970), 57–78 and passim; hereafter cited as JCRR.

10. T. H. Shen, "Agricultural Development in Free China," Cornell

International Agricultural Development Mimeograph 10 (Ithaca: Cornell University, May 1965); Lee Teng-hui, "China's Modernization and the United States of America," *Sino-American Relations* 15 (Spring 1989): 8–9.

11. Simon, "External Incorporation," 141–49.

12. Thomas B. Gold, *State and Society in the Taiwan Miracle* (Armonk, N.Y.: M. E. Sharpe, 1986), 70.

13. C. Martin Wilbur, "The Human Dimension," in Ramon Myers, ed., *Two Chinese States* (Stanford: Hoover Institution Press, 1978), 47.

14. Stephen Haggard, *Pathways from the Periphery* (Ithaca: Cornell, 1990), 90–92.

15. Maurice Scott, "Foreign Trade and Exchange," in James C. Hsiung, et al., *The Taiwan Experience, 1950–1980* (New York: Praeger, 1981), 180–82; Thomas Gold, "Entrepreneurs, Multinationals, and the State," in Winckler and Greenhalgh, *Contemporary Approaches*, 196–99.

16. Jan S. Prybyla, "Economic Development in Taiwan," in Chiu Hungdah, ed., *China and the Taiwan Issue* (New York: Praeger, 1979), 95; Haggard, *Pathways*, 92–93.

17. Robert Wade, *Governing the Market* (Princeton: Princeton University Press, 1990), 151.

18. 893.00/1–1251 Jack K. McFall, Assistant Secretary to Senator Tom Connally, chairman SFRC, bx 5633, RG 59, NA.

19. Wade, *Governing the Market*, 83.

20. Jacoby, *U.S. Aid*, 134.

21. Chang Peng-yuan, "Sino-American Scholarly Relations as Seen from Taiwan, 1949–1979," in Cecilia S. T. Chang, ed., *US-ROC Relations: From the White Paper to the Taiwan Relations Act* (New York: St. John's University Press, 1984), 72–75.

22. Jacoby, *U.S. Aid*, 144–48.

23. William C. Kirby, "Continuity and Change in Modern China: Economic Planning on the Mainland and on Taiwan, 1943–1958," *Australian Journal of Chinese Affairs* (July 1990): 123–36. The NRC, using Lend Lease funds, sent engineers to the U.S. for advanced training. Some of these individuals would later reach the highest levels in Taiwan as cabinet ministers, heads of state-run enterprises, and even premier. William C. Kirby, "The Chinese Wartime Economy," in Hsiung and Levine, *Bitter Victory*, 206–7.

24. Maurice Scott, "Foreign Trade," in Walter Galenson, ed., *Economic Growth and Structural Change in Taiwan: The Postwar Experience of the Republic of China* (Ithaca: Cornell, 1979), 315n14.

25. P'eng Huai-en called it a "planned free economy" in *Zhonghua Minguo Zhengzhi Tixi de Fenxi* (An analysis of the political system of the Republic of China) (Taipei: Times Press, 1983), 59. Regarding the debate among economists see Wade, *Governing the Market*, 220–24.

26. Wade, *Governing the Market*, 295.

27. PRC analysts, although crediting the U.S. with making Taiwan's economic miracle possible, also pointed out that U.S. assistance was extended as part of the nation's cold war strategy. Zhang Jiang, "Meiyuan yu Taiwan Jingji Fazhan," (American aid and the economic development of Taiwan), in Zi and He, *Meitai Guanxi*, 233–60.

28.   Shen, *JCRR*, 234–38.

29.   Memo William Gaud, administrator AID, and Orville Freeman, secretary of agriculture to the president, 5 April 1967, NSF Country File, bx 241, f: China Memos, vol. 9, 3/67–6/67, LBJ; Memo Rostow to the President 8 April 1967, NSF Memos to the President, bx 15, f: WWR, vol. 25, 4/1–15/67 [1 of 2], LBJ.

30.   Interview with Ambassador Arthur W. Hummel, Jr., Washington, D.C., May 1992.

31.   Interview with Ralph Clough, Washington, D.C., May 1993; *New York Times*, 1 July 1965, 1–2; Burton I. Kaufman, "Foreign Aid and the Balance-of-Payments Problem: Vietnam and Johnson's Foreign Economic Policy," in Robert A. Divine, ed., *The Johnson Years*, vol. 2 (Lawrence: University of Kansas Press, 1987), 80–84.

32.   NSC 146/2 "United States Objectives and Courses of Action with Respect to Formosa and the Chinese National Government," 6 November 1953, *FRUS 1952–54*, vol. 14, pt. 1, 307–30.

33.   793.5 MSP/2–2052 Memo of Conversation, bx 4221, RG 59, NA. NSC 162/2 "Review of Basic National Security Policy," 30 October 1953, explicitly called for the development of indigenous forces to deal with local aggression; *FRUS 1952–54*, vol. 2, pt. 1, *National Security Affairs* (Washington, D.C.: Government Printing Office, 1984), 489ff.

34.   "Status of Aid Programs for the Republic of China," 7 March 1956, Rankin Papers, bx 31, f: State Department, MUDD.

35.   Edward Friedman, "Real Interests of China and America in the Taiwan Area," in Jerome Cohen, Edward Friedman, Harold Hinton, and Allen S. Whiting, *Taiwan and American Policy* (New York: Praeger, 1971), 41–42.

36.   Memo Jenkins to McConaughy, 7 July 1953, Records of the Office of Chinese Affairs (CA), bx 41, f 430.1: US Aid to Nationalist China, RG 59, NA.

37.   FO 371/99268 (FC 10345/19) #550 Dening, 2 April 1952 and attached minute, 7 April 1952, Public Records Office, Kew, Great Britain (hereafter cited as PRO).

38.   Chow agreed to Chase's proposal in a letter, 13 February 1953, bx 2, f 11: Offensive Uses of Chinese Forces, 1953–56, RG 84, NA. Ironically one result of this was greater harassment of British shipping to Communist China.

39.   611.93/3–2553 Memo, Allison and State-JCS Meeting, 27 March 1953, *FRUS 1952–54*, vol. 14, pt. 1, 162–69, 172–75.

40.   Memo William Buell to McConaughy and Jenkins, 17 June 1954, CA Records, bx 49, f 430.1, RG 59, NA.

41.   #68 Wright, Taipei, 28 July 1964, National Security File, Country File China, bx 238, LBJ.

42.   Thomas Powers, *The Man Who Kept the Secrets: Richard Helms and the CIA* (New York: Pocket Books, 1979), 52–53, 415n11.

43.   793.5/8–3051 Memorandum of Conversation between General William C. Chase (chief of MAAG) and Robert W. Barnett, bx 4219, RG 59, NA.

44.   Joseph Burkholder Smith, *Portrait of a Cold Warrior* (New York: G. P. Putnam's Sons, 1976), 77.

45.   The history of CAT is ably told by William M. Leary in *Perilous Missions* (University Station: University of Alabama, 1984), 101–6 and passim; John Prados, *The Presidents' Secret Wars* (New York: William Morrow, 1986), 64–65.

46. Victor Marchetti and John D. Marks, *The CIA and the Cult of Intelligence* (New York: Dell, 1980), 121–26. The two operations complemented each other by providing trained personnel and machinery from Air Asia and CAT to Taiwan's domestic aerospace industry. Interview with Ambassador Arthur W. Hummel, Jr., Washington, D.C., May 1992.

47. This was done secretly, and the Department of Defense purposefully excluded the embassy not just from participation but from knowing about the agreements. Letter Ambassador Karl Rankin to Secretary of State, 30 June 1953, CA Records, bx 39, 306.11, RG 59, NA.

48. Ray S. Cline, *Secrets, Spies and Scholars: Blueprint of the Essential CIA* (Washington, D.C.: Acropolis Books, 1976), 177; Marchetti and Marks, *Cult of Intelligence*, 257. The SR-71 continued flying until 1971.

49. Interview with Ray Cline, former CIA station chief Taipei, Washington, D.C., May 1992; Gordon H. Chang, "JFK, China and the Bomb," *Journal of American History* 75 (March 1988): 1287–1310.

50. 690B.9321/11–3053 Allen, New Delhi, *FRUS 1952–54*, vol. 12, pt. 1, *East Asia and the Pacific* (Washington, D.C.: Government Printing Office, 1984), 179. John Ranelagh, *The Agency: The Rise and Decline of the CIA* (New York: Simon and Schuster, 1986), 221. The operation was so heavily classified that the U.S. ambassador to Burma, William Sebald, top officials at the State Department, and even Robert Amory, the CIA deputy director for intelligence, were not told; David Wise and Thomas B. Ross, *The Invisible Government* (New York: Random House, 1964), 131.

51. Alfred W. McCoy, *The Politics of Heroin in Southeast Asia* (New York: Harper, 1972), 127–30.

52. Evidence surfaced that the Nationalists had devised a plan called "Operation Heaven" calling for only token compliance. Despatch 573 "Some Observations on the Conduct of the First Phase of the Evacuation of Li Mi's Troops from Burma," 6 April 1954, *FRUS 1952–54*, vol. 12, pt. 1, 220n1.

53. Memcon Walter Bedell Smith and V. K. Wellington Koo, 3 March 1953, bx 187, Koo Papers, Columbia.

54. Despatch 617 "Chinese Nationalist Troops in Burma: A Summary," 21 May 1953, bx 2, f: 10-Troops in Burma, 1952–53, RG 84, NA.

55. Tucker, "John Foster Dulles," 244–51.

56. FO 371/106694 (DB 1041/37), R. F. G. Sarell, Rangoon, British Embassy, 25 July 1955, PRO.

57. FO 371/158464 (FCN 1021/3) Letter from Director Military Intelligence to Pedler, Far East, Foreign Ministry, 5 November 1961, PRO.

58. FO 371/158464 (FCN 1021/1) Letter E. E. Young, Tamsui to Arthur de la Mare, Far East, Foreign Office, 21 March 1961, PRO.

59. "If the United States could prevent the Formosa regime from raiding the mainland of China, our people cannot understand why she is unable to prevent that regime from sending supplies to its adherents in [Burma]." Letter Burmese Prime Minister to President Kennedy, 2 March 1961, POF Countries, bx 112a Brazil-Cameroon, f: Burma General 1961–63, JFK.

60. Cable E. Maung, Burma to Hammarskjold, 22 February 1961, Registry Archive Group 3/7, bx 151, f 240: Burma (1), UN; Wise and Ross, *Invisible Government*, 134–35; "United States Efforts to Effect Cessation of Government of

Republic of China's Support of Chinese Irregulars in Burma-Laos Border Area," 20 February 1961, NSF, bx 21, f: China General 2/20/61–2/28/61 (item 3b), JFK.

61. "United States Efforts," 4.

62. JCS 2118/97 "Utilization of Chinese (GRC) Armed Forces in Emergency," 17 March 1958, CCS 381 Formosa (11–8–48) sec. 35, RG 218, NA.

63. Friedman, "Real Interests," 46.

64. 455th NSC Meeting, 12 August 1960, Eisenhower Papers, Whitman File, NSC Series, bx 13, IKE.

65. Memo Bird to Radford, 3 February 1956, Chairman's Files, Adm. Radford, bx 6, f 091: China (1956), RG 218, NA. The Matador had a range of 600 to 650 miles and flew with a jet engine at an altitude of 35,000 feet.

66. During the 1958 Taiwan Straits crisis the U.S. also deployed Nike-Hercules anti-aircraft missiles to Taiwan and in August 1959 turned them over to Nationalists troops who had been specially trained at Fort Bliss, Texas. *New York Times*, August 10, 1959, p. 18.

67. *Renmin Ribao*, 8 May 1957, in *Survey of China Mainland Press* (hereafter cited as SCMP), #1528, 26.

68. "Courses of Action Relative to Communist China and Korea—Chinese Nationalists," JSPC 958/10 (JCS 2118/15), 29 January 1951, and "Courses of Action Relative to Communist China and Korea—Anti-Communist China," JCS 2118/17, 14 March 1951, CCS 381 FE (11–28–50) s.5, RG 218, NA.

69. "Working Paper on Support of China Mainland Resistance and Use of Nationalist Forces on Formosa," 2, 3, and 8, 24 January/21 March 1951, bx 40, f 410: Chinese Nationalist Armed Forces (TS), CA Records, NA.

70. 794A.5 MAP/2–551 Clubb to Parelman, *FRUS 1951*, vol. 7, pt. 2, *Korea and China* (Washington, D.C.: Government Printing Office, 1983), 1564–65.

71. Rankin to Clubb, 24 January 1951, ibid., 1523–27. Rankin was, in fact, right to worry about the military's efforts to circumvent civilian authority as can be seen repeatedly in the General Records of the Department of State available at the National Archives.

72. Jacoby, *U.S. Aid*, 118.

73. In 1951, the U.S. spent just 8.6 percent of its GNP on defense and international affairs outlays, which totaled 43.2 percent of the national budget. *Historical Tables, Budget of the United States Government, 1990* (Washington, D.C.: Government Printing Office, 1989), 39–41, 365.

74. 793.5/8–2351 Memo Perkins (CA) to Merchant (FE), bx 4219, RG 59, NA; 793.5MAP/8–1651 Memo Merchant to Rusk, bx 4221, RG 59, NA.

75. 893.00/5–951 Dean Rusk, Assistant Secretary to R. Allen Griffin, Director, Far East Division, ECA, bx 5633, RG 59, NA; 794A.5MAP/6–2251, #1389 Acheson, *FRUS 1951*, vol. 7, pt. 2, 1715–16.

76. Chase to Rankin, 5 October 1953, bx 11, f 501, RG 84, NA. MAAG believed that it had scored an important victory in drafting a thoroughly documented budget estimate for January through June 1954, but the triumph proved fleeting since the ad hoc nature of budget preparation would recur. 794A.5/18–853 #343 Rankin, Taipei, *FRUS 1952–54*, vol. 14, pt. 1, 341.

77. Memo Jenkins to McConaughy, 14 May 1953, CA Records, bx 41, f 430.1: US Aid to Nationalist China, RG 59, NA.

78.   793.5-MSP/10–753 Hope to McConaughy and 793.5-MSP/2–954 Hope to Drumright, bx 4222, RG 59, NA.

79.   "Working Paper on Support of China Mainland Resistance," 3.

80.   Chiang Ching-kuo took a leading role in finding alternative employment for retirees, many of whom helped to build the East-West highway. More than 60,000 men averaging 48 years old were processed by George Fry Associates, an American company. FO371/120951 (FC 1203/2) #37 A. A. E. Franklin, British Consulate Tamsui, 25 May 1956, PRO. The difficulty of finding employment for those demobilized, in order to retain their loyalty and prevent poverty, in a society lacking a large industrial base, contributed to the government's position. Payrolls in all kinds of enterprises were padded with redundant employees who happened to be military veterans.

81.   Memo Chase to Department of the Army, 20 February 1954, bx 2, f: 9-Chinese Army, and MAAG Program 1953–56, RG 84, NA.

82.   793.5/11–952 Transcript of meeting Chiang Kai-shek with General William C. Chase, bx 4219, RG 59, NA. Chiang Kai-shek believed abolition of the system on the mainland at the end of the Northern Expedition in 1928 contributed to the KMT's defeat by the CCP; Bruce J. Dickson, "The Lessons of Defeat: The Reorganization of the Kuomintang on Taiwan, 1950–52," *China Quarterly* 133 (March 1993): 75.

83.   793.00/10–351 Report on Formosa, *FRUS 1951*, vol. 7, pt. 2, 1820.

84.   Memo Gerald Stryker to Al Jenkins, 24 November 1954, CA Records, bx 49, f 430.1, RG 59, NA.

85.   "Taiwan," June 1960, p. 6. Whitman File, International Series, bx 10, f: Formosa (China) (Far East Trip) 6/12/60–6/26/60, IKE.

86.   Letter MacGregor, Hong Kong, to Emanuel Freedman, foreign editor, *New York Times*, 8 May 1955, Hanson Baldwin Papers, bx 11, f 563, Yale University Archives, Sterling Memorial Library, New Haven, Conn. (hereafter cited as Yale).

87.   RFE-7 "Republic of China Succession Problems," p. 4, Department of State, Bureau of Intelligence and Research, 17 January 1963, Thomson Papers, bx 18, f: Far East: Taiwan, 1958, 1962–64, JFK.

88.   Airgram CA-13487, 31 May 1963, and RFE-7 "Republic of China Succession Problem," JFK; Mei Wen-li, "The Intellectuals on Formosa," *China Quarterly* (July–September 1963): 68.

89.   893.00/11–2348 Krentz, Taipei, RG 59, NA. My thanks go to Steven Phillips for bringing this document to my attention.

90.   Cumings, *Cataract*, 532–44.

91.   The supposed conspirators, including a subordinate of General Sun, were themselves simply trying to propose a plan to Chiang for eliminating corruption in the armed services. Foreign Broadcast Information Service (hereafter cited as FBIS) CHI-88–062, 31 March 1988, 58.

92.   Robert P. Newman, "Clandestine Chinese Nationalist Efforts to Punish Their American Detractors," *Diplomatic History* 7 (Summer 1983): 205–22.

93.   There is a considerable literature by pro-Kuomintang writers and politicians accusing the U.S. of promoting independence activities: for example, Yin Chang-yi, Ch'ou Nung-yen Ho Lieh-chiu Ta-sheng K'ang-yi: T'ai-wan Li-shih yu T'ai-wan Ch'ien-t'u (Smoke Strong Cigarettes, Drink Strong Wine, Loudly Resist: Taiwan's History and Taiwan's Future) (Taipei: Ho T'ai-shih Yen-chiu-hui, 1988), 105.

94. "Study Unit Urges New China Policy," *New York Times*, 1 November 1959, 27.

95. Ch'en apparently felt humiliated and thought the U.S. government ought to have prevented it. Peng Ming-min, *A Taste of Freedom: Memoirs of a Formosan Independence Leader* (New York: Holt Rinehart & Winston, 1972), 109.

96. IR 7203 Intelligence Report "Taiwanese Independence Movements, 1683–1956," 8 August 1956, RG 59, NA; Kerr,*Formosa Betrayed* 464–65, 470.

97. FO 371/158462 (FCN 1015/5) #13 E. E. Young, Tamsui, 30 March 1961, PRO; Douglas Mendel, *The Politics of Formosan Nationalism* (Berkeley: University of California Press, 1970), 174. Of course, some Americans, particularly missionaries, took a strong interest in the independence movement.

98. Interview with Feldman, April 1991.

99. *Renmin ribao*, 24 May 1964, quoted in Chiu Hungdah, "China, the United States, and the Question of Taiwan," in Chiu, ed., *China and the Question of Taiwan* (New York: Praeger, 1973), 161.

100. Peng Ming-min, "Political Offenses in Taiwan: Laws and Problems," *China Quarterly* (July–September 1971): 471–82.

101. Letter John K. Fairbank to Hu Shih, 10 November 1960, John K. Fairbank Papers, HUG (FP) 12.8, bx 51, f: H, Harvard University Archives, Harvard University, Cambridge, Mass. (hereafter cited as Harvard).

102. Letter Robert Scalapino, 27 September 1966, James C. Thomson Papers, bx 18, f: Taiwan—OSI 1960 Campaign Issue, JFK.

103. Tien Hung-mao, *The Great Transition* (Stanford: Stanford University Press, 1989), 94.

104. Mark Mancall, "Taiwan, Island of Resignation and Despair," in Mancall, ed., *Formosa Today* (New York: Praeger, 1963), 38–39; Lei Chen, *Lei Chen Hui-i-lu* (Lei Chen memoirs) (Hong Kong: Ch'i shih Nien-tai She, 1978), 328–29; Mei, "The Intellectuals," 69–70.

CHAPTER 5

1. Warren Tozer, "Taiwan's 'Cultural Renaissance': A Preliminary View," *China Quarterly* (July–September, 1970): 89–90, 95.

2. Edel Lancashire, "Popeye and the Case of Guo Yidong, alias Bo Yang," *China Quarterly* (December 1982): 673–75.

3. Li Chi, director of the Academia Sinica's Institute of History and Philology lamented in October 1959 about the intellectual stagnation in Taiwan since 1949. Chang, "Sino-American Scholarly Relations," 35–37.

4. Mary Brown Bullock, "American Exchanges with China Revisited," in Joyce Kallgren and Denis Fred Simon, eds., *Educational Exchanges: Essays on the Sino-American Experience* (Berkeley: University of California, Institute of East Asian Studies Research Paper #21, 1987), 31–32. The government tried to stem the flow by limiting passports to graduate students and requiring a "going abroad" examination; Mei, "The Intellectuals," 74. It also required all males to complete military service before going overseas.

5. Walter Guzzardi, Jr., *The Henry Luce Foundation, A History: 1936–1986* (Chapel Hill: University of North Carolina Press, 1988), 112–15.

6.   John King Fairbank, *Chinabound* (New York: Harper & Row, 1982), 383; "Taiwan Research on Modern China," paper for board meeting, Ford Foundation, 8–9 December 1966, Ford Foundation Archives, New York, N.Y.

7.   Chang, "Sino-American Scholarly Relations," 43–52.

8.   C. Martin Wilbur, "Sino-American Relations in Scholarship as Viewed from the United States," in Chang, ed., *US-ROC Relations*, 99, 102.

9.   Marchetti and Marks, *Cult of Intelligence*, 150. The CIA's role was revealed in an exposé in *Ramparts* magazine in 1967.

10. Susan Yu, "American Cultural Center Changing Roles, Locales," *Free China Journal*, 10 December 1991, 5.

11. *Free China Journal*, 11 April 1991, 5.

12. 793.00/2–1154 Rankin, Taipei, bx 4207, RG 59, NA.

13. Despatch 507 Jones, Taipei, 8 May 1952, bx 14, f 570.1, RG 84, NA.

14. 793.00/7–1753 Despatch 164 David H. McKillop, Hong Kong, bx 4205, RG 59, NA.

15. Memo McConaughy to Allison, 4 February 1953, and Memo regarding telephone conversation with British Embassy, 3 April 1953, bx 40, f 350.5 ARCI, Records, RG 59, NA; B. A. Garside, *Within the Four Seas* (New York: Frederick C. Beil, 1985), 116–18.

16. Warren I. Cohen, *East Asian Art and American Culture* (New York: Columbia University Press, 1992), 144–45; Interview with Ray Cline, May 1992.

17. Cohen, *East Asian Art*, 146.

18. Friedman, "Real Interests," 43; Douglas Cater, *Power in Washington* (New York: Random House, 1964), 213–14.

19. Bachrack, *Committee of One Million*, 194, 220.

20. William Lederer, *A Nation of Sheep* (New York: W. W. Norton, 1961), 60.

21. Bachrack, *Committee of One Million*, 167–72.

22. George P. Cernada, *Taiwan Family Planning Reader* (Taichung, Taiwan: Center for International Training in Family Planning, 1970), 12.

23. Li, *Evolution*, 68–77.

24. Shen, *JCRR*, 215.

25. Seymour Topping, "Taiwan Program Curbs Births; Contraceptive Loop Is Praised," *New York Times*, 13 June 1965, 10; Li, *Evolution*, 69–74.

26. AID Administrator and Secretary of Agriculture memo to the President, n.d., NSF Country File, bx 241, f: China Memos, vol. 9, 3/67–6/67, LBJ.

27. Shen, *JCRR*, 218–19.

28. John R. Watt, *A Friend in Deed: ABMAC and the Republic of China, 1937–1987* (New York: ABMAC, 1992), 10. This section relies heavily on Watt's history.

29. Wilbur, "Sino-American Relations in Scholarship," 94.

30. Watt, *A Friend in Deed*, 15.

31. Murray Rubinstein, "The Churches of the Holy Spirit," *American-Asian Review* 6 (Fall 1988): 48.

32. Murray Rubinstein, "Taiwanese Protestantism in Time and Space, 1865–1988," *Journal of Oriental Studies* 27 (1989): 152, and "Taiwan Born Again: The Neo-Evangelical/Charismatic Community on Taiwan," *American Asian Review* 5 (Fall 1987): 64–65.

33. FO 371/158462 (FCN 1015/4) Report on a Visit to Tainan, 1961, PRO.

34. William P. Fenn, *Ever New Horizons: The Story of the United Board for Christian Higher Education in Asia, 1922–1975* (New York: United Board, 1980), 57–64, 74–115. The Board changed its name in 1955. Associated churches included Baptists, Episcopal, Lutheran, Methodist, Presbyterian, and Reformed.

35. Interview with Father John Witek, S.J., Washington, D.C., July 1993; William Klement, S.J., "25 Years on Taiwan," *The Jesuit* (Winter 1977): 7.

36. FO 371/158462 (FCN 1015/4) Report on a visit to Tainan, 1961, PRO.

37. Mendel, *Formosan Nationalism*, 195.

38. A.T. Steele, *The American People and China* (New York: McGraw-Hill, 1966), 262.

39. 793.00/6–2551 #334 Rankin, Taipei, bx 4199, RG 59, NA.

40. #193 Embassy to Washington, 6 November 1956, Rankin Papers, bx 29, f: China, Republic of, MUDD.

41. Letter Ambassador Rankin to President's Special Consultant Nash, 17 June 1957, *FRUS 1955–57*, vol. 3, 542–44.

42. Telephone Conversation, 24 May 1957, *FRUS 1955–57*, vol. 3, 528.

43. 793.00/5–2657 Memo McConaughy to Robertson, *FRUS 1955–57*, vol. 3, 534–35.

44. Memo of Discussion, 325th NSC Mtg., 27 May 1957, *FRUS 1955–57*, vol. 3, 541.

45. One writer in Taiwan argued that the incident reflected "envy of the living conditions and the status of Americans on the island. Envy, however, is derived from admiration." Mei, "The Intellectuals," 73.

CHAPTER 6

1. 793.00/4–2552 Despatch 491 Rankin, Taipei, RG 59, NA.

2. CIA, Office of National Estimates, "Prospects for Early Chinese Nationalist Military Action against the Mainland," 27 July 1961, NSF, bx 22, f: China General 7/28/61–7/31/61, JFK.

3. *China News*, Taipei, 17 or 18 March 1962, and Robert S. Allen and Paul Scott, "Chiang Scares JFK with His War Talk," *Miami News*, 25 April 1962, 13a, POF, bx 113a, f: China General 1962, JFK.

4. Letter Chiang Kai-shek to JFK, 15 March 1963, NSF Country File, bx 237-38, f: China Memos, vol. 4, 7/65–10/65, LBJ.

5. Letter Chiang Kai-shek to JFK, 5 September 1963, POF, bx 113a, f: China General 1963, JFK.

6. Despatch A-726 "Counterattack in 1963?" Clough, Taipei, 13 March 1963, Vice Presidential Security File—Government Agencies, bx 13, f: State Dept—Miscellaneous Cables 1961–63, LBJ.

7. Excerpts from Memcon Rusk and Chiang, 16 April 1964, NSF Country File, vol. 4, bx 238, LBJ; Memo for the Record: Views of Ambassador Wright, 12 May 1964, Thomson Papers, f: Far East: Taiwan 1958, 1962–64, JFK.

8. Memo Jenkins to Rostow, 7 March 1967, NSF Country File, bx 241, f: China Memos, vol. 9, 3/67–6/67, LBJ.

9. Message for Chiang from LBJ, NSF, Memos to the President, bx 14, f: Walt Rostow, vol. 23, 3/10–15/67 [1 of 2], LBJ.

10.   SC No. 10078/65, CIA, Office of Current Intelligence, "Probable Effects in China and Taiwan of a GRC Attack on the Mainland," 18 August 1965, NSF Country File Vietnam, bx 50–51, f: vol. 2: Special Intelligence Material 7/65–10/65, LBJ.

11.   Wang Jisi, "From Kennedy to Nixon: America's East Asia and China Policy," *Beijing Review*, 16–22 May 1988: 41–44. Re American conclusion that PRC fears genuine see #1539 Rice, Hong Kong, 19 February 1966, NSF Country File, bx 239, f: China Cables, vol. 5, 10/65–1/66, LBJ.

12.   Memorandum for the President, 15 December 1964, Memos to the President, bx 2: McGeorge Bundy, vol. 7, 10/1–12/31/64 [1 of 2], LBJ.

13.   George McT. Kahin, *Intervention* (Garden City, N.Y.: Doubleday, 1987), 287.

14.   *FRUS 1961–63*, vol. 1, *Vietnam 1961* (Washington, D.C.: Government Printing Office, 1988), 91, 431–36.

15.   Warning against allowing Nationalist troops to fight in Vietnam came from various quarters in the U.S. government, including consulate general analysts in Hong Kong. See #120 Rice, Hong Kong, 2 August 1965, NSF Country File, bx 237–38, f: China Cables, vol. 4, 7/65–10/65, LBJ. In December 1966 Chiang told Rusk he had reconsidered the idea of contributing uniformed troops lest settlement of the Taiwan question become part of the Vietnam denouement. Memo 4 May 1967, NSF Country File, bx 24–45, f: China—Visit of C. K. Yen 5/9–10/67 Briefing Book, LBJ.

16.   #315 Hummel, Taipei, 14 September 1965, NSF Country File, bx 237–38, f: China Cables, vol. 4, LBJ; Interview with Ray Cline, May 1992.

17.   Kahin, *Intervention*, 333.

18.   Ibid., 333; Yen Briefing Book, Harry Thayer Oral History, Foreign Affairs Oral History Program, Georgetown University, Washington, D.C. (hereafter cited as Georgetown).

19.   Gabriel Kolko, *Anatomy of a War* (New York: Pantheon, 1985), 211.

20.   Marilyn Young, *The Vietnam Wars, 1945–1990* (New York: HarperCollins, 1991), 192–209, 248.

21.   Kissinger biographer Walter Isaacson makes clear that Kissinger's place in the Harvard firmament was often uneasy. *Kissinger* (New York: Simon & Schuster, 1992), 95–101.

22.   Nixon discussed the China opening in *RN: The Memoirs of Richard Nixon* (New York: Grosset & Dunlap, 1978), 341, 522–25, 544–80. Henry Kissinger's account appeared in *The White House Years* (Boston: Little, Brown, 1979), 163–94, 684–787, 1049–96.

23.   Kissinger, *White House Years*, 171–77, 183–86.

24.   Warren I. Cohen, *America's Response to China* (New York: Columbia University Press, 1990), 190.

25.   U.S. Congress. Senate Committee on Foreign Relations. *U.S. Policy with Respect to Mainland China*. Hearings, 89th Cong., 2d sess., 1966.

26.   #180 McConaughy, Taipei, 16 July 1966, Thomson Papers, bx 11: Speeches/National Security Staff, f: LBJ 7/12/66 White Sulphur Springs—Diplomatic Reactions, JFK.

27.   #1086 Hummel, Taipei, 6 April 1966, NSF Country File bx 239, f: China Cables, vol. 6, 3/66–9/66, LBJ; #1240 7 May 1966, ibid., LBJ.

28. #993 Hummel, Taipei, 17 March 1966, NSF Country File, bx 239, f: China Cables, vol. 6, 3/66–9/66, LBJ; Memo Rusk to the President, n.d., NSF Country File, bx 244–45, f: China—Visit of C. K. Yen 5/9–10/67 Briefing Book, LBJ.

29. Richard Nixon, "Asia after Viet Nam," *Foreign Affairs* 46 (October 1967). Ambassador Arthur Hummel recalled that in 1965, when Nixon visited Taiwan and Hummel was chargé affaires, Nixon declared in a private conversation at the Grand Hotel that the Nationalists would never return to the mainland and that U.S.-PRC relations would have to be improved. Hummel noted that rooms at the Grand were known to be bugged. Interview with Ambassador Arthur W. Hummel, Jr., Washington, D.C., May 1992.

30. In fact the resumption was aborted because of the defection of a Chinese diplomat in the Netherlands shortly before the meeting was to have been held.

31. Kissinger, *White House Years*, 179–87. The Rogers speech came as a surprise to Nixon and Kissinger who had not cleared it and preferred to conduct their China opening in secret; Raymond L. Garthoff, *Detente and Confrontation: American-Soviet Relations from Nixon to Reagan* (Washington, D.C.: Brookings Institution, 1985), 219.

32. Kissinger insisted that Taiwan did not constitute a serious impediment to relations, but his judgment is suspect given that he knew little about China before Nixon launched him on his Chinese diplomacy; Harry Harding, *A Fragile Relationship: The United States and China since 1972* (Washington, D.C.: Brookings Institution, 1992), 398n61.

33. Garthoff, *Detente*, 223–24.

34. Harding, *Fragile Relationship*, 40–43.

35. Garthoff, *Detente*, 232–33.

36. James C. H. Shen, *The U.S. and Free China: How the U.S. Sold out Its Ally* (Washington, D.C.: Acropolis Books, 1983), 51.

37. Administrative History, chap. 7, pt. D, LBJ.

38. Ambassador Harvey Feldman, author of the dual representation concept, believed that Chiang finally relented in hopes that the idea would drive a wedge between Washington and Beijing. Interview with Ambassador Harvey Feldman, Virginia, April 1991.

39. Kusnitz, *Public Opinion*, 138; Kissinger, *White House Years*, 784.

40. Harvey J. Feldman, "Development of U.S.-Taiwan Relations, 1948–1987," in Feldman, Michael Y. M. Kau, and Ilpyong J. Kim, eds., *Taiwan in a Time of Transition* (New York: Paragon, 1988), 141, 170n20. Feldman was the Foreign Service officer in charge of the State Department Task Force on Chinese Representation in the UN at the time. William Glenn, "What Now, Generalissimo?" *FEER*, 13 November 1971, 17–20.

41. Kissinger, *White House Years*, 782, 1075.

42. Victor H. Li, ed., *The Future of Taiwan: A Difference of Opinion* (New York: M. E. Sharpe, 1980), 2.

43. Zbigniew Brzezinski, *Power and Principle* (New York: Farrar, Straus, Giroux, 1985), 198.

44. Haggard, *Pathways*, 161–88.

45. According to a study of 42 contemporary developing countries over a period of 100 years carried out by L. G. Reynolds and reported in the *Journal of Economic Literature* in 1983, "the single most important explanatory variable [in economic development] is political organization and the administrative competence of govern-

ment." Cited in James Riedel, "Economic Development in East Asia: Doing What Comes Naturally?" in Helen Hughes, ed., *Achieving Industrialization in East Asia* (New York: Cambridge University Press, 1988), 37.

46. This section draws on the substantial literature regarding dependency theory and the East Asian exceptions to it. My conclusions in the text rely most heavily upon Haggard, *Pathways*, and Winckler and Greenhalgh, *Contemporary Approaches*.

47. Thomas B. Gold, "Taiwan: In Search of Identity," in Steven M. Goldstein, ed., *Mini Dragons: Fragile Economic Miracles in the Pacific* (Boulder: Westview, 1991), 22–46.

48. Yen B-7, Visit of Vice President Yen Chia-kan, May 9–10, 1967, NSF Country File, bx 244–45, f: China—Visit of C. K. Yen, 5/9–10/67 Briefing Book, LBJ. Nevertheless, the government made a conscious decision not to neglect agriculture and continued investment in the rural sector.

49. Maurice Scott, "Foreign Trade," in Galenson, *Economic Growth*, 347.

50. Prybyla, "Economic Development," 84.

51. Gold, "Taiwan: In Search of Identity," 31; Ramon H. Myers, "The Economic Development of Taiwan," in Chiu, *China and the Question of Taiwan*, 55; *New York Times*, 9 June 1965, 65.

52. Prybyla, "Economic Development," 120.

53. Gold, *State and Society*, 79.

54. Dispatch A-512 Taipei, "Economic Trends," 15 February 1967, NSF Country File China, bx 242–43, f: Memos, vol. 12, 12/67–6/68, LBJ.

55. Jan S. Prybyla, "Economic Developments in the Republic of China," in Thomas Robinson, ed., *Democracy and Development in East Asia* (Washington, D.C.: American Enterprise Institute Press, 1991), 54.

56. David Bell, AID, memo for the President, 27 November 1964, White House Central Files, Confidential File, CO 50–1 (Formosa), LBJ; Shen, *JCRR*, 251–52.

57. Scott, "Foreign Trade," 348.

58. Memo Hornig to the president, 16 November 1967, White House Central Files, Executive, bx 22, f: CO 50–1, 11/15/66, LBJ.

59. Shen, *JCRR*, 31.

60. Ibid., 19.

61. *Far Eastern Economic Review* (27 October 1966): 207 (hereafter cited as *FEER*).

62. Memo Acting Secretary of State Katzenbach to the President, 7 April 1967, and Memo Charles L. Schultze, Director of the Bureau of the Budget to the president, 8 April 1967, and Memo William Gaud, Administrator AID and Orville Freeman, Secretary of Agriculture to the President, 5 April 1967, NSF Country File, bx 241, f: China Memos, vol. 9, 3/67–6/67, LBJ; Administrative History, chap. 7, pt. D, LBJ.

63. Administrative History, chap. 7, pt. D, LBJ.

64. "Economic Trends," 10.

65. Scott, "Foreign Trade," 348.

66. Tucker, *Patterns*, 60, 72–73.

67. UPI despatch, 2 August 1965, NSF Memos to the President, bx 4, f: McGeorge Bundy, vol. 13, August 1965, LBJ.

68.   It consumed some 55 percent even of the consolidated central and provincial annual budget, which better reflected the unavoidable internal expenditures. *New York Times*, 24 March 1968, 5.

69.   Annex III: "Countering the Chinese Communist Military Threat," in Communist China Long Range Study, June 1966, NSF Country File, China, bx 245, LBJ.

70.   Administrative History of the Department of State, vol. 1, chap. 7, pt. D: Taiwan, LBJ.

71.   The words quoted here actually come from a clearer restatement of the new policy in a November speech on Vietnam. Kissinger, *White House Years*, 224–25.

72.   Kusnitz, *Public Opinion*, 134–37, 168–69.

73.   Kissinger, *White House Years*, 220–22.

74.   Yung Wei, "Political Development in the Republic of China in Taiwan," in Chiu, *China and the Question of Taiwan*, 85.

75.   Mab Huang, *Intellectual Ferment for Political Reforms in Taiwan, 1971–1973* (Ann Arbor: Center for Chinese Studies, University of Michigan, 1976), 5–15.

76.   George Ball, former undersecretary of state, observed that "today the Nationalist government is like something from *Alice in Wonderland*. . . . [It is] anything but an example of a virile and militant democracy since the Taiwanese have little . . . voice in shaping their destinies." George W. Ball, *The Discipline of Power* (Boston: Little, Brown, 1968), 178–79.

77.   Republic of China—Questions and Answers, March 1965, Thomson Papers, bx 16: Far East, Communist China, 1/65–4/65, JFK.

78.   #441 Department to Taipei, October 1964, NSF Country File, China, bx 237–38, f: China Cables, vol. 2, September 1964–February 1965, LBJ.

79.   Peng tells his story in *A Taste of Freedom*; Robert L. Nichols Oral History, Georgetown, 25. Peng went back to Taiwan in November 1992 to campaign for the Democratic Progress Party, domestic political reform, discussed in chapter 8, having made his return possible; "Professor Peng Ming-min Speaks Out," *Taiwan Communique* (February 1993): 15–17.

80.   Richard Halloran, "Ex-Agent Sees 'Revolutionary Potential' on Taiwan," *New York Times*, 12 March 1972.

81.   Editorial, "The Forgotten Taiwanese," *New York Times*, 10 March 1972.

82.   Peng, *A Taste of Freedom*, 260.

83.   Trong R. Chai, "Taiwan for the Taiwanese: Taiwan Independence Movement, Its Characteristics and Prospects," in Jack F. Williams, ed., *The Taiwan Issue* (East Lansing: Michigan State University Press, 1975), 80–82. Chai served as president of WUFI after its formation in 1970.

84.   Charles Snyder, "That Sinking Feeling," *FEER* (19 September 1970):18.

85.   Leonard H. D. Gordon and Sidney Chang, "John K. Fairbank and His Critics in the Republic of China," *Journal of Asian Studies* 30 (November 1970): 137–49.

86.   *FEER* (29 August 1968): 434.

87.   Warren Tozer, "Taiwan's 'Cultural Renaissance': A Preliminary View," *China Quarterly* (July–September 1970): 81–99.

88.   Lancashire, "Popeye," 663–65.

89.   Ibid., 675–85.

90.   *The Asian Foundation Program Bulletin*, Special Issue, 1978, 28.

91.   Chang, "Sino-American Scholarly Relations," 36–37, 49, quote on p. 52;

David Finkelstein, "China Program," 5 January 1968, p. 14 and Finkelstein to Francis X. Sutton, "Why Taiwan?" 21 February 1968, Ford Foundation Archives.

92. Memo Rostow to the President, 1 May 1967, NSF Memos to the President, bx 16, f: vol. 27, May 1–15, 1967 [2 of 2], LBJ.

93. Memo Herman Pollack, Director, International Scientific and Technological Affairs to Donald F. Hornig, Director OST, 15 May 1968, NSF Country File China, bx 242–43, f: vol. 12, Memos 12/67–6/68, LBJ.

94. State Department Administrative History, vol. 1, chap. 11: Science and Technology: Section A-G, LBJ.

95. Walter Arnold, "Science and Technology Development in Taiwan and South Korea," *Asian Survey* 28 (April 1988): 444; Wilbur, "Sino-American Relations in Scholarship," 97–98.

96. Chang, "Sino-American Scholarly Relations," 81.

97. Wilbur, "Sino-American Relations in Scholarship," 102–7.

98. Leigh and Richard Kagan, "Oh Say, Can You See? American Cultural Blinders on China," in Edward Friedman and Mark Selden, eds., *America's Asia* (New York: Vintage, 1971), 11.

99. Warren I. Cohen, "While China Faced East: Chinese-American Cultural Relations, 1949–71," in Kallgren and Simon, *Educational Exchanges*, 44–57.

100. Marianthi Zikopoulos, ed., *Open Doors: 1987/88* (New York: Institute of International Education, 1988), 20.

101. Peter Kwong, *The New Chinatown* (New York: Noonday Press, 1987), 61.

102. Chen Hsiang-shui, *Chinatown No More* (Ithaca: Cornell University Press, 1992), 6–7.

103. Kwong, *New Chinatown*, 95–105; Chen, *Chinatown No More*, 11.

104. Kwong, *New Chinatown*, 29–32.

105. Administrative History, chap. 7, pt. D, LBJ.

106. Watt, *A Friend in Deed*, 22–24.

107. Ibid., 22–25.

108. Kusnitz, *Public Opinion*, 137.

109. Council on Foreign Relations, "The American Public's View of U.S. Policy toward China," survey conducted by the Survey Research Center, University of Michigan, May–June 1964. Reproduced in Steele, *American People and China*, 262.

110. Bachrack, *Committee of One Million*, 222, 232–33; Paul A. Marsh, "Growing Old with Chiang," *FEER* (5 February 1970): 29–31.

111. #1147 Rusk to Taipei, 7 May 1966, NSF Country File China, vol. 6, bx 239, LBJ.

112. Kusnitz, *Public Opinion*, 117.

113. Bachrack, *Committee of One Million*, 347n20.

CHAPTER 7

1. The idea of talks outside the formal Paris framework came from Nixon and Kissinger; George C. Herring, *America's Longest War* (New York: Alfred A. Knopf, 1986), 228. Stanley Karnow adds that Thieu was uncomfortable with the arrangement but had little choice; Stanley Karnow, *Vietnam* (New York: Viking, 1983), 624. Kissinger wrote about the pitfalls of excluding an ally from negotiations but, neverthe-

less, proved surprised and resentful when the South Vietnamese objected to his treaty draft; Kissinger, "The Vietnam Negotiations," *Foreign Affairs* 47 (January 1969): 225.

2. Walter LaFeber, *America, Russia and the Cold War, 1945–1990* (New York: McGraw-Hill, 1991), 273.

3. Shen, *Free China*, 13, 184–85.

4. Unger believes he was chosen because he was not identified with previous China policy and would not try to obstruct the shift in relations, but had the seniority to deal with Chiang Ching-kuo. Interview with Ambassador Leonard Unger, August 1993, Potomac, Md.

5. Banning Garrett and Bonnie Glaser, "From Nixon to Reagan: China's Changing Role in American Strategy," in Kenneth Oye, Robert Lieber, and Donald Rothchild, eds., *Eagle Resurgent: The Reagan Era in American Foreign Policy* (Boston: Little, Brown, 1987), 262.

6. Taipei was constrained by suspicion of the Soviets and concern about United States disapproval. Hard-line anticommunists successfully pushed Chow out of the foreign ministry; Ralph N. Clough, *Island China* (Cambridge: Harvard University Press, 1978), 168–70. President of the Central News Agency James C. M. Wei angrily dismissed the suggestion that Taipei would consider any such action "as if you are a helpless little bastard, as if you need a mafia godfather"; Frank Ching, "A Most Envied Province," *Foreign Policy* (Fall 1979): 144. See also John Garver, "Taiwan's Russian Option: Image and Reality," *Asian Survey* 18 (July 1978): 751–66.

7. Harding, *Fragile Relationship*, 50–52, 397–98n61.

8. Ibid., 46, 51.

9. Banning Garrett, "The Strategic Basis for Learning in U.S. Policy toward China, 1949–68," in George W. Breslauer and Philip E. Tetlock, eds., *Learning in U.S. and Soviet Foreign Policy* (Boulder: Westview, 1991), 228–33. The Pillsbury article appeared under the title "U.S.-Chinese Military Ties?" *Foreign Policy* (Fall 1975): 50–64.

10. Shen, *Free China*, 181–82.

11. Complaints from Taipei and Americans such as Barry Goldwater reversed the decision and Vice President Nelson Rockefeller made the trip.

12. Harding, *Fragile Relationship*, 70–73. Authors of the 30-page report were Richard Holbrooke and William Gleysteen, who had been drafted by Secretary of State Vance to serve on a special China task force in December 1976.

13. Linda Matthews, "Taiwan: Isle of Plenty . . . and Anxiety," *Los Angeles Times*, 13 November 1977, 1, 27; Jimmy Carter, *Keeping Faith: Memoirs of a President* (New York: Bantam, 1982), 188.

14. David Tharp, "Taiwan Sees Vance Speech as Severe Blow," *Christian Science Monitor*, 15 July 1977, 1.

15. Editorial, *China News*, 2 July 1977, *FBIS*, Republic of China, 8 July 1977, B2.

16. Linda Matthews, "The Two Chinas: Accommodations, but No Peace," *Los Angeles Times*, 11 December 1977.

17. Editorial, *United Daily News*, 18 July 1977, *FBIS*, Republic of China, 21 July 1977, B1.

18. "Foreign Spy Activity Found Rampant in U.S.," *Washington Post*, 9 August 1979, 1A.

19. David E. Kaplan, *Fires of the Dragon: Politics, Murder, and the Kuomintang* (New York: Atheneum, 1992), 240.

20.	Kaplan, *Fires*, 239. Wang would later mastermind the murder of Henry Liu; see chapter 8.

21.	Kusnitz, *Public Opinion*, 149n62.

22.	Kaplan, *Fires*, 281.

23.	The Senate Foreign Relations Committee's report *Activities of Certain Intelligence Agencies in the United States* was revealed in August 1979 but was not declassified. "Foreign Spy Activity," 1A; "Carter Pledges Not to Condone Spy Lawbreaking," 10 August 1979, 1A; Patrick E. Tyler, "Taiwanese Spies Said to Penetrate Top Agencies," 1 June 1982, 1A.

24.	Louis D. Bocardi, "Teng: Vance Trip Was Setback in U.S.-China Ties," *Washington Post*, 7 September 1977, 1A.

25.	Shen, *Free China*, 17, 216–17; Hao Yufan, "Solving the Dilemma in China Policy, 1978–1979: A Case Study of Normalization of U.S.-China Relations and the Taiwan Relations Act" (Ph.D. dissertation, Johns Hopkins School of Advanced International Studies, 1990), 198n119.

26.	Arthur M. Schlesinger, Jr., *The Imperial Presidency* (Boston: Houghton Mifflin, 1973), 127–207.

27.	Jaw-ling Joanne Chang, *United States–China Normalization* (Baltimore: Maryland Studies in East Asian Law and Politics, 1986), 157, 159, and passim.

28.	Roy Rowan, "Taiwan Gears up to Go It Alone," *Fortune* 99 (12 February 1979): 74.

29.	Michel Oksenberg of the National Security Council staff subsequently argued that secrecy was necessitated by the uncertainty that normalization would be successful given disagreement over arms sales and that it allowed the administration to control the pace of negotiations, as well as preventing the Taiwan lobby from picking draft agreements apart before the final package had been arranged. Michel Oksenberg, "Congress, Executive-Legislative Relations, and American China Policy," in Edmund S. Muskie, Kenneth Rush, and Kenneth W. Thompson, eds., *The President, the Congress and Foreign Policy* (Lanham, Md.: University Press of America, 1986), 215.

30.	Some Foreign Service officers recognized that dispatch of the mission had been a "very ill-considered move" given its high profile and the resentment engulfing the Taiwan government and people. Interview with former Director of the American Institute in Taiwan, David Dean, Washington, D.C., June 1991.

31.	Interview with Roger Sullivan, 18 November 1992; Ambassador Leonard Unger Oral History, Georgetown, 82–83; David Tawei Lee, "Congress Versus President on Foreign Policy: A Case Study of Taiwan Relations Act" (Ph.D. dissertation, University of Virginia, May 1987), 31–42. Stephen S. F. Chen, Deputy Representative of the CCNAA office, Washington, D.C., confirmed that the police did look the other way, that this behavior did make the subsequent negotiations more difficult, and that relations did not really return to normal for almost a year; interview, May 1992.

32.	Charles T. Cross, "Taiwan's Identity Crisis," *Foreign Policy* (Summer 1983): 51.

33.	Letter Hans Binnendijk, senior staff, Senate Foreign Relations Committee 1978–79, to the author, 10 August 1992.

34.	The issue of the legal challenges to be faced in reworking the U.S.-Taiwan relationship was raised by Victor Li in his study *De-Recognizing Taiwan* (Washington, D.C.: Carnegie Endowment, 1977).

35.   Lee, "Congress Versus President," 99. In fact, Holbrooke had given a higher priority to opening diplomatic relations with Vietnam rather than with China, but was outmaneuvered by Brzezinski and his staff.

36.   The Israelis talked about the uncertainty of U.S. pledges on Tel Aviv state-run radio December 16. "Taiwan's Fate Seen as Lesson in Israel," *Los Angeles Times*, 17 December 1978.

37.   Lee, "Congress Versus President," 174–81.

38.   Ibid., 188.

39.   Ibid., 222–25. Wolff's vocal criticism of Carter's approach led to publication of a volume he put together with David L. Simon, *Legislative History of the Taiwan Relations Act* (Jamaica, N.Y.: American Association for Chinese Studies, 1982).

40.   Richard M. Pious, "The Taiwan Relations Act: The Constitutional and Legal Context," in Louis W. Koenig, James C. Hsiung, and Chang King-yuh, eds., *Congress, the Presidency, and the Taiwan Relations Act* (New York: Praeger, 1985), 150–55.

41.   Lee, "Congress Versus President," 407–8; George McArthur, "Taiwan Indicates Its Intention to Remain Friends of Americans," *Los Angeles Times*, 21 December 1978.

42.   The Nationalists insisted on government-to-government mechanisms; see "President Chiang Ching-kuo's Five Principles on U.S.-ROC Relations in the Post-Normalization Period, December 29, 1978," in Tien Hung-mao, ed., *Mainland China, Taiwan, and United States Policy* (Cambridge: Oelgeschlager, Gunn & Hain, 1983), 215.

43.   Lee, "Congress Versus President," 42–46.

44.   Stephen P. Gibert, "The Isolation of Island China," in Gibert, ed., *Security in Northeast Asia* (Boulder: Westview, 1988), 122–23.

45.   Jay Matthews, "China Calls Bush Visit a Failure," *Washington Post*, 24 April 1980, A1–2.

46.   Analysts have suggested that the Reagan administration wanted to enlist China in a global united front against the declaration of martial law in Poland 13 December 1981. Banning Garrett, "China Policy and the Constraints of Triangular Logic," in Kenneth Oye, Robert J. Lieber, and Donald Rothchild, eds., *Eagle Defiant: United States Foreign Policy in the 1980s* (Boston: Little, Brown, 1983), 259.

47.   Chiang Ching-kuo, "Bitter Lessons and a Solemn Mission," Remarks to the Central Standing Committee of the KMT, 7 October 1981, in Tien, *Mainland China*, 243.

48.   Shen, *Free China*, 283–96.

49.   Although these terms did involve self-imposed constraints, Reagan apparently misunderstood, believing Beijing had sworn off a military solution under all circumstances; Lou Cannon, *President Reagan: The Role of a Lifetime* (New York: Simon and Schuster, 1991), 313.

50.   U.S. Senate, Committee on the Judiciary, Subcommittee on Separation of Powers, *Hearings on Taiwan Communique and Separation of Powers*, 97th Cong., 2d sess., 27 September 1982, 142.

51.   Garrett and Glasser, "From Nixon to Reagan," 285.

52.   William R. Kinter and John F. Copper, *A Matter of Two Chinas* (Philadelphia: Foreign Policy Research Institute, 1979), 27.

53. George Lenczowski, *Presidents and the Middle East* (Durham: Duke University Press, 1990), 130–34.

54. Prybyla, "Economic Development in Taiwan," 120.

55. Jack Williams, "Taiwan's Development Strategy since 1949: Prospects and Problems," in Williams, *The Taiwan Issue*, 46.

56. Gustav Ranis, "Industrial Development," in Galenson, *Economic Growth*, 255–56; Y. Dolly Hwang, *The Rise of a New World Economic Power: Postwar Taiwan* (New York: Greenwood, 1991), 16.

57. Norma Schroder, "Economic Costs and Benefits," in Ramon Myers, ed., *Two Chinese States* (Stanford: Hoover Institution Press, 1978), 35.

58. Clough, *Island China*, 166.

59. David Tharp, "American Salesmen Are Red-Carpet Visitors," *Christian Science Monitor*, 9 August 1977, B3.

60. Robert Gilpin, *The Political Economy of International Relations* (Princeton: Princeton University Press, 1987), 190–97; Jack F. Williams, "Big Dragon, Little Dragon: The Economies of Hong Kong and Taiwan and Their Future Relationship with the PRC," in Williams, *The Future*, 74.

61. Taiwan's heavy commitment to synthetic fibers followed in part from a 1961 study by an American think tank that recommended development of a petrochemical industry. One of the by-products proved to be synthetics. Low-end U.S. department stores such as Montgomery Ward, J. C. Penny, and Alexander's remained the largest buyers of Taiwan's synthetic garments through the 1970s; David Tharp, "Textile Exports Zoom to $2.5 Billion," *Christian Science Monitor*, 9 August 1977, 14B. Some analysts have questioned this recommendation to develop petrochemicals since Taiwan imported 25 percent of its oil; Williams, "Big Dragon, Little Dragon," 76.

62. Susan Greenhalgh, "Supranational Processes of Income Distribution," in Winckler and Greenhalgh, *Contemporary Approaches*, 76, 99n10.

63. William Armbruster, "The American Gamble," *FEER* (10 September 1976): 29–30.

64. Jeffrey Stein, "U.S. Trade Organization Planned with Taiwan," *Christian Science Monitor*, 12 November 1975, 23; Stein, "Economic Council Will Seek to Promote U.S.-Taiwan Trade," *Christian Science Monitor*, 18 March 1976.

65. Jay Matthews, "Taiwan's New Way to Win Allies—Borrow Money," *Washington Post*, 25 October 1977.

66. Fox Butterfield, "Taiwan Chafes as Accord Limits Textile Exports to U.S.," *New York Times*, 7 March 1978.

67. Norman Pearlstine, "Japan on a Smaller Scale," *Forbes* (26 June 1978): 35–36.

68. Theodore Hsi-en Chen, "Taiwan's Future," *Current History* 77 (September 1979): 73; Pearlstine, "Japan," 36.

69. Chang Chun-shyong, "The Economic Impact of American Investment in Taiwan, Republic of China," *Issues and Studies* (November 1988): 108, 113.

70. Robert G. Sutter, *Taiwan's Future: Implication for the United States* (Washington, D.C.: Congressional Research Service Issue Brief #IB79101, 1980), 2.

71. Prybyla, "Economic Development in Taiwan," 122.

72. Jimmy W. Wheeler and Andrew G. Caranfil, "Commercial Relations under the TRA," in William B. Bader and Jeffrey T. Bergner, eds., *The Taiwan Relations Act: A Decade of Implementation* (Indianapolis: Tango Press, 1989), 99.

73. Thomas J. Bellows, *Taiwan's Foreign Policy in the 1970s: A Case Study of Adaptation and Viability* (University of Maryland School of Law, Occasional Paper, Contemporary Asian Studies Series, 1977), 3.

74. Sutter, *Taiwan's Future*, 11.

75. In a biannual report to the Legislative Yuan, Chiang Ching-kuo asserted his government had had the capability beginning in 1974; *China Quarterly* 64 (December 1975): 808.

76. Clough, *Island China*, 117–18; George H. Quester, "Taiwan and Nuclear Proliferation," *Orbis* 18 (Spring 1974): 141–47.

77. Edward Schumacher, "Taiwan Team at MIT Seen to Have Military Purpose," *Washington Post*, 13 June 1976.

78. Edward Schumacher, "Taiwan Seen Reprocessing Nuclear Fuel," *Washington Post*, 29 August 1976; David Binder, "U.S. Finds Taiwan Developed A-Fuel," *New York Times*, 30 August 1976; Don Oberdorfer, "Taiwan to Curb A-Role," *Washington Post*, 23 September 1976.

79. Clough, *Island China*, 116n23.

80. Kusnitz, *Public Opinion*, 144.

81. *Aviation Week and Space Technology*, 23 October 1978, 24; "Carter Rejects Taiwan Bid for New Jet," *Los Angeles Times*, 25 October 1978.

82. Tyler, "Taiwanese Spies," 1A; Kaplan, *Fires*, 184–91.

83. Bill Kazer, "Taiwan Gets a Vote of Confidence," *FEER* (20 July 1979): 46.

84. Robert L. Downen, *The Tattered China Card: Reality or Illusion in United States Strategy?* (Washington, D.C.: Council for Social and Economic Studies, 1984), 75–78.

85. A. Doak Barnett, *The FX Decision: "Another Crucial Moment" in U.S.-China-Taiwan Relations* (Washington, D.C.: Brookings Institution, 1981), 2–3.

86. Ray S. Cline, "Ronald Reagan and the Taiwan Arms Sale," *Wall Street Journal*, 21 December 1981, 20. Cline, who was a longtime Nationalist supporter and a former CIA station chief in Taiwan, had been part of the Reagan campaign team. He departed after a pro-Taiwan outburst at a press conference in November 1980; John W. Garver, "Arms Sales, the Taiwan Question, and Sino-U.S. Relations," *Orbis* 26 (Winter 1983): 1014.

87. Some precedent apparently existed; Joseph Stilwell noted in his wartime diaries (1942) that CCK, "dressed like a coolie," turned up unexpectedly at the posts of rural officials. Joseph Lelyveld, "A 1 1/2-China Policy," *New York Times Magazine*, 6 April 1975, 76.

88. Huang, *Intellectual Ferment*, 81–101.

89. Ibid., 21–32, 41–59.

90. Clough, *Island China*, 63–65; Huang, *Intellectual Ferment*, 61, 74–80, 103–5.

91. *FEER* (8 January 1973): 13.

92. Fox Butterfield, "Elections in Taiwan a Setback for Regime," *New York Times*, 24 November 1977.

93. Tien, *The Great Transition*, 98–104.

94. George F. Will, "A Price for Taiwan," *Washington Post*, 21 December 1978, 15A.

95. Tien Hung-mao, "Taiwan in Transition: Prospects for Socio-Political Change," *China Quarterly* 64 (December 1975): 631.

96. Tien Hung-mao, "Social Change and Political Development in Taiwan," in

Feldman, Kau, and Kim, *Time of Transition*, 27; James Tyson, "Christians and the Taiwanese Independence Movement: A Commentary," *Asian Affairs* 14 (Fall 1987): 166.

97. Trong R. Chai, "The Future of Taiwan," *Asian Survey* 26 (December 1986): 1311; John Kaplan, *The Court Martial of the Kaohsiung Defendants* (Berkeley: University of California Press, 1981), tells the story in detail.

98. *New York Times*, 21 July 1981, 2, and 9 August 1981, 9.

99. Michael J. Glennon, "Liaison and the Law: Foreign Intelligence Agencies' Activities in the United States," *Harvard International Law Journal* 25 (Winter 1984): 3n5, 33–34; U.S. Congress, House of Representatives, Hearings before the House Subcommittee on Asian and Pacific Affairs and on Human Rights and International Organizations of the Committee on Foreign Affairs, *Taiwan Agents in America and the Death of Prof. Wen-chen Chen*, 97th Cong., 1st sess., 30 July and 6 October 1981 (Washington, D.C.: Government Printing Office, 1982); Kaplan, *Fires*, 141–52.

100. David Johnson, "Taiwan Chinese Bring Money to N.Y.—and Woes," *Los Angeles Times*, 23 October 1977.

101. Tien, *Mainland China*, xiii.

102. Robert G. Sutter, *China Quandary: Domestic Determinants of U.S. China Policy, 1972–1982* (Boulder: Westview, 1983), 35.

103. Harding, *Fragile Relationship*, 57.

104. *FEER* (28 May 1973): 22.

105. Fox Butterfield, "Free Congressional Trips to Taiwan Are Linked to the Nationalist Government," *New York Times*, 18 October 1975, 3. The PCF board was dominated by three retired air force generals who were also close associates of Chiang Ching-kuo.

106. Accusations were also made of direct payments to members of Congress. Jack Anderson and Les Whitten, "Chinese Agents Gave Gifts on Hill," *Washington Post*, 5 November 1977, 43E.

107. Bachrack, *Committee of One Million*, 274–75.

108. Wilbur, "The Human Dimension," 48.

109. Carol Chin, letter to author, October 1993.

110. Kusnitz, *Public Opinion*, 141–44.

111. "USOC Head Krumm Promises Decision Sometime Today," *Los Angeles Times*, 15 July 1976.

112. Hwang, *Rise of a New World*, 78–81; Glenn J. McLoughlin, *Taiwan: Science and Technology Policymaking* (Washington, D.C.: Congressional Research Service, 30 October 1989), 8–9.

113. Walter Arnold, "Science and Technology Development in Taiwan and South Korea," *Asian Survey* 28 (April 1988): 448–49.

114. Chang, "Sino-American Scholarly Relations," 60–69.

115. Smith Hempstone, "Taiwan's Anxious Boom," *Washington Post*, 23 July 1978.

116. Jospeh S. M. Lau, "Echoes of the May Fourth Movement in Hsiang-t'u Fiction," in Tien, *Mainland China*, 136–37, 139, 141–42.

117. C. T. Hsia, "Forward," in Jospeh S. M. Lau, ed., *Chinese Stories from Taiwan: 1960–1970* (New York: Columbia University Press, 1976), xxv.

118. Wilbur, "Sino-American Relations in Scholarship," 129; Fairbank, *Chinabound*, 439–40.

119. Chang, "Sino-American Scholarly Relations," 48–51.
120. Watt, *A Friend in Deed*, 25–35.
121. Ibid., 34–35.

CHAPTER 8

1. Ralph N. Clough, *Reaching across the Taiwan Strait* (Boulder: Westview, 1993), effectively explores all aspects of the developing relationship.

2. Gao Yingmao, "The Road of Modernization of the Two Coasts of the Taiwan Strait," *Lianhe Yuekan*, July 1981, in *FBIS*, 6 October 1981, W2. Between 1951 and 1959 there was already a significant Chinese presence in Tibet, which helped provoke the 1959 revolt in response to which Beijing used harsh repression; Melvyn C. Goldstein, "The Dragon and the Snow Lion: The Tibet Question in the Twentieth Century," in Anthony J. Kane, ed., *China Briefing, 1990* (Boulder: Westview, 1990), 136–39.

3. Shaw Yu-ming, *Beyond the Economic Miracle: Reflections on the Developmental Experience of the Republic of China on Taiwan* (Taipei: Kwang Hwa, 1988), 52–55.

4. James McGregor, "Taiwan Entrepreneurs Step around Sedition Laws and Secretly Turn a Profit on the Mainland," *Asian Wall Street Journal*, 2 May 1988.

5. Jia Qingguo, "Changing Relations across the Taiwan Strait: Beijing's Perceptions," *Asian Survey* 32 (March 1992): 279; Tien, "Politics in Taiwan's Democratic Reform," 17.

6. Shaw Yu-ming, "Taiwan: A View from Taipei," *Foreign Affairs* 63 (Summer 1985): 1060.

7. Mary McSherry, "You Can't Go Home Again," *National Review* (22 December 1989): 38.

8. Carl Goldstein, "One, but Also Two," *FEER* (4 May 1989): 27–28.

9. James Seymour, "Taiwan in 1988: No More Bandits," *Asian Survey* 29 (January 1989): 61; *FEER* (3 May 1990): 12.

10. Robert G. Sutter, *Taiwan: Recent Developments and U.S. Policy Choices* (Congressional Research Service Issue Brief #IB92038, 10 March 1992), 4–5. In 1992 it surpassed the U.S. and Japan and became second only to Hong Kong in investments on the mainland.

11. *U.S.-China Update* (New York: National Committee on U.S.-China Relations, July 1992), 3.

12. Lin Cheng-yi, "China, the U.S., and the Security of Taiwan" (Ph.D. dissertation, University of Virginia, 1987), 39, 45. The three links were articulated in the 1979 New Year's Day "Message to Taiwan Compatriots." It also called for four exchanges in academics, culture, sports, and technology.

13. Banquet toast, 5 March 1987, reported in *FBIS*, 6 March 1987, 1B.

14. Su Chi, deputy director of the Institute of International Relations at National Chengchi University, suggests a distinction between flexible diplomacy, which the government practiced before 1988 and which was largely reactive to policies of other governments, and pragmatic diplomacy, which Lee Teng-hui has pursued and which is "increasingly less a product of necessity and more a synthesis of the ROC's choice and circumstance." Su Chi, "The International Relations of the

NOTES TO PAGES 163–168 • 283

Republic of China during the 1990s," paper presented at the 22nd Sino-American Conference on Contemporary China, Center for Strategic and International Studies, June 1993, Washington, D.C., 11.

15. Chiu Hungdah, "Recent Chinese Communist Policy Toward Taiwan and the Prospect for Unification," *Issues and Studies* 27 (January 1991): 27–28.

16. Seymour, "Taiwan in 1988," 61; Shim Jae Hoon, "Money and Diplomacy," *FEER* (2 February 1989): 29–30; Jonathan Moore, "Pragmatic Diplomacy," *FEER* (20 April 1989): 26; Goldstein, "One, but Also Two," 27–28.

17. "Pragmatic" (advertisement), *New York Times*, 8 July 1991, 13A.

18. Sutter, *Taiwan: Recent Developments*, 11–12; Jim Mann, "U.S. Reportedly Refused Gulf Aid from Taiwan," *Washington Post*, 29 September 1990, 20A.

19. Julian Baum, "In Search of Recognition," *FEER* (18 July 1991): 26.

20. Shim Jae Hoon, "Money and Diplomacy," 29. Beijing broke relations with Grenada after its government established ties with Taipei; June Dreyer, "Taiwan in 1989: Democratization and Economic Growth," *Asian Survey* 30 (January 1990): 56.

21. Timothy Brook, *Quelling the People* (New York: Oxford, 1992), 108–69.

22. Ramon Myers, "Political Theory and Recent Political Developments in the Republic of China," *Asian Survey* 27 (September 1987): 1006. Martin Lasater emphasizes that the use of Graham was no accident; "Taiwan's International Environment," in Robinson, *Democracy and Development*, 96.

23. Selig S. Harrison, "Taiwan after Chiang Ching-kuo," *Foreign Affairs* 66 (Spring 1988): 792, 797.

24. Carl Goldstein, "A Two-Pronged Test," *FEER* (4 December 1986): 36.

25. Seymour, "Taiwan in 1988," 56. Although conservatives did try to block Lee, and many regarded him a figurehead, it was unclear how seriously to take any of their efforts. The coalition included Chiang Ching-kuo's brother Chiang Wei-kuo, the premier Lee Huan, and General Hau Pei-ts'un, later named premier by Lee Teng-hui.

26. Peter McKillop and Jeff Hoffman, "Fighting for Democracy," *Newsweek*, 14 January 1991, 31.

27. Peter Maass, "Youths Lead Campaign on Taiwan," *Washington Post*, 27 March 1990, 20A.

28. Sheryl WuDunn, "A Popular Vote Is Urged in Taiwan," *New York Times*, 5 July 1990, 4A; Tien Hung-mao, "Brothers in Arms: Political Struggle and Party Competition in Taiwan's Evolving Democracy," *Asian Update* (New York: Asia Society, December 1991).

29. Chiu Hungdah, "Constitutional Development and Reform in the Republic of China on Taiwan" (University of Maryland School of Law occasional paper #2, 1993), discusses the entire process.

30. "Taipei Square," *The Nation* 250 (23 April 1990): 562.

31. Nicholas D. Kristof, "A Dictatorship That Grew Up," *New York Times Magazine*, 16 February 1992, 16–17.

32. Ibid., 18–19.

33. McSherry, "You Can't Go Home," 38.

34. Jan S. Prybyla, "U.S.-ROC Economic Relations since the Taiwan Relations Act: An American View," *Issues and Studies* (November 1988): 74; *ROC Foreign Affairs Report* (Taipei: Government Information Office, 1993), 20–25. The United

States continued significantly to exceed the trade conducted with any one other country, but Taiwan's trade with its Asian neighbors calculated as a group surpassed that with the United States.

35. David Laux, "U.S.-Taiwan Economic Issues," Forum on American Economic Relations with Greater China: Challenges for the 1990s, American Enterprise Institute and the China Business Forum, February 1992.

36. The U.S. Congress passed a "sense of the Congress" resolution 17 November 1983 saying that Taiwan should be retained as a full member of the Asian Development Bank (ADB), eliciting strong protests from Beijing, which accused Washington of trying to create two Chinas; Wheeler and Caranfil, "Commercial Relations," 102.

37. Martin L. Lasater, *Policy in Evolution: The U.S. Role in China's Reunification* (Boulder: Westview, 1988), 138–39. According to the *Far Eastern Economic Review*, pressure came from Frederick Chien serving as head of the CCNAA in Washington and special U.S. emissary William Clark; Carl Goldstein, "An Alias to Save a Seat," *FEER* (23 January 1986): 36.

38. Frances Williams and Jonathan Moore, "Who Goes First?" *FEER* (1 February 1990): 37.

39. Julian Baum, "A Favour of Sorts," *FEER* (8 August 1991): 8.

40. Lin, "China, the U.S., and the Security of Taiwan," 352.

41. "Tobacco Trade Pressure Seen," *New York Times*, 5 April 1990, 6D; Philip J. Hilts, "U.S. Tobacco Ads in Asia Faulted," *New York Times*, 5 May 1990, 35A.

42. Wade, *Governing the Market*, 134.

43. Seymour, "Taiwan in 1988," 62. Nevertheless, according to Dr. Chang King-yuh, director of the Institute of International Relations in Taipei, in 1987 Taiwan was the third-largest market in the world for U.S. agricultural products. Martin L. Lasater, *U.S.-Republic of China Economic Issues: Problems and Prospects* (Washington, D.C.: Heritage Foundation, 1987), 13.

44. Wade, *Governing the Market*, 135n14.

45. At least part of the motivation was fear that the PRC might, at any moment, disrupt Taiwan's trade; Erland Heginbotham, "Taiwan's Economic Role in East Asian Development" (working paper, Taiwan Study Group, Sigur Center for East Asian Studies, George Washington University, Washington, D.C., January 1993), 7. For evidence of continued friction over the issue see Stuart Auerbach, "U.S. Assails Two Nations on Trade," *Washington Post*, 2 December 1992, 1C.

46. Nicholas Kristof, "Taiwan's Embarrassment of Riches," *New York Times*, 21 December 1986, 12.

47. Ibid., 12; Claudia Rosett, "Chiang Ching-kuo's China," *Wall Street Journal*, 30 October 1987, 22; Carl Goldstein, "Mountains of Green: Taipei Cannot Slow the Growth of Foreign Exchange Reserves," *FEER* (13 November 1986): 116.

48. Michael Westlake, "Hollow Gift Boxes," *FEER* (14 May 1987): 94–95.

49. Edwin J. Feulner, Jr.'s remarks, in Lasater, *U.S.-Republic of China Economic Issues*, 40.

50. Chu Yunpeng, "Taiwan's Trade Surplus, U.S. Responses, and Adjustment Policies," *Issues and Studies* (November 1988): 85. Chu's critique was fashioned from the vantage point of the Academia Sinica and the Graduate Institute of Industrial Economics at National Central University.

51. *The United States and the Republic of China: Democratic Friends, Strategic*

Allies, Economic Partners, Summary of Proceedings (Los Angeles: Claremont Institute, 1989), 7.

52. The maneuver, however, contributed to a still greater boost in the reserves as money flowed in for speculation in the foreign exchange, stock, and real estate markets. *International Herald Tribune*, 23 June 1989, 15.

53. Prybyla, "Economic Development in the Republic of China," 281n22.

54. Penelope Hartland-Thunberg, *China, Hong Kong, Taiwan and the World Trading System* (New York: St. Martin's Press, 1990), 117–18. Resistance to American life insurance companies was also cultural. People generally believed that buying life insurance would hasten one's death; Christopher Marchand, "A Win for Washington," *FEER* (6 April 1989): 79.

55. Jonathan Moore, "Into the Snake Pit," *FEER* (8 February 1990): 44.

56. Westlake, "Hollow Gift Boxes," 94.

57. Jeremy Mark, "Taiwan's Aerospace Sector Gets a Lift with McDonnell Deal to Build Jetliner," *Wall Street Journal*, 21 November 1991, 11A.

58. "Taiwan Backs Aircraft Deal," *New York Times*, 29 April 1992, 12D; Richard W. Stevenson, "Taiwan Company Backs off on McDonnell," *New York Times*, 19 May 1992, 1D.

59. Martin L. Lasater, *U.S. Interests in the New Taiwan* (Boulder: Westview, 1993), 212; Robert Sutter, Trip Report, 4 May 1993 (Washington, D.C.: Congressional Research Service, Library of Congress), 8.

60. Chu, "Taiwan's Trade Surplus," 93.

61. U.S. Department of Commerce, telephone inquiry, 7 July 1993.

62. *FEER* (11 January 1990): 50–52; Rhonda Richards, "Famous Amos Gets New Owner," *USA Today*, 18 September 1992, 1B.

63. James Hsiung, "Taiwan in 1984," *Asian Survey* 25 (January 1985): 97; Jonathan Moore, "Pirates' Charades," *FEER* (12 January 1989): 50. U.S. Trade Representative Mickey Kantor placed Taiwan on a "priority watch list" for copyright violations in May 1993; "Taiwan and Copyrights," *Washington Post*, 3 May 1993, 13A.

64. Louis Kraar, "Fighting the Fakes from Taiwan," *Fortune*, 30 May 1983, 114–16.

65. Harriet King, "Microsoft Nails Some Pirates," *New York Times*, 10 May 1992, 7F.

66. Stephen Haggard, "Policy, Politics and Structural Adjustment: The U.S. and the East Asian NICS," paper from the Conference on Economic Development Experiences of Taiwan and Its New Role in an Emerging Asia-Pacific Area, 8–10 June 1988, Institute of Economics, Academia Sinica, 503.

67. McLoughlin, *Science and Technology*, 10.

68. Hou Chi-ming, "The Role of Taiwan in International Economic Cooperation and Development" (unpublished paper, Chung-hua Institution for Economic Research, Taiwan, 1989), 18–19.

69. Benjamin Lu, director of the Economic Division, CCNAA, statement in Lasater, *U.S.-Republic of China Economic Issues*, 46–49; Ma Ying-jeou, National Chengchi University, Taipei, statement in Martin L. Lasater, ed., *Taipei Style*, vol. 2 of *Democracy in China* (Washington, D.C.: Heritage Foundation, 1987), 20. Given Taiwan's large trade deficit with Japan, a delay in completely opening Taiwan's economy to the Japanese through a multilateral accord enhanced the appeal of a bilateral agreement with the United States.

70. Sandy Kristoff, deputy assistant, Office of the U.S. Trade Representative, statement in Lasater, *U.S.-Republic of China Economic Issues*, 49–53.

71. Leslie H. Gelb, "Breaking China Apart," *New York Times*, 13 November 1991, 25A.

72. Harding, *Fragile Relationship*, 158–59. Calculations on the basis of total commercial deliveries and foreign military sales (FMS) agreements suggested a drop of $20 million a year, but if figured from total commercial sales and FMS deliveries, the volume increased from $473 million in 1983 to $683 million in 1988.

73. Harlan W. Jencks, "Taiwan in the International Arms Market," Taiwan Study Group, March 1993, 5.

74. Martin L. Lasater, "Military Milestones," in Stephen P. Gibert and William M. Carpenter, eds., *America and Island China: A Documentary History* (Lanham, Md.: University Press of America, 1989), 43–44; *1992 National Defense Report, Republic of China* (Taipei: Li Ming Cultural Enterprise Co., 1992), 151.

75. John F. Copper, "Taiwan in 1986: Back on Top Again," *Asian Survey* (January 1987): 87.

76. Baum, "A Favour of Sorts," 9.

77. Jencks, "International Arms Market," 24; "Taiwan Scraps Booster Plan," *Aviation Week and Space Technology*, 22 October 1990, 11; Kaplan, *Fires*, 481.

78. Benjamin Weiser, "Singlaub Suggested an Earlier Fund Diversion," *New York Times*, 20 March 1987, 1A and 14A; Theodore Draper, *A Very Thin Line: The Iran-Contra Affairs* (New York: Hill & Wang, 1991), 84–88.

79. R. Jeffrey Smith and Don Oberdorfer, "Taiwan to Close Nuclear Reactor," *New York Times*, 24 March 1988, 32A.

80. Shaw, "Taiwan: A View from Taipei," 1057.

81. Bonnie S. Glaser, "China's Security Perceptions: Interests and Ambitions," *Asian Survey* 33 (March 1993): 259, and discussions with the author.

82. Glaser, "China's Security," 262–67. The Chinese denied any offensive intent, noting that their defense budget for 1992 totalled only 2.27 percent of the U.S. defense budget. Even were estimates from the CIA credited, notes analyst Chen Qimao, chairman of the Academic Council of the Shanghai Institute for International Studies, the level would still be only 4 to 5 percent of the U.S. budget; Chen Qimao, "New Approaches in China's Foreign Policy: The Post–Cold War Era," *Asian Survey* 33 (March 1993): 246–48.

83. Jencks, "International Arms Market," 8; Thompson Lee, "Restoring the Balance," *Free China Review* (November 1992): 42–43.

84. Jencks, "International Arms Market," 10.

85. Ibid., 12–14.

86. Continued arrests and imprisonments in 1988, 1990, and 1991 were recorded by Jonathan Spence, "The Other China," *New York Review of Books*, 22 October 1992, 14; *Amnesty International Report, 1991* (Baltimore: John D. Lucas, 1991), 221; Tien, *Brothers in Arms*, 5.

87. Chou Yangsun and Andrew J. Nathan, "Democratizing Transition in Taiwan," *Asian Survey* (March 1987): 291.

88. Corinna-Barbara Francis, "Interview with Kang Ning-hsiang," *Bulletin of the Committee of Concerned Asian Scholars* 18 (1986): 63–64.

89. Jonathan Goldstein, "Barricaded Tarmac," *FEER* (11 December 1986): 16–17. Hsu did return and became head of the DPP.

90. Tien, *Brothers in Arms*, 5; Spence, "The Other China," 15.

91. Seymour, "Taiwan in 1988," 62.

92. Pell, "I Fully Support Self-Determination," 2.

93. Chao Chien-mai, "Interactions between Taiwan and Mainland China after the Tienanmen Massacre," *Issues and Studies* 26 (December 1990): 44.

94. Robert G. Sutter, *Taiwan's Elections: Implications for Taiwan's Development and U.S. Interests* (Congressional Research Service Issue Brief #90-11F, 7 December 1989), 10.

95. Chai, "The Future of Taiwan," 1311; Kaplan, *Fires*, 1–8, 376–489; Sutter, Trip Report, 9.

96. Kaplan, *Fires*, 481.

97. Yuen Ying Chan and Peter Kwong, "Trashing the Hopes of Tiananmen?" *The Nation*, 250 (23 April 1990): 560, 562–64.

98. Prohibitions against advocating independence were pursued during the campaign by the Central Election Commission acting under Article 54 of the ROC Election and Recall Law barring incitement to acts threatening internal or external security. The CEC had some success in controlling election bulletins, but the advocacy of *taidu* (Taiwan independence) continued largely unabated; Tammy C. Peng, "Restrictions on Platform Language Decreed," *Free China Journal*, 29 November 1991, 1.

99. Lena H. Sun, "Taiwan Election May Reflect Emerging Pride of a People," *Washington Post*, 21 December 1991, 16A; Neal E. Robbins, "Enter the Little Dragon," ibid., 15 December 1991, 5C.

100. According to the *China News*, 8 December 1991, a popular opinion survey conducted by the Chinese-language *China Times Express* in November 1991 found that a majority of Taiwan residents want neither reunification nor independence. Only 5.3 percent supported independence, and 22.6 percent favored reunification, whereas 52 percent indicated a preference for the status quo. Of those who spoke for independence only 3.9 percent considered themselves members of the KMT with the majority adhering to the DPP.
In the election 71 percent of the votes went to the KMT and just 24 percent to the DPP with other parties garnering 5 percent; *Washington Post*, 22 December 1991, 37A.

101. Gallup pollsters discovered that 60 percent of the Taiwanese believe that the PRC would invade if Taiwan tried to declare independence; Jerry Hoffman, "Ruling Party Wins Big in Taiwanese Election," *Washington Post*, 22 December 1991, 37A. Yang's threat was reported in *Renmin Ribao*, 3 October 1991, as cited in *FBIS*, 20 October 1991, 31–32.

102. The big loser in the campaign proved to be the New Tide faction of the DPP, only two of whose independence activists won their election bids. Former party chairman Huang Hsin-chieh pointed to the defeat of Lin Tso-shui, the architect of the independence strategy, as indicative of the mistake made by the DPP in focusing on that issue; Y. C. Chen, "DPP's Independence Platform Bombs; 'Wrong Move' Admitted," *Free China Journal*, 24 December 1991, 2.

103. Nicholas D. Kristof, "Taiwan Becomes a Tiger with an Identity Crisis," *New York Times*, 12 January 1992, 4E.

104. Li Shenzhi and Zi Zhongyun, "Jinghou Shinian de Taiwan" (Taiwan in the next ten years), in Zi and He, *Meitai Guanxi*, 7–12.

105. Spence, "The Other China," 14.

106. Tien Hung-mao, "Politics in Taiwan's Democratic Reform and Mainland-Taiwan Relations" paper presented at the Council on Foreign Relations, New York, N.Y., February 1993, 6–11.

107. This section draws heavily on Carl Goldstein, "The New China Lobby," FEER (6 November 1986): 44–45.

108. Jonathan Burton, "Creative Diplomacy," FEER (19 December 1991): 56.

109. Kristof, "A Dictatorship That Grew Up," 18.

110. Nicholas D. Kristof, "The Voice of Taiwan Speaks English," New York Times, 4 January 1992, 4.

111. Taiwan Studies Newsletter (Spring 1990): 27.

112. Taiwan Studies Newsletter (Fall 1989): 3–4; (Spring 1990): 26; and (Spring 1992): 10.

113. Taiwan Studies Newsletter (Fall 1989): 7–8.

114. Letter Terrill E. Lautz, vice president of the Henry R. Luce Foundation, to the author, 9 July 1992.

115. Hsu Cho-yun, "Summary," in Tien Mainland China, 96, 101.

116. Paul Blustein, "A Hidden U.S. Export: Higher Education," Washington Post, 16 February 1992, 4H; Kristof, "The Voice of Taiwan Speaks English," 4; Tsai Wen-hui, "The U.S. Educated Political Elite and Its Impact on the Modernization of the ROC on Taiwan," in Round Table Conference on Chinese and American Cultural and Educational Relations, 1947–1987 (Washington, D.C., 1987), 62.

117. Andrew Tanzer, "Brain Drain in Reverse," Forbes (7 April 1989): 114.

118. Ibid., 114–15; USA-ROC Taiwan Economic News 15 (May 1991): 26; Wade, Governing the Market, 191.

119. Anna Quindlen, "The Drive to Excel," New York Times Magazine, 22 February 1987, 32, 39.

120. U.S. Civil Rights Commission, Civil Rights Issues Facing Asian-Americans in the 1990s (Washington, D.C.: Government Printing Office, February 1992), 104–7; Quindlen, "Drive to Excel," 39.

121. Taiwan Studies Newsletter (Fall 1991): 12.

122. James Reardon-Anderson, Pollution, Politics and Foreign Investment in Taiwan: The Lukang Rebellion (Armonk, N.Y.: M. E. Sharpe, 1992), details the story of the movement.

123. "Taiwan Aims to Tighten Pollution Controls," South China Morning Post, 30 June 1986.

124. Taiwan 2000: Balancing Economic Growth and Environmental Protection (Taipei: Institute of Ethnology, Academia Sinica, 1989), i–iv, 16, 731–32.

125. Ho-ching Lee Liu, "ROC-U.S. Cooperative Relations in the Development of Science and Technology," Issues and Studies (November 1988): 124–29; David Dean, "U.S.-Taiwan Cooperation: Past Success, Future Challenges," Sino-American Relations 15 (Spring 1989): 18–19.

126. Watt, A Friend in Deed, 38–45.

127. Taiwan Studies Newsletter (Fall 1986): 12–17.

128. Taiwan Studies Newsletter (Fall 1985): 16–17; and (Spring 1986): 8.

129. Shaw, "A View from Taipei," 1054.

130. Gish Jen, "Challenging the Asian Illusion," New York Times, 11 August 1991, sec.II, 1, 12–13; Allen L. Woll and Randall M. Miller, Ethnic and Racial Images

in *American Film and Television* (New York: Garland, 1987), 189–96; Dick Stromgren, "The Chinese Syndrome: The Evolving Images of Chinese and Chinese-Americans in Hollywood Films," in Paul Loukides and Linda K. Fuller, *Beyond the Stars* (Bowling Green, Ohio: Bowling Green State University Popular Press, 1990), 63–77.

131.   Vincent Canby, "A Taiwan Artist Tells His Island's Story Obliquely," *New York Times*, 6 October 1993, C19; *Taiwan Studies Newsletter* (Fall 1989): 20; and (Spring 1991): 6.

132.   Columbia University scholar C. Martin Wilbur, in a lengthy review, insisted the volume was "unabashedly biased," inaccurate, and hostile. C. Martin Wilbur, "Fabricating History," *Issues and Studies* 22 (May 1986): 129–48.

133.   Helen C. Smith, "Taiwan Tempts Atlanta Director to Return, Teach," *Atlanta Constitution*, 16 December 1990, 8N.

134.   C. Martin Wilbur, "Sino-American Cultural Relations with Special Reference to Taiwan," *Sino-American Relations* 18 (Spring 1992): 35–36, 38.

135.   Kristof, "The Voice of Taiwan Speaks English," 4.

CHAPTER 9

1.   Hong Kong island, making up 32 square miles, was joined in 1860 by the Kowloon Peninsula and Stonecutter's Island, 3.75 square miles, and in 1898 by the New Territories, which included a strip further inland from the Kowloon area and 235 islands, all totaling 365 square miles.

2.   Gourlay, "Hong Kong and Taiwan," 1–6.

3.   Ibid., 5; Frank H. H. King, *The Hongkong Bank in Late Imperial China, 1864–1902: On an Even Keel*, vol. 1 of *The History of the Hongkong and Shanghai Banking Corporation* (New York: Cambridge, 1987), 46, 457.

4.   G. B. Endacott, *Hong Kong Eclipse* (New York: Oxford, 1978), 59.

5.   Arthur N. Young, *China and the Helping Hand, 1937–1945* (Cambridge: Harvard University Press, 1963), 22–23, 52–53, 189.

6.   John W. Garver, "The Nationalist-American Alliances, 1941–1963" paper given at the Conference on Patterns of Cooperation in the Foreign Relations of Modern China, Joint Committee on Chinese Studies, Wintergreen, Va., August 1987, 27; Chiu Hungdah, "The Hong Kong Agreement and American Foreign Policy," *Issues and Studies* 22 (June 1986): 77–78.

7.   William Roger Louis, *Imperialism at Bay* (New York: Oxford University Press, 1978), 229.

8.   Chiu Hungdah, "The Hong Kong Agreement and American Foreign Policy," 77–78.

9.   Transcripts of the Yalta Conference as published in the *New York Times*, 17 March 1955, 65 and 79.

10.   Louis, *Imperialism at Bay*, 285.

11.   #538 Stuart, Nanking, 4 March 1947, *FRUS 1947*, vol. 7, *The Far East: China* (Washington, D.C.: Government Printing Office, 1972), 55. In April 1949 Stuart cabled the department that "it would be splendidly foresighted . . . to end all colonial claims over these regions [including Hong Kong] and to prepare their peoples for real independence"; 893.00/4–1949 Stuart, Nanking, *FRUS 1949*, vol. 8, 253.

12. Jeffrey T. Richelson and Desmond Ball, *The Ties That Bind* (Boston: Allen & Unwin, 1985), 40.

13. Tillman Durdin, "U.S. Officer Joins Hong Kong Staff," *New York Times*, 8 September 1949, 15.

14. Harold B. Hinton, "Acheson Denies Hong Kong Pledge; Says Help Will Depend on Events," *New York Times*, 13 August 1949, 1.

15. The United States imposed economic and financial restrictions in December 1950. The development of export licensing policy toward Hong Kong can be traced through NSC 104/2, "U.S. Policies and Programs in the Economic Field Which May Affect the War Potential of the Soviet Bloc," 11 April 1951, *FRUS 1951*, vol. 1, *National Security Affairs; Foreign Economic Policy* (Washington, D.C.: Government Printing Office, 1979), 1059; NSC 122/1 "United States Export Licensing Policy toward Hong Kong and Macao," 6 February 1952, *FRUS 1952–54*, vol. 14, pt. 1, p. 5–8; NSC 152/3 "Economic Defense," 18 June 1954, *FRUS 1952–54*, vol. 1, pt. 2, *General: Economic and Political Matters* (Washington, D.C.: Government Printing Office, 1983), 1207.

16. Gourlay, "Hong Kong and Taiwan," 8; Norman J. Miners, *The Government and Politics of Hong Kong* (New York: Oxford University Press, 1975), 5. The British insisted that Hong Kong implemented the embargo effectively, with a wider range of control mechanisms than other nations employed and that it acted "as a sort of long-stop to cover up the shortcomings of other countries' controls"; CO 1030/284 #1071, "Hong Kong: Local Industry," 27 July 1955, PRO. The colony had, in fact, undertaken sweeping export controls in June 1951.

17. One of many documents making this point is 746G.5/1–851 #1949 Acheson to McConaughy, Hong Kong, bx 3599, RG 59, NA.

18. *New York Times*, 3 June 1951, 1.

19. Memcon Radford and Allison, 4 February 1953, *FRUS 1952–54*, vol. 14, pt. 1, 143. A similar offer was made to Karl Rankin a year earlier; 746G.5/1–352 #813 Rankin, Taipei, bx 3599, RG 59 NA. Grantham agreed that Hong Kong could be defended; Alexander Grantham, *Via Ports* (Hong Kong: Hong Kong University Press, 1965), 171.

20. Tracy Lee Steele, "Allied and Interdependent: British Policy during the Chinese Offshore Islands Crisis of 1958," in Anthony Gorst, Lewis Johnman, and W. Scott Lucas, eds., *Contemporary British History, 1931–1961* (New York: Pinter, 1991), 222. American intelligence also doubted an attack would come. See, for example, NIE-25 "Probable Soviet Courses of Action to Mid-1952," 2 August 1951, *FRUS 1951*, vol. 1, 123.

21. NSC 73, 1 July 1950 and NSC 73/4, 25 August 1950, *FRUS 1950*, vol. 1, *National Security Affairs; Foreign Economic Policy* (Washington, D.C.: Government Printing Office, 1977), 335.

22. 611.41/12–2951 #2903 Gifford, London, *FRUS 1952*, vol. 6, pt. 1, *Western Europe and Canada* (Washington, D.C.: Government Printing Office, 1986), 725.

23. Miners, *The Government and Politics of Hong Kong*, 14n4.

24. Grantham, *Via Ports*, 171.

25. 6ll.46G London, 26 November 1956, bx 3270, RG 59, NA.

26. Peter G. Boyle, *The Churchill-Eisenhower Correspondence, 1953–1955* (Chapel Hill: University of North Carolina Press, 1990), 137, 198.

27.   611.46G/6–2252 #3332 McConaughy, Hong Kong, FRUS 1952–54, vol. 14, pt. 1, 71.

28.   Memcon Radford and Allison, 4 February 1953, FRUS 1952–54, vol. 14, pt. 1, 143.

29.   Henry R. Lieberman, "Hong Kong Shaken as U.S. Bank Closes," New York Times, 6 January 1951, 5.

30.   446G.119/2–151 Barnett (CA) to Allison (FE), bx 1983, RG 59, NA; Henry R. Lieberman, "Hong Kong Press Likens U.S. Ban on Exports to 'Vicious Blockade,'" New York Times, 16 December 1950, 3.

31.   446G.119/2–951 Thorp to Matthews, FRUS 1951, vol. 7, 1899–1902; 446G.119/2–151 Bonbright and Rusk to Acheson, ibid., 1936–37; 446G.119/4–951 Marshall to Acheson, ibid., 1949–50.

32.   746G.00(W)/5–1151 #3354 McConaughy, Hong Kong, bx 3598, RG 59, NA; 746G.00(W)/7–1351 #165 McConaughy, Hong Kong, bx 3598, RG 59, NA.

33.   Grantham, Via Ports, 166.

34.   446G.119/7–3151 #188 McConaughy, Hong Kong and 446G.119/12–551 Despatch 1125 McConaughy, Hong Kong, bx 1983, RG 59, NA.

35.   746G.00(W)/5–853 #2941 Joint Weeka #19, bx 3599, RG 59, NA; Frank H. H. King, Hongkong and Shanghai Bank historian, claimed that the bank helped to finance the export of key commodities, such as bristles and duck feathers, from China via Japan to the U.S. with the connivance of American customs inspectors; King, The Hongkong Bank in the Period of Development and Nationalism, 1941–1984, vol. 4 of The History of the Hongkong and Shanghai Banking Corporation (New York: Cambridge University Press, 1991), 396.

36.   Gourlay, "Hong Kong and Taiwan," 9.

37.   CO 1030/860 Claude Burgess, Hong Kong to W. I. J. Wallace, London, 5 October 1959, PRO.

38.   447th NSC Meeting, 8 June 1960, Eisenhower Papers, Whitman File, bx 12: NSC Summaries of Discussion, IKE.

39.   NSC 6007/1 "U.S. Policy on Hong Kong," Kennedy Papers, NSF Series: Trips and Conferences, bx 283, f: NSC General, Papers on Military Policy, Boggs Memo, 14 March 1961 (5), JFK.

40.   P. Y. Tang to W. W. Rostow, 1 November 1961, NSF Country File, bx 22, f: China General, 1 November 1961–26 November 1961, JFK.

41.   Robert Trumbull, "Anti-U.S. Outcry Stirs Hong Kong," New York Times, 1 April 1962, 7.

42.   "Hong Kong Faces a Double-Squeeze," 17 March 1961, NSF Country File, bx 22, f: China General, 1 October 1961–31 October 1961, JFK.

43.   CO1023/101 #214 "KMT Guerilla Activity in Kwangtung," 7 February 1952, PRO. Non-Nationalist resistance in northeast China was supported through Operation TROPIC, which recruited in Hong Kong and flew from Japan via Korea using CAT/CIA aircraft. Such activities had to be kept secret from Taipei and from airline founder Chennault, whose intense loyalty to Chiang would have prompted him to inform the Generalissimo; Leary, Perilous Mission, 137–43.

44.   Donald M. Anderson Oral History, Georgetown, July 1992, 16.

45.   Smith, Portrait of a Cold Warrior, 148.

46. Darrell Garwood, *Under Cover: Thirty-Five Years of CIA Deception* (New York: Grove Press, 1985), 60–63.

47. Marchetti and Marks, *Cult of Intelligence*, 208; Powers, *The Man Who Kept the Secrets*, 276.

48. 611.41/1–2551 and 1–2751 Memcon Alan Watson, British liaison, with W. Bradley Conners, FE/P; and 611.41/3–2051 Memcon Watson with George L. Harris, FE/P, bx 2769, RG 59, NA.

49. FO 371/127290 (FC 10345/46) R. T. D. Ledward, Hong Kong to A. J. de la Mare, Washington, 21 August 1957, PRO.

50. CO 1023/101 Extract from Police Special Branch Summary, December 1953, PRO. The American consul general, Marshall Green, who served from 1961 to 1963 attempted to convince Washington that such Nationalist operations caused little damage to the Communists but seriously endangered Hong Kong; Marshall Green, "Evolution of U.S.-China Policy, 1956–1973: Memoirs of an Insider," unpublished paper, Washington, D.C., 13–14.

51. Leary, *Perilous Mission*, 91–92.

52. This policy on communist satellite countries was set forth in NSC 15/1; Leary, *Perilous Mission*, 93–94.

53. Grantham, *Via Ports*, 158–63.

54. GCD-6 "Hong Kong: Out of This World?" 1 January 1963, Thomson Papers, bx 13: Far East 1961–66, f: General—George C. Denny Newsletters 1–8, September 1962–January 1963, JFK, 3; #594 Trevelyan, Peking, 17 June 1955, CO 1030/377, PRO.

55. Grantham, *Via Ports*, 163.

56. CO 936/310 American press treatment of colonial affairs, March 1955, PRO.

57. The announcement from London came 30 May 1957, and Eisenhower noted in his 5 June press conference that continued American adherence to the existing levels did not seem to serve much purpose.

58. Steele, "Allied and Interdependent," 232.

59. Memcon, 24 October 1957, and Letter Lloyd to Dulles, 25 October 1957, *FRUS 1955–57*, vol. 27, *Western Europe and Canada* (Washington, D.C.: Government Printing Office, 1992), 814, 838.

60. Steele, "Allied and Interdependent," 232, 239. Britain's position on the UN changed again in the early 1960s.

61. Nevertheless, the governor of Hong Kong suspected that someday the United States would align itself with Communist China in some joint anticolonial action. His comments were sparked by the revelation 21 March 1955 of Franklin Roosevelt's wartime advocacy of returning Hong Kong to China; 746G.022/3–2255 Despatch 1568 Drumright, Hong Kong, bx 3599, RG 59, NA.

62. Steele, "Allied and Interdependent," 232; C.C.76 (57) minute 2, 25 October 1957, PRO.

63. NSC 6007/1 "U.S. Policy on Hong Kong," JFK.

64. Edwin W. Martin, *Divided Counsel: The Anglo-American Response to Communist Victory in China* (Lexington: University of Kentucky Press, 1986), 172.

65. Research Memorandum 110, "The Flow of Chinese Communist Refugees to Hong Kong," 23 May 1962, Hilsman Papers, bx 1: Countries, f: CC-Refugees 5/62, JFK.

66.   Grantham, *Via Ports*, 158.
67.   746G.00/12–952 #1475 Harrington, Hong Kong, bx 3598, RG 59, NA.
68.   Memo William B. Coolidge (INR/RFE) to Hilsman (INR), 21 May 1962, Hilsman Papers, bx 1: Countries, f: CC-Refugees 5/62, JFK; "Hong Kong: Out of This World?" 1 January 1963, James C. Thomson Papers, bx 13: Far East, 1961–66, f: General—George C. Denny Newsletters 1–8, September 1962–January 1963, JFK.
69.   Whiting to Hilsman, 23 May 1962, Roger Hilsman Papers, bx 1: Countries, f: CC—Refugees, May 1962, JFK; *New York Times*, 14 June 1962, 8.
70.   CO 968/349 Minutes and Correspondence regarding use of Hong Kong for military leaves, May–July 1953, PRO; Jan Morris, *Hong Kong: The End of an Empire* (New York: Penguin, 1990), 57.
71.   Jurgen Domes, "The Impact of the Hong Kong Problem and Agreement on PRC Domestic Politics," in Domes and Shaw Yu-ming, eds., *Hong Kong: A Chinese and International Concern* (Boulder: Westview, 1988), 81.
72.   *New York Times*, 2 September 1965, 3; and 5 September 1965, 3; and 6 September 1965, 2; #363 Rice, Hong Kong, 8 September 1965, NSF Country File China, vol. 4, bx 238, LBJ.
73.   "Contingency Planning for Hong Kong," n.d., NSF Country File China, bx 241, f: China Memos, vol. 10, 7/67–9/67, LBJ.
74.   A-454 "Hong Kong's Major Problems Affecting U.S. Policy Interests," 7 January 1966, Thomson Papers, bx 19: Southeast Asia, f: Baguio III 2/66 General and Background, JFK; Neville Maxwell, *India's China War* (New York: Pantheon, 1970), 227–29. Soviet attacks on China for permitting Hong Kong to remain in British hands continued sporadically. In 1972 Moscow denounced it as a major headquarters for the CIA in Asia; *New York Times*, 27 August 1972, 1.
75.   Seymour Topping, "What Goes in Hong Kong? Everything," *New York Times Magazine*, 11 April 1965, 48.
76.   "Hong Kong: Out of This World?" 16.
77.   #1366/67 "The Situation in Hong Kong," 11 July 1967, CIA Intelligence Memorandum, NSF Country File, bx 241, f: China Memos, vol. 10, 7/67–9/67, LBJ.
78.   REA-53 "The Confrontation in Hong Kong: Its Past and Its Future," 16 November 1967, INR Research Memorandum, 8, NSF Country File, China, vol. 11, bx 242, LBJ; *New York Times*, 18 May 1967, 1.
79.   "Recent Economic Development in Hong Kong, First Half of 1967," NSF Country File China, bx 242-43, f: vol. 11, Memos (cont.) 9/67–12/67, LBJ; *New York Times*, 15 September 1967, 37.
80.   #197313 Rusk to Hong Kong and London, 18 May 1967, NSF Country File, bx 241, f: China Cables, vol. 9, 3/67–6/67, LBJ.
81.   Jenkins to Rostow, 12 July 1967, NSF Country File, bx 241, f: China Memos, vol. 10: July–September 1967, LBJ.
82.   Melvin Gurtov and Byong-moo Hwang, *China under Threat* (Baltimore: Johns Hopkins University Press, 1980), 223.
83.   "Draft Contingency Plan on Hong Kong," replacement page 6, 25 August 1967, NSF Country File China, vol. 13, bx 243, LBJ.
84.   John Baylis, *Anglo-American Defense Relations 1939–1980: The Special Relationship* (New York: St. Martin's Press, 1981), 94–95.
85.   Memo 12 July 1967, NSF Country File China, bx 241, f: China Memos, vol. 10, 7/67–9/67, LBJ.

86.   *New York Times*, 5 April 1963, 72. For example, the United States Tariff Commission rejected efforts to mandate a 8.5 cent per pound fee on cotton textiles proposed in 1962.

87.   "The Economy of Hong Kong," 4 October 1967, Howard P. Jones Papers, bx 58, f: Hong Kong, Hoover Institution.

88.   Wade, *Governing the Market*, 94.

89.   Kayser Sung, "Changing Horizons," *FEER* (4 July 1968): 22.

90.   *New York Times*, 14 June 1963, 47.

91.   Green, "Evolution," 16–17.

92.   David Winder, "Hong Kong, Macao," *Christian Science Monitor*, 1 March 1972, 1, 3.

93.   Baylis, *Anglo-American Defense*, 101.

94.   Richelson and Ball, *The Ties That Bind*, 190–91. The facilities were operated by Australia's Defence Signals Directorate in cooperation with Britain's Government Communications Headquarters. Intelligence was shared with the U.S. under the 1947 UK-USA Security Agreement.

95.   "Hong Kong: Weighing the Odds," *The Economist*, 3 June 1989, 11.

96.   Stephan Haggard and Cheng Tun-jen, "State and Foreign Capital in the East Asian NICs," in Fred Deyo, ed., *The Political Economy of the New Asian Industrialism* (Ithaca: Cornell University Press, 1987), 120–21.

97.   Haggard, *Pathways*, 151–53.

98.   Louis Kraar, "Hong Kong's Short Haul," *Asia* (May–June 1981), 46–47.

99.   *New York Times*, 5 April 1978, 7D; Fox Butterfield, "An Asian Bank Challenges West," *New York Times*, 16 July 1978, sec. VI, 1; King, *Hongkong Bank, 1941–1984*, 769.

100.   Haggard, *Pathways*, 154.

101.   Robert Sutter, "Hong Kong: Issues for U.S. Policy," Issue Brief IB85015, Congressional Research Service, 10 December 1985, 7.

102.   Nayan Chanda, "Preventive Medicine: U.S.-Hong Kong Trade Pact Seeks to Avert Even Tougher Curbs," *FEER* (10 July 1986): 74–75.

103.   Andrew B. Brick, "Hong Kong: Now a Matter of U.S. Interest," Asian Studies Center Backgrounder, Heritage Foundation Washington, D.C., 18 October 1989, 12. Huang Chen-ya, a brain surgeon and founding member of the Hong Kong Affairs Society, insisted that the internationalization of Hong Kong would be the only way to ensure democracy; *South China Morning Post*, 19 June 1989, 6, in FBIS-CHI-89-116, 19 June 1989, 65.

104.   Actually, discontent with the slow pace of political change had been voiced earlier but accelerated appreciably in the wake of Tiananmen. See Suzanne Pepper, "The Struggle for Autonomy within the Chinese State: Birth and Death of Democracy in Hong Kong," Universities Field Staff International Reports #30, 1985.

105.   Yu Hung, "Guard against Certain Americans' Attempts to Encroach on Hong Kong Affairs," *Wen Wei Po*, Hong Kong, 25 November 1991, in FBIS-CHI-91-227, 25 November 1991, 4.

106.   Ibid., 5.

107.   Donald M. Anderson Oral History, Georgetown, 75.

108.   William McGurn, "Britain Sells out U.S. Interests in Hong Kong," *Wall Street Journal*, 31 July 1990, 12A.

109.   Stacy Mosher, "Declaring an Interest," *FEER* (3 June 1991): 11–12.

110. *New York Times*, 9 October 1989, 4D.

111. William H. Overholt, "Hong Kong and China: The Real Issues," paper given at Wingspread Conference on China and East Asia: Implications for American Policy, January 1991, Wisconsin.

112. In 1990 China's exports through Hong Kong totaled approximately $30 billion, some $10 billion of which went to the American market. Michael Taylor, "Trade Ebbs and Flows," *FEER* (16 May 1991): 67.

113. Harding, *Fragile Relationship*, 435–36n40.

114. McGurn, "Britain Sells Out," 12A; Pamela G. Hollie, "Hong Kong's Stake in America," *New York Times*, 1 August 1982, 17F.

115. Jan S. Prybyla, "The Hong Kong Agreement and Its Impact on the World Economy," in Domes and Shaw, *Hong Kong: A Chinese and International Concern*, 174, 178.

116. This became law in the 1982 British Nationality Act, wherein the citizens of the country's remaining colonial holdings were denied the right to settle in Britain.

117. In 1991 applications for such visas were undersubscribed, attesting to a return of some confidence to colony residents. David M. Lampton, et al., *The Emergence of "Greater China": Implications for the United States* (New York: National Committee China Policy Series, October 1992), 14.

118. "Hong Kong: Weighing the Odds," *The Economist*, 3 June 1989, 11.

119. Frank Ching, "One Country, Two Systems: The Future of Hong Kong," in Kane, *China Briefing, 1990*, 124–25.

120. Paul Lewis, "Asians to Press U.S. on Boat People," *New York Times*, 1 June 1990, 3A.

121. Nicholas D. Kristof, "Flow of Vietnamese to Hong Kong Seems Over, to Hong Kong's Relief," *New York Times*, 16 November 1992, 1.

122. Barbara Basler, "For Hong Kong, a New Governor, and a Much Different Style," *New York Times*, 14 June 1992, 7.

123. Sheryl WuDunn, "First Beijing Visit for Hong Kong's Governor," *New York Times*, 21 October 1992, 5A.

124. Ian Buruma, "The Last Days of Hong Kong," *New York Review of Books*, 12 April 1990, 43.

125. Kerry Dumbaugh and Michael Ipson, *The United States and Hong Kong's Future: Promoting Stability and Growth*, Summary Report (New York: National Committee on U.S.-China Relations, June 1990), 17.

126. Kerry Dumbaugh, "Hong Kong and China in the 1990s," in Joint Economic Committee Study, *China's Economic Dilemmas in the 1990s: The Problems of Reforms, Modernization and Interdependence*, vol. 2 (Washington, D.C.: Government Printing Office, 1991), 864n11.

127. Morris, *Hong Kong*, 111.

128. Anthony E. Sweeting, "The Reconstruction of Education in Post-war Hong Kong, 1945–1954: Variations in the Process of Policy Making" (Ph.D. dissertation, University of Hong Kong, 1989), cited in Gerald A. Postiglione, "The United States and Higher Education in Hong Kong: Preserving the High Road to China," paper given at the International Conference on America and the Asia-Pacific Region in the Twentieth Century, Beijing, May 1991, 4.

129. Letter by Grantham, 24 February 1950, cited in Postiglione, "The United States and Higher Education," 5–6.

130. Letter Terrill E. Lautz, vice president of the Henry Luce Foundation, to the author, 9 July 1992.

131. Fairbank, Chinabound, 379.

132. #349 Rankin, Taipei, 11 February 1952, bx 8, f: KMT, RG 84, NA; 793.00/3–253 Despatch 459 Rankin, Taipei, bx 4204, RG 59, NA.

133. NSC 5430, "Status of United States Programs for National Security as of June 30, 1954," pt. 7: The USIA Program, 18 August 1954, FRUS 1952–54, vol. 2, 1787.

134. Gary Catron, "Hong Kong and Chinese Foreign Policy, 1955–60," China Quarterly 51 (July–September 1972): 415.

135. Dumbaugh and Ipson, The United States and Hong Kong's Future, 15–16.

136. Richard H. Solomon, assistant secretary for East Asian and Pacific Affairs, "U.S. Policy toward Hong Kong," statement before the Subcommittee on East Asian and Pacific Affairs of the Senate Foreign Relations Committee, 2 April 1992, in U.S. Department of State Dispatch, 6 April 1992, 279.

137. Jack Anderson and Dale Van Atta, "Hong Kong Goes American," Washington Post, 3 June 1990, D7.

138. James P. Sterba, "Yankee Outpost," Wall Street Journal, 10 October 1985, 1 and 26.

139. Buruma, "The Last Days of Hong Kong," 42.

140. Geoffrey O'Brien, "Blazing Passions," New York Review of Books, 24 September 1992, 39.

141. Ibid., 39.

142. Desson Howe, "Target: America," Washington Post, 20 August 1993, 1D.

143. Bruce Lee's failure to be cast in the role contributed to his bitter decision to move permanently to Hong Kong where, he felt, his race would not preclude him from future opportunities.

144. Mary C. Turnbull, "Hong Kong: Fragrant Harbour, City of Sin and Death," in Robin W. Winks and James R. Rush, eds., Asia in Western Fiction (Honolulu: University of Hawaii Press, 1990), 129. This section draws heavily from Turnbull, 117–36.

145. Cohen, East Asian Art, 138.

146. A-478 Rice Hong Kong, 17 February 1967, NSF Country File, bx 240, f: China Cables, vol. 8, 12/66–3/67, LBJ.

147. Norman J. Miners, Hong Kong under Imperial Rule, 1912–1941 (New York: Oxford University Press, 1987), 250–54, 270–77 (quote on 276–77).

148. U.S. Congress, Asian Organized Crime, Senate Hearing before the Permanent Subcommittee on Investigations of the Committee on Governmental Affairs, 3 October and 5–6 November 1991 (Washington, D.C.: Government Printing Office, 1992), 14, 86.

149. "Chinese Crime Pays," FEER (12 January 1989): 30.

150. John Kifner, "New Immigrant Wave from Asia Gives the Underworld New Faces," New York Times, 6 January 1991, 20.

151. Gwen Kinkead, Chinatown (New York: HarperCollins, 1992), 96; Kaplan, Fires, 243, 515.

152. Robert J. Kelley, Ko-lin Chin, and Jeffrey Fagan, "The Dragon Breathes Fire: Chinese Organized Crime in New York City," paper for the Multinational

Conference on Asian Organized Crime, San Francisco, Calif., September 1991, 5, 15–16.

153.   John Pomfret, "INS Criticized for Not Acting to Stem Smuggling of Asians by Gangs," *Washington Post*, 9 February 1993, 4A; Eugene Robinson, "Worldwide Migration Nears Crisis," *Washington Post*, 7 July 1993, 1A.

154.   Albert Scardino, "Commercial Rents in Chinatown Soar as Hong Kong Exodus Grows," *New York Times*, 25 December 1986, 1.

CHAPTER 10

1.   Lampton, et al., *The Emergence of "Greater China,"* 18.

2.   Sutter, Trip Report, 7–8.

3.   "Yang Shangkun on China's Reunification," *Beijing Review*, 26 November–2 December 1990, 11, as quoted in Jia, "Changing Relations," 287.

4.   Ibid., 288n30.

BIBLIOGRAPHICAL ESSAY

Few authors have written about U.S.-Taiwan relations. Those who have done so generally have focused on particular crises rather than exploring the sweep of contacts over time. The single most comprehensive essay on American relations with Taiwan appears in the slim volume written before derecognition by Ralph Clough, *Island China* (Cambridge: Harvard University Press, 1978). A useful supplement is Stephen P. Gibert and William M. Carpenter, eds., *America and Island China: A Documentary History* (Lanham, Md.: University Press of America, 1989). Providing interesting insights, but to be used with great care given his enthusiasm for Chiang Kai-shek, is the memoir by U.S. ambassador to Taiwan Karl Rankin, *China Assignment* (Seattle: University of Washington Press, 1964). The most comprehensive study of American assistance to the Nationalist Chinese authorities on the island is Neil H. Jacoby, *U.S. Aid to Taiwan* (New York: Praeger, 1966). More specialized but also insightful is T. H. Shen, *The Sino-American Joint Commission on Rural Reconstruction* (Ithaca: Cornell University Press, 1970). The provocative question of how the relationship between Washington and Taipei has functioned is raised by Steve Chan, "The Mouse That Roared: Taiwan's Management of Trade Relations with the United States," *Comparative Political Studies* 20 (October 1987): 251–92.

A range of primary sources reinforces the insights of the books and articles discussed here. The most accessible is the United States Department of State series, *Foreign Relations of the United States*, which includes annual volumes on China, or East Asia and the Pacific, and on National Security Affairs. Materials from the presidential libraries augment these records, as do documents at the National Archives that were not included in the published volumes. Congressional hearings are particularly important for understanding U.S.-Taiwan relations. Also, manuscript collections for such people as Congressman Walter Judd or China lobby activist Marvin Liebman provide insights, as do oral history collections such as the Chinese Oral History

Project at Columbia University. Magazines, journals, and newspapers are essential for understanding the shifts in the relationship over time and for following developments in the cultural and social arenas. Especially useful is the *Far Eastern Economic Review*; see also *Asian Survey, China Quarterly, and Issues and Studies* (Taipei).

On the history of American–Nationalist Chinese relations on the mainland, the literature is rich and varied. Good general overviews are provided in Warren I. Cohen's classic, *America's Response to China* (New York: Columbia University Press, 1990); James K. Sheridan, *China in Disintegration: The Republican Era in Chinese History, 1912–1949* (New York: Free Press, 1975); and Michael Schaller, *The United States and China in the Twentieth Century* (New York: Oxford University Press, 1979). More specialized studies include the thoughtful and painstakingly researched volume by Dorothy Borg, *The United States and the Far Eastern Crisis of 1933–1938* (Cambridge: Harvard University Press, 1964), and examinations of the American role in reform by James C. Thomson, Jr., *While China Faced West* (Cambridge: Harvard University Press, 1969), and Arthur N. Young, *China and the Helping Hand, 1937–1945* (Cambridge: Harvard University Press, 1963). On the early wartime period, Waldo Heinrichs, *Threshold to War* (New York: Oxford University Press, 1988), places relations between Chiang and Washington in the broad context of international politics in the Pacific, while bilateral relations are the focus for Michael Schaller, *The U.S. Crusade in China, 1938–1945* (New York: Columbia University Press, 1979); Barbara Tuchman, *Stilwell and the American Experience in China, 1911–1945* (New York: Macmillan, 1970); and Herbert Feis, *The China Tangle* (New York: Atheneum, 1967). See also the memoirs by Claire Chennault, *The Way of a Fighter* (New York: G. P. Putnam's, 1949), and Theodore H. White, ed., *The Stilwell Papers* (New York: William Sloane, 1948). Astute reporting by American Foreign Service officers is reflected in Joseph W. Esherick, ed., *Lost Chance in China: The World War II Dispatches of John S. Service* (New York: Random House, 1974).

The most important volume on U.S.-Chinese relations in the civil war period derived from a path-breaking conference incorporated into a volume edited by Dorothy Borg and Waldo Heinrichs, *Uncertain Years* (New York: Columbia University Press, 1980). Other perspectives are provided by Robert M. Blum, *Drawing the Line* (New York: W. W. Norton, 1982), and William Stueck, *The Road to Confrontation* (Chapel Hill: University of North Carolina Press, 1981). American despair with the KMT provoked publication of the government exposé later edited and reprinted by Lyman P. Van Slyke as *The China White Paper, August 1949* (Stanford: Stanford University Press, 1967). On the central question of whether the U.S. should recognize the Chinese Communist government or remain tied to the Nationalists see Nancy Bernkopf Tucker, *Patterns in the Dust: Chinese-American Relations and the Recognition Controversy, 1949–1950* (New York: Columbia University Press, 1983).

American policy in the 1950s is explored through the most recently declassified U.S. archives and some documentary resources from China in Harry Harding and Yuan Ming, eds., *Sino-American Relations, 1945–1955* (Wilmington, Del.: Scholarly Resources, 1989); Warren I. Cohen and Akira Iriye, eds., *The Great Powers in East Asia, 1953–1960* (New York: Columbia University Press, 1990); and Nancy Bernkopf Tucker, "John Foster Dulles and the Taiwan Roots of the 'Two Chinas' Policy," in Richard H. Immerman, ed., *John Foster Dulles and the Diplomacy of the Cold War* (Princeton: Princeton University Press, 1990), 235–62. Gordon H. Chang's controversial *Friends and Enemies* (Stanford: Stanford University Press, 1990) looks at critical security issues in the 1950s and 1960s. On Chinese Nationalist involvement in Vietnam in the 1960s see George McT. Kahin's superb *Intervention* (Garden City, N.Y.: Doubleday, 1987).

The Taiwan Straits crises have intrigued scholars, who have viewed them from different perspectives in Jonathan Trumbull Howe, *Multicrises* (Cambridge: MIT Press, 1971); Tang Tsou, *The Embroilment over Quemoy* (Salt Lake City: University of Utah, 1959); O. Edmund Clubb "Formosa and the Offshore Islands in American Policy, 1950–1955," *Political Science Quarterly* 74 (1959): 517–31; Thomas E. Stolper, *China, Taiwan, and the Offshore Islands* (Armonk, N.Y.: M. E. Sharpe, 1985); and Gordon H. Chang and He Di, "The Absence of War in the U. S.-China Confrontation over Quemog and Matsu in 1954–1955: Contingency, Luck, Deterrence?" *American Historical Review* 98 (December 1993): 1500–24. Attitudes toward Taiwan during the period of normalization with the PRC are revealed in Henry Kissinger, *The White House Years* (Boston: Little, Brown, 1979); Richard Nixon, *RN: The Memoirs of Richard Nixon* (New York: Grosset & Dunlap, 1978); and Zbigniew Brzezinski, *Power and Principle* (New York: Farrar, Straus, Giroux, 1985). Quite a different viewpoint is expressed by the last ROC ambassador to the U.S., James C. H. Shen, *The U.S. and Free China: How the U.S. Sold out Its Ally* (Washington, D.C.: Acropolis Books, 1983).

The best effort to understand U.S.-China relations after 1972 comes from Harry Harding, *A Fragile Relationship* (Washington, D.C.: Brookings Institution, 1992). He also analyzes the role played by and the impact on Taiwan. Several edited volumes, although uneven, also provide insights, including Chiu Hungdah, ed., *China and the Taiwan Issue* (New York: Praeger, 1979), which is almost identical to *China and the Question of Taiwan* (New York: Praeger, 1973), with the same editor; Jack F. Williams, ed., *The Taiwan Issue* (East Lansing: Michigan State University Press, 1975); Ramon Myers, ed., *Two Chinese States* (Stanford: Hoover Institution Press, 1978); and Harvey Feldman, Michael Y. M. Kau, and Ilpyong J. Kim, eds., *Taiwan in a Time of Transition* (New York: Paragon, 1988). A particularly useful look at the 1980s comes from Banning Garrett and Bonnie Glaser, "From Nixon to Reagan: China's Changing Role in American Strategy," in Kenneth A. Oye, Robert J. Lieber, and Donald Rothchild, eds., *Eagle Resurgent: The Reagan Era in American Foreign Policy* (Boston: Little, Brown, 1987). Studies prepared for the Congress through the Congressional Research Service by Robert Sutter are especially illuminating: for example, *Taiwan's Future: Implications for the United States* (Issue Brief #IB79101, 1980), *Taiwan's Elections: Implications for Taiwan's Development and U.S. Interests* (Issue Brief #90-11F, 1989), and *Taiwan: Recent Developments and U.S. Policy Choices* (Issue Brief # IB92038, 1992). The case for closer relations between the U.S. and Taiwan has been made by several authors, including Martin L. Lasater, *The Taiwan Issue in Sino-American Strategic Relations* (Boulder: Westview, 1984), *Policy in Evolution* (Boulder: Westview, 1989), and *U.S. Interests in the New Taiwan* (Boulder: Westview, 1993); A. James Gregor, *The China Connection* (Stanford: Stanford University Press, 1986); and Robert L. Downen, *The Tattered China Card* (Washington, D.C.: Council for Social and Economic Studies, 1984).

On the crucial issue of ending formal diplomatic relations with Taiwan and the Taiwan Relations Act there have been numerous studies, including Lester Wolff and David L. Simon, *Legislative History of the Taiwan Relations Act* (Jamaica, N.Y.: American Association for Chinese Studies, 1982); Louis W. Koenig, James C. Hsiung, and Chang King-yuh, eds., *Congress, the Presidency and the Taiwan Relations Act* (New York: Praeger, 1985); and Victor Li, *De-Recognizing Taiwan* (Washington, D.C.: Carnegie Endowment, 1977). Congressional hearings are an important resource on this issue; see, for instance, U.S. Congress, Senate Committee on the Judiciary, Subcommittee on Separation of Powers, *Taiwan Communique and Separation of Powers*, 97th Cong., 2d sess., 1982; U.S. Congress, House Committee on Foreign Affairs, Subcommittee on Asian and Pacific Affairs, *Implementation of the Taiwan Relations Act*, 96th Cong., 2d sess., 1980.

The Nationalists were never passive witnesses to American politics. On their involvement see Ross Y. Koen, *The China Lobby in American Politics* (New York: Harper & Row, 1974); Stanley D. Bachrack, *The Committee of One Million* (New York: Columbia University Press, 1976); Robert P. Newman, "Clandestine Chinese Nationalist Efforts to Punish Their American Detractors," *Diplomatic History* 7 (Summer 1983): 205–22; and Carl Goldstein, "The New China Lobby," *Far Eastern Economic Review* (6 November 1986): 44–45. American public opinion toward Nationalist China is explored in Leonard Kusnitz, *Public Opinion and Foreign Policy: America's China Policy, 1949–1979* (Westport, Conn.: Greenwood Press, 1984), and in the influential A. T. Steele, *The American People and China* (New York: McGraw-Hill, 1966).

Intelligence gathering and covert operations, whether cooperative or competitive, have received attention from Ray S. Cline, *Secrets, Spies and*

Scholars (Washington, D.C.: Acropolis Books, 1976); William M. Leary, *Perilous Missions* (University Station: University of Alabama Press, 1984); and Victor Marchetti and John D. Marks, *The CIA and the Cult of Intelligence* (New York: Dell, 1980). Taiwan's efforts to penetrate the United States alarmed Michael J. Glennon, "Liaison and the Law: Foreign Intelligence Agencies' Activities in the United States," *Harvard International Law Journal* 25 (Winter 1984): 1–42; U.S. Congress, House Committee on Foreign Affairs, Subcommittee on Asian and Pacific Affairs and on Human Rights and International Organizations, *Taiwan Agents in America and the Death of Prof. Wen-chen Chen*, 97th Cong., 1st sess., 1981; and David E. Kaplan, *Fires of the Dragon* (New York: Atheneum, 1992).

Military issues often receive consideration in the general works mentioned here. The newspapers have provided a running account, but see also George H. Quester, "Taiwan and Nuclear Proliferation," *Orbis* 18 (Spring 1974): 141–47; A. Doak Barnett, *The FX Decision* (Washington, D.C.: Brookings Institution, 1981); and John W. Garver, "Arms Sales, the Taiwan Question, and Sino-U.S. Relations," *Orbis* 26 (Winter 1983): 999–1035.

Efforts to understand the workings of the Nationalist Chinese government have included the astute analyses by Lloyd Eastman, *The Abortive Revolution: China under Nationalist Rule, 1927–1937* (Cambridge: Harvard University Press, 1972), and *Seeds of Destruction: Nationalist China in War and Revolution, 1937–1949* (Stanford: Stanford University Press, 1984). A less negative judgment emerges from William C. Kirby, "Continuity and Change in Modern China: Economic Planning on the Mainland and on Taiwan, 1943–1958," *Australian Journal of Chinese Affairs* (July 1990): 121–41. He and Paul A. Cohen see elements shaped early that contributed to success in Taiwan. Cohen deals with the controversial issue of attitudes toward change in "The Post-Mao Reforms in Historical Perspective," *Journal of Asian Studies* 47 (August 1988): 529–32. Revision of the bleak assessment of the KMT war effort is attempted in James Hsiung and Steven I. Levine, eds., *China's Bitter Victory* (Armonk, N.Y.: M. E. Sharpe, 1992).

The impact of the Nationalist regime on Taiwan in the 1940s is most poignantly recounted by George Kerr, *Formosa Betrayed* (Boston: Houghton Mifflin, 1965). In addition to condeming the KMT, Kerr indicts the Americans for ignoring the calamity. The central 28 February 1947 incident is explored by Lai Tse-han, Ramon H. Myers, and Wei Wou, *A Tragic Beginning* (Stanford: Stanford University Press, 1992). Assumptions about a smoother transition are explored in Leonard Gordon, "American Planning for Taiwan, 1942–1945," *Pacific Historical Review* 37 (May 1968): 201–28. Critics did not see appreciable improvements for an extended period; see Mark Mancall, ed., *Formosa Today* (New York: Praeger, 1963).

Taiwan, nevertheless, finally developed into a prosperous, modern, and increasingly democratic entity. Discussions of how that change occurred abound but, again, tend to be partial. Among the most interesting are Tien

304 • BIBLIOGRAPHIC ESSAY

Hung-mao, *The Great Transition* (Stanford: Hoover Institution Press, 1989); Thomas B. Gold, *State and Society in the Taiwan Miracle* (Armonk, N.Y.: M. E. Sharpe, 1986); Thomas Robinson, ed., *Democracy and Development in East Asia* (Washington, D.C.: American Enterprise Institute, 1991); Robert G. Sutter, *Taiwan: Entering the Twenty-First Century* (New York: University Press of America, 1988); and for a Nationalist perspective, Shaw Yu-ming, *Beyond the Economic Miracle* (Taipei: Kwang Hwa, 1988).

Focusing more exclusively on the economic miracle are K. T. Li, *The Evolution of Policy behind Taiwan's Development Success* (New Haven: Yale University Press, 1988); Shirley W. Y. Kuo, Gustav Ranis, and John C. H. Fei, *The Taiwan Success Story* (Boulder: Westview, 1981); and Stephan Haggard, *Pathways from the Periphery* (Ithaca: Cornell University Press, 1990). Robert Wade has the distinction of making complicated economic issues understandable in *Governing the Market* (Princeton: Princeton University Press, 1990). He emphasizes the central role of the government in conjunction with a largely private market system in developing the economy and provides a useful discussion of how his interpretation differs from neo-classical, free market, and simulated free market theories. The other great debate focuses on the significance of U.S. assistance. Maurice Scott's essay in Walter Galenson, ed., *Economic Growth and Structural Change in Taiwan* (Ithaca: Cornell University Press, 1979), makes the case that though it was important it was not sufficient. Others who accentuate the U.S.'s role include Edwin A. Winckler and Susan Greenhalgh, eds., *Contemporary Approaches to the Political Economy of Taiwan* (Armonk, N.Y.: M. E. Sharpe, 1988). However critical, aid did not render Taipei dependent on the United States. See Richard E. Barrett and Martin K. Whyte, "Dependency Theory and Taiwan: Analysis of a Deviant Case," *American Journal of Sociology* 87 (March 1982): 1064–89.

On the extraordinary political developments in Taiwan of the 1980s and 1990s see some of the volumes already mentioned and the work of Tien Hung-mao, "Brothers in Arms: Political Struggle and Party Competition in Taiwan's Evolving Democracy," in *Asian Update* (New York: Asia Society, December 1991), and Chou Yangsun and Andrew J. Nathan, "Democratizing Transition in Taiwan," *Asian Survey* (March 1987): 277–99. That the future will not be easy becomes apparent in Denis F. Simon and Michael Y. M. Kau, *Taiwan: Beyond the Economic Miracle* (Armonk, N.Y.: M. E. Sharpe, 1992).

The changes are especially notable given the problems earlier confronted by critics of the regime. The status of intellectuals is examined by Mei Wen-li, "The Intellectuals on Formosa," *China Quarterly* (July–September 1963): 65–74; Mab Huang, *Intellectual Ferment for Political Reforms in Taiwan, 1971–1973* (Ann Arbor: Center for Chinese Studies, University of Michigan, 1976); Edel Lancashire, "Popeye and the Case of Guo Yidong, alias Bo Yang," *China Quarterly* (December 1982): 663–86; and on the general atmosphere, Warren Tozer, "Taiwan's 'Cultural Renaissance': A Preliminary View," *China Quarterly* (July–September 1970): 81–99. Attacks on American intellectuals included most prominently the campaign against the dean of American China scholars; see Leonard H. D. Gordon and Sidney Chang, "John K. Fairbank and His Critics in the Republic of China," *Journal of Asian Studies* 30 (November 1970): 137–49.

Although much has been written about the cause of Taiwan independence, little chronicles the movement. The most interesting studies are Douglas Mendel, *The Politics of Formosan Nationalism* (Berkeley: University of California Press, 1970); Peng Ming-min, *A Taste of Freedom: Memoirs of a Formosan Independence Leader* (New York: Holt Rinehart & Winston, 1972); John Kaplan, *The Court-Martial of the Kaohsiung Defendants* (Berkeley: University of California Press, 1981); and Mark J. Cohen, *Taiwan at the Crossroads* (Washington, D.C.: Asia Resource Center, 1988).

A constant variable in the relationship has been the People's Republic of China. Strong reactions in the 1950s were compiled into the volume *Oppose U.S. Occupation of Taiwan and "Two Chinas" Plot* (Peking: Foreign Language Press, 1958). A more scholarly examination appears in Zi Zhongyun and He Di, eds., *Meitai Guanxi Sishinian* (Forty years of U.S.-Taiwan relations) (Beijing: People's Press, 1991). The tremendous changes in Taiwan-PRC interaction are astutely commented upon in Ralph N. Clough, *Reaching across the Taiwan Strait* (Boulder: Westview, 1993).

On social/cultural interaction between the U.S. and Taiwan, it remains necessary to consult contemporary magazine and newspaper accounts. There are a small number of studies that do examine particular aspects of these issues. On health care see John R. Watt, *A Friend in Deed: ABMAC and the Republic of China, 1937–1987* (New York: ABMAC, 1992). On education see William P. Fenn, *Ever New Horizons: The Story of the United Board for Christian Higher Education in Asia, 1922–1975* (New York: United Board, 1980); Warren I. Cohen, "While China Faced East: Chinese-American Cultural Relations, 1949–71," in Joyce Kallgren and Denis Fred Simon, eds., *Educational Exchanges* (Berkeley: Institute of East Asian Studies, University of California, 1987), 44–57; C. Martin Wilbur, "Sino-American Relations in Scholarship as Viewed from the United States," and Chang Peng-yuan, "Sino-American Scholarly Relations as Seen from Taiwan, 1949–1979," both in Cecilia S. T. Chang, ed., *U.S.-ROC Relations* (New York: St. John's University, 1984), 35–145. On science see Walter Arnold, "Science and Technology Development in Taiwan and South Korea," *Asian Survey* 28 (April 1988): 437–50; and Glenn J. McLoughlin, *Taiwan: Science and Technology Policymaking* (Washington, D.C.: Congressional Research Service, 30 October 1989). On environmental issues directly involving U.S. companies see James Reardon-Anderson, *Pollution, Politics and Foreign Investment in China* (Armonk, N.Y.: M. E. Sharpe, 1992). Although the focus of the discussions is domestic, the literature on the *hsiang-t'u* movement touches on American influences: Joseph S. M. Lau, "Echoes of the May Fourth Movement in Hsiang-t'u Fiction," in Tien Hung-mao, ed., *Mainland China, Taiwan and U.S. Policy* (Cambridge: Oelgeschlager, Gunn & Hain, 1983); and C. T. Hsia, "Forward," in Jospeh S. M. Lau, ed., *Chinese Stories from Taiwan: 1960–1970* (New York: Columbia University Press, 1976).

Developments in American Chinatowns have received increased attention since the publication of Stanford M. Lyman's *Chinese Americans* (New York: Random House, 1974); see Peter Kwong, *The New Chinatown* (New York: Noonday Press, 1987); Chen Hsiang-shui, *Chinatown No More* (Ithaca: Cornell University Press, 1992); and Gwen Kinkead, *Chinatown* (New York: HarperCollins, 1992).

The literature on Hong Kong's relations with the United States is even thinner than that covering Taiwan-U.S. interaction. Generally it is necessary to examine works that focus on other subjects to see the U.S.–Hong Kong story. Notable exceptions include Chiu Hungdah, "The Hong Kong Agreement and American Foreign Policy," *Issues and Studies* 22 (June 1986): 76–91; Robert Sutter, *Hong Kong: Issues for U.S. Policy* (Issue Brief #IB85015, 1985); and Kerry Dumbaugh and Michael Ipson, *The United States and Hong Kong's Future* (New York: National Committee on U.S.-China Relations, 1990).

For historical background see Norman J. Miners, *The Government and Politics of Hong Kong* (New York: Oxford University Press, 1986), and *Hong Kong under Imperial Rule, 1912–1941* (New York: Oxford, 1987); G. B. Endacott, *Hong Kong Eclipse* (New York: Oxford, 1978); the somewhat overwhelming series by Frank H. H. King, *The History of the Hongkong and Shanghai Banking Corporation* (New York: Cambridge University Press, 1987–91); and Jurgen Domes and Shaw Yu-ming, eds., *Hong Kong: A Chinese and International Concern* (Boulder: Westview, 1988). Particularly helpful is the informative memoir by former governor Alexander Grantham, *Via Ports* (Hong Kong: Hong Kong University Press, 1965). Edwin W. Martin discusses the different perspectives on the civil war of Washington and London due to Hong Kong in *Divided Counsel* (Lexington: University of Kentucky Press, 1986). Unfortunately most histories of the colony are less scholarly, but at least they deliver a touch of local color, such as Kevin Rafferty, *City on the Rocks* (New York: Penguin, 1989); and Jan Morris, *Hong Kong: The End of an Empire* (New York: Penguin, 1990).

Grantham alludes to the mysterious U.S.–Hong Kong defense relationship, as does John Baylis, *Anglo-American Defense Relations 1939–1980* (New York: St. Martin's Press, 1981). Several books touch on the use of Hong Kong as a base for intelligence operations. See those already mentioned and Joseph Burkholder Smith, *Portrait of a Cold Warrior* (New York: G. P. Putnam's Sons, 1976); Darrell Garwood, *Under Cover* (New York: Grove Press, 1985); Thomas Powers, *The Man Who Kept the Secrets* (New York:

Pocket Books, 1979); and Jeffrey T. Richelson and Desmond Ball, *The Ties That Bind* (Boston: Allen & Unwin, 1985). Hong Kong's uncertain political future has generated more attention; see Frank Ching, *Hong Kong and China: For Better or for Worse* (New York: China Council of the Asia Society, 1985), and "One Country, Two Systems: The Future of Hong Kong," in Anthony Kane, ed., *China Briefing, 1990* (Boulder: Westview, 1990), 107–27; Jack F. Williams, *The Future of Hong Kong and Taiwan* (East Lansing: Michigan State University Press, 1985); Ian Buruma, "The Last Days of Hong Kong," *New York Review of Books*, 12 April 1990; and William H. Overholt, "Hong Kong and China after 1997: The Real Issues," in Frank J. Macchiarola and Robert B. Oxnam, eds., *The China Challenge* (Montpelier, Vt.: Capital City Press, 1991), 30–52.

Hong Kong's importance to the U.S. has most often been economic. For discussions of Hong Kong's economic development and its trade with the U.S. see Haggard, *Pathways*, noted earlier; and John P. Burns, "Hong Kong: Diminishing Laissez-Faire," in Steven M. Goldstein, ed., *Minidragons* (Boulder: Westview, 1991). On the related Greater China issue see David M. Lampton, et al., *The Emergence of "Greater China": Implications for the United States* (New York: National Committee on U.S.-China Relations, 1992) and the important forthcoming volume by Harry Harding. The *Far Eastern Economic Review* follows developments in Hong Kong closely.

The works cited above on American Chinatowns also reflect on the Hong Kong Chinese experience in the United States. For information on the Hong Kong–U.S. crime connection see U.S. Congress, Senate Committee on Governmental Affairs, Permanent Subcommittee on Investigations, *Asian Organized Crime* (Washington, D.C.: Government Printing Office, 1992) and the important forthcoming volume by Harry Harding.

In the cultural arena the best work on Hong Kong's influence on American fiction is Mary C. Turnbull, "Hong Kong: Fragrant Harbour, City of Sin and Death," in Robin W. Winks and James R. Rush, eds., *Asia in Western Fiction* (Honolulu: University of Hawaii Press, 1990).

INDEX

Abbott and Costello, 228
ABDA Agreement, 198, 199
Academia Sinica, 118, 188, 273n. 61;
American studies at, 120, 157; Asia
Foundation and, 82; collaboration
with U.S. National Academy of
Sciences, 82; Committee on
Scientific and Scholarly
Cooperation with the U.S., 187;
Ford Foundation support and, 81;
scientific research and, 192
Academy for the Performing Arts, 228
Acheson, Dean: as Atlanticist, 22; atti-
tude toward China/Asia, 22; China
policy and, 24; defense of Hong
Kong and, 200, 201; fall of China
and, 30–32; MacArthur and, 68;
National Press Club Speech (1950),
30, 35; recognition of PRC, 32;
relations with Nationalist Chinese,
22, 24, 68, 69, 72; as symbol to
Dulles, 38; Taiwan autonomy and,
29, 30
Africa: South Africa and Nationalist
Chinese uranium purchases, 146;
Soviet involvement in, 131; U.S.
intervention and, 94; Vanguard
Project and, 62

Agency for International Development
(AID), 57, 88; education and, 83;
end of economic aid to Taiwan
and, 62, 108, 110; facilitates
Nationalist Chinese participation
in Vietnam, 98; as front for
reformers in Taiwan, 59; health
care and, 87, 121; Investment
Guarantee Program, 109; popula-
tion control and, 86; Vanguard
Project and, 61
Aid to Refugee Chinese Intellectuals
(ARCI), 83, 210; educational sup-
port of, 226
Air America, 65
Air Asia, 65
Airforce General Hospital, 121
Allen, Richard V., 137
Allison, John M., 201
Ambler, Eric, 229
American Asiatic Fleet, 198
American Bureau for Medical Aid to
China (ABMAC): activities of, 87,
121, 158; origins of, 87; population
control and, 121; relocates head-
quarters to Taiwan, 191
American Chamber of Commerce, 142,
143

THE AUTHOR

Nancy Bernkopf Tucker is on the faculty of the Department of History and the School of Foreign Service at Georgetown University. She received her graduate degrees at Columbia University and taught at Colgate University and New York University. She is author of *Patterns in the Dust: Chinese-American Relations and the Recognition Controversy, 1949–1950* (1983) and numerous articles on American–East Asian relations for books and journals including *Foreign Affairs, Diplomatic History*, and the *Pacific Historical Review*. She is co-editor (with Warren I. Cohen) and contributor to *Lyndon Johnson Confronts the World* (1994). Professor Tucker has won the Stuart L. Bernath Lecture Prize of the Society for Historians of American Foreign Relations and received an International Affairs Fellowship from the Council on Foreign Relations which made it possible for her to serve in the Office of Chinese Affairs at the Department of State and the American Embassy in Beijing. She has also been a visiting scholar at the Institute of American Studies of the Chinese Academy of Social Sciences in Beijing and a resident scholar at the Charles Warren Center for Studies in American History at Harvard University.